Music Library Association
Index and Bibliography Series

David Farneth, Series Editor

1. *An Alphabetical Index to Claudio Monteverdi Tutte Le Opere,* edited by the Bibliography Committee of the New York Chapter, MLA, 1964.
2. *An Alphabetical Index to Hector Berlioz Werke,* edited by the Bibliography Committee of the New York Chapter, MLA, 1964.
3. *A Checklist of Music Bibliographies and Indexes in Progress and Unpublished,* compiled by the MLA Publications Committee Walter Gerboth, chair; Shirley Branner; and James B. Coover; 1965; 2nd ed. by James Pruett, 1969; 3rd ed. by Linda Solow, 1974; 4th ed. by Dee Baily, 1982.
4. *A Concordance of the Thematic Indexes to the Instrumental Works of Antonio Vivaldi,* by Lenore Coral, 1965; 2nd ed., 1972.
5. *An Alphabetical Index to Tomás Luis de Victoria Opera Omnia,* edited by the Bibliography Committee of the New York Chapter, MLA, 1966.
6. *An Alphabetical Index to Robert Schumann Werke. Schumann Index, Part 1,* compiled by Michael Ochs, 1967.
7. *An Alphabetical Index to the Solo Songs of Robert Schumann. Schumann Index, Part 2,* compiled by William J. Weichlein, 1967.
8. *An Index to Maurice Frost's "English & Scottish Psalm & Hymn Tunes,"* by Kirby Rogers, 1967.
9. *Speculum: An Index of Musically Related Articles and Book Reviews,* compiled by Arthur S. Wolff, 1970; 2nd ed., 1981.
10. *An Index to "Das Chorwerk," Vols. 1–110,* compiled by Michael Ochs, 1970.
11. *Bach Aria Index,* compiled by Miriam Whaples, 1971.
12. *Annotated Bibliography of Writing about Music in Puerto Rico,* compiled by Annie Figueroa Thompson, 1975.
13. *Analyses of Twentieth-Century Music, 1940–1970,* compiled by Arthur Wenk, 1975.
14. *Analyses of Twentieth-Century Music, 1970–1975,* compiled by Arthur Wenk, 1976; 2nd ed., 1984.
15. *Analyses of Nineteenth-Century Music: 1940–1975,* compiled by Arthur Wenk, 1976; 2nd ed., 1940–1980, 1984.
16. *Writings on Contemporary Music Notation,* compiled by Gerald Warfield, 1976.

Musical Memorials for Musicians

A Guide to Selected Compositions

R. Michael Fling

MLA Index and Bibliography Series, No. 29

The Scarecrow Press, Inc.
Lanham, Maryland, and London
and
Music Library Association, Inc.
2001

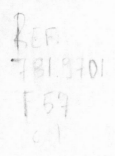
SCARECROW PRESS, INC.

Published in the United States of America
by Scarecrow Press, Inc.
4720 Boston Way, Lanham, Maryland 20706
www.scarecrowpress.com

4 Pleydell Gardens, Folkestone
Kent CT20 2DN, England

British Library Cataloguing-in-Publication Information Available

Library of Congress Cataloging-in-Publication Data
Fling, Robert Michael, 1941–
   Musical memorials for musicians : a guide to selected compositions /
R. Michael Fling.
      p. cm. — (MLA index and bibliography series, ISSN 0094-6478 ; no. 29)
   Includes bibliographical references and indexes.
   ISBN 0-8108-4013-8 (alk. paper)
   1. Music—Bio-bibliography. 2. Musicians—Songs and music—History and
criticism. 3. Memorial music. I. Title. II. MLA index and bibliography series ; 29.
ML128.B3 F57 2001
016.7815'9—dc21   00-054912

In memoriam

Milton "Chris" Blazakis

Contents

Preface

Throughout recorded history the deaths of noble and heroic persons have inspired poets and musicians to create songs of lamentation.[1] Literary and musical genres such as the Latin *planctus* and related vernacular forms were widespread in the Middle Ages in praise of real as well as mythical persons. Among the earliest surviving examples with music notation is the *Planctus Karoli*, preserved in a tenth-century manuscript as a lament on the death of the emperor Charlemagne (d. 814).[2] Singers and poets were motivated not only by the passing of persons of eminent station. In the late-fourteenth century a variant of the practice emerged that offered opportunities for an even more specialized musical expression of grief: the *déploration* to memorialize the musical and personal ties that a composer had with a deceased mentor or colleague.

The earliest known *déploration* for a musician pays homage to the fourteenth-century French composer and poet Guillaume de Machaut (ca. 1300–1377). It is a setting for four voices by (François?) Andrieu of two poems by Eustache Deschamps, who was Machaut's pupil in poetry.[3] The text makes reference to Machaut and to the people and places associated with him, and the music includes quotations from his works. In the fifteenth century this practice gained popularity. Johannes Ockeghem initiated a veritable cascade of musical lamentation when he mourned the death of Burgundian composer Gilles Binchois (ca. 1400–1460); Ockeghem (ca. 1410–1496) was then himself honored with *déplorations* by Johannes Lupus and Josquin des Prez; and Josquin (ca. 1440–1521) in turn was mourned in musical works by Nicolas Gombert, Benedictus Appenzeller, and Hieronymus Vinders.

In ensuing centuries composers carried on this tradition in a variety of forms and styles, exemplified in France in the early-seventeenth to mid-eighteenth centuries by instrumental works characterized as *tombeaux* ("tombs"), usually in a single movement for lute, harpsichord, or viol, such as those of Louis Couperin and Johann Jakob Froberger in honor of the lutenist Blancrocher (d. 1652?), and in the eighteenth century by François Couperin's instrumental chamber suites, called *apothéoses,* in memory of Jean-Baptiste Lully (1632–1687) and Arcangelo Corelli (1653–1713). In seventeenth-century England, William Byrd set a solo vocal lament for Thomas Tallis (ca. 1505–1585), as Henry Purcell did for Matthew Locke (ca. 1620–1677); Mozart (1756–1791) was memorialized in choral cantatas by his contemporaries Carl Cannabich and Franz Danzi. In the nineteenth century, elegiac sentiments were prominent in the works of many composers, though works of that period often were regarded more as vehicles for expressing general feelings about sadness and death than as epicedia for departed friends or heroes. Notable exceptions include funeral marches for piano by Stephen Heller and Sigismund Neukomm in honor of Frédéric Chopin (1810–1849), keyboard works by Franz Liszt to memorialize Richard Wagner (1813–1883), and Tchaikovsky's piano trio "à la mémoire d'un grand artiste," the Russian pianist and pedagogue Nicolai Rubinstein (1835–1881), who was director of the Moscow Conservatory where Tchaikovsky was a colleague.

Alongside these works that express private and personal feelings of grief have coexisted musical memorials conceived and presented under the sponsorship of musical organizations. These usually have taken the form of collections of works by several composers, commissioned or compiled for the occasion by an influential individual or, more often, a publisher or organization. The first collective publication of *déplorations* occurred in 1545, when the Antwerp publisher Tielman Susato printed works memorializing Josquin by Vinders, Appenzeller, and Gombert in his edition of Josquin's seventh book of chansons. The collective format has flourished particularly in the twentieth century, in examples such as the 1920 issue of the French journal *La revue musicale* dedicated to the memory of Claude Debussy (1862–1918); this special issue bore the title *Le tombeau de Debussy*, and its musical supplement included short memorial pieces by ten composers written at the invitation of the editor. In 1949 the United Nations Educational, Scientific, and Cultural Organization (UNESCO) commissioned several works to be performed at a memorial concert in Paris to commemorate the 100th anniversary of the death of Chopin. In 1971 the American journal *Perspectives of new music* honored Igor Stravinsky (1882–1971) with an issue that included new memorial works by six composers.[4]

Several music historians have discussed aspects of memorial music, usually in the context of narrowly defined chronological periods, musical genres, geographical locations, or of individual musicians.[5] Other scholars have taken broader views, but have commented only on a few masterworks.[6] No source provides anything approaching a comprehensive survey of *déplorations* for musicians. The present listing is a first step toward filling that lacuna.

Obstacles to this compilation have been many, primarily because the criteria that usually define a musical genre are in this case irrelevant. Musical laments are not limited to particular forms, styles, media of performance, chronological periods, geographical locations, or vocal texts and languages. In addition, these works are known by a plethora of descriptive terms. During the Middle Ages and Renaissance, composers and publishers employed more than thirty different terms, seemingly interchangeably, to identify vocal *déplorations*, sometimes using different descriptive terms for the same music from one vocal partbook to another.[7] Today, common descriptive terms that denote feelings of sadness or lamentation may fill several columns in standard lists of synonyms,[8] and many of these terms have at various times been used as the titles, subtitles, and tempo indications for works of lamentation.

Despite this abundance and confusion of equivalent or related descriptors, several conventions of nomenclature now are in common use. *Déploration* normally is reserved for late-medieval and early-Renaissance vocal compositions; *tombeau* usually refers to memorial works for lute, harpsichord, or viol that were composed in France between the mid-seventeenth and mid-eighteenth centuries (though use of this term was revived by twentieth-century composers); "dump" is considered an English equivalent of *tombeau*; *apothéose* usually is reserved for a small corpus of instrumental laments composed in France around 1725; variants of "elegy" have referred to many kinds of vocal or instrumental laments since the time of the classical Greeks, but the term came to be particularly favored by late-Renaissance English composers of part-songs and lute-songs, and later by nineteenth-century composers of purely instrumental works; and the meaning of "dirge" is commonly limited to a song, often march-like, that is performed at a burial. Although these and related definitions can be found in most music dictionaries and encyclopedias, their susceptibility to varying shades of meaning has precluded their systematic adoption as indexing terms. None of these terms appears in recent editions of *Library of Congress subject headings*.[9] The Library of Congress does provide a subject heading for "Memorial music," but its use has been inconsistent and infrequent.[10] In short, there are no convenient or all-inclusive labels for this music.

Until the twentieth century, the titles or subtitles of these works were usually the most prominent indicators of their mournful purpose. Most composers included as part of a memorial work's title the name of the musician being remembered, together with some evocative word or phrase about death or sadness. Today, however, a composer is as likely to use a generic title such as "Sonata" for such a work, and to identify it as a memorial piece only in a dedicatory phrase or prefatory note. The texts of such dedications are quoted only in the most thorough catalogs and bibliographies, and they rarely are indexed anywhere. Consequently the fact that many of these works are dedicated as memorials to deceased friends often can be discovered only with the scores in hand, or through chance references in the secondary literature.

An additional impediment is that composers sometimes dedicate works to individuals who are otherwise uncelebrated, and who may or may not be musicians. Also, many compositions have funereal titles or musical characteristics but have no dedications in the published, manuscript, or recorded manifestations of the work, or in associated literature. Efforts to discover more information about obscure dedicatees or about the particular circumstances surrounding the composition of a work are often unsuccessful; when standard music reference works or literature about the composers do not provide particulars in this respect, such works have been omitted from this listing.

Despite the many obstacles to discovery and verification of *déplorations*, the compiler has made a systematic examination of bibliographies and catalogs of music, pertinent related literature, and published music scores in an effort to identify them. Among the works that have been examined are all of the biographical entries and lists of composers works in several multivolume music encyclopedias (including *The New Grove dictionary of music and musicians, Die Musik in Geschichte und Gegenwart*, and Robert Eitner's *Quellen-Lexikon*[11]); entries in bibliographies documenting earlier publications (including all citations for pre-1800 published scores in Series A of the *Répertoire international des sources musicales*, and of nineteenth-century publication activity in Pazdirek's *Universal-Handbuch der Musikliteratur aller Zeiten und Völker*); and the contents of about ninety linear feet of topical bibliographies and composer thematic catalogs in the reference section of a large academic music library. Online keyword searches were performed in the databases of the Research Libraries Information Network (RLIN), and the Online Computer Library Center (OCLC) for musical works that incorporate any of a broad range of words or phrases such as "tombeau" and "in memoriam" in their titles. The compiler also has routinely examined the dedications and program notes in new scores and recordings that have crossed his desk over a period of more than two decades for clues to memorial works for musicians.

In a majority of cases the composer's intent to memorialize a person is obvious from a work's title, subtitle, dedication, or accompanying program notes. Works with ambiguous dedication phrases that could apply equally to a living or dead person, such as "Hommage to . . ." are normally excluded unless the date of composition or first publication is known to fall within the first decade following the dedicatee's death, or unless there is some collateral evidence to verify the composer's memorial intent, such as a statement by the composer in published writings, or information that is transmitted by a member of the composer's family or musical circle. Indirect evidence also can sometimes be found in the music itself, such as the use of recognizable quotations of music written by the deceased, together with quotations of funeral music, such as the *Dies irae* sequence of the requiem mass.

This guide cannot be considered in any way "complete," nor can exhaustive coverage ever be fully realized. It is impossible to peruse a detailed catalog of works by every composer who ever lived, or to examine every pertinent related secondary source. We also cannot know what is in the mind of a composer during the creation of a work unless the composer chooses to articulate it. The purely serendipitous nature of discovery of many of the entries herein calls to question how many others eluded the compiler.

User Guide

Arrangement is alphabetical by name of dedicatee. Following the recommendation of *The Chicago manual of style*,[12] accented vowels and consonants are alphabetized as if unaccented, so that *ü*, *ö*, and *ä* are treated as *u*, *o*, and *a* rather than as *ue*, *oe*, and *ae* and so on. Collective works are listed first after dedicatee name, followed by individual compositions. Works published in collections and also published separately are listed as individual works under the composers' names, with cross-references to the contents of the collective work. Entries normally include the following elements, depending upon availability of information. DEDICATEE: Name, profession, birth and death dates. If multiple forms or spellings of the name are in common use, the one adopted by the Library of Congress is the preferred form for the heading. WORK TITLE AND DEDICATION: Dedication phrases are quoted as found in the source of information, frequently the published score. Longer dedications are quoted in the note area. COMPOSITION DATE: Enclosed in parentheses. PERFORMANCE MEDIUM (if not obvious from the title): Doubling instruments are separated by a slash, e.g., clarinet/bass clarinet; alternate instruments are enclosed in parentheses, e.g., piano (or organ). If voicings of multipart vocal works are specified, the usual abbreviations are used (SATB), with baritone (Bar) and mezzo-soprano (Mz). PUBLICATION DATA: The earliest known publication is cited. Works originally published by firms or their successors that are still in operation are presented *italicized* in a shortened form (consult the Abbreviations of Publishers and Sources for full name and address information), followed by the publisher's edition number if any is known. A published score may have multiple edition numbers, or none at all. Sometimes publishers even list alternate numbers for the same edition in different manifestations of their own catalogs. Publisher numbers cited herein were taken from whatever edition or source was conveniently at hand. Works originally published by firms not known to be now in operation are presented with the additional place of publication, and a full statement of the publisher name. Works not known by the compiler to have been published are designated "Unpublished"; in these instances the compiler's source of information is cited in abbreviated form (see the Abbreviations of Publishers and Sources for full citations). NOTES: Additional notes are added to many entries in order to clarify the circumstances of composition or publication; to cite modern editions or reprints of pre-twentieth century works; to cite *RISM-A1* or *RISM-B1* numbers for pre-1800 publications; recordings of improvisatory or electronic works; full quotation of dedication statements that are longer than a stock phrase; and any other data that the compiler found to be of interest about a particular composition.

Notes

1. Portions of this preface were originally published in the compiler's "Musical laments on the deaths of musicians: Toward a bibliography of compositions," in *Music reference services quarterly* 1/1 (1992): 3-13, and are quoted here with the permission of The Haworth Press, Inc.

2. "A solis ortu usque ad occidua" in Bibliothèque nationale (France), manuscript Latin 1154. Recorded on *The Best of Gregorian chants*, vol. 2 (Madacy Records VPJ9120).

3. This and other examples mentioned in this preface are cited in full in the main text.

4. The collective memorials included in this compilation are dedicated to Vincenzo Bellini, John Cage, Pablo Casals, Frédéric Chopin, Jacopo Corsi, Paul Dessau, Claude Debussy, Johann Dilherr, Paul Dukas, Henry Gagnon, Mikhail Glinka, Victor Gonzales,

Joseph Haydn, David Roger Jones, William Lawes, Kenneth Leighton, Maria Malibran, Salvatore Martirano, Caspar Othmayr, Ignacy Jan Paderewski, Charles H. H. Parry, Charles Peaker, Willem Pijper, Gioachino Rossini, Pierre Schaeffer, Franz Schubert, Roger Sessions, Dmitri Shostakovich, Igor Stravinsky, and Samuel Webbe.

5. See in the Select Bibliography, for example, the works by Geary and Rubin on the Renaissance *déploration*; by Abbate, Borren, Brenet, Goldberg, Mussat, Rollin, and Vendrix on the Baroque *tombeau*; by Johnston, Reich, Schuhmacher, and Traub on the Baroque funeral motet; by Burke, Hilfiger, and Piccardi on the funeral march; by Rownd and Schneider on memorial works for piano; and by Bergmann, Hudson, Rice, and Kappner on memorial works by and about specific musicians.

6. See, for example, works by Schrade, Robertson, and Mies listed in the Select Bibliography.

7. Frances Rubin, "Car atropos," pp. 2–7, lists the following terms as used for this purpose during the Renaissance: *Naenia, threnodia, epicedia, carmina exsequidia, requiem, planctus* or *planh*, dump, remembrance, dirge, funeral song, funeral tears, lament, elegy, epitaph, *déploration, complainte, hommage, chanson triste, regrêt, tombeau, plainte, chant lugubre, apothéose, musicalische Exequie, Klaglied, Begrabnisgesang, Begrabnislied, Grablied*, and *Musikermotette*.

8. See, for example, *Roget's international thesaurus*, 4th ed., rev. by Robert Chapman (New York: Harper & Row, 1984), which includes five columns of terms under the general headings "Sadness" and "Lamentation," and these are only those terms that are commonly used by speakers of English.

9. *Library of Congress subject headings*, 22nd edition (Washington, DC: Library of Congress, 1999).

10. As of mid-1999, the *OCLC* Online Union Catalog included only thirty-three scores with this subject heading, of which twenty memorialized individual persons (five being musicians); The *RLIN* bibliographic file included seventy-one scores with this subject heading, of which forty-two memorialized individual persons (twenty-three being musicians). The *OCLC* and *RLIN* union catalogs each contain millions of bibliographic records from thousands of libraries.

11. For full citations of the resources mentioned in this paragraph, see*NGrove, MGG, EitnerQL, RISM-A1, Pazdirek, RLIN*, and *OCLC* in the Key to Abbreviated Publishers and Sources.

12. *The Chicago manual of style*, 14th ed. (Chicago: University of Chicago Press, 1993).

But the public . . . loves everything connected with a funeral.
—George Bernard Shaw, *Music in London 1890–94*

Musical Memorials for Musicians

ABEL, CARL FRIEDRICH, German composer, gambist; b. Dec. 22, 1723; d. June 20, 1787.

Mozart, Wolfgang Amadeus, 1756–1791. *Sonate pour le forte-piano ou clavecin avec accompagnement d'un violon* [Sonatas, violin, piano, K. 526, A major] (1787). Piano (or harpsichord) with violin accompaniment. Published Vienna: F. A. Hofmeister 128, 1787. Modern edition in Mozart, *Sonaten und Variationen für Klavier und Violine,* vol. 2, ed. Eduard Reeser, Neue Ausgabe sämtlicher Werke, Ser. VIII, Wg. 23, vol. 2 (*Bärenreiter* BA4540, 1965). The final movement quotes Abel's piano trio, op. 5 no. 5. Since the work was completed two months after Abel's death, *WSF,* vol. 5, p. 319, conjectured that Mozart intended this sonata as a memorial to Abel.

ABRAVANEL, MAURICE, Greek-American conductor; b. Jan. 6, 1903; d. Sep. 22, 1993.

Lazarof, Henri, 1932– . *Three pieces for orchestra: In memoriam Maurice Abravanel* (1994). Published *Merion* 446-41083, 1995. CONTENTS: Preambolo—Lamentazione—Finale.

ABSIL, JEAN, Belgian composer; b. Oct. 23, 1893; d. Feb. 2, 1974.

Legley, Vic, 1915–1994. *Hommage à Jean Absil* (1980). Saxophone quartet and band. Unpublished. Source: *Londeix.* Recorded by the Belgian Guides Symphonic Band, cond. by Norbert Nozy (René Gailly CD87123, 1996).

ACE, JOHNNY, American rhythm-and-blues vocalist; b. June 9, 1929; d. Dec. 25, 1954.

Dillard, Varetta, 1933–1993. *Johnny has gone* (1955). Pop song. Recorded as a single on Savoy Records, 1955. Reissued on *Ladies sing the blues,* Roots of rock 'n' roll, vol. 12 (Savoy Records SJL2256, 1981).

ADAM, ADOLPHE, French composer; b. July 24, 1803; d. May 3, 1856.

Dietsch, Pierre-Louis-Philippe, 1808–1865. *Deux messes de requiem* (1856). Mixed voices and organ. Published Paris: Regnier,

1856. According to *NGrove*, one of these masses is dedicated to the memory of Adam.

ADASKIN, JOHN, Canadian conductor, violoncellist; b. Mar. 28, 1908; d. Mar. 4, 1964.

Glick, Srul Irving, 1934– . *Elegy for orchestra* (1964). Published *Canadian*. Composed in memory of three Toronto violoncellists who died in 1964: John Adaskin, Isaac Mammot, and Rowland Pack.

AGRICOLA, ALEXANDER, Netherlands composer; b. 1447?; d. Aug. 1506.

Isaac, Heinrich, ca. 1450–1517. "Musica, quid defles?" in *Symphoniae iucundae atque adeo quatuor vocum, ab optimis quibusque musicis compositae, ac iuxta ordinem tonorum dispositae, quas vulgo mutetas appellare solemus, numero quinquaginta duo.* Published Wittenberg: G. Rhaw, 1538. *RISM-B1*: 1538/8. Subtitle: Epitaphion Alexandri Agricolae Symphonistae regis. Modern edition in George Rhaw, *Musikdrucke aus den Jahren 1538 bis 1545 in praktischer Neuausgabe*, vol. 3, ed. Hans Albrecht (*Bärenreiter* BA3133, 1959). Attributed to Isaac by Ludwig Fischer in his review of the Albrecht edition in *Die Musikforschung* 16 (1963): 206, and by Martin Picker in "A letter of Charles VIII of France concerning Alexander Agricola," *Aspects of Medieval and Renaissance Music: A birthday offering to Gustav Reese*, p. 665–672, ed. Jan LaRue (New York: Pendragon, 1978).

AHLE, JOHANN RUDOLPH, German organist, composer; b. Dec. 24, 1625; d. July 9, 1673.

Ahle, Johann Georg, 1651–1706. "Ach! Ach! ihr Augen, Ach!" in *Der Gläubigen . . . Adel und Würde . . . bey Beerdigung des . . . Johann Rudolph Ahlen . . . den 11. Julij lauffendes 1673. Iahrs* (1673). Voices (5). Published Mühlhausen: Johann Hüter, 1673. *RISM-A1*: A-470. Johann Rudolph was the father of Johann Georg.

ALAIN, JEHAN ARISTE, French organist, composer; b. Feb. 3, 1911; d. June 20, 1940.

Dupré, Marcel, 1886–1971. "Virgo Mater: à la mémoire de Jehan Alain," in his *Offrande à la Vierge,* op. 40 (1944). Organ. Published *Bornemann* SB5338, 1945. CONTENTS: Virgo Mater—Mater dolorosa—Virgo mediatrix.

Duruflé, Maurice, 1902–1986. *Prelude et fugue sur le nom d'Alain,* op. 7: *à la mémoire de Jehan Alain, mort pour la France* (1942). Organ. Published *Durand* 13159, 1943. Alain was killed in action at Petits-Puis, near Saumur.

Fleury, André, 1903–1995. *In memoriam: Hommage à Jehan Alain* (1990). Organ. Published *ChantM*, 199– .

Langlais, Jean, 1907–1991. *Mort et résurrection: In memoriam Jehan Alain* (1990). Organ. Published *Leduc* AL28159, 1990.

ALBÉNIZ, ISAAC, Spanish composer; b. May 29, 1860; d. May 18, 1909.

    Charles, Agustin, 1960– . *Da niente . . . .: A la memoria de Isaac Albéniz* (1990). Piano solo with chamber ensemble. Published *EMEC*, 1990.

    Garcia Roman, José, 1945– . "Epitafio a Isaac Albéniz," in his *Ocho canciones para coro mixto.* Mixed chorus. Published *EMEC* 8489921113, 1999. CONTENTS: Romance de la luna, luna—Baladilla de los tres rios—Cancion tonta—La senorita del abanico—Serenata—Balada interior—En la amplia cocina, la lumbre—Epitafio a Isaac Albéniz.

    Séverac, Déodat de, 1872–1921. *Sous les lauriers roses* (1919). Piano. Published Paris: Rouart, Lerolle 11080, 1920. Alternate title on caption: *Soir de Carnaval sur la Côte Catalane.* "Fantaisie dédiée à la mémoire des maitres aimés, E. Chabrier, I. Albéniz et Ch. Bordes"—dedication in score.

ALBERT, STEPHEN, American composer; b. Feb. 6, 1941; d. Dec. 30, 1992.

    MacCombie, Bruce, 1943– . *Elegy to the memory of Stephen Albert: For chamber ensemble.* Quartet for clarinet, violin, violoncello, piano. Published *Helicon* EA765, 1994. Includes musical references to Albert's *Symphony Riverrun.*

    Schwantner, Joseph, 1943– . *Concerto for percussion and orchestra: To the memory of Stephen Albert* (1994). Published *Helicon* EA8092, 1994.

ALBRECHT, JOHANN LORENZ, German music scholar; b. Jan. 8, 1732; d. Nov. 29, 1768.

    Albright, William, 1944–1998. *1732: In memoriam Johannes Albrecht* (1983). Organ with optional narration in English. Published *Henmar* 67129, 1986. The title is the year of Albrecht's birth.

ALESSANDRO, RAFFAELE D', Swiss composer, pianist; b. Mar. 17, 1911; d. Mar. 17, 1959.

    Diethelm, Caspar, 1926–1997. *Epitaph für Raffaele d'Alessandro,* op. 39 (1963). String orchestra. Unpublished. Source: *Diethelm.*

AMATI, NICOLA, Italian luthier; b. Dec. 3, 1596; d. Apr. 12, 1684.

    David, Johann Nepomuk, 1895–1977. "Nicola Amati in memoriam," in his *Vier Trios,* op. 33 (1928–1935). Trio for violin, viola, violoncello. Published *Breitkopf* 5598, 1948. CONTENTS: Nicola Amati in memoriam—Antonio Stradivario in memoriam—Giuseppe Guarneri del Gesù in memoriam—Jacobo Stainer in memoriam.

AMENGUAL ASTABURUAGA, RENÉ, Chilean composer; b. Sep. 2, 1911; d. Aug. 2, 1954.

Heinlein, Federico, 1912–1999. *Silencio: A la memoria de René Amengual* (1957). Voice and piano. Unpublished. Source: *Chile.* Text by A. Storni.

AMNER, RALPH, English vocalist; d. Mar. 3, 1664.

Child, William, 1606–1697. "Let poets ne'er puzzle," in *Catch that catch can, or, The musical companion containing catches and rounds for three and four voyces, to which is now added a second book containing dialogues, glees, ayres, & ballads, &c, some for two/three/foure voyces.* Voices (3). Published London: W. Godbid for J. Playford, 1667. *RISM-B1*: 1667/6. Modern microfilm edition in *Early English books, 1641–1700*, vol. 148:6 and 157:8 (Ann Arbor, MI: University Microfilms, 1964).

ANDERSEN, ALF, Norwegian flutist; b. Nov. 25, 1928; d. June 24, 1962.

Nordheim, Arne, 1931– . *Epitaffio: Alf Andersen in memoriam* (1963; rev. 1977). Orchestra and electronic tape. Published *Hansen* 4090, 1980. Recorded by the Oslo Philharmonic Orchestra, cond. by Herbert Blömstedt on *Musique électronique norvégienne* (Philips Records 836–896, 197–).

ANDERSON, BARRY, New Zealand composer, pianist; b. Feb. 22, 1935; d. May 27, 1988.

Montague, Stephen, 1943– . *In memoriam: Barry Anderson and Tomasz Sikorski* (1989–91). Ensemble of string quartet, percussion (2), electronics, tape; a revision of the composer's 1989 string quartet. Published *UMP*, 1991. "In memoriam . . . was inspired by my close friendship with these two men, and uses short thematic and harmonic material from their works"—note in score.

ANDERSON, BRUCE C., American pianist; b. 1955; d. Jan. 4, 1991.

Mumford, Jeffrey, 1955– . *The clarity of remembered spirits: In memoriam Bruce Anderson.* Viola solo. Published *Presser* 114-40939, 1999.

ANDERSON, MARIAN, American contralto; b. Feb. 17, 1899; d. Aug. 4, 1993.

Singleton, Alvin, 1940– . *Somehow we can* (1994). String quartet.

Published *EurAmer*, 1994. Commissioned by the Eastman School of Music in memory of Marian Anderson.

ANSERMET, ERNEST, Swiss conductor; b. Nov. 11, 1883; d. Feb. 20, 1969.

Sutermeister, Heinrich, 1910–1995. *Consolatio philosophiae: Scène dramatique in memoriam Ernest Ansermet* (1977). High voice and orchestra. Published *Schott-M* 6817, 1978. Text from Boethius. CONTENTS: Le chemin de la vérité—Les tentations—La violence—L'amour—La gloire—La folie du temps—La consolation de la philosophie—La prière.

ARISTOXENOS, Greek music scholar; b. 354 B.C.

Xenakis, Iannis, 1922– . *Nomos alpha: À la mémoire d'Aristoxène de Tarente, de Evariste Galois et de Felix Klein* (1965–66). Violoncello solo. Published *Boosey*, 1966.

ARMSTRONG, LOUIS, American jazz trumpeter; b. July 4, 1900; d. July 6, 1971.

Broege, Timothy, 1947– . "Le tombeau de Louis Armstrong," in his *Partita no. 2 "Le Lardon"* (1972). Harpsichord. Published Arlington, VA: Plucked Strings Editions, 198–? CONTENTS: Le tombeau de Igor Stravinsky—Death dance: Yasuari Kawabata—Death dance: John Berryman—Death dance: Yukio Mishima—Le tombeau de Louis Armstrong.

Dickerson, Roger, 1934– . *A musical service for Louis: A requiem for Louis Armstrong* (1972). Orchestra, with optional wordless mixed chorus. Published *Peer-S* 60820-956, 1973.

Wilson, Dana Richard, 1946– . *I remember . . . .: Louis and Clifford and Miles and Dizzy.* Trumpet solo in the jazz idiom. Published *ITG*, c1997, as special supplement to *ITG journal* 23/1 (Sept. 1998). A memorial to jazz trumpeters Louis Armstrong, Clifford Brown, Miles Davis, and Dizzy Gillespie.

ARNOLD, SAMUEL, English organist, composer; b. Aug. 10, 1740; d. Oct. 22, 1802.

Callcott, John Wall, 1766–1821. *I heard a voice from heaven: Part of the burial service at the funeral of Samuel Arnold* (1802). Motet. Published London: s.n., 1802. Later edition in *Singer's library of concerted music*, ed. John Pyke Hullah, Sacred series, no. 19, London: Addison, Hollier & Lucas, 1859–1863.

AST, RENÉ VAN, Dutch violoncellist; b. 1937; d. Mar. 4, 1985.

Hamburg, Jef, 1956– . *Elegie: In memoriam René van Ast* (1985). Septet for guitars (3), flute, viola, violoncello, harp. Published *Done-*

mus, 1985. Also in a revised version for bass flute, saxophone, bass clarinet, percussion: *Donemus*, 1986.
AYESTARÁN, LAURO, Uruguayan musicologist; b. July 9, 1913; d. July 22, 1966.
Biriotti, Leon, 1929– . *Symphony no. 3: Homeneje a la memoria de Lauro Ayestarán* (1968). Orchestra. Unpublished. Source: *IUL*.

BACEWICZ, GRAZYNA, Polish composer; b. Feb. 5, 1913; d. Jan. 17, 1969.
Luciuk, Juliusz, 1927– . *Lamentazioni in memoriam Grazyna Bacewicz* (1970). Orchestra. Published *PWM*.
BACH, CARL PHILIPP EMANUEL, German composer; b. Mar. 8, 1714; d. Dec. 14, 1788.
Loudová, Ivana, 1941– . *Posey for Emanuel: In memory of C. P. E. Bach* (1981). Jazz quintet (oboe, clarinet, piano, double bass, percussion). Published *Cesky*, 1981? Also known as *Bouquet for Emanuel*.
Mozart, Wolfgang Amadeus, 1756–1791. *Menuetto avec trio pour le piano-forte* [Minuets, piano, K. 355, D major] (1791?). Published Vienna: T. Mollo 179, 1801. Interpretation of the work as a tombeau for C. P. E. Bach is by Peter Schleuning, "Mozart errichtet ein Denkmal: Das Menuett D-Dur KV 355," *Zwischen Aufklarung & Kulturindustrie: Festschrift für Georg Knepler zum 85 Geburtstag* (Hamburg: Bockel, 1993), vol. 1, pp. 83–94.
BACH, JOHANN CHRISTIAN, German-English composer; b. Sep. 5, 1735; d. Jan. 1, 1782.
Mozart, Wolfgang Amadeus, 1756–1791. *Grand concert pour le clavecin ou forte-piano: Avec l'accompagnement des deux violons, alto, et basse, deux hautbois, et deux cors: oeuvre IV, livre [1]* [Concertos, piano, orchestra, K. 414, A major] (1782). Published Vienna: Artaria, 1785. The theme of the Andante movement is taken from an overture of J. C. Bach composed in 1763 for a revival of Galuppi's *La calamita dei cuori*. *WSF* thus surmised that the concerto was intended as a memorial tribute to Bach, whose death day he described in a letter to his father (April 10, 1782) as "a sad day for the world of music" ("Schade für die musikalische Welt!"). Modern edition in Mozart, *Konzerte für ein oder mehrere Klaviere und Orchester mid Kadenzen*, ed. Wolfgang Rehm, Neue Ausgabe sämtlicher Werke, Ser. V, Wg. 15, vol. 8 (*Bärenreiter* BA4524, 1960).
Schmittbaur, Joseph Aloys, 1718–1809. "Hülle dich, in düstren

Trauerschlein: Auf den Tod des grossen Bachs in London," in *Blumenlese für Klavierliebhaber,* Part 2, 14th week. Cantata for voice, flute, violins (2), violoncello, harpsichord. Published Speyer: Rath Bossler, 1782. *RISM-A1*: S-1820.

BACH, JOHANN SEBASTIAN, German composer; b. Mar. 21, 1685; d. July 28, 1750.

> **Abbott, Alain, 1938– .** *Le tombeau de Bach* (1974). Saxophone quartet. Unpublished. Source: *Londeix.*
>
> **Bach, Carl Philipp Emanuel, 1714–1788.** *Exempel nebst achtzehn Probe-Stücken in sechs Sonaten zu Carl Philipp Emanuel Bachs Versuche über die wahre Art das Clavier zu spielen auf XXVI. Kupfer-Tafeln* [Sonatas, keyboard instrument, H. 75. Fantasia] (1753). Published Berlin: Verlegung des Auctoris, gedruckt by D. F. Henning, 1753. The Fantasia in C-minor (the "Hamlet" fantasy) is from the *Probestücke* composed to accompany C. P. E. Bach's *Versuch über die wahre Art das Clavier zu spielen* (Essay on the true art of keyboard playing) of 1753. Facsimile edition: *The collected works for solo keyboard by Carl Philipp Emanuel Bach, 1714–1788,* 6 vols. (New York: Garland, 1985), vol. 1, p. 58–59. This Fantasia is republished in Hans-Günter Ottenberg, *C. P. E. Bach,* trans. Philip J. Whitmore (*OUP,* 1987), pp. 79–84, and elsewhere. Attribution as a lament for his father is by Wolfgang Wiemer, "Carl Philipp Emanuel Bachs Fantasie in c-moll: ein Lamento auf den Tod des Vaters?" *Bach Jahrbuch* 74 (1988): 163–177.
>
> **Denéréaz, Alexandre, 1875–1947.** *Concerto grosso for organ solo and orchestra: À la mémoire de J.-S. Bach* (1908). Unpublished. Source: *Beckmann.*
>
> **Gárdonyi, Zoltán, 1906–1986.** *Praeludium et fuga per organo: In memoriam J. S. Bach* (1943). Organ. Published *EMB* Z5095, 1950.
>
> **Hamilton, Iain, 1922–2000.** *Le tombeau de Bach: Reflections on six chorales* (1985). Organ. Published *Presser* 413-41142, 1989.
>
> **Hovland, Egil, 1924– .** *Le tombeau de Bach,* op. 95 (1978). Suite for orchestra. Published *Norsk* 9305, 1979. CONTENTS: Entrée—Rondeau—Air—Gavotte—Menuett—Gigue—Sortie.
>
> **Hrabovskyi, Leonid Oleksandrovych, 1935– .** "Aria: In memoriam Johann Sebastian Bach," in his *Homages: Seven pieces for guitar.* Published *Duma,* 1996. CONTENTS: Ciaccona: In memoriam Henry Purcell—Aria: In memoriam Johann Sebastian Bach—Impromptus: In memoriam Franz Schubert—Prelude: In memoriam Frédéric Chopin—A little cake-walk: In memoriam Scott Joplin—Chorale: In

memoriam Johannes Brahms—Amoroso: In memoriam Sergei Prokofiev.

Kraehenbuehl, David, d. 1997. *Sonata sopra B-A-C-H: Tombeau de Bach.* Piano. Unpublished. Source: Recorded by Martha Braqden on *Random walks: Piano music of David Kraehenbuehl* (New World Records NW80584, 2000).

Krenek, Ernst, 1900–1992. *Parvula corona musicalis,* op. 122*: Ad honorem Johannes Sebastiani Bach* (1950). String trio. Published *UE* 30201, 1993. Composed for the bicentennial of Bach's death. CONTENTS: Argumentum—Symphonia—Invocationes—Contrapunctivarii—Corona—Clausula.

Pousseur, Henri, 1929– . *Ballade berlinoise: À la mémoire de Brahms, Mahler, Schoenberg et . . . J. S. Bach* (1974–77). Piano. Published *Zerboni* 8373, 1979.

Reger, Max, 1873–1916. *Suite for organ in E minor,* op. 16*: Den Manen Joh. Seb. Bachs* (1894–95). Published London: Augener 310, 1896. Subsequent editions published by *Schott-M.*

Rosenvald, Helmuth, 1929– . *In memoriam J. S. Bach.* Violoncello and organ. Unpublished. Source: *Beckmann.*

Söderstrom, Gunno, 1920– . *Sonatina for piano: Bach-Handel in memoriam* (1984). Published *STIM.*

Tan, Dun, 1957– . *St. Matthew Passion* (in preparation 2000). Source: *New York Times,* April 2, 2000, Arts & Leisure section, announcing its preparation for performance by the Internationale Bachakadamie Stuttgart at a festival honoring the 250th anniversary of Bach's death. Tan's publisher is *Schirmer.*

Wallborn, Hartmut. *Ouvertürensuite: In memoriam J. S. Bach.* String orchestra. Published *DVfM.*

Wesley, Samuel, 1766–1837. "Eulogium de Johanne Sebastiano Bach" (1810), in *The Anglican hymns and Roman Catholic motets of Samuel Wesley,* by Holmes Ambrose. Chorus (ATB). Published Boston University (Ph.D. thesis), 1969, available in reprint from Bell & Howell Information and Learning Company (formerly University Microfilms). Text from Horace ("Unde nil maius"). Edited from British Library Ms. Add. 14340.

Winstin, Robert Ian. *In memoria J. S. Bach.* For "virtual orchestra" (digitally sampled, computer controlled orchestral sounds). Unpublished. Recorded by the composer (Editions de la rue Margot CCC6660, 1992).

BACH, WILHELM FRIEDEMANN, German composer; b. Nov. 22, 1710; d. July 1, 1784.

Bach, Carl Philipp Emanuel, 1714–1788. *Clavier-Sonaten und freye Fantasien nebst einigen Rondos . . . für Kenner und Liebhaber . . . 6. Sammlung* [Fantasias, piano, H. 289] (1786) . Wq. 61/3. Published Leipzig: Im Verlage des Autors, 1787. *RISM-A1*: B-93. Facsimile edition: *The collected works for solo keyboard by Carl Philipp Emanuel Bach, 1714–1788,* 6 vols. (New York: Garland, 1985), vol. 2, pp. 424–39. The fantasia in B-flat major in this collection quotes a polonaise of W. F. Bach, thus the conjecture that the work is a tombeau for him made by Peter Schleuning, "Mozart errichtet ein Denkmal: Das Menuett D-Dur KV 355," *Zwischen Aufklarung & Kulturindustrie: Festschrift für Georg Knepler zum 85 Geburtstag* (Hamburg: Bockel, 1993), vol. 1, pp. 83–94.

BAIRD, TADEUSZ, Polish composer; b. July 26, 1928; d. Sep. 2, 1981.

Pstrokonska-Nawratil, Grazyna, 1947– . *Fresco IV "alla campana": Tadeusz Baird in memoriam* (1984). Piano and orchestra. Unpublished. Source: *No/Gro.*

BAKFARK, BÁLINT, Hungarian lutenist; b. 1507; d. Aug. 15, 1576.

Terényi, Ede, 1935– . *In memoriam Bakfark: Simfonie.* String orchestra. Published *EditMuz,* 1983.

BALAKIREV, MILY, Russian composer; b. Jan. 2, 1837; d. May 29, 1910.

Liapunov, Sergei Mikhailovich, 1859–1924. "Dem Andenken M. A. Balakirewa," op. 52, no. 1, in his *Lieder und Romanzen,* vol. 10. Song. Published *Zimmermann,* 1913. In vol. 10 of 13 published 1902–1926. Text incipit "Der Tod nahm dich hinweg."

BANKS, DON, Australian composer; b. Oct. 25, 1923; d. Sep. 5, 1980.

Sitsky, Larry, 1934– . *Fantasia no. 3: In memory of Don Banks* (1980). Trumpet and string orchestra. Published *Seesaw,* 1990. A free transcription of Ferruccio Busoni's *Sonatina brevis in signo Joannis Sebastiani Magni* for piano.

BARBIROLLI, SIR JOHN, English conductor; b. Dec. 2, 1899; d. July 29, 1970.

Denniston, Donald Edwards, 1944– . *Ode for small orchestra,* op. 12: *In memory of Sir John Barbirolli* (1970). Unpublished. Source: *BCP.*

BARIÉ, AUGUSTIN, French organist; b. Nov. 18, 1883; d. Apr. 22, 1915.

Dupré, Marcel, 1886–1971. *Trois préludes et fugues pour grand orgue* [Préludes et fugues, organ, op. 7. No. 2] (1912). Published *Leduc* AL16405, 1920. The 2nd of the preludes and fugues was dedicated upon publication "à la mémoire d'Augustin Barié, organiste de Saint-Germain-des-Prés"—dedication in score.

BARLOW, DAVID, English composer; b. May 20, 1927; d. June 9, 1975.

Weisgarber, Elliot, 1919– . *Northumbrian elegy* (1977). Orchestra. Published *Canadian.* "Written in memory of David Barlow, late of the University of Newcastle Faculty of Music, and long-time friend of the composer"—*Canadian.*

BARRAQUÉ, JEAN, French composer; b. Jan. 17, 1928; d. Aug. 17, 1973.

Young, Douglas, 1947– . *Le tombeau de Barraqué* (1974). Piano. Unpublished. Source: *NGrove.*

BARRIOS MANGORÉ, AGUSTIN, Paraguayan guitarist; b. May 5, 1885; d. Aug. 7, 1944.

McConnell, David Edward. *Preludio: À la mémoire de Augustin Barrios.* Guitar. Published in the journal *Guitar international* (Jan. 1989).

BARROWS, JOHN, American hornist, composer; b. Feb. 12, 1913; d. Jan. 11, 1974.

Heiden, Bernhard, 1910–2000. *Variations for solo tuba and nine horns: Written for Harvey Phillps and dedicated to the memory of John Barrows* (1974). Published *AMP* 7451, 1977.

Wilder, Alec, 1907–1980. *John Barrows* (1977). Horn and chamber orchestra. Published Virginia Beach, VA: A Moll Dur AMD9HE1, 1979.

BARTÓK, BÉLA, Hungarian composer; b. Mar. 25, 1881; d. Sep. 26, 1945.

Ancelin, Pierre, 1934– . *Stèle pour trio à cordes,* op. 20: *À la mémoire de Béla Bartók* (1965). Trio for violin, viola, violoncello. Published *Choudens* AC20218, 1966?

Arma, Paul, 1905– . *À la mémoire de Béla Bartók: Poème musical* (1981). String orchestra and percussion. Published *EMB* Z12154, 1982. "Pour le centenaire de sa naissance: 25 Mars 1881"—note in score.

————. "Pour Béla Bartók," in his *Trois epitaphes* (1945). Piano. Published *EMT* TR001082, 1969. CONTENTS: Pour Romain Rolland—Pour ceux qui ne sont jamais revenus: Mes amis torturés, massacrés—Pour Béla Bartók.

Bárdos, Lajos, 1899–1987. *Bartók emlékére = In memoriam Bela Bartók* (1965). Chorus (3 equal voices). Published *EMB*, 196–? Text by L. Bóka.

Bausznern, Dietrich von, 1928–1980. *In memoriam Béla Bartók* (1974). Pianos (2). Unpublished. Source: *Siwe.*

Bloch, Augustyn, 1929– . *Infiltrazioni per due violini: Béla Bartók in memoriam* (1995). Violins (2). Unpublished. Source: *KdG.* First performance 1995, Budapest, Ildikó Line and Zsombor Tamási.

Clementi, Aldo, 1925– . *Tre piccoli pezzi: Omaggio a Bartók* (1950). Piano 4-hands. Published *Zerboni* 6829, 1950.

Eröd, Iván, 1936– . *Bartók emlékezete = In memory of Bartók,* op. 66b (1985). Piano. Unpublished. Source: *KdG.*

Godár, Vladimir, 1956– . *Le tombeau de Bartók* (1995). Orchestra. Unpublished. Source: *KdG.*

Kilar, Wojciech, 1932– . *Oda: Béla Bartók in memoriam* (1957). Violin, brasses (13), percussionists (6–7). Published *PWM*, 1960.

Kohs, Ellis B., 1916– . *Etude for piano: In memory of Bartók* (1946). Published *ACE*, 1946.

Kósa, György, 1897–1984. *In memoriam Bartók* (1947). Piano. Unpublished. Source: *Hungar.*

Ligeti, György, 1923– . "Adagio. Mesto: Béla Bartók in memoriam," in his *Musica ricercata per pianoforte* (1951–53). Published *Schott-M* 7718, 1995. No. 9 of 11 pieces.

Lopes Graça, Fernando, 1906–1994. *In memoriam Béla Bartók: 8 suites for piano* (1960–75). Unpublished. Source: *Lopes.*

Lutoslawski, Witold, 1913–1994. *Muzyka zalobna = Musique funèbre: À la mémoire de Béla Bartók* (1958). Suite for string orchestra (46 to 66 strings). Published *PWM* 5600, 1958. CONTENTS: Prologue—Metamorphoses—Apogée—Epilogue.

Pires, Filipe, 1934– . *In memoriam Béla Bartók* (1970). String quartet. Unpublished. Source: *NGrove.*

Ránki, György, 1907– . *Quartetto per archi = String quartet: In memoriam Bartók Béla* (1987). Published *EMB* Z13318, 1988.

Rautavaara, Einojuhani, 1928– . "Epitaph to BÉla BArtók [sic]," in his *Two preludes and fugues for violoncello and piano,* op. 36 (1955). Published *Fazer*, 1969. CONTENTS: Nimesta EinAr EnGlunD [On the name of Einar Englund]—Epitafi BÉla BArtok. Rautavaara transcribed the Bartók movement for string orchestra in 1986.

Saxton, Robert, 1953– . *Sonata for piano* (1981). Published *Chester* 55666, 1985.

Serly, Tibor, 1901–1978. *Lament: Homage to Béla Bartók* (1958). String orchestra. Published *Peer-S* 60661-766, 1963.

Sugár, Reszo, 1919– . *Concerto for orchestra: In memoriam Béla Bartók* (1962). Published *EMB* 210, 1967.

Szelényi, István, 1904–1972. *Hommage à Bartok* (1947). Orchestra. Published Leeds, UK; New York: The Arts Council, 1947. Also arranged for piano: Budapest: Korda Testverek, 1948. New edition of the piano version published: *Schott-M* 8756, 1997.

Takács, Jenö, 1902– . "Dialogue nocturne für Béla Bartók," in his *Vier Epitaphe,* op. 79 (1964). Piano. Published *Doblinger* 681671, 1966. CONTENTS: Praeludium für Paul Hindemith—Elegie für Claude Debussy—Fragment für Alban Berg—Dialogue nocturne für Béla Bartók.

Tansman, Alexandre, 1897–1986. *Sonata no. 5 for piano: À la mémoire de Béla Bartók* (1955). Published *UE* 12498, 1956.

Tassone, Pasquale, 1949– . *Unknown memory: Tribute to Bartók* (1981). Trio for violin, clarinet, piano. Unpublished. Source: *BCP*. First performance August 31, 1981, Siena, Italy.

Turchi, Guido, 1916– . *Concerto breve: Alla memoria di Béla Bartók* (1947). String quartet. Published *Zerboni* 5067, 1955.

Valls, Manuel, 1920–1984. *Tema con variaciones: Sobre la muerte de Béla Bartók* (1946). Sextet for oboe, bassoon, string quartet. Unpublished. Source: *Catalan.* First performance October 21, 1948, Barcelona.

Veress, Sándor, 1907–1992. *Threnos: In memoriam Béla Bartók* (1945). Orchestra. Published *Zerboni* 4715, 1952. Identified in *NGrove* as "Sirató ének [Threnody] in memoriam Béla Bartók."

Zinsstag, Gérard, 1941– . *String quartet no. 2: In memoriam Béla Bartók* (1994–95). Published *Modern* TME218, 1998.

BATES, DAVID SNOW, American composer; b. 1936; d. Nov. 1974.

Riley, Dennis, 1943–1999. *Elegy* (1975). Violoncello and string orchestra. Published *Peters* 66696, 1975.

BATTISHILL, JONATHAN, English organist, composer; b. May 1738; d. Dec. 10, 1801.

Wesley, Charles, 1757–1834. *Elegy to the memory of Jonathan Battishill* (1801). Chorus (SATB). Published London: s.n., 1801. Source: *BPL.*

BAUSZNERN, DIETRICH VON, German composer; b. Mar. 12, 1928; d. Jan. 20, 1980.

Hummel, Bertold, 1925– . *In memoriam,* op. 74: *To the memory of*

Dietrich von Bausznern (1980). Organ and percussion. Published *Schott-M* 7182, 1984. CONTENTS: Invocation—Toccata—Requiem—Choral "Wenn wir in höchsten Nöten sein."

BEAUCAMP, ALBERT MAURICE, French composer, conductor; b. May 13, 1921; d. Sep. 22, 1967.

Murgier, Jacques, 1912– . *Concertino for violin and piano: In memoriam Albert Beaucamp* (1968). Published *Leduc*, 1968.

BEAUREGARD, LAWRENCE, French flutist; d. Sep. 4, 1985.

Boulez, Pierre, 1925– . *Memoriale (. . . explosante-fix . . . originel): Pour flûte solo et huit instruments: En souvenir de Lawrence Beauregard* (1985). Solo flute with octet of horns (2), violins (3), violas (2), violoncello. Published *UE* 18657, 1985. An earlier version of this work (*Explosante-fix . . .*) was written for the collection *In memoriam Igor Fedorovich Stravinsky: Canons and epitaphs*, Set I (q.v.).

BECKER, CARL FERDINAND, German organist, composer; b. July 14, 1804; d. Oct. 26, 1877.

Kirchner, Theodor, 1823–1903. "Andante," in his *Gedenkblätter: Zwölf Musikstücke zur Erinnerung an die Einweihung des neuen Königl. Conservatoriums für Musik zu Leipzig,* op. 82 (1843–87). Piano. Published Leipzig: J. Rieter-Biedermann 1508, 1887. No. 9 of 12 short piano pieces memorializing Conrad Schleinitz, Felix Mendelssohn, Robert Schumann, Moritz Hauptmann, Ferdinand David, Ignaz Moscheles, Ernst Friedrich Richter, Carl Ferdinand Becker, Ernst Ferdinand Wenzel, and Louis Plaidy.

BEELER, WALTER, American band director, educator; b. May 8, 1908; d. June 6, 1973.

Tull, Fisher, 1934– . *Concerto grosso for brass quintet and symphonic band: In memory of Walter Beeler* (1980). Published *Boosey* QMB449, 1985.

BEETHOVEN, LUDWIG VAN, German composer; b. Dec. 16, 1770; d. Mar. 26, 1827.

Castérède, Jacques, 1926– . *In memoriam Ludwig van Beethoven* (1975). Orchestra. Unpublished. Source: *Mussat.*

Czerny, Carl, 1791–1857. *Hommage à Beethoven: Six fantaisies en forme de rondeaux sur des mélodies choisies des compositions vocales de Beethoven,* op. 466. Piano. Published *Simrock*; London: R. Cocks, 1837.

Darcy, Robert, 1910–1967. *String quartet: À la mémoire de Beethoven.* Published *CeBeDeM.*

Heinrich, Anthony Philip, 1781–1861. *To the spirit of Beethoven: An echo from America to the inauguration of Beethoven's monument at Bonn.* Orchestra. Unpublished. Source: *Heinrich.* Undated autograph manuscript is at the Library of Congress.

Hüttenbrenner, Anselm, 1794–1868. *Nachruf an Beethoven in Akkorden am Pianoforte von seinem innigsten Verehrer Anselm Hüttenbrenner* (1827). Piano. Published Vienna: T. Haslinger VN5039, 1827.

Lachner, Franz, 1803–1890. *Elegie for 5 violoncellos,* op. 160 (1834). Published Leipzig: Bertholf Senff 915. Modern edition by Bernhard Pauler: Winterthur: Amadeus Verlag BP2073, 1983. The editor of the 1983 edition names Hugo Riemann as the source of attribution of the work as a memorial to Beethoven.

Liszt, Franz, 1811–1886. *Kantate zur Inauguration des Beethoven-Monuments zu Bonn* [Festkantate zur Enthüllung des Beethoven-Denkmals in Bonn] (1845). Vocal soloists (SSTTBB), chorus (STB), orchestra. Published *Peters* 8710, 1989, in a reconstruction by Gunther Massenkeil. The full score survives only in Liszt's incomplete holograph in the Liszt Museum in Weimar (Ms. B.14). Composed for the inauguration of the Beethoven Monument in Bonn, Germany (August 13, 1845). Text by Bernhard Wolff.

Liszt, Franz, 1811–1886. *Zur Säcularfeier Beethovens: Cantate* (1870). Vocal soloists (SATB), chorus, orchestra. Published Leipzig: Kahnt, 1870? Text by A. Stern. First performed in Weimar May 29, 1870, for the Beethoven Centenary celebrations of the Allgemeiner Deutscher Musikverein in Weimar.

Mayr, Giovanni Simone, 1763–1845. *Cantata per la morte di Beethoven* (1827). Soloists (STB), chorus (SATB), orchestra. Published *Peters.* Text possibly by Mayr. Manuscript is located at Civico Instituto Musicale "Gaetano Donizetti" in Bergamo. Additional information in Lawrence Sisk, "Giovanni Simone Mayr's cantata for the death of Beethoven," *Beethoven newsletter* 2/2 (Summer 1987): 27–29.

Meyerbeer, Giacomo, 1791–1864. "Au tombeau de Beethoven," in his *40 mélodies à une et à plusieur voix* (1845). Women's chorus (SSA) with bass soloist. Published Paris: Brandus & Cie. 5100, between 1848–1851, as the final work in the collection. Also published separately as *Der Wanderer und die Geister an Beethovens Grabe* (Vienna: F. Glögl, 1855?). Text by Ferdinand Braun; French translation by Maurice Bourges.

Miller, Julius, 1782–1851. *Apotheose auf Ludwig van Beethoven: Cantate für Männerstimmen.* Four-part men's chorus. Published Amsterdam: s.n., 1845? Source: *CPM.*

Schumann, Robert, 1810–1856. *Fantasie for piano in C major,* op. 17 (1936). Published *Breitkopf* 6053, 1839. The fantasie was begun by Schumann with the intent that proceeds from the sale would be donated for the erection of the Beethoven monument in Bonn. The initial working title for the planned three-movement sonata was *Grand Sonata for Beethoven,* with movements titled: Ruins—Trophies—Palms.

Seyfried, Ignaz, Ritter von, 1775–1841. *Requiem: Den Manen Ludwig van Beethovens gewidmet* (1833). Men's solo voices (4), chorus, muted trumpets (2), violoncellos (3), double bass, timpani, organ. Published Vienna: T. Haslinger 6513, 1835? Manuscript in the Österreichische Nationalbibliothek, Vienna, is dated 1833. Performances in Vienna and Prague in 1835 were noted in the *Allgemeine musikalische Zeitung,* vol. 37, p. 446.

————. *Libera [me, Domine], welches bei Beethoven's Leichbegängniss . . . am 29. März 1827 . . . gesungen worden ist* (1827). Men's chorus (TTBB). Published Vienna: T. Haslinger, 1827. Later edition in Ludwig van Beethoven's *Studien im Generalbass, Contrapunkt und in der Compositionslehre,* ed. Ignaz von Seyfried (Vienna: Haslinger, 1832). Reprint of the 1853 Leipzig/Hamburg/New York edition: *Olms,* 1967. Performed at Beethoven's funeral.

Shostakovich, Dmitri, 1906–1975. "Adagio," in his *Sonata for viola and piano,* op. 147 (1975). Published *Schirmer,* 1975. The third movement (Adagio) is dedicated to the memory of Beethoven.

Tanaka, Karen, 1961– . *At the grave of Beethoven* (1999). String quartet. Published *Chester* CH61656, 1999. Includes quotations from Beethoven's string quartet op. 18, no. 3.

Tower, Joan, 1938– . *Concerto for piano and orchestra: Dedicated to the memory of Beethoven* (1985). Published *AMP* 8011, 1986.

Valcárcel, Edgar, 1932– . *Montaja 59 para Ludwig: In memoriam Ludwig van Beethoven* (1971). Sextet for clarinet, string quartet, piano, and lights. Published *Seesaw.*

Webbe, Samuel, 1770–1843. *Funeral march in honour of Beethoven.* Piano. Published London: s.n., 1828. Source: *CPM.*

BELAIEV (BELAIEFF), MITROFAN PETROVICH, Russian music publisher; b. Feb. 22, 1836; d. Jan. 10, 1904.

Glazunov, Aleksandr Konstantinovich, 1865–1936. *Elegie for string quartet,* op. 105 (1929). Published *Belaieff* 3328, 1929. Composed for the 25th anniversary of Belaiev's death. Uses the "B-la-F" (Bb-A-F) motive also used by Glazunov in earlier compositions in honor of the still-living Belaiev.

Rimsky-Korsakov, Nikolay, 1844–1908. *Nad mogiloi,* op. 61: *Pamiati M. P. Bieliaeva* (1904). Prelude for orchestra. Published *Belaieff* 2551, 1905. Also arranged by the composer for piano 4-hands. New edition in Rimsky-Korsakov, *Sochineniia dlia orkestra,* Polnoe sobranie sochinenii [Works], vol. 23 (*Muzyka,* 1966).

Taneev, Sergei Ivanovich, 1856–1915. *String quintet no. 2,* op. 16, *in C major: À la mémoire de M. P. Belaieff* (1904). Quintet for violins (2), violas (2), violoncello. Published *Belaieff* 2546, 1905.

BELATI, TITO, Italian composer, music publisher; b. 1865; d. 1941.

Bartolucci, Mariano, 1881–1976. *In memoriam di Tito Belati.* Band. Published *Belati,* 1941?

BELL, WILLIAM, American tubist; b. Dec. 25, 1902; d. Aug. 7, 1971.

Benson, Warren, 1924– . *Canon for tuba and hand drum* (1971). Published *CFischer,* 1979.

Gould, Morton, 1913–1996. *Tuba suite: For Bill Bell in memoriam* (1971). Solo tuba with horns in F (3). Published *Chappell* 0047779-465, 1972. CONTENTS: Prelude—Chorale—Waltz—Elegy—Quickstep.

Schuller, Gunther, 1925– . *Five moods: In memory of William Bell* (1973). Tubas (4). Published *AMP,* 1976. "Five moods, dedicated to Mr. Bell's memory, tries to capture in vignette portraits the different characteristic traits of this remarkable man"—composer's note in score.

White, Donald H., 1921– . "In memory of 'The Boss'," in his *Tetra ergon: Four pieces* (1972). Bass trombone and piano. Published Nashville, TN: Brass Music Press, 1975. Published in International Trombone Association series, no. 2. CONTENTS: For Van [Haney]—In memory of "The Boss"—In memory of "The Chief" [i.e., Emory Remington]—In memory of "Dottie" [i.e., Dorothy Ziegler].

Wilder, Alec, 1907–1980. *Elegy: Written in tribute to and in memory of William Bell* (1971). Tuba solo with brass choir. Published New York: Wilder Music W197, 1974.

BELLASIO, PAOLO, Italian composer, organist; b. May 20, 1554; d. July 10, 1594.

Anonymous. "Ben f'ul nome fatale. D'incerto in morte del cav. P.

Bellasio," in *Il quinto libro de madrigali a cinque, del cavalier Paolo Bellasio.* Voices (5). Published Verona: Francesco Dalle Donne, 1595. *RISM-A1*: B-1718. An anonymous madrigal dedicated to the deceased Bellasio, and inserted into this posthumous edition of Bellasio's madrigals, compiled by Francesco Stivori.

BELLINI, VINCENZO, Italian composer; b. Nov. 3, 1801; d. Sep. 23, 1835.

Alla memoria di Vincenzo Bellini: Album per pianoforte. Published *Ricordi* 49317-49353, 1885. CONTENTS: Studio elegiaco / by Carlo Andreoli, 1840–1908—Mazurka / by Hans von Bronsart, 1830–1913—Pagine per l'Album Bellini, op. 7 / by Gius. Buonamici, 1846–1914—Polacca / by Eduardo Carracciolo—Melodia / by Benjamino Cesi, 1845–1907—Dolcezza fugace e meteora / by Ernesto Coop, 1802–1879—Ahi sugli estini non sorge fiore / by Michel Esposito, 1855–1929—Notturno / by Gabrielli Ferrari, 1860–1921—Pensiero romantico, op. 288 / by Disma Fumagalli, 1826–1893—Idylle-Impromptu, op. 61 / by Giuseppi Gariboldi, 1833–1905—M'abbandono / by Bernardo Geraci, 1825–1889—? . . . / by Stefano Golinelli, 1818–1891—Minuetto nello stile antico, a 4 mani, op. 220 / by Henri Herz, 1803–1888—Pensiero elegiaco / by Ferdinand Hiller, 1811–1885—Elegia, op. 170 / by Alfred Jaell, 1832–1882—Ricordanza / by Adolf Jensen, 1837–1879—Andante / by Friedrich Kiel, 1821–1885—Un fiore sulla tomba di Bellini / by Arnold Krug, 1849–1904—Agitazione: Impromptu / by Theodor Kullak, 1818–1882—Fantasia / by Franz Lachner, 1803–1890—2me Elegie, op. 207 / by Ignaz Leybach, 1817–1891—Recueillement / by Franz Liszt, 1811–1886—Racconto / by Giuseppe Martucci, 1856–1909—Canzone / by Constantino Palumbo, 1843–1928—Etude, op. 141 / by Pierre Perny, 1822–1908—Lontana! Canto senza parole, op. 10 / by Eugenio Pirani, 1852–1939—Andante sostenuto e Presto assai agitato / by Alfonso Rendano, 1853–1931—Romance / by Anton Rubinstein, 1829–1894—Scherzo sopra due note / by Paolo Serrao, 1830–1907—Notturno / by Giovanni Sgambati, 1841–1914—Berceuse / by Francesco Simonetti, 1846–1904—Barcarola, op. 59 / by Wilhelm Speidel, 1826–1899—Nostalgia: Notturno, op. 310 / by Fritz Spindler, 1817–1905—Canzone alla Siciliana / by Ludwig Stark, 1831–1844—Danse russe / by Piotr Ilyich Tchaikovsky, 1840–1893—Pagina d'album (Minuetto) / by Marie Wieck, 1832–1916.

Alary, Giulio, 1814–1891. *Sulla tomba di Bellini, l'amico dolente*

(1835). Voice and piano. Published *Ricordi* 8841, 1835.

Bergamo, Petar, 1930– . *Gloria: Alla memoria Vincenzo Bellini* (1967). Strings (13). Unpublished. Source: *NGrove.*

Bonica, Pietro. *A Vincenzo Bellini: Elegia per violino e piano-forte* (1866). Unpublished. Source: *SBN.* Manuscript at the Conservatorio di Santa Cecilia, Rome.

Bornacini, Giuseppe, 1802–1881. *In memoria di Vincenzo Bellini* (1836). Ode for soprano. Published *Ricordi* 9016, 1836.

Donizetti, Gaetano, 1797–1848. *Messa di requiem* [Requiems, In. 183, D minor] (1835). Soloists (SATBB), chorus (SATB), orchestra. Published Milan: Francesco Lucca, 1870. Modern facsimile ed. of the 1870 vocal score published under the auspices of the Donizetti Society: London: Egret House, 1974. New edition of vocal score: *Ricordi* 131956, 1975. Holograph full score is in the library of the Naples Conservatory.

————. *Sinfonia per orchestra sopra i migliori motivi di Vincenzo Bellini* (1836). Published *Ricordi* 9089, 1836. Modern edition: *B&S* BS20. The autograph is in the Paris Conservatory Library.

————. *Venne sull'ali ai zeffiri: Lamento per la morte di Bellini* (1835). Voice and piano. Published *Ricordi* 9022, 1835. Modern edition in a collection of 12 solo songs and 4 duets, *Donizetti per camera* (Naples: B. Girard). Text by Andrea Maffei. Dedicated to Maria Malibran.

Florimo, Francesco, 1800–1888. *Sinfonia funèbre in morte di Bellini* (1835). Orchestra. Published in an edition for piano 4-hands *Ricordi* 9439, 1836. Autograph score at Naples Conservatory library.

Gandolfi, Antonio. *Marcia funebre: In occasione del trasporto delle ceneri di Vincenzo Bellini da Parigi a Catania* (1864). Piano. Published Milan: Paolo De Giorgi 2149. Composed for the proposed transference of Bellini's remains from Paris to Catania, Italy.

Gorgni, Giuseppe. *Una lagrima sulla tomba di Donizetti: Elegia per pianoforte,* op. 2. Published *Ricordi* 25541, 1853.

Jaell, Alfred, 1832–1882. *Elegia per pianoforte,* op. 170: *Omaggio alla memoria di V. Bellini.* Published Naples: Associazione musicale industriale 253, 1885. Also published in *Alla memoria di Vincenzo Bellini* (q.v.).

Kullak, Theodor, 1818–1882. *Agitazione: Impromptu per pianoforte alla memoria di Vincenzo Bellini.* Published Naples: Associazione musicale industriale 251. Also published in *Alla memoria di Vincenzo Bellini* (q.v.).

Nicolai, Otto, 1810–1849. *Marcia funèbre in morte di Vincenzo Bellini* (1835). Orchestra. Published *Ricordi* 8909, 1835.

Pacini, Giovanni, 1796–1867. *Messa di requiem per il trasporto delle ceneri del sommo Bellini* (1864). Unpublished. Source: *NGrove.* Composed for the proposed transference of Bellini's remains from Paris to Catania, Italy. Manuscript is in the Seminario di Lucca. Recorded by the Cappella musicale S. Cecilia di Lucca, Orchestra lirico-sinfonica del Teatro del Giglio di Lucca, cond. by Gianfranco Coisma (Bongiovani GB2059-2, 1988).

Pedrotti, Carlo, 1817–1893. *In morte di Bellini* (1835). Voice and piano. Published *Ricordi* 8997, 1835.

Pirani, Eugenio, 1852–1939. *Lontana!: Canto senza parole alla memoria di Vincenzo Bellini,* op. 10. Piano. Published Naples: Associazione musicale industriale 276, after 1835. Also published in *Alla memoria di Vincenzo Bellini* (q.v.).

Platania, Pietro, 1828–1907. *Pensiero sinfonico* (1886). Orchestra. Unpublished. Source: *NGrove.* Composed for the dedication of the Bellini monument in Naples.

————. *Bellini e Meyerbeer: Sinfonia caratteristica a grande orchestra* (July 31, 1864). Vocal soloists (SMzTB) with orchestra. Unpublished. Source: *NGrove.* Text by Luigi de Brun ("Salvete o divi geni del canto"). Manuscript at the Conservatorio Santa Cecilia, Rome.

Rossi, Lauro, 1812–1885. *In morte di Vincenzo Bellini* (1835). Soprano and orchestra (or piano). Published *Ricordi* 8984, 1835. Text by Adele Curti.

BENZ, ALBERT, Swiss composer, bandmaster; b. Mar. 10, 1927; d. 1988.

Favre, Pascal, 1949– . *Dies aeterna: Hommage à Albert Benz = Huldigung an Albert Benz* (1988). Brass band. Published *Ruh* ER01534, 1990.

BERBERIAN, CATHY, American mezzo-soprano; b. July 4, 1925; d. Mar. 6, 1983.

Berio, Luciano, 1925– . *Requies: In memoriam Cathy Berberian* (1983–85). Chamber orchestra. Published *UE* 19149, 1985.

Bussotti, Sylvano, 1931– . *In memoriam Cathy Berberian* (1984). Voice with flute, viola, piano. Published *Ricordi.* Text by Bussotti.

Cage, John, 1912–1992. *Nowth upon Nacht: In memoriam Cathy Berberian* (1984). Song. Published *Peters* 67039, 1984. Text from *Finnegan's wake* by James Joyce.

BERG, ALBAN, Austrian composer; b. Feb. 9, 1885; d. Dec. 24, 1935.

Absil, Jean, 1893–1974. *Passacaille,* op. 101: *In memoriam Alban Berg* (1959). Piano. Published *CeBeDeM,* 1966.

Ali-Sade, Frangis, 1947– . *Sonata for piano no. 1: To the memory of Alban Berg* (1970). Published *Sikorski* (publication "in preparation" according to *Sikorski* web site in 2000).

Brindle, Reginald Smith, 1917– . *Epitaph for Alban Berg: On the 20th anniversary of his death: 24–XII–55* (1955). String orchestra. Published *Zerboni,* 1956.

Casanova, André, 1919– . *Trio for flute, bass clarinet, viola,* op. 3: *In memoriam Alban Berg.* Published Paris: A. Casanova, 1946?

Durme, Jef van, 1907–1965. *Ballade for orchestra no. 1,* op. 18 (1938). Published *CeBeDeM.*

Israel-Meyer, Pierre, 1933–1979. *Le tombeau d'Alban Berg* (1960). Suite for string orchestra. Published *Eschig,* 1965.

Kasparov, Yuri, 1955– . *Epitaph: In memory of Alban Berg* (1989). Quartet for violin, oboe, harp, percussion. Unpublished. Source: *ConCom.* Recorded by the Moscow Contemporary Music Ensemble (Olympia Records OCD283, 1991).

Krenek, Ernst, 1900–1992. *Streichtrio in zwölf Stationen,* op. 237: *Dem Andenken Alban Bergs gewidmet* (1985). String trio. Published *Bärenreiter* BA7042, 1986.

Petric, Ivo, 1931– . *Quatuor: À la mémoire d'Alban Berg* (1985). String quartet. Published *Slovensk* 1188, 1987.

Reimann, Aribert, 1936– . *String trio: Dem Andenken Alban Bergs* (1986–87). Published *Schott-M* 7581, 1989.

Scelsi, Giacinto, 1905–1988. "Passage du poète: À la mémoire d'Alban BERG," in his *Four poems* (1936–1939). Piano. Published *Salabert* EAS18376, 1986. CONTENTS: Une dernièr fois la terre—Comme un cri traverse un cerveau—Chemin du rêve—Passage du poète: À la mémoire d'Alban BERG.

Stromholm, Folke, 1941– . *In memoriam Alban Berg,* op. 9 (1967). String quartet (or string orchestra). Published *NMIC,* 1967.

Takács, Jenö, 1902– . "Fragment für Alban Berg," in his *Vier Epitaphe,* op. 79 (1964). Piano. Published *Doblinger* 681671, 1966. CONTENTS: Praeludium für Paul Hindemith—Elegie für Claude Debussy—Fragment für Alban Berg—Dialogue nocturne für Béla Bartók.

Vega, Aurelio de la, 1925– . *String quartet in five movements: In memoriam Alban Berg* (1957). Unpublished. Source: *NGrove.* First performance April 20, 1958, Washington, D. C., First Interamerican Music Festival, by the Claremont Quartet, to which the work is dedicated.

Vogel, Wladimir, 1896–1984. *Epitaffio per Alban* Berg (1936). Piano. Published *Ricordi* 128798, 1969. Based on a tone row derived from the words "Alban Berg aufs Grab Friede" ("Alban Berg upon the grave's peace").

BERG (MONTANUS), JOHANN VAN, Flemish music printer; d. Aug. 7, 1563.

Meiland, Jacob, 1542–1577. "Plerides pie rides, Epitaphium Joannis Mountain," in *Thesauri musici tomus tertius, continens cantiones sacras quas vulgo motetas vocant ex optimis musicis secletas.* Voices (6). Published Nuremberg: Berg & Neuber, 1564. *RISM-B1*: 1564/3.

BERG, JOSEF, Czech composer; b. Mar. 8, 1927; d. Feb. 26, 1971.

Istvan, Miloslav, 1928–1990. *In memoriam Josef Berg* (1972). Orchestra. Published *Cesky*; *Boosey*.

BERGENSON, ARON VICTOR, Swedish theorist, pedagogue; b. Oct. 2, 1848; d. May 18, 1914.

Paulson, Gustaf, 1898–1966. *Symphony no. 5, op. 51: Aron Bergenson in memoriam* (1948). Published *STIM*.

BERGER, WILHELM GEORG, Romanian composer; b. Dec. 4, 1929; d. Mar. 8, 1993.

Firca, Gheorghe, 1935– . *Epitaph: In memoriam Wilhelmi Bergeri* (199–). Organ. Unpublished. Source: *Beckmann*.

Terényi, Ede, 1935– . *Die Trompeten Gottes: In memoriam Wilhelm Georg Berger* (1995). Organ. Unpublished. Source: *Beckmann*.

BERGH, SVERRE, Norwegian composer; b. Nov. 2, 1915; d. Dec. 9, 1980.

Davies, Peter Maxwell, 1934– . *The Bairns of Brugh: For Sverre Bergh in memoriam* (1981). Sextet for piccolo, bass clarinet, piano, marimba, viola, violoncello. Published *Boosey* FSB515, 1983.

BERKELEY, SIR LENNOX, English composer; b. May 12, 1903; d. Dec. 26, 1989.

Berkeley, Michael, 1948– . "Fierce tears II," in his *Fierce tears I & Fierce tears II* (1990). Oboe and piano. Published *OUP* 193555018, 1994. "Fierce tears I" is a memorial to the English oboist Janet Craxton. Both pieces develop a line from "Elegy: In memoriam Benjamin Britten," which is the final movement of Michael Berkeley's oboe concerto. Sir Lennox Berkeley was the father of Michael Berkeley.

BERNSTEIN, LEONARD, American conductor, composer; b. Aug. 25, 1918; d. Oct. 14, 1990.

Asia, Daniel, 1953– . *Symphony II: Celebration symphony in memory of Leonard Bernstein* (1989–90; rev. 1992). Published Tucson: D. Asia Music, 1992. CONTENTS: Ma tovu—Ashrrenu—L'kha dodi—Hine El yeshuati—Hallaluyah. Program notes on the work are at http://www.danielasia.com.

Avshalomov, David, 1946– . *Elegy for Leonard Bernstein* (1989). String orchestra. Unpublished. Source: Recorded by the Moscow Symphony Orchestra, cond. by Daniel Avshalomov (Marco Polo 8.225035, 2000). Avshalomov studied with Bernstein at Tanglewood. The memorial dedication and the date of composition are both from the composer's notes accompanying the recording.

Cunningham, Michael G., 1937– . *In memoriam Leonard Bernstein,* op. 152 (1992). Clarinet and piano. Published *Media*, 1995.

Dubois, Pierre Max, 1930– . "Rapsodie: À Leonard Bernstein," in his *Bouquet d'hommages* (199–). Alto saxophone and piano. Published *Billaudot* 6126, 1997. CONTENTS: Prélude: À Albert Roussel—Barcarolle: À Darius Milhaud—Rapsodie: À Leonard Bernstein—Aria: À Jacques Ibert—Presto: À Francis Poulenc—Scherzo: À Dimitri Shostakovitch.

Franke, Bernd, 1959– . *Music for trumpet, harp, violin and orchestra: In memoriam Leonard Bernstein* (1990–1993). Published *Breitkopf*.

Glick, Srul Irving, 1934– . *In memoriam Leonard Bernstein* (1993). Chorus (SATB) and piano. Published *Thompson*, 1995. CONTENTS: Psalm 23—What I have learned is this (Ecclesiastes)—Lenny—Memorial kaddish.

Hutchison, Warner, 1930– . *Tombeau for Leonard Bernstein* (1991). Clarinet, percussion, strings. Published Las Cruces, NM: Cornucopia Music.

Leitner, Ernst Ludwig, 1943– . *Requiem: In memoriam Leonard Bernstein* (1993). Soprano, chorus (SATB), with ensemble of trumpets (2), horn, trombone, tuba, percussion, organ, harp, piano. Published *Doblinger* 45439, 1993.

Pizer, Elizabeth Hayden, 1954– . *Elegy in amber: In memoriam Leonard Bernstein* (1993). String orchestra. Unpublished. Source: OCLC. Recorded by the Slovak Radio Symphony Orchestra, cond. by Robert Stankovsky on *Desertscapes: A portrait of American women composers* (MMC Recordings 2026, 1997).

Rouse, Christopher, 1949–. *Concerto for trombone and orchestra: In memoriam Leonard Bernstein* (1991). Published *Helicon* EA731, 1991. Commissioned by the New York Philharmonic for its 150th anniversary. Awarded the 1993 Pulitzer Prize in Music.

BIGGIE SMALLS, American rap musician; b. 1972; d. Mar. 9, 1997. See: NOTORIOUS B. I. G.

BINCHOIS, GILLES, Burgundian composer; b. 1400?; d. Sep. 20, 1460.

Busnois, Antoine, ca. 1430–1492. A lament reportedly composed by Busnois for Binchois is lost. Source: *Houdoy.*

Dufay, Guillaume, 1400?–1474. "En triumphant de cruel dueil" in his *Cantiones*, ed. by Heinrich Besseler, Opera omnia, vol. 6, Corpus mensurabilis musicae, vol. 1/6. Voices (3). Published *AIM*, 1964. Text incipit in the Besseler edition: "Je triomphe de crudel dueil." Manuscript source: Oporto, Biblioteca publica municipal, Manuscript 714 (ca. 1467), f. 76–77. The designation of the work as a lament for Binchois is by David Fallows, "Two more Dufay songs reconstructed," *Early music* 3 (Oct. 1975): 358–360.

Ockeghem, Johannes, ca. 1410–1496. "Mort tu as navre de ton dart," in *Les musiciens de la cour le Bourgoyne au XVe siècle (1420–1467),* ed. Jeanne Marix. Voices (4). Published *Oiseau-L,* 1937. Facsimile of the original manuscript is published in *Dijon Bibliothèque publique ms 517,* intro. by Dragan Plamenac, Publications of medieval music manuscripts, vol. 12 (Brooklyn: Institute of Medieval Music, 1971?).

BLACK, RALPH, American arts administrator; b. July 11, 1919; d. Feb. 13, 1989.

Gould, Morton, 1913–1996. *Notes of remembrance* (Aug. 1989). Orchestra. Published *Schirmer* 3812, 1990. "He was a 'circuit rider' for the American Symphony Orchestra League in helping orchestras 'keep the faith'. . . . Dedicated to the American Symphony Orchestra League in memory of Ralph Black"—note in score.

BLACK, ROBERT CARLISLE, American composer, conductor; b. 1950; d. Nov. 14, 1993.

Bauer, Ross, 1951– . *Stone soup: Dedicated to the memory of Robert Black* (1995). Quintet for flute/piccolo, clarinet/bass clarinet, violin, violoncello, piano. Published *Peters* 67688, 1997.

BLANCROCHER, French lutenist; d. 1652?

Froberger, Johann Jacob, 1616–1667. "Le tombeau sur la mort de M. Blancheroche [sic]," in his *Orgel- und Clavierwerke III.* Denkmaler der Tonkunst in Osterreich, vol. 21. Published *DTÖ*, 1903.

Manuscript source: Klosterbibliothek, Minoritenkonvent, manuscript (without signature).

Couperin, Louis, ca. 1626–1661. "Le tombeau de M. de Blancrocher," in *Manuscrit Bauyn: Pièces de clavecin ca. 1660, avec une introduction de François Lesure.* Harpsichord. Published *Minkoff* 2826606522, 1977, which is a facsimile of the manuscript source, Bibliothèque nationale (France), Ms. Vm7 674–75. In modern notation in *Oeuvres complètes de Louis Couperin*, ed. Paul Brunold (*Oiseau-L*, 1936).

Dufaut, François, 17th cent. "Le tombeau de M. Blanrocher [sic]," in *Manuscrit Vaudry de Saizenay: Tablature de luth et de théorbe de divers auteurs* (1699). Published *Minkoff* 2826606859, 1980, which is a facsimile of the manuscript source, Besançon, Bibliothèque de la ville, Ms. 279.152, 279.153. In modern notation in *Oeuvres de Dufaut*, rev. ed. by André Souris, historical introduction by Monique Rollin (Paris: Éditions du Centre national de la recherche scientifique, 1988).

Gaultier, Denis, d. 1672. "Andromède (tombeau de Blancrocher)," published in *Rhétorique*. Lute. The identification of the work as a tombeau is from manuscript sources other than *Rhétorique* (see the concordances there).

BLISS, SIR ARTHUR, English composer; b. Aug. 2, 1891; d. Mar. 27, 1975.

Williamson, Sir Malcolm, 1931– . *Piano trio: In memory of Sir Arthur Bliss* (1976). Published *Weinberger*, 1976.

BODIG, RICHARD D., American gambist; b. Feb. 12, 1923; d. May 26, 1998.

Goldstein, David, 1918– . *Daybreak for viol quartet (treble, two tenors, and bass): In memory of Richard D. Bodig* (1999). Published Albany, CA: PRB Productions CC033, 1999. "Richard Bodig was very proud of his Armenian descent. Therefore it seemed right to use an Armenian folk song as a basis for a piece in his honor. . . . The piece is in four sections: 1. The melody is presented. 2. He goes off to war (to the hospital) almost gaily. 3. He is overwhelmed by cruel reality. 4. He does not come home"—program note in score.

BÖHM, KARL, Austrian conductor; b. Aug. 28, 1894; d. Aug. 14, 1981.

Zimmermann, Udo, 1942– . *Songerie: Dem Andenken von Karl Böhm* (1982). Chamber orchestra. Published *DVfM* 1730, 1983. CONTENTS: Hymnus—Psalmus—Canticum marianum—Hymnus—Psalmus.

BOIELDIEU, FRANÇOIS-ADRIEN, French composer; b. Dec. 16, 1775; d. Oct. 8, 1834.

Thomas, Ambroise, 1811–1896. *Hommage à Boieldieu: Cantata* (1875). Men's voices and winds. Published *Heugel*, 1875. Composed for the Boieldieu centenary.

BONHAM, JOHN HENRY (BONZO), English rock drummer; b. May 31, 1948; d. Sep. 25, 1980.

Rouse, Christopher, 1949– . *Bonham: For eight percussionists* (1988). Published *Helicon* EA672FS, 1989. "The work is an ode to rock drumming and drummers, most particularly Led Zeppelin's legendary drummer, the late John ('Bonzo') Bonham. The core ostinato of the score, played by the drum set, is taken from Led Zeppelin's 'When the levee breaks,' although there are references to other Led Zeppelin songs as well. . . ."—composer's note in score.

BONNET, JOSEPH, French organist; b. Mar. 17, 1884; d. Aug. 2, 1944.

Schulé, Bernard, 1909–1996. "Toccate-choral: À la mémoire de mon maitre Joseph Bonnet" (1944), in his *Enluminures: 6 pièces,* op. 12. Organ. Published Paris: Rouart, Lerolle, 1946. "Toccate-choral" is no. 6 of the set.

BORDES, CHARLES, French choral conductor; b. May 12, 1863; d. Nov. 8, 1909.

Séverac, Déodat de, 1872–1921. *Sous les lauriers roses* (1919). Piano. Published Paris: Rouart, Lerolle 11080, 1920. "Fantaisie dédiée à la mémoire des maitres aimés, E. Chabrier, I. Albéniz et Ch. Bordes" —dedication in score. Alternate title on caption: *Soir de carnaval sur la côte catalane.*

BORODIN, ALEXANDER, Russian composer; b. Nov. 12, 1833; d. Feb. 27, 1887.

Glazunov, Aleksandr Konstantinovich, 1865–1936. *Stenka Razine: Poème symphonique,* op. 13: *À la mémoire d'Alexandre Borodin* (1885). Orchestra. Published *Belaieff* 465, 1888. Reprint: *Belaieff,* 1977. Composed in 1885, prior to Borodin's death. Dedication added apparently at publication.

Rimsky-Korsakov, Nikolay, 1844–1908. *Svetlyi prazdnik vskresnaia uvertiura = Ouverture "La grande Pâque Russe": À la mémoire de Moussorgski et de Borodine* (1888). Orchestra. Published *Belaieff* 245, 1890. Popularly known in English as *Russian Easter overture.* New edition in Rimsky-Korsakov, *Sochineniia dlia orkestra,* Polnoie sobranie sochineni [Works], vol. 21 (*Muzyka,* 1958).

BOSKOVICH, ALEXANDER URIAH, Israeli composer; b. Aug. 16, 1907; d. Nov. 5, 1964.

    Seter, Mordecai, 1916– . *Meditation* (1967). Orchestra. Published *Israeli* IMI128, 1977.

    Yannay, Yehuda, 1937– . *Statement: In memoriam A. U. Boskovich* (Nov. 1964). Flute. Published *Israeli*, 1972.

BOULANGER, LILI, French composer; b. Aug. 21, 1893; d. Mar. 13, 1918.

    Blanc de Fontbelle, Cécile, 1905– . *A la mémoire de Lily Boulanger*. Piano. Published Paris: M. Senart, 1924.

    Migot, Georges, 1891–1976. *Piano trio: À la mémoire de Lili Boulanger* (1918). Published Paris: M. Senart, 1920.

    Musgrave, Thea, 1928– . *Cantata for a summer's day: Dedicated to the memory of Lili Boulanger* (1954). Vocal quartet (or small chorus) and speaker with flute, clarinet, string quartet, double bass (or flute, clarinet, small string orchestra). Published *Novello*.

    Naoumoff, Emile, 1962– . *Impression: In memoriam Lili Boulanger* (1992). Bassoon and piano. Published *Schott-M* FAG24, 1996.

    Rorem, Ned, 1923– . *String quartet no. 2: To the memory of Lili Boulanger* (1950). Published *Peer-S* 61305-757, 1971.

    Wuorinen, Charles, 1938– . *Evolutio* (1961). Organ. Published *Peters* 67362, 1961. Also transcribed for chamber orchestra as *Evolutio transcripta* (*Peters* 67363). Wuorinen received the Lili Boulanger prize in 1961. Nadia Boulanger suggested to him that he dedicate this work to the memory of her deceased sister. Nadia Boulanger attended the first performance by Leonard Raver, April 8, 1962, at the Church of the Advent, Boston.

BOULANGER, NADIA, French pedagogue; b. Sep. 16, 1887; d. Oct. 22, 1979.

    Amlin, Martin, 1953– . "Sixths: Nadia Boulanger in memoriam," in his *Six etudes for piano* (1973–80). Unpublished. Source: *BCP.* CONTENTS: Thirds—Fourths—Fifths—Sixths: Nadia Boulanger in memoriam—Sevenths—Tenths.

    Schulé, Bernard, 1909–1996. *Hommage à Nadia Boulanger: Sonata,* op. 159 (1988). Violoncello and piano. Published Neuchatel, Switzerland: Schulé, 1988.

BOULNOIS, JOSEPH, French organist, composer; b. Jan. 28, 1884; d. 1918.

    Dupré, Marcel, 1886–1971. *Trois préludes et fugues pour orgue* [Préludes et fugues, organ, op. 7. No. 3] (1912). Published *Leduc*

AL16405, 1920. The 3rd of the preludes and fugues was dedicated post-composition "à la mémoire de Joseph Boulnois, organiste de Saint-Louis-d'Antin."

BOURDIN, ROGER, French baritone; b. June 14, 1900; d. Sep. 14, 1974.

Calvi, Gérard, 1922– . *Sept simples: En mémoire de Roger Bourdin.* Flute solo. Published *Leduc* AL25861, 1980. CONTENTS: Paisible—Brutal—Méditatif—Cocasse—Veloce—Secret—Performant.

BRAGA SANTOS, JOLY, Portuguese composer, conductor; b. May 14, 1924; d. July 18, 1988.

See: **SANTOS, JOLY BRAGA.**

BRAHMS, JOHANNES, German composer; b. May 7, 1833; d. Apr. 3, 1897.

Hrabovskyi, Leonid Oleksandrovych, 1935– . "Chorale: In memoriam Johannes Brahms," in his *Homages: Seven pieces for guitar.* Published *Duma*, 1996. CONTENTS: Ciaccona: In memoriam Henry Purcell—Aria: In memoriam Johann Sebastian Bach—Impromptus: In memoriam Franz Schubert—Prelude: In memoriam Frédéric Chopin—A little cake-walk: In memoriam Scott Joplin—Chorale: In memoriam Johannes Brahms—Amoroso: In memoriam Sergei Prokofiev.

Lunssens, Martin, 1871–1944. *Symphony no. 3: Symphonie française: En mémoire de Brahms.* Unpublished. Source: *Lunssens.*

Parry, Sir Charles Hubert Hastings, 1848–1918. *Elegy for Brahms* (1897). Orchestra. Unpublished. Source: *Parry.* Autograph manuscript is at the Royal College of Music, London. First performance November 9, 1918, London, Royal College of Music, at the Parry Memorial Concert, cond. by Sir Charles Villiers Stanford. Recorded by the London Philharmonic, cond. by Matthias Bamert (Chandos Records CHAN7006, 1995).

Reinecke, Carl, 1824–1910. *String trio,* op. 249 (1898?). Published *Breitkopf* PB1671, 1901. New edition by Michael A. Kimbell and Nandor Szederkenyi (*MusicaRara*, 1996). "The string trio op. 249 was probably composed around 1898, not long after the Cello sonata op. 238 (dedicated to the shades of Brahms), and like the latter suggests a deeply moving homage to Brahms"—preface to *MusicaRara* edition.

————. *Sonata for violoncello and piano no. 3,* op. 238: *Den Manen Johannes Brahms* (1898). Published *Breitkopf* 21890, 1898.

Rheinberger, Josef, 1839–1901. *Mass in G minor (Sincere in memoriam),* op. 187: *Johannes Brahms (+ 3.4.1897) zum Gedächtnis*

(1897). Solo voices ad libitum (SSA), women's chorus (SSA), organ. Published *Forberg* 2400, 1897. Reprint: Stuttgart: Carus-Verlag 501871, 1989. Composed between February 14 and April 9, 1897. The last four movements were completed after Brahms's death.

Rihm, Wolfgang, 1952– . *Ernster Gesang: Für Orchester* (1996). For the centennial of Brahms's death. Conductor Wolfgang Sawallisch "invited me to compose an orchestral piece for him and the Philadelphia Orchestra, a piece that should in a specific way establish a connection to Brahms. . . . For months I sang and played through *Lieder* and piano pieces from his late period. . . . The mystery of the *Vier ernste Gesänge* only revealed itself to me in those days of unceasing contact to his world"—composer's note in score.

BRAIN, AUBREY, British hornist; b. July 12, 1893; d. Sep. 21, 1955.

Jacob, Gordon, 1895–1984. *Sextet for piano and winds* (1957). Sextet for piano, flute, oboe, clarinet, horn, bassoon. Published *MusicaRara* 1070, 1962. "This work was written in memory of Aubrey Brain, the great horn player and father of the equally distinguished Dennis Brain. Very shortly after its first performance [Summer 1956] by the Dennis Brain Ensemble, Dennis Brain himself was killed in a motor accident. The work can therefore be regarded as a double tribute to the memory of father and son" —preface to score.

BRAIN, DENNIS, British hornist; b. May 17, 1921; d. Sep. 1, 1957.

Jacob, Gordon, 1895–1984. *Sextet for piano and winds* (1957). Sextet for piano, flute, oboe, clarinet, horn, bassoon. Published *MusicaRara* 1070, 1962. "This work was written in memory of Aubrey Brain, the great horn player and father of the equally distinguished Dennis Brain. Very shortly after its first performance [Summer 1956] by the Dennis Brain Ensemble, Dennis Brain himself was killed in a motor accident. The work can therefore be regarded as a double tribute to the memory of father and son"—preface to score.

Poulenc, Francis, 1899–1963. *Elegie: In memory of Dennis Brain* (1957). Horn and piano. Published *Chester* 1607, 1958.

BREITENGASER, WILHELM, German composer; b. 1495?; d. Dec. 23, 1542.

Othmayr, Caspar, 1515–1553. "Non secus atque olim," in *Selectissimae symphoniae compositae ab excellentibus musicis, antehac non aeditae*. Voices (4). Published Nuremberg: Berg & Neuber, 1546. *RISM-B1*: 1546/8. Modern edition in Othmayr, *Abteilung Ausgewahlter Werke einzilner Meister*, Ausgewahlte Werke, vol. 4, ed. Hans Albrecht, Das Erbe deutscher Musik, vol. 26 (*Peters*, 1956).

BREMNER, JAMES, Scottish-American composer, teacher; d. Sep. 1780.

Hopkinson, Francis, 1737–1791. *Sing to his shade a solemn strain: Ode in memory of Mr. James Bremner.* Recitative and air. Unpublished. Text and music by Hopkinson. The music is lost; the text is reprinted in *Hopkinson.*

BRENNAND, CHARLES, American violoncellist; b. 1929; d. July 29, 1976.

Suderburg, Robert, 1936– . *Chamber music I: Entertainments: Dedicated to the memory of Charles Brennand* (1967; rev. 1983). Duo for violin and violoncello. Published *Presser* 114-40398, 1984.

BRITTEN, LORD BENJAMIN, English composer; b. Nov. 22, 1913; d. Dec. 4, 1976.

Berkeley, Michael, 1948– . "Elegy: In memoriam Benjamin Britten," in his *Concerto for oboe and string orchestra* (1977). Published *OUP* J2029, 1982. CONTENTS: Moderato—Allegro vivace—Elegy: In memoriam Benjamin Britten.

Crosse, Gordon, 1937– . *Dreamsongs: Second elegy,* op. 43 (1978). Small orchestra. Published *OUP* J2604, 1986. "*Dreamsongs* is dedicated to the memory of Benjamin Britten. The origin of all the thematic ideas in one of his most well-loved pieces is, I hope, obvious. But if it isn't, then no matter because they are not quotations and they are developed in a manner totally different from that of Britten"—composer's note in score.

Denniston, Donald Edwards, 1944– . *Evening music,* op. 23: *In memory of Lord Benjamin Britten* (1979). Tenor and orchestra. Unpublished. Source: *BCP.* CONTENTS: The night wanderer / text by Douglas Shea—Instrumental passage: The evening air; Night has fallen / text by Alfred, Lord Tennyson—Instrumental passage: The evening star / text by Percy Bysshe Shelly.

Fricker, Peter Racine, 1920–1990. *Sinfonia for 17 winds,* op. 76: *In memoriam Benjamin Britten* (1976–77). Unpublished. Source: *Stoneham.*

Henze, Hans Werner, 1926– . *String quartet no. 5: In memoriam Benjamin Britten* (1976–77). Published *Schott-M* 6715, 1977.

Hoddinott, Alun, 1929– . *Hymnus ante somnum,* op. 97, no. 2: *In memoriam Benjamin Britten* (1979). Male chorus (TTTTBBBB) and organ. Published Cardiff: University College Cardiff Press, 1983. Text by Prudentius.

Hummel, Bertold, 1925– . *Adagio für Streicher,* op. 62a: *In memo-*

riam Benjamin Britten (Dec. 4, 1976). Trio for violin, viola, violoncello. Published *Schuberth* JS103, 1977.

Knussen, Oliver, 1952– . *Autumnal,* op. 14: *Benjamin Britten in memoriam* (1976–77). Violin and piano. Published *Faber* 0571505848, 1980. *Autumnal* is the first part of a triptych of chamber works (with *Sonya's lullaby* for piano, op. 16, and *Cantata* for oboe and string trio, op. 15); these works may be performed separately or together.

Lister, J. Rodney, 1951– . "O Lord, my God, though I forsake Thee: In memoriam Benjamin Britten," in *Three sacred songs* (1976–77). Soprano and violin. Published *ACA*, 1977? CONTENTS: Stedde fast cross, inmong all other / text anon. 14th cent.—O Lord, my God, though I forsake Thee / text by W. H. Auden—Generosity / text by Christopher Smart.

Pärt, Arvo, 1935– . *Cantus in memory of Benjamin Britten* (1977). String orchestra with bell. Published *UE* 17498, 1981.

Standford, Patric, 1939– . *Three motets,* op. 36: *In memoriam Benjamin Britten* (1976–77). Chorus (SATB). Published *Redcliffe* RES18, 1977. CONTENTS: Ave Verum Corpus—Flos Florum—Alma Redemptoris Mater.

Stevenson, Ronald, 1928– . *Sonata serenissima: In memoriam Benjamin Britten* (1973–77). Piano. Published *Bardic*, 1987.

Whittenberg, Charles, 1927–1984. *In memoriam Benjamin Britten* (1977). Percussion. Unpublished. Source: *NGrove*.

Williamson, Sir Malcolm, 1931– . *The lion of Suffolk: For Benjamin Britten* (1977). Organ. Published *Weinberger*, 1979.

Wills, Arthur, 1926– . *Missa: In memoriam Benjamin Britten.* Chorus (SATB) and organ. Published Croydon: Addington Press AP101, 1978.

BRIZZI, GAETANO, Italian composer; b. 1804; d. 1876.

Amadei, Roberto, 1840–1913. *Elegia sullo Stabat di Rossini: Alla memoria di Gaetano Brizzi.* Violin and piano. Published Bologna: Brizzi e Comp. 79, 187–?

BROWN, CLIFFORD ("BROWNIE"), American jazz trumpeter; b. Oct. 30, 1930; d. June 26, 1956.

Golson, Benny, 1929– . "I remember Clifford," recorded on *Meet the Jazztet*: Argo LP664, 1960. Jazz sextet: Art Farmer (trumpet), Benny Golson (tenor saxophone), Curtis Fuller (trombone), McCoy Tyner (piano), Addison Farmer (bass), Lex Humphries (drums). CONTENTS: Serenate—It ain't necessarily so—Avalon—I remember

Clifford—Blues march—It's all right with me—Park Avenue petite—Max nix—Easy living—Killer Joe. Piano arrangement by Jack Reilly is published in Reilly, "Voicings: Putting it all together," *Piano today* 18/2 (Spring 1998): 41–43.

Wilson, Dana Richard, 1946– . *I remember . . .: Louis and Clifford and Miles and Dizzy.* Trumpet solo in the jazz idiom. Published *ITG*, c1997, as special supplement to *ITG journal* 23/1 (Sept. 1998). A memorial to jazz trumpeters Louis Armstrong, Clifford Brown, Miles Davis, and Dizzy Gillespie.

BRUCH, MAX, German composer; b. Jan. 6, 1838; d. Oct. 2, 1920.

Ermatinger, Emil, 1931– . *Lichtung: Study in memory of Max Bruch* (1964). Band. Published *ELWE,* 1964?

BRUCKNER, ANTON, Austrian composer; b. Sep. 4, 1824; d. Oct. 11, 1896.

Goller, Vinzenz, 1873–1953. *Festpräludium für Orgel: In memoriam Anton Bruckner: Festgabe anlässlich des Einzuges Anton Bruckners in die Walhalla* (1937). Organ. Published *Böhm* 8716, 1937? "Gift for the entry of Anton Bruckner into Valhalla."

Hummel, Bertold, 1925– . *In memoriam Anton Bruckner, op. 91.* Organ. Published *Böhm* 12464-72, 1990.

Kelemen, Milko, 1924– . *Archetypon II für Anton: In honor of the centenary of Anton Bruckner's death* (1994–95). Orchestra. Published *Sikorski,* 1995. CONTENTS: Tremendum—Mirum—Energicum—Sanctum—Fascinans—Majestas.

Müller, Franz Xaver, 1870–1948. *In memoriam Anton Bruckner.* Organ. Unpublished. Source: *Beckmann.* Müller's manuscripts are at the Stift St. Florian in Markt St. Florian, Austria.

BRUNA, PABLO, Spanish organist, composer; b. June 22, 1611; d. June 26, 1679.

Briz, Juan, 1950– . *Diferencias, op. 53: In memoriam Pablo Bruna.* Piano. Published *EMEC,* 1981.

BUCCHI, VALENTINO, Italian composer; b. Nov. 29, 1916; d. May 9, 1976.

Vlad, Roman, 1919– . *Ricordando Valentino Bucchi: Variazioni su sei note per 14 strumenti.* Chamber orchestra. Published *B&S* BSM7, 1977. Also known as "In memoriam Valentino Bucchi."

BUKOWSKI, RYSZARD, Polish composer; b. 1916; d. May 19, 1988.

Pstrokonska-Nawratil, Grazyna, 1947– . *Plomienie = Flames: Ryszard Bukowski in memoriam* (1988). Harpsichord and strings. Unpublished. Source: *No/Gro.*

BULL, OLE, Norwegian violinist; b. Feb. 5, 1810; d. Aug. 17, 1880.
Blessner, Gustave, fl. 19ᵗʰ cent. *Ole Bull in memoriam.* Organ. Published Philadelphia: Oliver Ditson.

BÜLOW, HANS VON, German pianist, conductor; b. Jan. 8, 1830; d. Feb. 12, 1894.
Kistler, Cyrill, 1848–1907. *Trauerklänge,* op. 64, C minor: *Erinnerung an Hans von Bülow* (1894). Organ. Published *Breitkopf,* 1894?

BURGMÜLLER, NORBERT, German composer; b. Feb. 8, 1810; d. May 7, 1836.
Mendelssohn-Bartholdy, Felix, 1809–1847. *Trauermarsch für Harmoniemusik,* op. 103: *Zum Begräbniss Norbert Burgmüller* (May 8, 1836). Wind band. Published Leipzig: J. Rieter-Biedermann; *Novello,* 1868. New edition in *Felix Mendelssohn Bartholdy's Werke,* Ser. 7, no. 29a, ed. Julius Rietz (*Breitkopf:* 1874–77). Composed for the funeral of Burgmüller. Adapted for concert band by Erik Leidzen: *AMP,* 1954. Also published in a version for orchestra.

BURKHARD, WILLY, Swiss composer; b. Apr. 17, 1900; d. June 18, 1955.
Huber, Klaus, 1924– . *In memoriam Willy Burkhard: Zwei Orgelstücke* (1955). Organ. Published *Bärenreiter* BA4462, 1965.

BUSONI, FERDINANDO, Italian clarinetist; b. June 24, 1834; d. May 12, 1909.
Busoni, Ferruccio, 1866–1924. *Fantasia nach Johann Sebastian Bach: Alla memoria di mio padre Ferdinando Busoni, il 12 maggio 1909* (1909). Piano. Published *Breitkopf* 3054, 1909? Ferdinando was the father of Ferruccio.

BUSONI, FERRUCCIO BENVENUTO, Italian-German pianist, composer; b. Apr. 1, 1866; d. July 27, 1924.
Gruenberg, Louis, 1884–1964. *The creation: A Negro sermon for voice and eight instruments,* op. 23. Voice with ensemble of flute, clarinet, bassoon (or violoncello), timpani, percussion, viola, piano. Published *UE* 8327, 1926. New edition: *GunMar,* 1989. Text by James Weldon Johnson. "To the memory of my beloved master and friend Ferruccio Busoni"—note in score.
Loos, Armin, 1904–1971. *Symphony: In memoriam Ferruccio Busoni* (1944). Published *Mobart,* 1978.
Luening, Otto, 1900–1996. *Lyric scene: In memory of Ferruccio Busoni* (1958). Flute and strings. Published *Peters* 66008, 1958.
———. *Sonata for piano: In memoriam Ferruccio Busoni* (1975).

Published *ACA*, 1975. Another edition: *Bardic*, 1988.

Smalley, Robert, 1943– . *Gloria tibi Trinitas I: In memory of Ferruccio Busoni* (1965; rev. 1969). Orchestra. Published *Faber*.

Vogel, Wladimir, 1896–1984. *Preludio, interludio lirico, postludio* (1954). Orchestra. Published *Ricordi* 128831, 1955. Composed for the 30th anniversary of Busoni's death. "Interludio" movement is also known by the titles "Branle lyrique," and "Pezzo lirico."

————. *Sinfonia fugata: Dem Andenken Ferruccio Busonis* (1925–28). Orchestra. Published *Bote*.

BUTTERWORTH, GEORGE SAINTON KAYE, English composer; b. July 12, 1885; d. Aug. 5, 1916.

Vaughan Williams, Ralph, 1872–1958. *A London symphony: To the memory of George Butterworth* [Symphonies, no. 2, G major] (1913; rev. 1920). Published *Stainer* 2230, 1920. The revised version of 1920 bears the dedication to Butterworth's memory, and is the first published version of this symphony.

BUXTEHUDE, DIETRICH, German organist, composer; b. 1637 (ca.); d. May 9, 1707.

Eben, Petr, 1929– . *Hommage à Buxtehude: Toccata fugue for organ* (1987). Published *Schott-M* 7543, 1987. "This work was commissioned by the Ministry of Education and Cultural Affairs of Schleswig-Holstein/West Germany on the occasion of Dietrich Buxtehude's 350th birthday"—note in score. *Eben* states that the work also honors the 280th anniversary of Buxtehude's death. Based on motives from Buxtehude's *Prelude, fugue, and ciacona* in C major, and *Prelude and fugue* in G minor.

Froidebise, Pierre, 1914–1962. "In memoriam Dietrich Buxtehude," in his *Sonatine for organ* (1939). Published *CeBeDeM*, 1958. CONTENTS: In memoriam Samuel Scheidt—In memoriam Louis Vierne—In memoriam Dietrich Buxtehude.

BUXTEHUDE, JOHANNES, German organist, composer; b. 1602; d. Jan. 22, 1674.

Buxtehude, Dietrich, 1637–1707. *Fried-und freudenreiche Hinfarth des alten grossglaubigen Simeons bey seeligen ableiben des Weiland wohl-ehrenbesten, gross-achtbaren und kunstreichen Herrn Johannis Buxtehuden . . . welcher im 72. Jahr seines Alters am 22. Januarii des 1674. Jahres alhier zu Lubeck mit Fried und Freude aus dieser angst und unruhe-vollen Welt abgeschieden . . . Dem Sellig-verstorbenen, als seinem hertzlich geliebten Vater zur schuldigen Ehren und Christlichen Nachruhme in 2. Contrapuncten abgesungen* *von Dieterico Buxtehuden.* . . . [Mit Fried und Freud]. For alternate soprano and bass voice with acc. of four string instruments. Published Lübeck: U. Wettstein, 1674. *RISM-A1*: B-5200. Facsimile reprint: Lübeck: E. Robert, 1937. In modern notation in *Buxtehude's Werke*, vol. 2, ed. by the Oberleitung der Glaubensgemeinde Ugrino (Klecken: Ugrino, 1925–1958). Text is from Martin Luther's translation of Luke II. Johannes was Dietrich's father.

BUZZOLLA, ANTONIO, Italian composer, conductor; b. Mar. 2, 1815; d. Mar. 20, 1871.

    Lago, Nicodemo, fl. 19th cent. *Adagio funèbre: Per la morte dell'esimio maestro Antonio Buzzolla.* Organ. Published *Ricordi.*

BYRD, WILLIAM, English composer; b. 1543; d. July 4, 1623.

    Fort, Bernard, 1954– . *Le tombeau de William Byrd* (1982). Harpsichord and electronic tape. Published Paris: Centre de Documentation de la Musique Contemporaine, 1982.

    Jenkins, Joseph Willcox, 1928– . *Rounds and sounds,* op. 35: *In memory of Messrs. Purcell and Byrd.* Men's chorus (TTBB), strings, percussion. Published by the composer (c/o *ASCAP*).

CAAMAÑO, ROBERTO, Argentine composer; b. July 7, 1923; d. 1993.

    Ortiz, Pablo, 1956– . *Impromptu: Dedicated to the memory of Maestro Roberto Caamaño* (1994). Piano. Unpublished. Source: *IUL.* Includes motives from *Oneiron* / by Gerardi Gardini; *Riprap* / by Eric Moe; *Le tombeau de Couperin* / by Maurice Ravel; *Variaciones Gregorianas* / by Roberto Caamaño; *Il Prigioniero* / by Luigi Dallapicola.

CACCINI, FRANCESCA, Italian composer; b. Sep. 18, 1587; d. 1640 (ca.).

    Uyttenhove, Yolande, 1925– . *Le tombeau de Francesca Caccini,* op. 180. Piano. Published *CeBeDeM* D20005652, 2000.

CAGE, JOHN, American composer; b. Sep. 5, 1912; d. Aug. 12, 1992.

    A chance operation: The John Cage tribute. Avant garde works by and for Cage, compiled for a memorial recording (Koch International Classics 3-7238-2, 1993). Only the works that appear to have been prepared specifically for this recording, or that include memorial dedications are listed here. The descriptions in quotations are by the composers from the accompanying booklet. MEMORIAL CONTENTS: *First four-language word event in memoriam John Cage* (1992) / by Jackson MacLow, 1922– and Anne Tardos ["A collaborative three-by-four foot collage and acrylic painting on linen, which is also a visual poem and a performance score. It includes words and phrases from eight of Mr. Cage's books—each one appearing not only in English but also in French, German and Hungarian translations by Ms. Tardos—as well as letters and phonemes from his name and several versions of two portraits of Mr. Cage. The realization . . . comprises four superimposed duo-performances of this score/painting. In these performances Tardos and MacLow speak and sing the linguistic elements and either observe silence or produce various 'informal percussion' sounds to realize the portraits of Mr. Cage." A photo of the collage is reproduced in the booklet.]— *Six melodies variations for solo violin* (1993) / by Christian Wolff, 1934– [". . . uses the violin sounds of John Cage's *Six melodies for violin and keyboard* and some music of the early American composers William Billings and Daniel Read, somewhat in the manner of John Cage's 'cheap imitation' procedures (Cage has also drawn on Billings' work)."]—*A cage went in search of a bird* (1993) / by Ken Nordine [Word jazz poem recited by Nordine with electronics. Nordine's voice is familiar to millions from commercial voiceovers, which he does for a living. He claims to have invented the "word jazz" art form. The poem is printed in the booklet.]— *Chance/choice: A group composition offered in memory of John Cage* (1993) / by members of the musical group Oregon: Ralph Towner, 1940– , Paul McCandless, 1947– , and Glen Moore, 1941– [Trio for synthesizers, reeds, double bass ". . . a collective improvisation/composition performed by three of the members of the group. The compositional approach is one that we have been developing in our 23 years as an ensemble, and it certainly benefits from the existence and influences of John Cage."]—*Factory preset* (1993) / by Robert Ahsley, 1930– [Electronic sounds.]—*In memoriam John Cage: Call waiting* (1992) / by John Cale, 1942– [Electronic sounds ". . . originally produced for the FluxAttitudes Exhibition at the New Museum of Contemporary Art. Recorded on a cassette, it played on a deck that would endlessly loop the tape creating a continuous soundtrack for the exhibit. By programming the track marks of that piece and using the repeat function, you can approximate the original intent. If you have a good portable disc player, then try it while walking through a local art museum"]. Composers and performers in other works on the recording are Laurie Anderson, Larry Austin, Earle Brown, John Cage, Takahisa Kosugui, Kronos Quartet, Meredith Monk, Patrick Moraz, Yoko Ono, Ryuichi Sakamoto, James Tenney, David Tudor, David Van Tieghem, Roger Zahab, and Frank Zappa.

Chambers, Wendy Mae, 1953– . *12² [i.e. Twelve-squared]: A voodoo tone poem in memory of John Cage* (1994). Percussion ensemble (12 players). Published *WholeSum*, 1996.

Cornicello, Anthony, 1964– . *Le città invisibili I: Agarttha: In memoriam John Cage* (1992). Percussion quartet. Published *APNM*, 1993.

Finnissy, Michael, 1946– . *John Cage: In memory of John Cage* (1992). Piano. Published *OUP*, 1992.

Grosso, Cheryl Ann. *Homage in metal* (1992; rev. 1997). Solo percussion. Published *SmithPubs*, 1999. "Homage in metal is dedicated to the memory of John Cage. It was inspired by the polyphonic style of Cage's *Constructions* for percussion ensemble"—composer's note in score.

Ichiyanagi, Toshi, 1933– . *In memory of John Cage* (1992–93). Piano. Published *Schott-J* SJ1086, 1994.

Jeney, Zoltán, 1943– . *Fungi: Epitaphium John Cage* (1992). Alto flute. Published *EMB* Z14023, 1992.

Samuel, Gerhard, 1924– . *Dirge for John Cage* (1992). Bassoon and percussion. Published *MMB*, 1996.

Tan, Dun, 1957– . *C-A-G-E: Fingering for piano: In memory of John Cage* (1993). Published *Schirmer*, 1993.

CAMPO, CONRADO DEL, Spanish violinist, composer; b. Oct. 28, 1878; d. Mar. 17, 1953.

Garcia Roman, José, 1945– . *Elocuencias: In memoriam Conrado del Campo.* Nonet for flutes (2), oboe, clarinet, bassoon, horn, trumpet, trombone, piano. Published *Alpuerto*, 1979.

Turina de Santos, José Luis. *Crucifixus: In memoriam Conrado del Campo.* Ensemble of violins (8), violas (6), violoncellos (4), double basses (2), piano. Published *Alpuerto*, 1979.

CAPUZZI, GIUSEPPE ANTONIO, Italian violinist, composer; b. Aug. 1, 1755; d. Mar. 28, 1818.

Donizetti, Gaetano, 1797–1848. *Symphony in D minor: Per la morte di Capuzzi* (1818). Published *Litolff* 8365, 1979. Edited by Marc Andreae from the autograph score located in the Bibliothèque Nationale, Paris (Ms. 4133). Composed for Capuzzi's funeral.

Mayr, Giovanni Simone, 1763–1845. *Cantata per la morte di Antonio Capuzzi* (1818). Solo voices (2), chorus, orchestra. Unpublished. Source: *Bergamo.* Text ("O voi d'Orobia alme bennate") by Muletti. Autograph manuscript is at the Biblioteca civica in Bergamo.

CARDEW, CORNELIUS, English composer; b. May 7, 1936; d. Dec. 13, 1981.

Frey, Jürg, 1953– . *In memoriam Cornelius Cardew* (1993). Piano. Published *EWP* 2010, 1994.

Lombardi, Luca, 1945– . *Winterblumen: In memoriam Cornelius Cardew* (1982). Flute and harp. Published *Zerboni* 9038, 1983.

CARDOSO, LINDEMBERGUE ROCHA, Brazilian composer; b. June 30, 1939; d. 1989.

Ficarelli, Mario, 1937– . *Potencias: In memory of Lindembergue Cardoso.* Sextet for trombones (4), bass drums (2). Published *Brazilian* 104793, 1994.

Oliveira, Alda de Jesus, 1945– . *In memoriam: A memórie de Lindembergue Cardoso* (1989). Voice, piano, vibraphone, percussion. Published Salvador, Bahia, Brazil: UFBA, Escola de Música, 1989.

CARMICHAEL, HOAGY, American pianist, composer of popular music; b. Nov. 22, 1899; d. Dec. 27, 1981.

Jamal, Ahmad, 1930– . "I remember Hoagy," recorded on *I remember Duke, Hoagy and Strayhorn:* Telarc Jazz CS33339, 1995. Jazz trio. Performed by Ahmad Jamal (piano), Ephriam Wolfolk (bass), Arti Dixson (drums). Unpublished.

CARRILLO, JULIÁN, Mexican composer; b. Jan. 28, 1875; d. Sep. 9, 1965.

Marie, Jean-Etienne, 1917– . *Le tombeau de Carrillo* (1966). Piano tuned in microtones (2 players) with electronic tape of second piano tuned in microtones. Published *Jobert* JJ772, 1967.

CARUSO, ENRICO, Italian tenor; b. Feb. 27, 1873; d. Aug. 2, 1921.

Sadero, Geni, 1886–1961. *Amuri, amuri = Amore, amore: Canzone dei carrettieri siciliani.* Published Milan: G. Sadero, 1923, in series Raccolta nazionale delle musiche italiane, Ser. IV: Le piu belle canzoni d'Italia, no. 1005. "Alla memoria di Enrico Caruso che questo canto predilessa"—note in score. Words in Sicilian dialect, with English and Italian translations. "Geni Sadero" is a pseudonym of Eugenia Scarpa.

CARVER, ROBERT, Scottish composer; b. 1490 (ca.).

Stevenson, Ronald, 1928– . *In memoriam Robert Carver: 12-part motet.* Voices unacc. (or with optional organ). Unpublished. Source: *Tempo* 166 (1988): 72. Text "Domino Roberto Carwor" in Latin and aureate Scots by James Reid Baxter. First performance November 30, 1988, Edinburgh, Old St. Paul's Church, Cappella Nove, cond. by Alan Taverner. Recorded by them on *20th century Scottish choral music* (Linn Records CKD014, 1994).

CASADESUS, JEAN, French pianist; b. July 7, 1927; d. Jan. 20, 1972.

Korte, Karl, 1928– . *Pale is the good prince: In memory of Jean Casadesus* (1973). Oratorio for mixed chorus, soprano soloist, pianos (2), percussion, narrator. Published *E-V* 362-03167, 1973. Text from love songs and tomb songs of ancient Egypt, translated by Milton Kessler and Gerald E. Kadish.

CASALS, PABLO, Spanish violoncellist; b. Dec. 29, 1876; d. Oct. 22, 1973.

Homenaje a Pablo Casals. Violoncello and piano. Published Barcelona: Ministerio de Educación y Ciencia, 1977. Works commissioned for the centenary of the birth of Casals. CONTENTS: Tres transparencias de un preludio be Bach, "A la memoria de Pau Casals" / by Leonardo Balada, 1933– —Tiempos, "Música para un centenario Casals" / by Carmelo A. Bernaola, 1929– —Ricercare a Paul Casals, "a la memoria de Pau Casals" / by Manuel Castillo, 1930– —In memoriam Pau Casals / by Joaquim Homs, 1906– —El pont, "Homenatge a Pau Casals" / by Federico Mompou, 1893–1987—Microrapsodia, "a la memoria de Pau Casals" / by Xavier Montsalvatge, 1912——Sonata a la breve, "a Pablo Casals in memoriam" / by Joaquin Rodrigo, 1901–1999.

Balada, Leonardo, 1933– . *Homage to Casals* (1975). Orchestra. Published *Schirmer* 47924, 1979. Based on the Catalonian folk melody "El cant del aucells" (The song of the birds).

Cervelló, Jordi, 1935– . *Sonata for violoncello: A la memória de Pau Casals* (1977). Published *EMEC*, 1991.

Gange, Kenneth, 1939– . *Prelude on the death of Pablo Casals.* Organ. Unpublished. Source: *Beckmann.*

Ginastera, Alberto, 1916–1983. *Glosses sobre temes de Pau Casals: To Pau Casals in memoriam* (1976). Orchestra. Published *Boosey* HPS1132, 1978?

Hummel, Bertold, 1925– . *Fantasia II for violoncello solo,* op. 97a: *In memoriam Pablo Casals* (1993). Published *Zimmermann* 3086, 1993. For thematic material "I chose the letters of the name 'CASA(L)S' that can be used musically, the sequence of notes 'B-A-C-H' as well as the first line of the Gregorian chant 'Te deum laudamus'"—preface in score.

Lasón, Aleksander. *Concerto for violoncello and orchestra: Pablo Casals in memoriam* (1985–87). Published *Tonos* 7424, 1987.

CASELLA, ALFREDO, Italian composer; b. July 25, 1883; d. Mar. 5, 1947.

Petrassi, Goffredo, 1904– . *Elogio per un'ombra: Per Alfredo Casella venticinque anni dopo* [i.e. 25 years after his death] (1971). Violin solo. Published *Zerboni* 7463, 1972.

Solares, Enrique, 1910– . *Partita para cuerdas = Partita for strings: A la memoria de mi querido maestro Alfredo Casella* (1946–47; rev. 1949). String orchestra. Published Washington, D. C.: Pan American Union 22-40; *Peer-I*, 1959.

CASSADO, GASPAR, Spanish violoncellist; b. Sep. 13, 1897; d. Dec. 24, 1966.

Halffter, Ernesto, 1905–1989. *Fantaisie espagnole: À la mémoire de Gaspar Cassado, en hommage* (1952). Violoncello and piano. Published *Eschig* ME8789, 1992. Completed in August–September 1952; the memorial dedication is a later addition.

CAUDELLA, EDOARDO, Romanian violinist, composer; b. June 3, 1841; d. Apr. 15, 1924.

Enesco, Georges, 1881–1955. *Impressions d'enfance,* op. 28: *À la mémoire d'Edouard Caudella* (1940). Violin and piano. Published *Salabert* EAS15219, 1952.

CAVALLI, PIER FRANCESCO, Italian composer; b. Feb. 14, 1602; d. Jan. 17, 1676.

Cavalli, Pier Francesco, 1602–1676. *Missa pro defunctis: Requiem a otto voci, con il responsorio Libera me a cinque voci* (1675). Voices (8) and continuo. Published *Zerboni* 7671, 1978, edited by Francesco Busse. Composed by Cavalli to be sung twice a year after his death, once in St. Mark's Cathedral, Venice, and once in S. Lorenzo.

Monferrato, Natale, ca. 1603–1685. *Missa pro defunctis.* Cavalli's will stipulated that on the eighth day after his death, a Requiem specially composed by his successor should be sung in S. Lorenzo by the choir and musicians of St. Mark's Cathedral. That Requiem is possibly one of the masses in Monferrato's collection *Messe et Magnificat a quattro voci*, opera XVIIII (Venice: Sala, 1681).

CHABRIER, EMMANUEL, French composer; b. Jan. 18, 1841; d. Sep. 13, 1894.

Séverac, Déodat de, 1872–1921. *Sous les lauriers roses* (1919). Piano. Published Paris: Rouart, Lerolle 11080, 1920. Alternate title on caption: *Soir de carnaval sur la côte catalane.* "Fantaisie dédiée à la mémoire des maitres aimés, E. Chabrier, I. Albéniz et Ch. Bordes"— dedication in score.

CHALLENDER, STUART, Australian conductor; b. Feb. 19, 1948; d. Dec. 13, 1991.

Sculthorpe, Peter, 1929– . *Threnody* (1991–92). Violoncello solo. Published *Faber* 057151412X, 1993. "Threnody is dedicated to the memory of the conductor Stuart Challender, who died of AIDS in December 1991. Considering that he conducted [Sculthorpe's composition] *Kakadu* on many occasions, it seems fitting that this lament should be sung for him"—composer's note in score.

CHAMBONNIÈRES, JACQUES CHAMPION DE, French composer; b. 1601?; d. Apr. 1672.

Anglebert, Jean Henry d', 1628–1691. "Le tombeau de M. de Chambonnières," in his *Pièces de clavecin, livre premièr.* Harpsichord. Published Paris: L'autheur, 1689. *RISM-A1*: A-1222. Facsimile reprint in Anglebert, *Pièces de clavecin*, Monuments of music and music literature in facsimile, Ser. 1, vol. 4 (*Broude*, 1965). In modern notation in Anglebert, *Pièces de clavecin*, ed. Kenneth Gilbert, Le Pupitre, vol. 54 (*Heugel*, 1979).

CHAMPAGNE, CLAUDE, Canadian composer; b. May 27, 1891; d. Dec. 21, 1965.

Duchow, Marvin, 1914–1979. *Seven chorale preludes in traditional style: In memoriam: À la mémoire de Claude Champagne.* Organ. Published *Berandol*, 1970.

CHANCE, JOHN BARNES, American composer; b. Nov. 20, 1932; d. Aug. 6, 1972.

Mailman, Martin, 1932– . *A simple ceremony,* op. 53: *In memoriam John Barnes Chance.* Symphonic band with unison voices. Published *Boosey* QMB405, 1978. Text from Ordinary of the Mass.

CHATZIDAKES, MANOS, Greek composer; b. June 23, 1925; d. June 15, 1994.

Antoniou, Theodore, 1935– . *Lament for Manos* (1995). Clarinet solo. Published *GunMar* MG024, 1997. Alternate transliterations of dedicatee name: Hadjidakis, Hadzikakis.

CHÁVEZ, CARLOS, Mexican composer, conductor; b. June 13, 1899; d. Aug. 2, 1978.

Galindo, Blas, 1910–1993. *Concertino for violin and string orchestra: En homenaje a Carlos Chávez* (Dec. 27, 1978). Published *UNAM* 9683611273, 1989.

Halffter, Rodolfo, 1900–1987. *Elegia for string orchestra,* op. 41: *In memoriam Carlos Chavez* (1978). Published *UNAM* 968580396X, 1982.

Harrison, Lou, 1917– . *Threnody for Carlos Chávez* (1979). Sudanese gamelan degung and viola. Published *Lingua.*

CHERUBINI, LUIGI, Italian composer, teacher; b. Sep. 14, 1760; d. Mar. 15, 1842.

Rossini, Gioachino, 1792-1868. "Chant des Titans" (1861), in *Quaderni Rossiniani,* vol. 8. Unison bass voices (4), orchestra. Published Pesaro: Fondazioni Rossini, 1959. Text by Emilien Pacini. Written for and first performed at a Dec. 22, 1861, concert in Paris to raise funds for a monument to Cherubini. Subsequently the work was performed Apr. 15, 1866, in Vienna at a concert to raise funds for a monument to Mozart.

CHOPIN, FRÉDÉRIC, Polish composer; b. Mar. 1, 1810; d. Oct. 17, 1849. For the centennial of Chopin's death, the United Nations Educational, Scientific, and Cultural Organization (UNESCO), in cooperation with the French Broadcasting Company, commissioned Lennox Berkeley, Carlos Chávez, Oscar Esplá, Howard Hanson, Jacques Ibert, Bohuslav Martinu, Andrzej Panufnik, Florent Schmitt, Alexandre Tansman, and Heitor Villa-Lobos to compose piano and chamber works for a memorial concert in Paris at the Salle Gaveau on Oct. 3, 1949. The concert featured Hélène Pignari at the piano. These works were published, and are listed below among works by other composers.

Mouvements du cour: Un hommage à la mémoire de Frédéric Chopin. Songs on poems of Louise de Vilmorin. Published *Heugel,* 1949. CONTENTS: Prélude, "Une forêt surgit des flots" / by Henri Sauguet, 1901-1989—Mazurka, "Les bijoux aux poitrines" / by Francis Poulenc, 1899-1963—Valse, "Le flot du silence ne porte" / by Georges Auric, 1899-1983—Scherzo impromptu, "Promesse au coeur de vos sourires" / by Jean Françaix, 1912-1997—Étude, "Seigneur venez à mon secours" / by Leo Preger, 1907-1965—Ballade nocturne, "Dame du soir" / by Darius Milhaud, 1892-1974—Postlude: polonaise, "Dans les campagnes de Pologne" / by Henri Sauguet, 1901-1989.

Baur, Jürg, 1918– . "Erinnerung an Chopin," in his *Erinnerungen: Fünf Stücke und Bearbeitungen* (1941-43). Violongello and piano. Published *Tonger* 2296, 1991. CONTENTS: Erinnerung an Chopin—Rhapsodie nach Bach—Fantasie—Präludium—Gavotte.

Berkeley, Sir Lennox, 1903–1989. *Three mazurkas: Hommage à Chopin* (1949). Piano. Published *Chester* 2316, 1951. Composed for and no. 3 performed at the UNESCO memorial concert.

Bollinger, Samuel, 1871–1941. *In memory of Chopin.* Piano. Published St. Louis: Bollinger Alumni Assoc., 1940.

Casella, Alfredo, 1883–1947. *Sei studi,* op. 70. Piano. Published *Curci* 4020, 1944? "La presente collana di 'studi' vuol essere un umile omaggio di ammirazione e di gratitudine verso le memorie di F. F. Chopin e di M. Ravel"—dedication in score.

Castérède, Jacques, 1926– . *Pour un tombeau de Frédéric Chopin.* Piano. Published *Billaudot* 5354, 1994. CONTENTS: Prélude—Valse—Scherzo—Nocturne.

Chávez, Carlos, 1899–1978. *Etudes no. 1–4 for piano* (1949). Nos. 1–3 published New York: Mills Music, 1969; no. 4 published *Mexicanas*, 1949. Composed for and no. 4 performed at the UNESCO memorial concert.

Debussy, Claude, 1862–1918. *Etudes pour piano: À la memoire de Frédéric Chopin* (1915). Published *Durand* 9406-9407, 1916.

Esplá, Oscar, 1886–1975. *Sonata español para piano,* op. 53. Published *UMEsp* 18657, 1952. Composed for the 1949 UNESCO memorial concert.

Françaix, Jean, 1912–1997. *Nocturne: À la mémoire du grand Frédéric Chopin* (1994). Piano. Published *Schott-M* 8471, 1996.

Garcia Abril, Antón, 1933– . *Canciones de Valldemosa: A Federico Chopin "in memoriam"* (1976). High voice and piano. Published *Alpuerto* 8486230268, 1985. CONTENTS: A Federico Chopin—Jardin de Valldemosa—Pareja en sombra sobre fondo de oro—Agua me daban a mi—Canción de anillos—No por amor, no por tristeza—Preludios de Mallorca—Horas de Valldemosa—Chopin, tal vegada a Valldemosa. Texts in Spanish and Catalan by various authors.

Glazunov, Aleksandr Konstantinovich, 1865–1936 (transcriber). Chopin, Frédéric, 1810–1849. *Chopiniana,* op. 46: *Suite à la mémoire de Frédéric Chopin* (1893). Published *Belaieff* 863, 1894. New edition: *Belaieff,* 1979. Glazunov's orchestration for ballet performance of piano pieces by Chopin: Polonaise, op. 40—Nocturne, op. 15—Mazurka, op. 50—Tarentelle, op. 43.

Gniot, Walerian Jozef, 1902–1977. *Pamieci Chopina = In memory of Chopin* (1948). Chorus and orchestra. Unpublished. Source: *NGrove.* Text by J. Kasprowicz.

Hanson, Howard, 1896–1981. *Pastorale for solo oboe, strings, and harp*, op. 38. Published *CFischer* W2247, 1952. Originally for oboe and piano, which version was composed for the 1949 UNESCO memorial concert.

Heller, Stephen, 1813–1888. *Aux mânes de Frederic Chopin: Élegie et marche funèbre*, op. 71 (1849). Piano. Published *Breitkopf* 8358, 1850. Includes quotations from Chopin's Préludes, op. 28, nos. 4 and 6.

Hrabovskyi, Leonid Oleksandrovych, 1935– . "Prelude: In memoriam Frédéric Chopin," in his *Homages: Seven pieces for guitar.* Published *Duma*, 1996. CONTENTS: Ciaccona: In memoriam Henry Purcell—Aria: In memoriam Johann Sebastian Bach—Impromptus: In memoriam Franz Schubert—Prelude: In memoriam Frédéric Chopin—A little cake-walk: In memoriam Scott Joplin—Chorale: In memoriam Johannes Brahms—Amoroso: In memoriam Sergei Prokofiev.

Ibert, Jacques, 1890–1962. *Etude-caprice pour un tombeau de Chopin* (1949). Violoncello solo. Published *Leduc* AL20951, 1950. Composed for the 1949 UNESCO memorial concert.

Jong, Marinus de, 1891–1984. *15 Fantasy-walsen*, op.118: *In memoriam Frédéric Chopin* (1960). Piano. Published *CeBeDeM.*

Jongen, Joseph, 1873–1953. *Ballade for orchestra*, op. 136: *Hommage à Frédéric Chopin* (1949). Published *Elkan.*

Koszewski, Andrzej, 1922– . *Muzyka fa-re-mi-do-si: Pamieci Fryderyka Chopina w 150 rocznice urodzin* (1960). Chorus (SATB) unacc. Published *PWM* 5425, 1968. For the 150th anniversary of Chopin's birth. The motive fa-re-mi-do-si (F-D-E-C-H [i.e. B natural]) is based on Chopin's name: *FreDEric CHopin.* Text is a repetition of these syllables.

Lombardi, Daniele, 1940– . *Quattro studi alla memoria di Chopin.* Piano. Published *EdiPan*, 1982. Graphic notation.

Martinu, Bohuslav, 1890–1959. *Mazurka-nocturne*, op. post.: *Mémorial à Chopin* (1949). Quartet for oboe, violins (2), violoncello. Published *Eschig*, 1970. Composed for the 1949 UNESCO memorial concert.

Migot, Georges, 1891–1976. *Symphonie: À la mémoire de Chopin.* Published *Baron.* Though listed in *ASCAP* as available from publisher M. Baron, no work with this title and dedication is found in *Migot.*

Neukomm, Sigismund, Ritter von, 1778–1858. *Élegie harmonique* *pour piano ou physharmonica* (1849). Published Vienna: A. Diabelli; Leizpig: A. Cranz; etc., 1849. Title varies slightly among editions. "Une fleur sur la tombe de notre amie Chopin, décede à Paris"—dedication quoted in *Neukomm.*

Panufnik, Andrzej, 1914–1991. *Hommage à Chopin: Five vocalises* (1949; rev. 1955). Soprano and piano. Published *Boosey*, 1955. An arrangement for flute and string orchestra (1966) was published by *Boosey*, 1968. Composed for the 1949 UNESCO memorial concert, where it was performed as *Suite polonaise.*

Rimsky-Korsakov, Nikolay, 1844–1908. *Pan voevoda* (1902–03). Opera in four acts. Published St. Petersburg: V. Bessel, 1903. New edition in Rimsky-Korsakov, *Pan voevoda*, Polnoe Sobranie sochinenii [Works], vol. 13 (*Muzyka*, 1955). Libretto by I. F. Tiumenev.

Schickele, Peter, 1935– . *Epitaphs for piano.* Published *E-V* 160-00202, 1981. "*Epitaphs* is a set of tributes written over a period of thirteen years; the composers to whom homage is paid represent each century from the 16th through the 20th"—note in score. CONTENTS: Orlando di Lasso—Michael Praetorius—Domenico Scarlatti—Frédéric Chopin—Igor Stravinsky.

Schmitt, Florent, 1870–1958. *Le chant de la nuit,* op. 120*: Ode à Frédéric Chopin* (1949). Chorus (SATB) and orchestra (or piano). Published *Durand* 13501, 1951. Composed for the UNESCO concert.

Schoemaker, Maurice, 1890–1964. *Le tombeau de Chopin: Variations sur le prélude no. 20* (1949). Pianos (2). Published *CeBeDeM*, 1963. Composed for the centenary of Chopin's death.

Scholtz, Hermann, 1845–1918. *Elegie auf den Tod F. Chopins.* Piano. Published Breslau: J. Hainauer, 1857.

Tansman, Alexandre, 1897–1986. *Le tombeau de Chopin* (1949). String quintet (or string orchestra). Published New York: Leeds, 1951. Composed for the 1949 UNESCO memorial concert.

Villa-Lobos, Heitor, 1887–1959. *Hommage à Chopin* (1949). Piano. Published *Eschig* ME6730, 1955. Composed for the 1949 memorial concert. CONTENTS: Nocturne—Ballade.

CHORON, ALEXANDRE ETIENNE, French theorist; b. Oct. 21, 1771; d. June 28, 1834.

Dietsch, Pierre-Louis-Philippe, 1808–1865. *6e messe (Ier Requiem): Dédiée à la mémoire d'A. Choron.* Mixed voices (STB). Published Paris: Regnier.

CHRESTOU, GIANNES, Greek composer; b. Jan. 8, 1926; d. Jan. 8, 1970. Alternate transliteration: Christou, Jani.

Antoniou, Theodore, 1935– . *Moirologhia for Jani Christou* (1970). Baritone voice and piano. Alternatively, for baritone voice, piano, and any combination of flute, clarinet, guitar, percussion instruments (2), double bass. Published *Bärenreiter* BA6135, 1972.

Felciano, Richard, 1930– . *Lamentations for Jani Christou* (1970). Ensemble of flute, oboe, horn, trumpet, trombone, tuba, violoncello, double bass, piano, percussion, electronic tape. Published *ECS*, 1970.

Papaioannou, Giannes Andreou, 1911–1989. *Five characters for brass quintet: In memory of Yannis Christou* (1970). Quintet for trumpets (2), horn, trombone, tuba. Unpublished. Source: *Papaioannou.* First performance April 21, 1970. Manuscript located at the Historical Archives Dept. of the Benaki Museum in Athens.

CIMAROSA, DOMENICO, Italian composer; b. Dec. 17, 1749; d. Jan. 11, 1801.

Gianella, Louis, ca. 1778–1817. *Concerto lugubre,* op. 7: *Composé et exécuté pour les funérailles de l'immortel Cimarosa* (1801). Flute (or violin) with concertato accompaniment of oboe, horns, trumpets, timpani. Published Paris: La Syrene 20, 1801? Modern edition: *Concerto lugubre,* ed. Claudio Scimone (*Zanibon,* 1978). First performed at Cimarosa's funeral.

CLARK, EDWARD, English conductor; b. May 10, 1888; d. Apr. 29, 1962.

Williamson, Sir Malcolm, 1931– . *Planctus: Monody for men's voices: In memoriam Edward Clark.* Published *Weinberger,* 1962. Text from "David's lament for Jonathan" by Peter Abelard (d. 1142).

CLEMENS NON PAPA, JACOB, Netherlands composer; b. 1510?; d. 1556?

Vaet, Jacobus, 1529–1567. "Continuo lachrimas, in mortem Clementis non Papae," in *Novum et insigne opus musicum, sex, quinque et quatuor vocum, cuius in Germania hactenus nihil simile usquam est editum.* Voices (6). Published Nuremberg: Berg & Neuber, 1558. *RISM-B1*: 1558/4. The collection is reproduced in facsimile with an introduction by Howard Mayer Brown in the series Renaissance music in facsimile, vol. 27–29 (New York: Garland: 1986). The work is published in modern notation in Vaet, *Sämtliche Werke,* vol. 3, ed. Milton Steinhardt (*DTÖ,* 1963).

CLEMENTI, MUZIO, Italian pianist, composer; b. Jan. 23, 1752; d. Mar. 10, 1832.

Neukomm, Sigismund, Ritter von, 1778–1858. *Elégie harmonique* *sur la mort de Clementi* (Mar. 18, 1832). Orchestra. Unpublished. Source: *Neukomm*, p. 106.

CLIQUET-PLEYEL, HENRI, French composer; b. Mar. 12, 1894; d. May 9, 1963.

> **Sauguet, Henri, 1901–1989.** *Le souvenir . . . déjà: À la mémoire de Henri Cliquet-Pleyel* (1966). Equal voices (2). Unpublished. Source: *Sauguet*. Text by Jean Gacon.

COLANDER, ANTON, German organist, composer; b. 1590; d. before April 1622.

> **Schütz, Heinrich, 1585–1672.** *Ich bin die Auferstehung und das Leben: Achtstimmige motette,* SWV 464 (1620?). Chorus (SSAATTBB) with optional continuo. Published *Peters* 4177, 1935. Later edition in Schütz, *Trauermusiken,* ed. Werner Breig, Neue Ausgabe sämtlicher Werk, vol. 31 (*Bärenreiter*, 1970). Text from John 11:25–26. Composed before 1620, possibly on the death of Schütz's friend and pupil Anton Colander. The original publication of this work announced in the Leipzig Booksellers' catalog of 1620 is lost. See Albert Göhler, *Verzeichnis der in den Frankfurter und Leipziger Messkatalogen der Jahre 1564 bis 1759 angezeigten Musikalien* (Leipzig: Kahnt, 1902; reprint: Frits Knuf, 1965).

COLTRANE, JOHN, American jazz musician; b. Sep. 23, 1927; d. July 17, 1967.

> **Baker, David, 1931– .** *Coltrane in memoriam* (1967). Jazz ensemble. Published Chicago: Music Workshop Publications, 1970.

> **Baraglioli, Jean-Pierre, 1957– .** *Epitaphe: John Coltrane,* op. 86 (1979). Soprano saxophone and piano. Published *Billaudot*, 1979.

> **Lemeland, Aubert, 1932– .** *Epitaph to John Coltrane* (1981). Soprano saxophone and piano. Published *Billaudot* 3218, 1981.

> **Stadlmair, Hans, 1929– .** *Monodie: In memoriam John Coltrane "Love supreme"* (1991). Saxophone solo. Published *Thiasos* 5031, 1998.

CONSOLO, ERNESTO, Italian pianist; b. Sep. 15, 1864; d. Mar. 21, 1931.

> **Dallapiccola, Luigi, 1904–1975.** *Partita for orchestra: Alla memoria de Ernesto Consolo* (1930–32). Published Milan: Carisch 17114, 1934. The last movement is with soprano solo (Latin words). CONTENTS: Passacaglia—Burlesca—Recitativo e fanfara—Naenia B. M. V. (con soprano solo).

COOKE, DERYCK, English musicologist; b. Sep. 14, 1919; d. Oct. 26, 1976.

Matthews, Colin, 1946– . *Night music: Deryck Cooke in memoriam* (1977). Orchestra. Published *Faber* 0571505341, 1978.

COOLIDGE, ELIZABETH SPRAGUE, American patron, composer; b. Oct. 30, 1864; d. Nov. 4, 1953.

Enesco, Georges, 1881–1955. *String quartet no. 2, op. 22, no. 2, in G major: À la mémoire de Madame Elisabeth Shurtleff Coolidge* (1951–52). Published *Salabert* EAS17555, 1956.

Milhaud, Darius, 1892–1974. *Septuor à cordes, op. 408: À la mémoire de Mrs. Elizabeth Sprague Coolidge* (1964). Septet for violins (2), violas (2), violoncellos (2), double bass. Published *Heugel* PH256, 1964. Commissioned by the Library of Congress, home of the Elizabeth Sprague Coolidge Foundation in the Library of Congress.

Poulenc, Francis, 1899–1963. *Sonata for flute and piano: À la memoire de Madame Sprague Coolidge* (1957). Published *Chester* 1605, 1958.

COPLAND, AARON, American composer; b. Nov. 14, 1900; d. Dec. 2, 1990.

Kolb, Barbara, 1939– . *Voyants* (1990–92). Piano and chamber orchestra. Published *Boosey* HPS1229, 1995. "*Voyants* is dedicated to the memory of Aaron Copland who passed away while this work was being written"—note in score.

Nickerson, Joe, 1951– . *Lament in memoriam Aaron Copland* (1991). Flute and harpsichord. Unpublished. Source: *Bedford.*

Ramey, Phillip, 1939– . *Cantus arcanus: In memoriam Aaron Copland* (1990). Orchestra. Unpublished. Source: *Koshgarian.*

CORBETTA, FRANCESCO, Italian guitarist, composer; b. 1615; d. Mar. 1681.

Visée, Robert de, ca. 1650–ca. 1725. "Le tombeau de Mr Françesque Corbet," in his *Livre de guittarre dedié au Roy.* Published Paris: H. Bonneuil, 1682. *RISM-A1:* V-2117. Facsimile edition: *Minkoff* 2826601083, 1973. In modern notation in Visée, *Oeuvres complètes pour guitare,* ed. Robert W. Strizich, Le pupitre, vol. 15 (*Heugel,* 1969).

CORELLI, ARCANGELO, Italian composer; b. Feb. 17, 1653; d. Jan. 8, 1713.

Anonymous. *Le triomphe des Mélophilètes.* An "Idyll in music." Unpublished. Text by Pierre Bouret. The work is lost, but a description survives in the *Mercure de France* (Dec. 1725). Marc Pincherle, in *Corelli: His life and work* (New York: Norton, 1956), conjectures a connection between this work and the *Apothéoses* by Couperin for Corelli and Lully: either that Bouret and his collaborator reworked and expanded the works by Couperin, or that Couperin composed the music of the *Triomphe* and then retained only the instrumental parts for publication, and from them formed the *Apothéose* for Lully.

Couperin, François, 1668–1733. "Parnasse, ou L'apothéose de Corelli," in his *Les goûts-réunis, ou Nouveaux concerts à l'usage de toutes les sortes d'instruments de musique, augmentés d'une grande sonade en trio intitulée Le parnasse, ou L'apothéose de Corelli* (1724). Trio sonata. Published Paris: L'autheur, Boivin, Le Clerc, 1724. *RISM-A1*: C-4275. Facsimile reprint: *Minkoff* 2826606964, 1979. New edition in *Oeuvres complètes de François Couperin*, ed. Maurice Cauchie, vol. 10 (*Oiseau-L*, 1932–1933).

CORIGLIANO, JOHN, American violinist; b. Aug. 28, 1901; d. Sep. 1, 1975.

Corigliano, John, 1938– . *Concerto for clarinet and orchestra* (1977). Published *Schirmer* 47959, 1982. Begun shortly after the death of the composer's father, and completed in 1977. Slow movement ("Elegy") features a solo violin in addition to the clarinet. The elder Corigliano was concertmaster of the New York Philharmonic.

CORSI, JACOPO, Florentine patron, composer; d. 1604.

Gagliano, Marco da, 1582–1643. "Fuggi lo spirito," in his *Di Marco da Gagliano: Il secondo libro di madrigali a cinque voci*. Published Venice: A. Gardano, 1604. *RISM-B1*: 1604/17. A collection of 5-voice madrigals, including three that memorialize Corsi (one by Gagliano, two by other composers). MEMORIAL CONTENTS: Fuggi lo spirito / by Marco da Gagliano, 1582–1643—Portate aure del ciel / by Pietro Strozzi, 1560–1604—Corso hai di questa / by Giovanni Del Turco, 1577–1647.

COUPERIN, FRANÇOIS, French composer; b. Nov. 10, 1668; d. Sep. 11, 1733.

Ravel, Maurice, 1875–1937. *Le tombeau de Couperin: Suite pour piano* (1914–17). Published *Durand* 9569, 1918. CONTENTS: Prélude—Fugue—Forlane—Riguadon—Menuet—Toccata. Each of the six movements is dedicated to a friend of the composer killed in World War I, including the French musicologist Joseph de Marliave ("Toccata"). Four of the movements are also arranged as a suite for orchestra.

COWELL, HENRY, American composer; b. Mar. 11, 1897; d. Dec. 10, 1965.

Diemer, Emma Lou, 1927– . *Homage to Cowell, Cage, Crumb, and Czerny* (1981). Pianos (2). Published *Plymouth*, 1983.

Harrison, Lou, 1917– . "Reel: Homage to Henry Cowell" (1978), in *12 x 11: Piano music in twentieth-century America,* compiled and ed. by Maurice Hinson. Published *Hinshaw*, 1979.

Montague, Stephen, 1943– . *Strummin': In memoriam Henry Cowell* (1975; rev. 1981). Piano with lights, electronic tape. Published *Modern* 1779, 1975.

CRAXTON, JANET, English oboist; b. May 17, 1929; d. July 1981.

Berkeley, Michael, 1948– . "Fierce tears I," in his *Fierce tears I & Fierce tears II* (1983). Oboe and piano. Published *OUP* 193555018, 1994. "Fierce tears II" is a memorial to the composer's father, Sir Lennox Berkeley. Both pieces develop a line from "Elegy: In memoriam Benjamin Britten," which is the final movement of Michael Berkeley's oboe concerto.

Davies, Peter Maxwell, 1934– . *First grace of light* (1991). Oboe solo. Published *Boosey* 9877, 1995. "Composed for Nicholas Daniel to perform at a concert in memory of Janet Craxton for BBC Radio 3 on 7 November 1991"—note in score.

CRISTINI, CESARE MARIO, Italian operatic stage designer; b. Dec. 7, 1906; d. Aug. 14, 1970.

Eaton, John, 1935– . *Piano trio: In memoriam Mario Cristini* (1971). Published *Shawnee*, 197–? Later edition: *AMP* HL50507890, 1987.

DADI, MARCEL, Tunisian-French guitarist; b. Aug. 20, 1951; d. July 17, 1996.

Dyens, Roland, 1955– . *Deux hommages à Marcel Dadi* (1997). Guitar. Published *Orphée* PWYS44, 1997. CONTENTS: Notes indescrètes—Tristemusette. Dadi died in the crash of TWA flight 800.

DAHL, INGOLF, German composer; b. June 9, 1912; d. Aug. 7, 1970.

Kubik, Gail, 1914–1984. *Sonatina for clarinet and piano: In memory of Ingolf Dahl* (1959). Published *MCA* 17771-028, 1971. The memorial dedication is printed in the published edition, though composed before Dahl's death.

Westin, Philip L. *In memoriam Ingolf Dahl* (1972). Band. Unpublished. Source: *Symphony news* 24/5 (1973): 24. First performance Oct. 30, 1973, Los Angeles Music Center, by the California Wind Symphony, the composer conducting.

DALLAPICCOLA, LUIGI, Italian composer; b. Feb. 3, 1904; d. Feb. 19, 1975.

Crosse, Gordon, 1937– . *Concerto for violoncello and orchestra,* op. 44: *In memoriam Luigi Dallapiccola* (1979). Published *OUP* J2441, 1979.

Felciano, Richard, 1930– . *Angels of Turtle Island: To the memory of Luigi Dallapiccola, teacher and friend* (1972). An "environment" for soprano, flute, violin, percussion, and live electronics. Published *ECS* 697, 1984. "Turtle Island" is the Hopi Indian name for America. The dedication apparently was added after composition.

Harper, Edward, 1941– . *Ricercari: In memoriam Luigi Dallapiccola for 11 players* (1975). Ensemble of flute, clarinet, bass clarinet, horn, trumpet, violin, viola, double bass, piano, harp, percussion. Published *OUP* N6889, 1978.

Lumsdaine, David, 1931– . *Sunflower: To the memory of Luigi Dallapiccola* (1975). Chamber orchestra. Published *UE.*

Lutyens, Elisabeth, 1906–1983. *Pietà* (1975). Harpsichord. Published *UE-L,* 1988.

Nono, Luigi, 1924–1990. *Con Luigi Dallapiccola: Per 6 esecutori di percussione e live electronic* (1979). Percussionists (6), loudspeakers (2), pickups (3), ring modulators (3), sine-wave generators (3) with optional amplification. Published *Ricordi* 132946, 1988. Based on a theme from Dallapiccola's opera *Il prigioniero.* Recorded during the concert *Zeitfluss 1993* at the Salzburg Festival (Col Legno WWE 1CD 81871, 1994).

Peragallo, Mario, 1910–1996. *Emircal: Sequenza in 12 episodi: In memoriam Luigi Dallapiccola* (1980). Orchestra and electronic tape. Published *Zerboni* 8667, 1981.

Petrassi, Goffredo, 1904– . "Ode a Luigi Dallapiccola," in his *Odi per quartetti d'archi* (1973–75). String quartet. Published *Zerboni* 9422, 1986. CONTENTS: Ode a Luigi Dallapiccola—a Riccardo Malipiero—a Guido Turchi—Ode al ruscello I. S. J. S. B. First performance (this movement only) in Sienna, Italy, 1975. Movements may be performed separately, or together in any order.

Saxton, Robert, 1953– . *Piccola musica per Luigi Dallipiccola* (1981). Quintet for flute, oboe, viola, violoncello, piano/celesta. Published *Chester,* 1981.

Schwantner, Joseph, 1943– . *Canticle of the evening bells: Consortium IX* (1975). Flute and chamber ensemble. Published *Peters* 66678, 1976. "For Arthur Weisberg and the Contemporary Chamber

Orchestra and to the memory of Luigi Dallapiccola"—caption in score. Based on *A ringing bell*, by Ch'ang Yu.

Sessions, Roger, 1896–1985. *Five pieces: To the memory of Luigi Dallapiccola* (1974–75). Piano. Published *Merion*, 1976. CONTENTS: Lento—Con fuoco—Andante, leggero e grazioso—Molto agitato: In memoriam L. D., Feb 19, 1975 (April 6, 1975)—Molto adagio.

Shackelford, Rudy, 1944– . *Epitaffio: Alla memoria di Luigi Dallapiccola* (1975). Guitar. Published *Zerboni* 8237, 1979. "Several passages in this work are paraphrased from Gordon Binkerd's setting of Robert Herrick's poem 'Let not thy Tombstone' for unaccompanied chorus SATBB"—composer's introduction to score.

DANZI, FRANZ, German composer; b. June 15, 1763; d. Apr. 13, 1826.

Kont, Paul, 1920– . *Quintet for winds: In memoriam Fr. Danzi* (1961). Quintet for flute, oboe, clarinet, horn, bassoon. Published *Doblinger* 10697, 1963.

DARKE, HAROLD, English organist, composer; b. Oct. 29, 1888; d. Nov. 28, 1976.

Popplewell, Richard, 1935– . *Elegy: In memory of Harold Darke.* Organ. Published *Banks*, 1980.

DAVID, FERDINAND, German violinist; b. June 19, 1810; d. July 18, 1873.

Kirchner, Theodor, 1823–1903. "Un poco agitato," in his *Gedenkblätter: Zwölf Musikstücke zur Erinnerung an die Einweihung des neuen Königl. Conservatoriums für Musik zu Leipzig,* op. 82 (1943–87). Violin and piano. Published Leipzig: Rieter-Biedermann 1508, 1887. No. 6 of 12 short pieces memorializing Conrad Schleinitz, Felix Mendelssohn, Robert Schumann, Moritz Hauptmann, Ferdinand David, Ignaz Moscheles, Ernst Friedrich Richter, Carl Ferdinand Becker, Ernst Ferdinand Wenzel, and Louis Plaidy.

DAVIS, MILES, American jazz trumpeter, bandleader; b. May 25, 1926; d. Sep. 28, 1991.

Heider, Werner, 1930– . *Steps for Miles: In memoriam Miles Davis* (1991). Piano. Published *Tre Media* 276, 1997.

Wilson, Dana Richard, 1946– . *I remember . . . .: Louis and Clifford and Miles and Dizzy.* Trumpet solo in the jazz idiom. Published *ITG*, c1997, as special supplement to *ITG journal* 23/1 (Sept. 1998). A memorial to jazz trumpeters Louis Armstrong, Clifford Brown, Miles Davis, and Dizzy Gillespie.

DEANS, KENNETH N. (BUDDY), American saxophonist, educator; b. July 12, 1947; d. Jan. 10, 1984.

Hartley, Walter S., 1927– . *Sonata elegiaca: For alto saxophone and piano* (1987). Published *Tenuto* 49401420, 1989. "Sonata Elegiaca . . . reflects the composer's feelings of loss, on the recent departures from this life of several valued friends and companions in the art of music, including two considerably younger than himself: the composer-pianist Brian Israel and the saxophonist Kenneth Deans"—note in score.

Taggart, Mark Alan, 1956– . *Lament and credo* (1984). Saxophones (11). Unpublished. Source: Lee Patrick, "Mark Alan Taggart: The man and his saxophone music," *Saxophone journal* 21/6 (May–June 1997): 64–70.

Tull, Fisher, 1934– . *Threnody for solo saxophone: In memoriam Kenneth N. Deans.* Published *Boosey* WSB20, 1988. "The thematic germ consists of the interval B-D produced from the initials of his nickname 'Buddy' Deans"—note in score.

DEBUSSY, CLAUDE, French composer; b. Aug. 22, 1862; d. Mar. 25, 1918.

Le tombeau de Claude Debussy. Principally for piano. Published *RevueMus* (Dec. 1920): supplément musical. "Dix compositions inédites pour le piano, les instruments et la voix écrites à l'intention et dédiées à la mémoire de Debussy"—subtitle of publication. CONTENTS: La plainte, au loin du faune / by Paul Dukas, 1865–1935—L'accueil des muses / by Albert Roussel, 1869–1937—Hommage / by Gian Francesco Malipiero, 1882–1973—Hommage à Debussy / by Eugene Goossens, 1893–1962—Sostenuto rubato / by Béla Bartók, 1881–1945—Et Pan, au fond des blés lunaires / by Florent Schmitt, 1870–1958—Fragment des Symphonies pour instruments à vent / by Igor Stravinsky, 1882–1971—Duo pour violon et violoncello / by Maurice Ravel, 1875–1937—Homenaje [Guitar] / by Manuel de Falla, 1876–1946—Que me font ses vallons [Voice and piano] / by Erik Satie, 1866–1925.

Ansermet, Ernest, 1883–1969 (transcriber). Debussy, Claude, 1862–1918. *Six épigraphes antiques.* Suite for orchestra. Published *Durand* 12935, 1939. Original for pianos (2). Transcription by Ansermet for orchestra is inscribed in the score "à la mémoire de Claude Debussy je dédie ce travail ou j'ai essayé de mettre à exécution le désir qui avait été sien."

Bartók, Béla, 1881–1945. "Sostenuto, rubato. Beli fiam, beli" (1920), in his *Improvizációk magyar parasztdalokra = Eight improvisations on Hungarian peasant songs*, op. 20. Piano. Published

UE, 1922. Originally published in *Le tombeau de Claude Debussy* (q.v.).

Beers, Jacques, 1902–1947. *Sur le tombeau de Debussy* (1946). Piano. Published *Donemus*, 1946.

Chamisso, Olivier Mayran de. *Prélude à la mémoire de Debussy.* Guitar. Published *Combre* C5076, 1987.

Dukas, Paul, 1865–1935. *La plainte, au loin, du faune: Pièce écrite pour le "Le tombeau de Claude Debussy"* (1920). Piano. Published *Durand*, 1921. Originally published in *Le tombeau de Claude Debussy* (q.v.).

Engel, Paul, 1949– . *Impromptu: Claude Debussy in memoriam.* Ensemble of flute, clarinet, bass trombone, violin, violoncello double bass, piano, and percussionists (3). Published *Orlando.*

Falla, Manuel de, 1876–1946. *Homenaje: Le tombeau de Debussy* (1920). Guitar. Published *Chester* GA105, 1926. Originally published in *Le tombeau de Claude Debussy* (q.v.). Also arranged for piano solo: *Chester*, 1921. In the 1930s Falla orchestrated the work and published it as the second movement ("à C. Debussy") of his *Homenajes* (*Chester*; *Ricordi*, 1953).

Goossens, Sir Eugene, 1893–1962. *Hommage à Debussy,* op. 28 (1920). Piano. Published *Chester* 2087, 1921. Originally published in *Le tombeau de Claude Debussy* (q.v.).

Hemel, Oscar van, 1892–1981. *In memoriam Claude Debussy: Overleden in 1918* (1968). Carillon. Published *Donemus*, 1968. Also published in Hemel, *Werken voor Beiaard* (*Donemus*, 1992). Composed for the 50th anniversary of Debussy's death. CONTENTS: Danse sacrée—Danse profane—Rigaudon—Passacaille.

Malipiero, Gian Francesco, 1882–1973. *A Claudio Debussy* (1920). Piano. Published *Chester* 2077a, 1921. Originally published in *Le tombeau de Claude Debussy* (q.v.).

Migot, Georges, 1891–1976. *Pour un hommage à Claude Debussy* (1924). Guitar. Published *EMT* TRGC1559, 1980.

Milhaud, Darius, 1892–1974. *Amours de Ronsard,* op. 132: *À la mémoire de Claude Debussy* (1934). Vocal quartet (SATB) or chorus with small orchestra. Published Paris: R. Deiss 7534, 1937. Text by Pierre de Ronsard (d. 1585).

Nin, Joaquin, 1879–1949. *Mensaje a Claudio Debussy: Boceto sinfónico = Message à Claude Debussy: Esquisse symphonique* (1925). Piano. Published *Eschig* ME2502, 1929. "Epigraphe: Lorsque les yeux de Claude Debussy se fermèrent à jamais sur la nuit de la mort, une soudaine angoisse vint répandre au coeur des musiciens d'Espagne une inapaisable nostalgie"—note in score.

Ohana, Maurice, 1914–1992. *Le tombeau de Claude Debussy* (1962). Soprano with zither, flute, orchestra. Published *Amphion*, 1967. Composed for the centenary of Debussy's birth.

Poulenc, Francis, 1899–1963. *Dialogues des Carmelites* (1956). Opera in 3 acts. Published *Ricordi-P* R1471, 1957. "À la mémoire de ma mère, qui m'a révélé la musique, de Claude Debussy, qui m'a donné le goût d'en écrire, de Claudio Monteverdi, Giuseppe Verdi, Modeste Moussorgski, qui m'ont servi ici de modèles"—dedication in score. Text by Georges Bernanos.

Ravel, Maurice, 1875–1937. *Sonata for violin and violoncello in four parts: À la mémoire de Claude Debussy* (1920). Published *Durand* 10170, 1922. The first movement was originally published as "Duo pour violon et violoncelle" in *Le tombeau de Claude Debussy* (q.v.).

Roussel, Albert, 1869–1937. *L'accueil des muses: Écrit pour le tombeau de Claude Debussy* (1920). Piano. Published *Durand* 9954, 1920. Originally published in *Le tombeau de Claude Debussy* (q.v.).

Satie, Erik, 1866–1925. "Élegie" (1920), in his *Quatre petites mélodies*. Voice and piano. Published *Eschig*, 1920. Originally published as "Que me font ses vallons" in *Le tombeau de Claude Debussy* (q.v.). "À la mémoire de Claude Debussy, en souvenir d'une douce amitié de 30 ans"—dedication in score. Text by Lamartine.

Sauguet, Henri, 1901–1989. *Plus loin qui la nuit et le jour* (1960). Tenor solo with mixed chorus unacc. Published *Salabert*, 1961. Text by Louis Emié.

Schmitt, Florent, 1870–1958. *Et Pan, au fond des blés lunaires, s'accouda* (1920). Piano. Published *Durand* 9950, 1920. Also published in *Le tombeau de Claude Debussy* (q.v.). Version for orchestra published as no. 1 ("Tristesse de Pan") of Schmitt's *Mirages* (*Durand* 11750, 1925).

Seroux, Maurice de. *Hommage à Claude Debussy.* Piano. Published Paris: M. Senart 6885, 1925.

Stravinsky, Igor, 1882–1971. *Symphonies of wind instruments: À la mémoire de Claude-Achille Debussy* [Symphonies d'instruments à vent] (1920; rev. 1947). Published *Boosey* HPS672, 1952 (rev. version). The concluding section was originally published in a version for piano as "Fragment des Symphonies pour instruments à vent à la mémoire de Claude Achille Debussy," in *Le tombeau de Claude Debussy* (q.v.).

Tailleferre, Germaine, 1892–1983. *Hommage à Debussy: Suivi de très vite* (1920). Piano. Published Paris: Musik Fabrik, 1998.

Takács, Jenö, 1902– . "Elegie für Claude Debussy," in his *Vier Epitaphe,* op. 79 (1964). Piano. Published *Doblinger* 681671, 1966. CONTENTS: Praeludium für Paul Hindemith—Elegie für Claude Debussy—Fragment für Alban Berg—Dialogue nocturne für Béla Bartók.

DEGAETANI, JAN, American mezzo-soprano; b. July 10, 1933; d. Sep. 15, 1989.

Adler, Samuel, 1928– . *Bridges to span adversity* (Sept. 24, 1989). Harpsichord. Published *Presser* 110-40687, 1991. "In celebration of the life of my good friend and colleague Jan DeGaetani (1933–1989)"—note in score.

Smit, Leo, 1921–1999. *White diadem: 7 songs about poets and poetry: In memoriam Jan De Gaetani* (1989). Mezzo-soprano (or soprano) and piano. Published *Presser* 111-40171, 2000. Texts by Emily Dickinson.

DE GROOTE, STEVEN, South African-born pianist; b. 1954; d. May 22, 1989.

Liebermann, Lowell, 1961– . *Nocturne no. 2 for piano,* op. 31: *In memory of Steven De Groote* (1990). Published *Presser* 110-40715, 1996.

DELAMARTER, ERIC, American composer, organist; b. Feb. 18, 1880; d. May 17, 1953.

Beversdorf, Thomas, 1924–1981. *Three epitaphs for brass quartet: In memory of Eric DeLamarter* (1955). Quartet for trumpets (2), trombones (2); or for trumpets (2), horn, trombone. Published *Southern* SS6, 1966.

DELIUS, FREDERICK, English composer; b. Jan. 29, 1862; d. June 10, 1934.

Mann, Leslie, 1923–1977. *Prelude and fugue for small orchestra,* op. 12 (1955). Published *Canadian.*

DEMESSIEUX, JEANNE, French organist; b. Feb. 14, 1921; d. Nov. 11, 1968.

Labric, Pierre, 1891–1972. *Hommage à Jeanne Demessieux* (1969). Organ. Published *Durand* 14044, 1970. "À la mémoire de mon Amie Jeanne Demessieux en modeste témoignage d'admiration, de reconnaissance et d'affection"—dedication in score. Published edition includes also the text of a memorial poem to Demessieux by Félicie Casanova.

DENISOV, EDISSON VASILEVICH, Russian composer; b. Apr. 6, 1929; d. Nov. 23, 1996.

Bräm, Thüring, 1944– . *Le tombeau pour Edison Denisov* (1996). Quintet for soprano saxophone, oboe, violin, violoncello, vibraphone. Unpublished. Source: *SNB*, vol. 1999/16. Manuscript is at the Schweizerische Landesbibliothek, Bern.

Darbellay, Jean-Luc, 1946– . *Luce: Hommage an Edison Denisov über die Noten e-d-es* (1997). Saxophone and violoncello. Unpublished. Source: *SNB*, vol. 1999/16. Manuscript is at the Schweizerische Landesbibliothek, Bern.

DESMOND, PAUL, American jazz saxophonist; b. Nov. 25, 1924; d. May 30, 1977.

Schmitz, Manfred, 1939– . *Memory-Suite: Reverence to Paul Desmond.* Tenor saxophone and piano. Published *DVfM*.

DES PREZ, JOSQUIN, b. 1440?; d. Aug. 27, 1521.

See: **JOSQUIN DES PREZ.**

DESSAU, PAUL, German composer; b. Dec. 10, 1894; d. June 27, 1979.

Gemeinschaftskomposition: In memoriam Paul Dessau. Ensembles for strings. Published *Peters* 13352, 1985. CONTENTS: Sonata per archi: Ommagio a Paul Dessau / by Friedrich Schenker, 1942– —D: für 15 Streicher / by Reiner Bredemeyer, 1929–1995 —Für P. D.: für 15 Streicher / by Friedrich Goldmann, 1941– .

Henze, Hans Werner, 1926– . *Barcarola: In memoriam Paul Dessau* (1979). Orchestra. Published *Schott-M* 6899, 1980.

DEUTSCH, MAX, Austrian-born conductor, composer; b. Nov. 17, 1892; d. Nov. 22, 1982.

Bussotti, Sylvano, 1931– . "Max Deutsch in memoriam" (1983), in his *Due concertanti.* Published *Ricordi* 134083, 1985. CONTENTS: Max Deutsch in memoriam (piccolo and double bass)—Naked angel face (2 double basses).

DIAGHILEV, SERGE, Russian impressario; b. Mar. 31, 1872; d. Aug. 19, 1929.

Dukelsky, Vladimir, 1903–1969. *Epitaph on the death of Diaghilev* (1932). Soprano solo, chorus (SATB), orchestra. Published *Boosey.* Dukelsky used the name Vernon Duke as a composer of light music.

Markevitch, Igor, 1912–1983. *Rébus: Suite: À la mémoire de Serge Diaghilew* (1931). Ballet with orchestral accompaniment. Published *Schott-M*, 1931. The original 1931 publication was a limited edition of 25 copies. New edition: *Boosey* HPS997, 1983. The full ballet was first performed December 15, 1931 at the Salle Gaveau, Paris, Orchestre symphonique de Paris, cond. by Roger Desormier, choreography by Léonide Massine.

Prokofiev, Sergey, 1891–1953. *Sur le Borysthène: Poème chorégraphique en 2 tableaux,* op. 51: *À la mémoire de Serge de Diaghileff* [Na Dnepre] (1932). Ballet in two scenes. Published Berlin; New York: Editions Russe de Musique RMV520, 1932 (reduction for piano). New edition: *Belwin*, 1980. Full score not published. Orchestral score for the suite from the ballet first published by *Muzyka*, 1972. Scenario by Prokofiev and Serge Lifar.

DIEREN, BERNARD VAN, Dutch composer, author; b. Dec. 27, 1884; d. Apr. 24, 1936.

ApIvor, Denis, 1916– . *Four Chaucer songs,* op. 1 (1936). Baritone voice and string quartet. Unpublished. Source: *NGrove.*

Stevenson, Ronald, 1928– . "In memoriam Bernard van Dieren," in his *20th-century music diary,* op. 41 (1956–59). Canon for piano. Unpublished. Source: "Piano music of Stevenson," *Musical opinion* 92 (1969): 292–95. No. 9 of 16 movements. Recorded by Joseph Banowetz on *Piano music [of Ronald Stevenson]* (Altarus Records AIR-CD9089, 1993).

DIETRICH, ALBERT HERMANN, German conductor, composer; b. Aug. 28, 1829; d. Nov. 19, 1908.

Thoma, Xaver, 1953– . *Trauermusik,* op. 22a: *In memoriam Albert Dietrich.* String orchestra. Published *Bella* M20430044.

DIETRICH, JOSEF HEINRICH, German choral conductor; b. Jan. 21, 1874; d. 1956.

Huber, Paul, 1918– . *Symphonic adagio: In memoriam J. H. Dietrich* (1959). Brass band. Published *Milgra* ME88WZ, 1977. Arranged 1977 for concert band, which is the published edition.

DILHERR, JOHANN MICHAEL, German poet, musician; b. Oct. 14, 1604; d. Apr. 8, 1669.

Tauben-Rast der Christen-Seelen . . . bei . . . Leichenbegängniss des . . . ohann Michael Dilherrn. . . . Voices, viols, continuo. Published Nuremberg: W. Endter, 1669. *RISM-B1*: 1669/4. CONTENTS: Hör liebe Seel; Es ist genug, mein Geist / by Paul Hainlein, 1626–1686—Der gerechten Seelen sind in Gottes Hand / by Heinrich Schwemmer, 1621–1696.

DINICU, GRIGORAS, Romanian composer; b. Apr. 3, 1889; d. Mar. 28, 1949.

Filip, Vasile, 1900–1983. *Suita romaneasca: In memoriam lui Grigoras Dinicu.* Orchestra. Published Bucurest: ESPLA, 1953.

DOLPHY, ERIC, American jazz musician; b. June 20, 1928; d. June 29, 1964.

Rolin, Etienne, 1952– . *Memoire pour Dolphy* (1980–83). Bass clarinet solo. Published *Fuzeau* 2708, 1988. "This work renders hommage to the jazzman Eric Dolphy, the first musician who knew how to tame the bass clarinet into a solo virtuoso instrument"—note in score.

Sapieyevski, Jerzy, 1945– . *Requiem dla Eric Dolphy* (1967). Soprano with string quartet, double bass, piano, percussion. Published Warsaw: Przedstawicielstwo Wydawnictwo Polskich, 1967. Text is repetition of "Eric Dolphy."

Smith, William Overton, 1926– . *Elegy for Eric: In memory of Eric Dolphy* (1964). Octet for flute (or alto saxophone), clarinet (or baritone saxophone), trumpet, trombone, vibraphone, percussion, violin, double bass. Published New York: MJQ Music, 1967.

Willis, Larry. "Poor Eric" (1965), recorded on *Right now*: Blue Note Records ST84215, 1965. Jazz ensemble: Jackie McLean (alto saxophone), Larry Willis (piano), Bob Cranshaw (bass), Clifford Jarvis (drums). CONTENTS: Eco—Poor Eric—Christel's time—Right now.

DONIZETTI, GAETANO, Italian composer; b. Nov. 29, 1797; d. Apr. 8, 1848.

Ambrosioni, Pietro. *Un fiore alla memoria di Donizetti: Elegia sopra motivi della Lucrezia Borgia,* op. 17. Flute and piano. Published *Ricordi* 24218, ca. 1851. Paraphrases themes from Donizetti's opera *Lucrezia Borgia.*

Giosa, Nicola de, 1820–1885. *Messa da requiem* (1848). Unpublished. Source: *NGrove.* First 20th-century performance at the 23rd Valle D'Itria Festival, Martina Franca, Italy, 1997, reviewed in the monthly journal *Opera* (1997 special annual issue): 106–108.

Krakamp, Emanuele, 1813–1883. *Pochi momenti consacrati alla memoria di Donizetti: Fantasia concertante.* Flute and piano. Published Milan: Giovanni Canti 2229, ca. 1850.

Lillo, Giuseppe, 1814–1863. *Un fiore sulla tomba di Donizetti: Rimembranze de' Martiri (Poliuto),* op. 10. Piano. Published Naples: Girard e Cie 9186, ca. 1850. Paraphrases themes from Donizetti's opera *Poliuto.*

Montuoro, A. G. *Les derniers moments de Donizetti: Elegie* (after

1875). Voice and piano. Published Rome: L. Franchi 1480. Text by Achille de Lauzieres.

Ponchielli, Amilcare, 1834–1886. *A Gaetano Donizetti* (1875). Cantata for solo voices, chorus, orchestra. Published *Ricordi*, 1877. Text by Ghislanzoni. First performance September 13, 1875, on the occasion of the removal of Donizetti's remains to the basilica of S. Maria Maggiore in Bergamo.

DONOSTIA, JOSÉ ANTONIO DE, Basque composer; b. Jan. 10, 1886; d. Aug. 30, 1957.

Migot, Georges, 1891–1976. *Trois pièces a cappella: Au père Donostia in memoriam* (April 1957). Equal voices (3) unacc. Published Paris: Editions Ouvrières, 1957. CONTENTS: Quasimodo—Pâques—Hymne de la Trinité.

DOWLAND, JOHN, English composer; b. 1563; d. Feb. 1626.

Blyton, Carey, 1932– . *Lachrymae: Five songs for high voice and string quartet: In memoriam John Dowland* (1956). Published *Faber*, 1974. Later edition: Enfield, Middlesex, UK: Modus Music, 1998? Songs composed in 1956 and originally published that year by the composer in a vocal score; instrumental interludes added in 1960. CONTENTS: Prelude—Madrigal / text by William Drummond—Interlude I—To the moon / text by Percy Bysshe Shelley—Interlude II—The open door / text by Francis Weiss—Interlude III—The sick rose / text by William Blake—Interlude IV—Sonnet / text by Samuel Daniel—Postlude.

DRUCKMAN, JACOB, American composer, teacher; b. June 26, 1928; d. May 24, 1996.

Maw, Nicholas, 1935– . "Tombeau: JD May 1996," in his *Sonata for solo violin* (1996-97). Published *Faber* 0571519261, 1999. Muted throughout this movement. CONTENTS: Scena—March-burlesque—Tombeau—Flight.

DUBUT [PIERRE?], French lutenist; b. 1644; d. 1692?

Visée, Robert de, ca. 1650–ca. 1725. "Le tombeau for Mr. Dubut," in *Manuscrit Vaudry de Saizenay: Tablature de luth et de théorbe de divers auteurs* (1699). Lute. Published *Minkoff* 2826606859, 1980, which is a facsimile of the manuscript source, Besançon, Bibliothèque de la ville, Ms. 279.152, 279.153.

DUFAUT, [FRANÇOIS?], French lutenist; d. 1652?

Dupré d'Angleterre, fl. 17th cent. "Le tombeau de Dufaux: Allemande de Dupré d'Angleterre," in *Manuscrit Milleran: Tablature de luth française, compiled by René Milleran (ca. 1690).* Lute. Pub-

lished *Minkoff* 2826606530, 1976, which is a facsimile of manuscript source Bibliothèque nationale (France), Ms Rés. 832, fol. 15v.
Gallot, Jacques, d. ca. 1690. "Entrée, Le sommeil de du Fault," in his *Pièces de luth: Composées sur differens modes.* Published Paris: H. Bonneuil, ca. 1673–1675. Facsimile of Bonneuil's 1684 edition published with introduction by François Lesure (*Minkoff* 2826606719, 1978). In modern notation in *Gallot.*
Migot, Georges, 1891–1976. *Le tombeau de Du Fault, joueur de luth* (1923). Piano. Published *Leduc*; Paris: M. Senart EMS6241, 1923. First published in *RevueMus* (Nov. 1, 1923): supplément musical.
DUFAY, GUILLAUME, Burgundian composer; b. 1400?; d. Nov. 27, 1474.
    Barbe, Helmut, 1927– . "Exaudi preces: In memoriam Guillaume Dufay," in his *Preces: Fünf leichte Stücke nach gregorianischen Motiven = Five easy pieces after Gregorian airs.* Organ. Published *ProOrgano* 1032, 1991. CONTENTS: Exaudi preces—Veni Creator Spiritus—Da pacem Domine—Pange lingua—O lux beata.
    Busnois, Antoine, ca. 1430–1492. A lamentation for Dufay by Busnois mentioned in the Cambrai Cathedral records of 1475 is lost. Source: *Houdoy.*
    Dufay, Guillaume, 1400?–1474. "Ave Regina celorum III," in his *Compositiones liturgicae minores,* ed. by Heinrich Besseler, Opera omnia, vol. 5, Corpus mensurabilis musicae, vol. 1/5. Voices (4). Published *AIM,* 1966. Edited from Biblioteca apostolica vaticana, codex San Pietro B80 (1464). Dufay's last testament requested that this antiphon be sung at his deathbed. It includes the trope "Miserere tui labentis Dufay."
    Hemart, Jean, fl. 1469–1484. A lamentation for Dufay by Hemart mentioned in the Cambrai Cathedral records of 1475 is lost. Source: *Houdoy.*
    Ockeghem, Johannes, ca. 1410–1496. A lamentation for Dufay by Ockeghem mentioned in the Cambrai Cathedral records of 1475 is lost. Source: *Houdoy.*
DUKAS, PAUL, French composer; b. Oct. 1, 1865; d. May 17, 1935.
    Le tombeau de Paul Dukas. Piano. Published *RevueMus* (May–June 1936): supplément musical. CONTENTS: Tombeau de Paul Dukas / by Florent Schmitt, 1870–1958—Pour le tombeau de Paul Dukas / by Manuel de Falla, 1876–1946—Prélude sur le nom de Paul Dukas / by Gabriel Pierné, 1863–1937—À la mémoire de Paul Dukas / by

Joseph Guy Marie Ropartz, 1864–1955—Hommage à Paul Dukas (Sonada de adiós) / by Joaquin Rodrigo, 1901–1999—Pièce à la mémoire de Paul Dukas / by Julian Krein, 1913– —Pièce pour le tombeau de Paul Dukas / by Olivier Messiaen, 1908–1992—Le sommeil d'Iskender / by Tony Aubin, 1907–1981—Hommage à Paul Dukas / by Elsa Barraine, 1910– .

Falla, Manuel de, 1876–1946. *Pour le tombeau de Paul Dukas* (1935). Piano. Published *Ricordi*, 1974. First published in *Le tombeau de Paul Dukas* (q.v.). In the 1930s Falla orchestrated the piece as the third movement ("À Paul Dukas [Spes vita]") of his *Homenajes*. Published *Ricordi*, 1953.

Rodrigo, Joaquin, 1901–1999. *Sonade de adios* (1935). Piano. Published *Eschig* ME7670, 1966. First published as "Hommage à Paul Dukas" in *Le tombeau de Paul Dukas* (q.v.).

Schmitt, Florent, 1870–1958. "Stèle pour le tombeau de Paul Dukas," in his *Chaîne brisée,* op. 87 (1936). Piano. Published *Durand* 12806, 1937. First published in *Le tombeau de Paul Dukas* (q.v.). CONTENTS: Stèle pour le tombeau de Paul Dukas—Barcarolle des sept vierges—Branle de sortie.

DUPONT, JACQUES, French stage designer; b. Jan. 16, 1909; d. Apr. 21, 1978.

Sauguet, Henri, 1901–1989. *String quartet no. 3: To the memory of Jacques Dupont* (1979). Published *Eschig* ME8708, 1990.

DU PRÉ, JACQUELINE, English violoncellist; b. Jan. 20, 1945; d. Oct. 19, 1987.

Lewis, Paul. *In memoriam Jacqueline Du Pré.* Violoncello and piano. Published *Simrock* 4035, 1998.

Stevenson, Ronald, 1928– . *Concerto for violoncello and orchestra* (1992–94). Unpublished. Source: *Tempo* 196 (April 1996): "First performances." First performance December 8, 1995, Edinburgh, Moray Welsh, Scottish National Orchestra, cond. by Walter Weller.

Zuckmantel, Diethelm, 1955– . *Clach: In memoriam Jacqueline du Pré* (1988). Organ. Published *Gravis* EG170, 1988.

DUPRÉ, MARCEL, French organist, composer; b. May 3, 1886; d. May 30, 1971.

Darasse, Xavier, 1934–1992. *Organum II: À la mémoire de mon maître Marcel Dupré* (1978). Organ. Published *Salabert* EAS17334, 1978.

Gárdonyi, Zsolt, 1946– . *Hommage à Marcel Dupré* (1976). Organ. Published *Impero* 9041, 1978.

Madsen, Trygve, 1940– . *Le tombeau de Dupré,* op. 69 (1989). Organ. Published *NMIC,* 1989.

DURAND, AUGUSTE, French music publisher; b. July 18, 1830; d. May 31, 1909.

Busser, Henri, 1872–1973 (transcriber). Debussy, Claude, 1862–1918. *Printemps: Suite symphonique: À la mémoire d'Auguste Durand.* Arr. for piano 4-hands by Henry Busser. Published *Durand* 8551, 1912. The original version by Debussy for orchestra and wordless chorus (1887), and Debussy's own transcription for voices with piano (1904) were composed prior to Durand's death, and carry no dedication to his memory. After the original orchestral score was destroyed in a fire, Busser created under Debussy's direction a new transcription for piano 4-hands without chorus (1912), and a reorchestration (1913), also without chorus. It is Busser's transcription for piano that includes the memorial dedication.

DURUFLÉ, MAURICE, French organist, composer; b. Jan. 11, 1902; d. June 16, 1986.

Massini, Ian de. *Déploration sur le nom de Duruflé.* Chorus (16 parts) and percussion. Unpublished. Source: Recorded by The Cambridge Voices, cond. by Ian de Massini on *Music for St.-Étienne-du-Mont* (Herald AV Publications HAVPCD234, 2000).

DUSSEK, JOHANN LADISLAUS, Bohemian composer; b. Feb. 12, 1760; d. Mar. 20, 1812.

Clifton, Arthur, 1784?–1832. *La morte di Dussek: Elegiac sonata* (1816). Piano with violin (obligato) and violoncello (ad libitum). Published *Chappell* 376, 1816. New edition: *Kallisti,* 1998. Clifton published under the name Philip Antony Corri.

Neukomm, Sigismund, Ritter von, 1778–1858. *Elégie harmonique sur la mort de mon amie Dussek, en forme de fantaisie* (April 19, 1812). Piano. Published *Breitkopf* 2465, 1814. New edition: *Belwin,* 1980. Concludes with a funeral march that was published separately, arranged for orchestra: *Simrock,* 1812.

DVOŘÁK, ANTONÍN, Bohemian composer; b. Sep. 8, 1841; d. May 1, 1904.

Heilner, Irwin, 1908– . *Concerto for violin and orchestra: In memory of Dvořák* (1952). Published *ACA,* 1952.

Holbrooke, Joseph Charles, 1878–1958. "Elegia e poem: Hommage à Dvořák," in his *Hommages: Grand suite no. 3* (1905). Orchestra. Published *Novello,* 1910. CONTENTS: Festival: Hommage à Wagner—Serenata: Hommage à Grieg—Elegia e poem: Hommage à

Dvořák—Introduction and Russian dance: Hommage à Tchaikovsky. **Suk, Josef, 1874–1935.** *Symphonie "Asrael,"* op. 27 (1906). Orchestra. Published *Breitkopf* PB2069, 1907. New edition: *Asrael: Symfonie pro velky orchestr,* op. 27, ed. Karel Srom (Prague: Statni hudebni vydavatelstvi, 1965). Asrael is the angel of death. "To the highly esteemed memory of Dvořák and Otilie"—caption in score. The symphony was begun as a memorial to Dvořák, who was Suk's father-in-law. During the course of composition, Suk's wife Otilie (Dvořák's daughter) also died, hence the dual memorial dedication.

EDWARDS, JOHN S., American orchestra executive; b. July 23, 1912; d. Aug. 10, 1984.

> **Erb, Donald, 1927– .** *Concerto for brass and orchestra: Dedicated to the memory of John S. Edwards* (1986). Brass parts are for trumpets (3), horns (4), trombones (3), tuba. Published *Merion* 446-41057, 1989.

EISLER, HANNS, German composer; b. July 6, 1898; d. Sep. 6, 1962.

> **Blake, David, 1936– .** *Symphony: In memory of my teacher Hans [sic] Eisler.* Chamber orchestra. Published *Novello* 89010900, 1981.

> **Jappelli, Nicola.** *Auferstanden aus Ruinen: In memoriam Hanns Eisler.* Guitars (2). Published *Sinfonica,* 1998.

> **Lombardi, Luca, 1945– .** *Non requiescat: Musica in memoria di Hanns Eisler* (1973). Chamber orchestra. Published *Moeck* 5154, 1975.

ELGAR, SIR EDWARD, English composer; b. June 2, 1857; d. Feb. 23, 1934.

> **Brent-Smith, Alexander, 1889–1950.** *Elegy: In memory of Edward Elgar* (1939). Soloists (SB), chorus, orchestra. Published *Novello* 16731, 1939. Text from multiple Biblical sources.

> **Collins, Anthony, 1893–1963.** *Elegy in memory of Edward Elgar.* Orchestra. Published London: Patterson's Publs., 1956. Based on a phrase possibly intended for Elgar's third symphony.

ELKUS, ALBERT, American composer; b. Apr. 30, 1844; d. Feb. 19, 1962.

> **Leplin, Emanuel, 1917–1972.** *Elegy for Albert Elkus* (1962). Orchestra. Unpublished. Source: *BMI-71.*

ELLER, HEINO, Estonian composer; b. Mar. 7, 1887; d. June 16, 1970.

> **Sumera, Lepo, 1950– .** *In memoriam* (1972). Orchestra. Published Tallin, Estonia: EMF, 1978.

ELLINGTON, EDWARD K. ("DUKE"), American composer, bandleader; b. Apr. 29, 1899; d. May 24, 1974.

Beadell, Robert, 1925– . *Elegy for the Duke* (1975). Band. Unpublished. Source: *Rehrig*.

Blake, Ran, 1935– . "Duke dreams," recorded on *Duke dreams: The legacy of Strayhorn-Ellington*: Soul Note SN1027, 1981. Piano.

Feather, Leonard, 1914–1994. *I remember Duke.* Jazz band. Published *Camerica*. Published edition arr. by Tommy Newsom.

Heider, Werner, 1930– . *D. E. memorial: Duke Ellington zum Gedenken* (1975). Trombone solo. Published *Litolff* 8361, 1976.

Hilse, Walter, 1941– . *In memoriam Duke Ellington.* Organ. Unpublished. Source: Recorded by Walter Hilse on *Aeolian-Skinner Organ Company*, The Great Organ Builders of America series, vol. 3 (JAV Recordings 103, 1998).

Quibel, Bob. *À la mémoire de Duke Ellington: Suite pour quintette de cuivres.* Quintet for trumpets (2), horn, trombone, tuba. Published *Martin* R1809, 1982.

Wonder, Stevie, 1950– . "Sir Duke" (1976), recorded on *Songs in the key of life*: Tamla Records T13-340C2, 1976. Soul song. Vocals by the composer, with various ensembles. CONTENTS: Love's in the need of love today—Have a talk with God—Village ghetto land—Contusion—Sir Duke—I wish—Knocks me off my feet—Pastime paradise—Summer soft—Ordinary pain—Isn't she lovely—Joy inside my tears—Black man—Ngiculela; Es una historia; I am singing—If it's magic—As—Another star.

EMOND, CLAUDE, French lutenist; d. 17ᵗʰ century.

Gallot, Jacques, d. ca. 1690. "Allemande, Départ de Mr. Emont," in his *Pièces de luth: Composées sur différents modes.* Published Paris: H. Bonneuil, 1684. Facsimile reprint: *Minkoff* 2826606719, 1978. In modern notation in *Gallot*.

ENCLOS, HENRI DE L', French lutenist; b. 1592?; d. 1649.

Gaultier, Denis, d. 1672. "Consolation aux amis du Sr. Lenclos," "Resolution des amis du sr. Lenclos sur sa mort," and "Le tombeau de Monsr. de Lenclos." Lute. Published in *Rhétorique,* p. 70–72 in transcriptions volume.

ENESCO, GEORGES, Romanian composer; b. Aug. 19, 1881; d. May 4, 1955.

Grigoriu, Theodor, 1926– . *Omagiu lui Enescu: Piesa simfonica* (1960). Solo violins (4) with four groups of violins. CONTENTS: Preludiu—Melopeea—Polifonia. Published *EditMuz,* 1962.

Taranu, Cornel, 1934– . *Epitaph pour Enesco: Sinfonia brevis I* (1971). Timpani, harp, string orchestra. Published *Salabert*, 1971.

ERVIN, BOOKER, American jazz saxophonist; b. Oct. 31, 1930; d. Aug. 31, 1970.

Parlan, Horace, 1931– . "Lament for Booker," recorded on *Lament for Booker Ervin*: Enja Records 2054, 1975. Jazz quartet and quintet: Booker Ervin (tenor saxophone), Kenny Drew and Horace Parlan (piano), Nils-Henning Orsted Pedersen (bass), Alan Dawson (drums). CONTENTS: Blues for you / by Booker Ervin (recorded at the Berlin Jazz Festival, 1965)—Lament for Booker / by Horace Parlan (recorded in Copenhagen, 1975). The melody and chord changes for "Lament for Booker" are reproduced in manuscript facsimile on the container of the CD recording.

ESHPAI, IAKOV, Russian composer; b. Oct. 30, 1890; d. Feb. 20, 1963.

Eshpai, Andrei, 1925– . *Pesni gornykh i lugovykh Mari = Songs of the mountain and meadow Maris* (1983). Orchestra. Published Moscow: Sov. Kompozitor 7147, 1985. Memorializes his composer-father, who was of Mari extraction and a scholar of Mari national music.

———. *Symphony no. 3: To the memory of my father* (1964). Published Moscow: Izdatelstvo Muzyka, 1967.

ESPLÁ, OSCAR, Spanish composer; b. Aug. 5, 1886; d. Jan. 6, 1975.

Montsalvatge, Xavier, 1912– . "Berceuse a la memoria de Oscar Esplá" (1987), in his *Tres obras para la mana izquierda*. Piano left-hand. Published *UME* 22373, 1992. CONTENTS: Si, a Mompou—Berceuse a la memoria de Oscar Espla—Una pagina para Rubinstein.

EVANS, BILL, American jazz pianist; b. Aug. 16, 1929; d. Sep. 15, 1980.

Bestor, Charles, 1924– . *In memoriam Bill Evans* (1989). Orchestra. Published North Amherst, MA: Tamar Music Publ.

FABRICIUS, JAKOB, German composer; d. Aug. 14, 1652.

Hasse, Nikolaus, ca. 1617–1672. *Grab-Lied über den . . . Hintritt des . . . Herrn Jacobi Fabricii . . . den 14. Augusti itzlauffenden 1652 Jahrs . . . entschlaffen* (1652). Voices (5). Published Rostock: Johann Richel, 1652. *RISM-A1*: H-2316

FAIRBANK, JANET, American soprano; b. 1903; d. 1948.

Pinkham, Daniel, 1923– . *Epitaph: In memoriam, Janet Fairbank*

(1948). Harpsichord (or piano). Published *CFE*, 1952.

FALABELLA, ROBERTO, Chilean composer; b. 1926; d. 1958.

Schidlowsky, León, 1931– . *Triptico: A la memoria de Roberto Falabella Correa* (1959). Orchestra. Published Santiago: Universidad de Chile, Instituto de Extension Musical, 1959.

FALLA, MANUEL DE, Spanish composer; b. Nov. 23, 1876; d. Nov. 14, 1946.

Arizaga, Rodolfo, 1926– . *Endecha: In memoriam Manual de Falla* (1968). Guitar. Published Buenos Aires: Editorial Argentina de Musica EAM145, 1968.

Asencio, Vicente, 1908– . *Elegia a Manuel de Falla* (1946). Ballet for piano. Published *Piles*, 1947. Also arranged by the composer for guitar (no. 2, "Elegia," in the *Suite de homenajes* (*Schott-M*, 1964)); and for orchestra (1946). The orchestral version formed the basis of the ballet *Llanto a Manuel de Falla* (1953).

Azpiazu Iriarte, José de, 1912–1986. *Homenaje a Manual de Falla: Jota para guitarra.* Published *UMEsp* 19400, 1948.

Caamaño, Roberto, 1923–1993. *Lamento,* op. 13: *En la tumba de Manuel de Falla* (1952). Voice (without words) and piano. Published *Ricordi-BA* BA10864, 1953.

Cruz, Ivo, 1901– . "A Manuel de Falla," in his *Homenagens = Hommages* (1955). Piano. Published Lisbon: Sassetti; *Mercury*, 1958. CONTENTS: A Richard Strauss—A Manuel de Falla—A Oscar da Silva.

Cruz de Castro, Carlos, 1941– . *Sagitario: A Manuel de Falla "in memoriam."* Unspecified woodwind, brass, and string instruments (1 or more of each), piano, percussion (1 player). Published *EMEC*, 1983.

Escudero, Francisco, 1913– . *Concerto for piano and orchestra: Homenaje a Manuel de Falla* (1946). Published *EMEC*, 1999. Winner of the Falla National Prize for 1946. Dedication may be a later addition.

Falcón, Juan José, 1936– . *Abora: Dedicada a la memoria de Manuel de Falla* (1977). Octet for flute, English horn, clarinet, trumpet, violoncello, xylophone, percussion, piano. Unpublished. Source: *Falcón.* Available from: Las Palmas de Gran Cataria: Archivio de Compositores Canarios, Museo Canario.

Fernández Alvez, Gabriel, 1943– . *Peñalara: In memoriam Manual de Falla* (1976). Oboe, clarinet, bassoon, percussion (2), organ, harpsichord, strings. Published *Alpuerto*, 1978.

Garcia Abril, Antón, 1933– . *Nocturnos de la Antequeruela: A Manuel de Falla en el 50 aniversario de su muerte* (1996). Piano and string orchestra. Published *Bolamar* 8488241275, 1996. Composed for the 50th anniversary of Falla's death.

———. *Balada de los Arrayanes: A Manuel de Falla en el 50 aniversario de su muerte* (1996). Piano. Published *Bolamar* 8488241313, 1996. Composed for the 50th anniversary of Falla's death.

Garcia Roman, José, 1945– . *Elegia-homenaje a Manuel de Falla: Beata mors* (1973). The second work of a trilogy for orchestra. Published Granada: Universidade de Granada, Secretariado de Publicaciones, 1974. Awarded the Falla prize for composition in 1973.

Grau, Eduardo, 1919– . *Elegia a Manuel de Falla* (1959). Guitar. Published Buenos Aires: Randolph RG1005, 1965.

Groba, Rogelio, 1930– . *In memoriam Manuel de Falla: Cantata de cámara para voces y conjunto instrumental* (1977). Vocal soloists (SSAATTBarBar) with violins (4), violas (2), violoncellos (2), timpani, pianos (2), vibraphone, xylophone, percussionists (3). Published *Alpuerto*, 1977. Text by the composer. CONTENTS: Mors—Fertur infortunium—In sepultus.

Lopes Graça, Fernando, 1906–1994. *Para o túmolo de Manuel de Falla* (1961). Chorus. Unpublished. Source: *NGrove.*

Malipiero, Gian Francesco, 1882–1973. *Dialoghi I: Con Manuel de Falla, in memoria* (1955–56). Chamber orchestra. Published *Ricordi*, 1957. The first of eight *Dialoghi* for various instrumental combinations. Though the memorial dedication is applied only to *Dialoghi I*, elsewhere Malipiero wrote ". . . they grew out of a homage to Manuel de Falla, written in October 1955, which seemed to me almost a conversation with my dead friend. Continuing to converse with myself and with the instruments at my disposal, the [other] Dialoghi were born as if by magic. . . . Spiritually they can all be said to be dedicated to De Falla, in friendly homage to his memory"—quoted in *Malipiero,* p. 283.

Pittaluga, Gustavo, 1906– . *Hommage pour le tombeau de Manuel de Falla* (1953). Harpsichord. Published *Ricordi* 10868, 195–?

Tansman, Alexandre, 1897–1986. *Concerto for guitar and orchestra: Hommage à Manuel de Falla* (1954). Unpublished. Source: *Pocci.*

Turull, Xavier, 1922– . *Ronda: A la memòria de Manuel de Falla.* Guitar and string orchestra. Published *Boileau* B3107, 1996. Also published for guitar and piano (*Boileau* B3123, 1996).

Valls, Manuel, 1920–1984. *Quatre peces per a piano: Homenatje a Manuel de Falla* (1947). Unpublished. Source: *Catalan.* First performance 1974, Barcelona, by L. Guiu.

FARKAS, PHILIP, American hornist, teacher; b. Mar. 5, 1914; d. Dec. 21, 1992.

Tull, Fisher, 1934– . *Lament: In memoriam Philip Farkas.* Quintet for horns (4) and tuba; or for horns (5). Published *Southern* SU233, 1995.

FARMER, THOMAS, English composer; d. 1690?

Purcell, Henry, ca. 1659–1695. "Elogy upon the death of Mr. Thomas Farmer, B. M.," in *Orpheus britannicus: A collection of all the choicest songs for one, two, and three voices . . . the second book, which renders the first compleat.* Soprano, chorus (SB), continuo. Published London: J. Heptinstall for Henry Playford, 1702. *RISM-A1*: P-5983. Facsimile reprint: *Broude,* 1965, in the series Monuments of music and music literature in facsimile. Text by Nahum Tate ("Young Thirses fate ye hills and groves deplore").

FARNAM, W. LYNNWOOD, Canadian organist; b. Jan. 13, 1885; d. Nov. 23, 1930.

Tournemire, Charles, 1870–1939. "Domenica IV post Pascha," in his *L'orgue mystique.* Organ. Published *Heugel,* 1931. No. 21 in the cycle. "En témoignage de reconnaissance et à la mémoire de son confrère et ami Lynnwood Farnam, organist and choirmaster, Church of the Holy Communion, New York"—dedication in score.

Willan, Healey, 1880–1968. *Elegy: In memory of a great artist, a valued friend and fellow-student* (1933). Organ. Published *Gray* SC851-5, 1949.

FARRAR, ERNEST BRISTOWE, English composer, organist; b. July 7, 1885; d. Sep. 18, 1918.

Bridge, Frank, 1879–1941. *Sonata for piano: To the memory of Ernest Bristowe Farrar* (1921–24). Published London: Augener, 1925. New edition: *Stainer,* 1979. Farrar was a pacifist killed in World War I.

FAUGES, GUILLAUME, French composer; fl. 1460.

Compère, Loyset, d. 1518. "Omnium, bonorum plenum," in his *Opera omnia,* vol. 4, ed. by Ludwig Finscher, Corpus Mensurabilis Musicae, vol. 15, p. 32–38. Voices (4). Published *AIM,* 1958. Known as the "singers prayer." Concludes with prayers for a number of "magistri cantilenarum" and "cantores," most still living at the time of composition (ca. 1470–1474): Dufay, Johann Dussart (i.e. Johannes de Sarto), Busnois, Caron, Georget de Brelles, Tinctoris, Ockeghem, Josquin, Corbet, Hemart (i.e. Martin Hanard), Fauges, and the poet Jehan Molinet. Manuscript source: Trent codices Tr. 91, fol. 33b.

FAURÉ, GABRIEL, French composer; b. May 12, 1845; d. Nov. 4, 1924.

Baker, Michael, 1942– . *À Gabriel Fauré in memoriam,* op. 23 (1974). Chamber orchestra. Published *Canadian,* 1974. Composed to commemorate the 50th anniversary of the death of Fauré.

Calmel, Roger, 1921– . *Le tombeau de Gabriel Fauré: Pour la formation musicale.* Vocal solfège. Published *Billaudot* 4494.

Castelnuovo-Tedesco, Mario, 1895–1968. "Elegy (Hommage à Fauré)," in his *Six pieces in form of canons,* op. 156 (1952). Piano. Published *Ricordi* 1623, 1954. CONTENTS: Ninna nanna (Cradle song)—Marcetta (Little march)—Toccata—Elegy (Hommage à Fauré)—Valse (Hommage à Chabrier)—Tarantella (Omaggio a Casella).

Enesco, Georges, 1881–1955. *Quartet for piano and strings no. 2,* op. 30, in D minor: À la mémoire de mon maître Gabriel Fauré (1944). Quartet for piano, violin, viola, violoncello. Published *Edit-Muz,* 1968.

Huybrechts, Albert, 1899–1938. *Sicilienne: Hommage à Gabriel Fauré* (1934). Piano. Published *CeBeDeM,* 1934.

Milhaud, Darius, 1892–1974. *String quartet no. 12,* op. 252: À la mémoire de Gabriel Fauré (1945). Published *Salabert* EAS14788, 1948. For the centenary of Fauré's birth.

Schmitt, Florent, 1870–1958. *In memoriam for orchestra,* op. 72 (1934). Published *Durand* 12682, 1937. CONTENTS: Cippus feralis—Scherzo sur le nom de Gabriel Fauré. The second movement also is published for piano as *Hommage sur le nom de Gabriel Fauré.*

FELDMAN, MORTON, American composer; b. Jan. 12, 1926; d. Sep. 3, 1987.

Adams, John, 1947– . *Eros piano* (1989; rev. 1990). Piano and chamber orchestra. Published *Hendon,* 1989. "Eros Piano began as an elegy on the death of Morton Feldman. . . . [It] became an homage to both [Feldman and Toru Takemitsu]"—notes accompanying the recording by Paul Crossley (piano), Orchestra of St. Luke's: *John Adams conducts American elegies* (Elektra/Nonesuch 79249-2, 1991).

Cherney, Brian, 1942– . *Déploration: Hommage à Morton Feld-*

man (1988). Harpsichord. Unpublished. Source: *Canadian*. Based on material from Josquin's *déploration* for Ockeghem. First performance October 22, 1988, Toronto, The Music Gallery, by Vivienne Spiteri.

Fulkerson, James, 1945– . *For Morty: To the memory of Morton Feldman* (1987). Trombone and piano with electronic tape. Published *Donemus*, 1992. "This score is a tribute to the sound world so fully explored by Morton Feldman and mourns his passing. It consists of composed fragments, mobiles, an electronic tape environment, and interactive listening schemes" —note in score.

———. *For Morty Feldman II* (1991). Tuba solo and pre-recorded tape. Published *Donemus*, 1992.

Garcia, Orlando Jacinto, 1954– . *On the eve of the 2nd year anniversary of Morton's death* (1989). Chorus (SATB) unacc. Published *Kallisti*, 1998.

———. *For Morton: In memory of Morton Feldman* (1987). Trio for clarinet, percussion, violoncello. Unpublished. Source: *AMC*.

Genge, Anthony, 1952– . *In memoriam Morton Feldman*. Trio for flute, piano, percussion. Published *Canadian*, 1988.

Goor, Joost van de, 1956– . *Voor Morton Feldman* (Oct. 1987). Carillon. Published *Donemus*, 1988.

Kotonski, Wlodzimierz, 1925– . *Bucolica: Morton Feldman in memoriam* (1989). Flute solo. Published *Moeck* 5441, 1993.

Nogueira, Ilza, 1948– . *In memoriam Morton Feldman* (1988). Soprano and percussion. Unpublished. Source: *No/Gro*.

Paccione, Paul, 1952– . *Stations: To Morton Feldman* (1987). Piano. Published in *Perspectives* 27 (Winter 1989): 174–78. "Dedicated to the memory of composer Morton Feldman. . . . The title refers to points of arrival and departure, both as a tribute and as a suggestion of the musical mood and structure" —note with score.

Takemitsu, Toru, 1930–1996. *Twill by twilight: In memory of Morton Feldman* (1988). Orchestra. Published *Schott-J* SJ1053, 1989.

Wolff, Christian, 1934– . *For Morty* (1987). Trio for glockenspiel, vibraphone (motor off), piano (or other instrumentation). Published *Peters* 67275, 1987.

FELTKAMP, JOHANNES HENDRICUS, Dutch flutist; b. May 28, 1896; d. May 10, 1962.

Ketting, Piet, 1904–1984. *Preludium e fughetta: In memoriam Johann Feltkamp* (1970). Alto flute and piano. Published *Donemus*, 1970.

FENMEN, MITHAT, Turkoman pianist, composer; b. Jan. 24, 1916; d. 1982.

 Baran, Ilhan, 1934– . *Navi anadolu: Piyanist Mithat Fenmen in anisina = Blue anatolia: In memory of Mithat Fenmen, the pianist.* Piano. Published *Yayincilik* 9758303031, 1999.

FENNELLY, PRISCILLA PROXMIRE, American vocalist, musicologist; b. Oct. 19, 1936; d. Oct. 1978.

 Fennelly, Brian, 1937– . *Scintilla prisca: In memoriam Priscilla Proxmire Fennelly* (1979). Violoncello and piano. Published *Margun* MM74, 1987. "Scintilla prisca was written in 1979 at the suggestion of cellist David Moore and was dedicated to the composer's first wife, Priscilla Proxmire, whose name forms the hexachordal basis of the work"—introduction to score.

FERGUSON, HOWARD, English composer, pianist; b. Oct. 21, 1908; d. Nov. 1, 1999.

 Bennett, Richard Rodney, 1936– . *In memory of Howard Ferguson* (2000). Performance medium not identified. Unpublished. Source: *Tempo* 212 (April 2000): 62, announcing the premiere on Jan. 29, 2000, Oxford, Holywell Music Room.

 Finzi, Gerald, 1901-1956. *Eclogue*, op. 10: *For piano and string orchestra: Reduction for 2 pianos by Howard Ferguson.* Published *Boosey* M060111891, 2000. "This publication is dedicated to the memory of Dr. Howard Ferguson (1908–1999), whose death occurred during the preparation of the computer-set score"—note in score. The work was completed in the late 1920s, revised in the late 1940s, and first performed in January 1957 at the Victoria and Albert Museum, London, by Kathleen Long (piano), the Kalmar Orchestra, cond. by John Russell.

FERRIER, KATHLEEN, English contralto; b. Apr. 22, 1912; d. Oct. 8, 1953.

 Hemel, Oscar van, 1892–1981. *Le tombeau de Kathleen Ferrier: Passacaille et psaume 125* (1954). Alto voice and orchestra. Published *Donemus*, 1954.

FEUERMANN, EMANUEL, Austrian-American violoncellist; b. Nov. 22, 1902; d. May 25, 1942.

 Goldschmidt, Berthold, 1903–1996. *Concerto for violoncello and orchestra* (1932; rev. 1954). Published *Boosey* HPS1284, 1992. Originally composed at Feuermann's request as a work for violoncello and piano. The original work was lost during World War II, but Goldschmidt recomposed it as this concerto in the 1950s in memory of Feuermann. Premiered in a studio broadcast with the BBC Scottish Orchestra, August 1954.

Stutschewsky, Joachim, 1892–1982. *Suitah Yi'sreelit = Israeli suite: In memoriam Emanuel Feuermann* (1942). Violoncello and piano. Published *Israeli*, 1980.

FÉVIN, ANTOINE DE, French composer; b. 1474; d. Jan. 1512.

Mouton, Jean, d. 1522. "Qui ne regretteroit le gentil Févin," in *Motetti novi e chanzoni franciose a quatro sopra doi.* Voices (4). Published Venice: Andrea Antico, 1520. *RISM-B1*: 1520/3. Facsimile reprint: *Minkoff* 2826608142, 1982. In modern notation in Dragan Plamenac, "Deux pièces de la Renaissance tirées de fonds Florentins," *Revue belge de musicologie* 6 (1952): 12–23.

FINK, REGINALD H., American trombonist; b. June 20, 1931; d. Nov. 3, 1996.

Hartley, Walter S., 1927– . *Memorial music* (1998). Duo for tenor and bass trombones. Published *Nichols* 084, 1999. "Ray Premru and Reginald Fink were distinguished trombonists. Premru also a composer and Fink the author of a much-used instrumental manual. Both were fellow students with me at Eastman over 40 years ago, and both died recently of cancer"—Introduction to score.

FINZI, GERALD, English composer; b. July 14, 1901; d. Sep. 27, 1956.

Parrott, Ian, 1916– . *Hands across the years: In memoriam Gerald Finzi* (1980). Organ. Unpublished. Source: *ConCom.* First performance Aug. 8, 1983, Harrogate, Yorkshire.

Williamson, Sir Malcolm, 1931– . *Sonata for piano no. 2: In memory of Gerald Finzi* (1957; rev. 1970–71). Published *Weinberger*, 1972. Original version titled *Janua Coeli.*

FISCHER, EDWIN, Swiss pianist; b. Oct. 6, 1886; d. Jan. 24, 1960.

Casanova, André, 1919– . *Quatre intermezzi, op. 28: In memoriam Edwin Fischer* (1967). Piano. Published *Billaudot* 1278, 1970.

FISK, CHARLES BRENTON, American organ builder; b. Dec. 16, 1925; d. Dec. 16, 1983.

Pinkham, Daniel, 1923– . *Proclamation: To the memory of Charles Fisk* (1984). Organ. Published *ECS* 4034, 1986.

FLESCH, CARL, Hungarian violinist, pedagogue; b. Oct. 9, 1873; d. Nov. 14, 1944.

Brustad, Bjarne, 1895– . *Concerto for violin and orchestra no. 4: Professor Carl Flesch in memoriam* (1961). Published *Lyche*, 1971.

FLETCHER, JOHN, English tubist; b. 1941; d. 1987.

Premru, Raymond Eugene, 1934–1998. *Concerto for tuba and or-*

chestra: Dedicated to the memory of my friend John Fletcher (1991–92). Published *Tuba*, 1994.

FLEURET, MAURICE, French music journalist; b. June 22, 1932; d. May 22, 1990.

Lenot, Jacques, 1945– . *Maurice Fleuret in memoriam: Pour orgue et 8 instruments à vent* (1990). Organ with octet of flute, English horn, clarinet, bassoon, horns (2), trumpet, trombone. Published *Salabert* EAS18943, 1990.

Xenakis, Iannis, 1922– . *Knephas* (1980). Mixed chorus unacc. Published *Salabert* EAS18909, 1933. "The title means 'darkness' and refers to the sombre thoughts occasioned by the dramatic and untimely death of the music scholar and personal friend Maurice Fleuret"—introduction to score.

FLEURY, LOUIS, French flutist; b. May 24, 1878; d. June 11, 1925.

Pierné, Gabriel, 1863–1937. *Sonata da camera pour trois instruments,* op. 48*: À la mémoire de Louis Fleury* (1927). Trio for flute, violoncello, piano. Published *Durand* 11324, 1927.

FORNEROD, ALOYS, Swiss violinist; b. Nov. 16, 1890; d. Jan. 8, 1965.

Chatton, Pierre-André. *Concert à la mémoire d'Aloys Fornerod.* Chamber orchestra. Published *Suisse.*

FORTNER, WOLFGANG, German composer; b. Oct. 12, 1907; d. Sep. 5, 1987.

Kruyf, Ton de, 1937– . *Adagio: In memoriam Wolfgang Fortner* (1987). Orchestra. Published *Donemus*, 1987.

FOSS, AAGE, Danish baritone; b. 1853; d. Apr. 3, 1894.

Langgaard, Rued, 1893–1952. *Aftenklokker: In memoriam kgl. Operasanger Aage Foss, dod 3. April 1894* (1915; rev. 1939). Baritone with orchestra. Published *SUDM*. Text by Holger Drachmann.

FOSTER, STEPHEN, American song composer; b. July 4, 1826; d. Jan. 13, 1864.

Bennett, Robert Russell, 1894–1981. *Commemoration symphony: Stephen Foster* (1959). Orchestra with ad libitum vocal soloists (ST) and chorus (SATB). Published *Chappell*, 1960. Written for the Pittsburgh Centennial, and based on themes of Pittsburgh native Foster.

Engel, Carl, 1883–1944. *Way down south in Dixie: To the memory of Stephen Collins Foster.* Operetta in one act for 11 soloists, children's chorus, orchestra. Published Boston: Birchard, 1924. Includes musical quotes from Foster songs. Libretto by Frederick H. Martens.

Ives, Charles Edward, 1874–1954. *Second orchestral set* (1909–15). Chorus and orchestra. Published *Schirmer*, 1915. New edition:

New York: Peer. The first movement, titled "Elegy to our forefathers," was earlier called "Elegy to Stephen Foster," and quotes Foster's song "Old black Joe."

Rupprecht, Paul. *Foster's memorial march: Stephen C. Foster, born 1826, Pittsburgh, died 1864.* Voice and piano. Published Pittsburgh: H. R. Basler Music Typographer & Printer, 1895. Includes first verse and refrain of Foster's song "Old folks at home."

Tucker, Henry, 1826?–1882. *Oh! Let him rest: Ballad and chorus: Tribute to the memory of the late Stephen C. Foster* (1864). Solo voice, chorus (SATB), piano. Published New York: Wm. Pond 5992, 1864.

FOX, CHARLOTTE MILLIGAN, Irish folksong collector; b. 1864; d. 1916.

Scott, Cyril, 1879–1970. *Requiem: Dedicated to the memory of Charlotte Milligan-Fox.* Voice and piano. Published London: Elkin & Co. Ltd., 1917.

FOX, VIRGIL, American organist; b. May 3, 1912; d. Oct. 25, 1980.

Faxon, Nancy Plummer, 1915– . *Fanfare in memory of Virgil Fox* (1990). Octet for trumpets (3), trombones (3), timpani, organ. Published *Nichols* 052, 1995. Composed for a concert commemorating the 10th anniversary of the death of Fox.

Hebble, Robert, 1934– . *Symphony of light: In memory of Virgil Fox* (1986). Organ. Published *Hinshaw* HMO150, 1986.

FRANCK, CÉSAR, Belgian organist, composer; b. Dec. 10, 1822; d. Nov. 8, 1890.

Machl, Tadeusz, 1922– . *Tryptyk = Triptych: Dedicated to the memory of César Franck.* Large organ. Published *WMAA*, 1976. CONTENTS: Improwizacja—Fuga—Toccata.

Ropartz, Joseph Guy Marie, 1864–1955. *Pêcheur d'islande: À la mémoire vénérée de mon maître César Franck* (1893). Incidental music for voices and orchestra to the 4-act drama by Pierre Loti and Louis Tiercelin. Published *Choudens* AC9043, 1893.

Tournemire, Charles, 1870–1939. *Triple choral,* op. 41: *À la mémoire de mon maître vénérée César Franck* (1910). Organ. Published Lyon: Janin JF1300, 1912. New edition, ed. by Maurice Duruflé: Paris: Schola Cantorum, 1962.

FRASI, FELICE, Italian composer, organist; b. 1805; d. Sep. 8, 1879.

Ponchielli, Amilcare, 1834–1886. *Elegia funebre in onore di Felice Frasi,* op. 89 (1881). Piano. Published *Ricordi* 47711, 1881. Frasi was a teacher of Ponchielli at the Milan conservatory. The work was first performed in Nov. 1881 at the unveiling of a bust in Frasi's honor.

FREITAS BRANCO, PEDRO DE, Portuguese composer; b. Oct. 12, 1896; d. Mar. 24, 1963.

    Cassuto, Alvaro Leon, 1937– . *In memoriam Pedro de Freitas Branco* (1963). Orchestra. Published *Schirmer.*

    Santos, Joly Braga, 1924–1988. *Requiem à memoria de Pedro de Freitas Branco* (1964). Vocal soloists, chorus, orchestra. Unpublished. Source: *Perkins.*

FREUDENTHAL, JOSEF, German-American composer; b. Mar. 1, 1903; d. May 5, 1964.

    Fromm, Herbert, 1905–1995. *Chamber cantata: For 4 voices and 8 instruments* (1965). Vocal soloists (SATB) with octet of flute, oboe, clarinet, bassoon, horn, piano, viola, violoncello. Published *TCL* 748, 1966. "This work is dedicated to the memory of Dr. Josef Freudenthal (1903–1964)"—caption in score. Text by Judah ha-Levi.

FRIEDERICH, JOHANN, German composer; d. Dec. 8, 1629.

    Dietrich, Marcus, fl. 1630. "Ode discolos tetrastrophos," in *Christliche Leichpredigt . . . bey . . . Leichenbestattung des . . . Herrn M. Johannes Freiderici . . . welcher am 8. Decembr Anno 1629 entschlaffen.* Published Leipzig: Friedrich Lankisch, 1629. *RISM-A1:* D-3012.

FRIEDMAN, IGNAZ, Polish pianist; b. Feb. 14, 1882; d. Jan. 26, 1948.

    Helps, Robert, 1928– . "Valse mirage: To the memory of Lewis Lane and Ignaz Friedman" (1977), in *Waltzes by 25 contemporary composers.* Piano. Published *Peters* 66735, 1978.

FROBERGER, JOHANN JAKOB, German organist, composer; b. May 19, 1616; d. May 7, 1667.

    Froberger, Johann Jakob, 1616–1667. "Allemande," in his *10 suittes de clavessin . . . mis en meilleur ordre et corrigée d'un grand nombre de fautes.* Harpsichord. Published Amsterdam: Mortier, 1710? *RISM-A1:* F-2033. Modern edition as "Suite no. 20, Allemande" in Froberger, *Suiten für Klavier,* ed. Guido Adler (*DTÖ,* vol. 13, 1959). In the *Hintze Manuscript* that also contains this Allemande (Yale University School of Music, Ms Ma. 21.H59), it is identified as a meditation by Froberger on his future death: "Metitation faict sur ma mort future la quelle se jove lentement avec discretion. di Gio. Gia. Frob."

FROMM, PAUL, American patron of contemporary music; b. Sep. 28, 1906; d. July 4, 1987.

Carter, Elliott, 1908– . *Remembrance: In memory of a great patron and believer in music of our time, Paul Fromm* [Occasions. Remembrance]. Orchestra. Published *Hendon*, 1988. The second of "Three occasions." Others titled: *A celebration of some 100 x 150 notes*, and *Anniversary.* "Each may be performed separately or all three together as a suite"—program note in score.

Johnston, Ben, 1926– . *Journeys: In memory of Paul Fromm* (1988). Chorus (SSATB) and orchestra. Published *SmithPubs*, 1989.

O'Brien, Eugene, 1945– . *Mysteries of the horizon: In memory of Paul Fromm* (1987). Chamber orchestra. Published *MMB*, 1987.

Shapey, Ralph, 1921– . *In memoriam: For my friend, Paul Fromm, 1906–1987* (July 1987). Solo voices (SBar) with nonette of flute, oboe, clarinet, bassoon, horn, string quartet. Published *Presser* 005-0009, 1987.

FUCHS, ROBERT, Austrian composer, pedagogue; b. Feb. 15, 1847; d. Feb. 19, 1927.

Whithorne, Emerson, 1884–1958. *Fata Morgana,* op. 44*: Dedicated to the memory of my master Robert Fuchs* (1928). Symphonic poem. Published New York: Cos Cob Press, 1930.

GADE, NIELS, Danish composer; b. Feb. 22, 1817; d. Dec. 21, 1890.

Grieg, Edvard, 1843–1907. "Gade," in his *Lyriske stykker = Lyrische Stücke,* op. 57 (1893). Piano. Published *Peters* 2657a, 1893. CONTENTS: Svundne dager = Vanished days—Gade—Illusion—Hemmelighet = Secret—Hun danser = She dances—Hjemlengsel = Homesickness.

Langgaard, Rued, 1893–1952. *Toccata: Zum Andenken Niels W. Gade* (1911; rev. 1938). Organ. Published *Hansen* 1401, 1912.

Matthison-Hansen, Johann Gottfred, 1832–1909. *Sorgemusik helliget Niels W. Gades Minde = Trauermusik dem Andenken Niels W. Gade gewidmet,* op. 29. Piano (or organ). Published *Hansen* 10764.

Piutti, Carl, 1846–1902. *In memoriam,* op. 21*: Pastorale und Fuge über Gade.* Organ. Published Leipzig: J. Rieter-Biedermann 1737, 1891.

GAGNON, HENRI, Canadian organist, composer; b. Mar. 6, 1887; d. May 17, 1961.

Le tombeau de Henri Gagnon: Pour orgue. Organ. Published Québec: Editions Jacques Ostiguy, 1987. Collection compiled by Lucien Poirier. CONTENTS: Élegie; Antiennes nos. 1–2; Prélude à l'introït du

IXe dimanche après la pentecote; Prélude sur l'alleluia de la Fête de Saint-Michel / by Henri Gagnon, 1887–1961—Prélude; In paradisum / by Antoine Bouchard, 1932– —Prières nos. 1–2 / by Claude Champagne, 1891–1965—Lumen / by Joseph Antonio Thompson, 1896–1974—Hymne Pascal / by Marius Cayouette, 1904–1985—Basilicale / by François Brassard, 1908–1976—Variations sur le nom de Henri Gagnon / by Antoine Reboulot, 1914–1967.

GAIL, EDMÉE-SOPHIE, French vocalist, composer; b. Aug. 28, 1775; d. July 24, 1819.

> **Neukomm, Sigismund, Ritter von, 1778–1858.** *Elégie sur la mort de Sophie Gail* (Nov. 20, 1819). Piano. Unpublished. Source: *Neukomm*, p. 83.

GALLON, JEAN, French composer; b. June 25, 1878; d. June 23, 1959.

> **Revel, Pierre, 1901– .** *Triptyque* (1962). Harpsichord (or piano). Published *EMT* TR00792, 1962.

GALLOT, JACQUES, French lutenist; d. 1690?

> **Visée, Robert de, ca. 1650–ca. 1725.** "Le tombeau du vieux Gallot, Allemande," in *Manuscrit Vaudry de Saizenay: Tablature de luth et de théorbe de divers auteurs* (1699). Published *Minkoff* 2826606859, 1980, which is a facsimile of the manuscript source: Besançon, Bibliothèque de la ville, Ms. 279.152, 279.153. In modern notation in *Gallot*.

GARANT, SERGE, Canadian composer, conductor, pianist, teacher; b. Sep. 22, 1929; d. Nov. 1, 1986.

> **Joachim, Otto, 1910– .** *Requiem: In memoriam Serge Garant* (1976; rev. 1986). Guitar. Unpublished. Source: *Canadian*.

GARCIA GUERRERO, ALBERTO, Chilean pianist; b. Feb. 6, 1886; d. Nov. 7, 1959.

> **Schafer, R. Murray, 1933– .** *In memoriam Alberto Guerrero* (1959). String orchestra. Published *Arcana*, 1985.

GARLAND, JUDY, American pop vocalist; b. June 10, 1922; d. June 22, 1969.

> **Rands, Bernard, 1934– .** *Ballad 1: To Ann—and the memory of Judy Garland* (1970). Mezzo-soprano with quintet for flute, tenor trombone, double bass, piano, percussion. Published *UE-L* 15414, 1971. Text by Gilbert Sorrentino.

GARRETA, JULIO, Spanish composer; b. Mar. 12, 1875; d. Dec. 2, 1925.

> **Montsalvatge, Xavier, 1912– .** *Elegia a Juli Garreta* (1946). Sardana band (Cobla). Unpublished. Source: *Montsalvatge*.

GATTI, CARLO, Italian composer; b. Dec. 19, 1876; d. Mar. 3, 1965.

Coscia, Silvio, 1899– . *Dramatic elegy: To the memory of my beloved teacher, academician Professor Carlo Gatti.* Band. Published *Baron,* 1967.

GAULTIER, DENIS, French lutenist, composer; b. 1600?; d. Jan. 1672.

Gallot, Jacques, d. ca. 1690. "Allemande, Le bout de l'an de Monsieur Galutier," in his *Pièces de luth composées sur differens modes par Jacques de Gallot avec Les folies d'Espagne enrichies de plusieurs beaux couplets.* Published Paris: H. Bonneuil, 167–? New edition in *Gallot.*

Gaultier, Denis, d. 1672. "Allemande grave de Mr. Gaultier," in *Livre de tablature des pieces de luth de Mr. Gaultier Sr. de Neve et de Mr. Gaultier son cousin sur plusieurs diferents modes, avec quelques reigles qu'il faut observer pour le bien toucher.* Published Paris: Veuve Gaultier, 1672. *RISM-B1:* 1672/6. Modern edition: "Allemande grave, dite tombeau de Gaultier par lui-même," in *Rhétorique.* Gaultier may or may not have intended this as a tombeau for himself, since it was designated as such only in manuscript copies and not in the printed edition of 1672 (see Tessier's notes in the modern edition).

Mouton, Charles, 1626–after 1699. "Oraison funebre de Monsieur Gautier," in *Rhétorique.* Lute. Edited from a manuscript at Roudnice, Czechoslovakia: Ms Lobkowicz (KK 80).

GAVINIÉS, PIERRE, French violinist, composer; b. May 11, 1726; d. Sep. 9, 1800.

Gaviniés, Pierre, 1726–1800. *Trois sonates pour le violon composées par la célèbre Gaviniés, avec accompagnement de violoncelle ad libitum, dont l'une en fa mineur, dite son tombeau, dédiées d'apres ses dernières intentions à son amie Kreutzer* [Sonatas, violin, violoncello, op. posth.]. Violin with violoncello accompaniment ad libitum. Published Paris: Naderman 1640, 1801. *RISM-A1:* G-746. Later edition: Berlin: Lischke, 1828? The first of the three sonatas (F minor) is titled "Le tombeau de Gaviniés."

GAYE, MARVIN, American rhythm-and-blues vocalist; b. Apr. 2, 1939; d. Apr. 1, 1984.

Commodores (Musical group). "Nightshift," recorded on *Nightshift*: Motown Records 6124ML, 1984. Pop song. Also released on single 45rpm recording (Motown 1773MF). Also dedicated to the memory of vocalist Jackie Wilson. Words and music by W. Orange, D. Lambert, F. Golde.

Turnage, Mark-Anthony, 1960– . *Ekaya: Elegy in memory of Marvin Gaye* (1984). Orchestra. Published *Schott-L*, 1986. ". . . He freed a lot of people, but it seems the good die young"—quote at end of score from the song "Abraham, Martin and John" by Dick Holler.

GEOFFRAY, CÉSAR, French choral conductor, composer; b. Feb. 20, 1901; d. Dec. 24, 1972.

Regel, Hans Wolfgang, 1929– . *Requiem: À la mémoire de César Geoffray* (1974). Chorus (5 parts), solo speaking voice, speaking chorus, violins, double bass. Published *ACoeur*, 1990.

GERHARD, ROBERTO, Catalonian composer; b. Sep. 25, 1896; d. Jan. 5, 1970.

Bassett, Leslie, 1923– . *Sounds remembered.* Violin and piano. Published *Peters* 66490, 1975. "*Sounds remembered* is an hommage to Roberto Gerhard (1896–1970), the distinguished Spanish-British composer, pupil of Schoenberg, and my colleague and friend since 1960. . . ."—composer's note in score.

Mestres i Quadreny, Josep, 1929– . *Homenatge a Robert Gerhard* (1976). Variations for piano solo, with 9 instruments ad libitum. Unpublished. Source: *Catalan.* Chance composition. A portion of the manuscript score (in graphic notation) is published in *Catalan.* A score reproduced from manuscript is held by Carnegie Mellon University Library.

Reynolds, Roger, 1934– . *Promises of darkness* (1975). Ensemble of flute, clarinet, violin, trumpet, horn, violoncello, piano, percussion, trombone, bassoon, contrabassoon. Published *Peters* 66655, 1976. "*The promises of darkness* was commissioned by Arthur Weisberg for the Contemporary Chamber Ensemble. It was written in memory of Roberto Gerhard and represents a personal response to his music, humanity and intellect"—note in score.

GERSHWIN, GEORGE, American composer; b. Sep. 26, 1898; d. July 11, 1937.

Call, Audrey, 1905– . *Elegy to the memory of George Gershwin* (1939). Orchestra. Unpublished. Source: *ASCAP.*

Twardowski, Romuald, 1930– . *Capriccio in blue: George Gershwin in memoriam* (1979). Violin and piano. Published *PWM* 8436, 1982.

GESUALDO, DON CARLO, Neapolitan lutenist, composer; b. 1560; d. Sep. 8, 1613.

Moran, Robert, 1937– . *In memoriam Don Carlo Gesualdo.* Chamber ensemble and electronic tape. Unpublished. Source: *BMI-78.*

GHEDINI, GIORGIO FEDERICO, Italian composer; b. July 11, 1892; d. Mar. 25, 1965.

Farina, Edouardo, 1939– . *Elegia per Ghedini* (1966). Violin and string orchestra. Published *Ricordi* 13097900, 1966.

Zanettovich, Daniele, 1950– . *Musica per cinque: In memoria di Giorgio Federico Ghedini* (1971). Quintet for violin, viola, violoncello, double bass, piano. Published *Pizzicato* NO24.

GIANNEO, LUIS, Argentine composer; b. Jan. 9, 1897; d. Aug. 15, 1968.

Lasala, Angel E., 1914– . *Homenaje a Luis Gianneo* (1968). Guitar. Published *Ricordi-BA* BA13083.

GIBSON, SIR ALEXANDER, Scottish conductor; b. Feb. 11, 1926; d. Jan. 13, 1995.

MacMillan, James, 1959– . *Inés de Castro* (1996). Opera in 2 acts. Published *Boosey*. Libretto adapted by MacMillan from the play by John Clifford. Premiered at the 1996 Edinburgh festival.

GILELS, EMIL, Russian pianist; b. Oct. 19, 1916; d. Oct. 14, 1985.

Rumson, Gordon, 1960– . *Poem for Emil Gilels* (1995). Piano. Published *Sikesdi*, 1995.

Smirnov, Dmitrii, 1948– . *Epitafiia = Epitaph: In memoriam Emil Gilels* (1985). Piano and organ. Published *Schirmer*; *Sikorski*.

GILLES, JOSEPH, French organist, composer; b. May 21, 1903; d. Oct. 12, 1942.

Dupré, Marcel, 1886–1971. "Virgo mediatrix: À la mémoire de Joseph Gilles," in his *Offrande à la Vierge,* op. 40 (1944). Organ. Published *Bornemann* SB5338, 1945. CONTENTS: Virgo Mater—Mater dolorosa—Virgo mediatrix.

GILLESPIE, JOHN BIRKS ("DIZZY"), American jazz trumpeter b. Oct. 21, 1917; d. Jan. 6, 1993.

Wilson, Dana Richard, 1946– . *I remember . . .: Louis and Clifford and Miles and Dizzy.* Trumpet solo in the jazz idiom. Published *ITG*, c1997, as special supplement to *ITG journal* 23/1 (Sept. 1998). A memorial to jazz trumpeters Louis Armstrong, Clifford Brown, Miles Davis, and Dizzy Gillespie.

GILSON, PAUL, Belgian composer, teacher; b. June 15, 1865; d. Apr. 3, 1942.

Brenta, Gaston, 1902– . *In memoriam Paul Gilson* (1950). Orchestra. Published *CeBeDeM.*

GINASTERA, ALBERTO, Argentine composer; b. Apr. 11, 1916; d. June 25, 1983.

Brncic, Gabriel, 1942– . *Piano trio: A la memoria d'Alberto Ginastera* (1983). Unpublished. Source: *Catalan.*

GINTER, FRANZ, Netherlands lutenist; d. 1706.

Saint-Luc, Jacques Alexandre, b. 1663. "Le tombeau de Mr. François Ginter," in *Österreichische Lautenmusik zwischen 1650 und 1720,* ed. Adolf Koczirz. Lute. Published *DTÖ,* vol. 50, 1918. Edited from Österreichische Nationalbibliothek, MS Sm.1586.

GLENN, CARROLL, American violinist; b. Oct. 28, 1918; d. Apr. 25, 1983.

Adler, Samuel, 1928– . *Double portrait: For violin and piano.* Published *Southern* ST785, 1989. "Commissioned by Carey Lewis and Ronald Nead to honor the memory of two great artists and two beautiful people, Carroll Glenn and Eugene List"—note in score.

GLINKA, MIKHAIL IVANOVICH, Russian composer; b. June 1, 1804; d. Feb. 15, 1857.

Eleven variations on a theme by Glinka (1957). Piano. Published *AMP* 7729, 1977. Variations on "Vanya's Song" from Glinka's opera *Ivan Susanin,* compiled in 1957 to honor the centenary of Glinka's death. CONTENTS: Variation 1 / by Eugene Knapp—Variations 2 & 3 / by Vissarion Shebalin, 1902–1963—Variation 4 / by Andrei Eshpai, 1925– —Variation 5 / by Rodion Shchedrin, 1932– —Variation 6 / by Georgii Sviridov, 1915–1998—Variation 7 / by Iurii Levitin, 1912– —Variations 8–9 / by Dmitri Shostakovich, 1906–1975—Variation 10 / by Dmitri Kabalevsky, 1904–1987—Variation 11 / by Dmitri Shostakovich, 1906–1975.

Balakirev, Milii Alekseevich, 1837–1910. *Kantata na otkrytiye pamyatnika M. I. Glinke v Peterburge* (1902–04). Soprano, chorus, orchestra. Published Leipzig: Gutheil, 1904. Text by V. Glebov. Composed for the unveiling of the Glinka memorial in St. Petersburg, planned for 1904 but postponed until 1906.

Erdeli, Kseniia Aleksandrovna, 1878–1971. *Elegiia: Pamiati Glinki* (1946). Harp. Published Moscow: Gosudarstvennoe Muzykalnoe Izdatelstvo 21071, 1950.

Stravinsky, Igor, 1882–1971. *Mavra: Opéra bouffe: À la mémoire de Pouchkine, Glinka et Tschaikovsky* (1922; rev. 1947). Opera in one act. Published Paris; New York: Editions Russe de Musique, 1925. Revised edition: *Boosey* HPS843, 1947. Libretto by Boris Kochno after Pushkin's *The little house of Kolomma.*

GLUCK, CHRISTOPH WILLIBALD, German composer; b. July 2, 1714; d. Nov. 15, 1787.

Beecke, Notger Ignaz Franz von, 1733–1803. *Musikalische Apotheose des Ritters Gluck: In Musik gesetz und der Wittwe Frau von Gluck zugeeignet.* Solo voices (SATB), orchestra. Published *Schott-M* 86, 1788. *RISM-A1:* B-1635.

Vernier, Jean Aimé, 1769–after 1838. *Le tombeau de l'immortel chevalier Gluck* (1788). Harpsichord (or piano). Published Paris: Mme Baillou, 1788. *RISM-A1:* V-1290.

GLUCK, MARIANNE NANETTE, Austrian soprano; b. 1759?; d. Apr. 22, 1776.

Beecke, Notger Ignaz Franz von, 1733–1803. *Klagen über den Tod des grosen Saengerinn Nanette von Gluck.* Soprano, violins (2), viola, bass, harpsichord. Published Augsburg: Konrad Heinrich Staye, 1776. *RISM-A1:* B-1628. Marianne Nanette was Christoph Willibald Gluck's niece (daughter of his sister Maria Anna Rosine) whom he adopted. Contemporary accounts describe her excellent soprano voice, which was trained by the famous castrato Giuseppe Millico.

GOLDMAN, EDWIN FRANKO, American bandmaster; b. Jan. 1, 1878; d. Feb. 21, 1956.

Ward, Robert, 1917– . *Night fantasy* (1962). Concert band. Published *Highgate*, 1962. Commissioned by Richard Franko Goldman in memory of his father Edwin Franko Goldman.

GOMES, CARLOS, Brazilian composer; b. July 11, 1836; d. Sep. 16, 1896.

Zandonai, Riccardo, 1883–1944. *Homenagem a Carlos Gomes: Lembrança do 1o centenario de independencia do Brasil* (1922). Chorus and orchestra. Published Sao Paulo: Estabel Graphico Musical "Paulista" J. Mari & Cia, 1936. Composed 1922 for the centennial of Brazilian independence; first published 1936 in honor of the centennial of Gomes's birth. Text by Antonio Zampedri. Zandonai's autograph of the vocal score was also published in facsimile in 1936 as *Hymno triumphal a Carlos Gomes para coro e grande orchestra* (Sao Paulo: De Rosa 00568, 1936).

GONZALES, VICTOR, Spanish-French organist; b. May 21, 1877; d. June 3, 1956.

Le tombeau de Gonzalez. Organ. Published Paris: Editions musicales de la Schola Cantorum S5595P, 1956. Published in series Orgue e liturgie, no. 38. CONTENTS: Choral-prélude "O dieu, la gloire qui t'es due" / by Alexandre Cellier, 1883–1968—Offertoire sur une chanson espagnole / by Seth Bingham, 1882–1972—Thème et variations sur le nom de Victor Gonzalez / by Gaston Litaize,

1909–1991—Introduction et aria, "à la mémoire de Victor Gonzalez" / by Jean-Jacques Grunenwald, 1911–1982—Complainte / by Marie-Louise Girod-Parrot, 1915– —Lacrymae / by Olivier Alain, 1918–1994—Prélude sur les jeux d'anches, "à la mémoire de Victor Gonzalez" / by Georges Robert, 1928– .

GOOSSENS, SIR EUGENE, English conductor, composer; b. May 26, 1893; d. June 13, 1962.

Still, William Grant, 1895–1978. *Festive overture: Dedicated to the memory of Eugene Goossens* (1944). Orchestra. Published *CFischer* 05343, 1944. Dedication on the holograph is "To my friend, Rudolph Dunbar." Memorial dedication to Goossens appears later in the published version.

GOTTLIEB, VICTOR, American violoncellist; d. 1963?

Dahl, Ingolf, 1912–1970. *Elegy concerto for violin and small orchestra: In memoriam Victor Gottlieb* (1963–70; rev. 1971). Published Hackensack, NJ: J. Boonin, 1974. Gottlieb was a musician at Universal Pictures before he was blacklisted in the 1950s. Composition was begun in 1963, but the work was left incomplete at Dahl's death in 1970. Completed by Donal Michalsky in 1971, and first performed Nov. 21st of that year by Eudice Shapiro (Gottlieb's widow) with the University of Southern California Chamber Orchestra as part of a memorial concert of Dahl's music.

GOTTSCHALK, LOUIS MOREAU, American pianist, composer; b. May 8, 1829; d. Dec. 18, 1869.

Heimburger, Edward. *Elegy on the death of L. M. Gottschalk.* Piano. Published Rochester, NY: Jos. P. Shaw, 1870.

Hoffman, Richard, 1831–1909. *In memoriam L. M. G.* Piano. Published New York: Wm. Pond, 1870. New edition in *Piano music in nineteenth century America*, compiled and ed. by Maurice Hinson (*Hinshaw,* 1975).

GOULD, GLENN, Canadian pianist; b. Sep. 25, 1932; d. Oct. 4, 1982.

Ashkenazy, Benjamin, 1940– . *Izkor: In memoriam Glenn Gould* (1986). English horn and piano soloists with orchestra. Published *Donemus,* 1986.

Louie, Alexina, 1949– . *O mangnum mysterium: In memoriam Glenn Gould* (1983; rev. 1984). Strings (44). Published *Canadian.*

Rak, Stepán, 1945– . *Romance Ontario: To the memory of Glenn Gould.* Guitar. Unpublished. Source: *OCLC.* Recorded by the composer on *Dedications* (Nimbus Records NI5239, 1989).

Rossum, Frederic van, 1939– . *In memoriam Glenn Gould,* op. 43

(1984). Piano. Published *Billaudot* 5869, 1989.

Titmus, Clive. *Tombeau for Glenn Gould.* Guitar. Unpublished. Source: Recorded by the composer on *La Musette* (DoReMi 71131, 1999).

GOULD, MORTON, American composer; b. Dec. 13, 1913; d. Feb. 21, 1996.

Ferritto, John, 1937– . *Ballad in blue: In memoriam Morton Gould.* String orchestra. Published *Squirrel* BSMSO-100, 1997.

GRAINGER, PERCY, Australian-American pianist, composer; b. July 8, 1882; d. Feb. 20, 1961.

Finnissy, Michael, 1946– . *Folk song set: In memory of Percy Grainger* (1969–70; rev. 1975–76). Soprano with ensemble of English horn, clarinet, flugelhorn, percussion, string quartet, double bass. Published *UE-L*, 1970. Revised 1975–1976 for mezzo-soprano with sextet of flute, clarinet, piano, violin, viola, violoncello. Another version 1975–1976 is for mezzo-soprano, flute, oboe, percussion, piano.

GRANADOS, ENRIQUE, Spanish composer; b. July 28, 1867; d. Mar. 24, 1916.

Cruz, Zulema de la, 1958– . *Nucleofonia: In memoriam Enrique Granados* (1980). Octet for soprano saxophone, bass clarinet, trumpet, piano, vibraphone, string trio. Published *Alpuerto*, 1981.

Garcia Laborda, José Maria, 1946– . *Cántico: In memoriam Enrique Granados* (1980). High voice with instrumental ensemble. Published *Alpuerto*, 1981?

Garcia Roman, José, 1945– . *O tempora: In memoriam Enrique Granados.* Solo voices (STB) with instrumental ensemble. Published *Alpuerto*, 1981?

GREENBERG, NOAH, American conductor, musicologist; b. Apr. 9, 1920; d. Jan. 9, 1966.

Perle, George, 1915– . *Songs of praise and lamentation* (1974). Chorus and orchestra. Published *Mobart*, 1976. "Commissioned by the Dessoff Choirs and dedicated to the memory of Noah Greenberg"—note in score. Texts from the Psalms, from Rilke's *Sonnets to Orpheus*, and "In eius memoriam," an original poem for the occasion by John Hollander. Music incorporates the incipits from Ockeghem's *déploration* for Binchois, Josquin's *déploration* for Ockeghem, and Vinders's lamentation for Josquin.

GRÉTRY, ANDRÉ ERNEST MODESTE, French composer; b. Feb. 8, 1741; d. Sep. 24, 1813.

Berton, Henri Mouton, 1767–1844. "Stances sur la mort de Grétry," in *Menestrel: Journal de chant avec accompagnement de piano ou harpe . . . Ier année, no. 1.* Song. Published Paris: S. Gaveaux 148, 1816? *RISM-A1:* B-2354.

Gaubert, Denis, fl. 19ᵗʰ cent. *Passage de l'Achéron par Grétry, et sa réception aux Champs-Elysées: Mélange d'aire arrangés par piano* (1813). Published Paris: Sieber fils, 1813.

Reicha, Anton, 1770–1836. *Hommage à Gretry* (1814). Vocal soloists, chorus, orchestra. Unpublished. Source: *NGrove*, which locates the manuscript score at the Paris Conservatory (MS 12010). According to *Reicha* this manuscript contains a cantata-parody of Grétry's opera *Zémire et Azor.*

GRIEG, EDVARD, Norwegian composer; b. June 15, 1843; d. Sep. 4, 1907.

Heilmann, Harald, 1924– . *Fantasie for organ,* op. 179*: In memoriam Edvard Grieg.* Published *Merseburger* 1895, 1998.

Whiting, George Elbridge, 1840–1923. *Melody: Homage to Grieg.* Organ. Published *Presser*, 1908.

GRIGNY, NICOLAS DE, French organist, composer; b. Sep. 8, 1672; d. Nov. 30, 1703.

Gerber, René, 1908– . *Le tombeau de Nicolas Grigny* (1947). Trio for trumpet, violin, organ. Unpublished. Source: *Beckmann.* CONTENTS: Sarabande—Comptine—Berceuse—Ronde.

Migot, Georges, 1891–1976. *Le tombeau de Nicolas de Grigny* (1931). Organ (or piano). Published *Leduc* AL18124, 1933. "Sur un air auvergnat." An unpublished orchestral version exists under the title *Pour saluer Antoine d'Auvergne.*

GROVES, SIR CHARLES, English conductor; b. Mar. 10, 1915; d. June 20, 1992.

Davies, Peter Maxwell, 1934– . *Sir Charles his pavan* (1992). Orchestra. Published *Schott-L* 12438, 1994.

GRUNWALD, HUGO, German-American pianist; b. Mar. 17, 1869; d. Oct. 2, 1956.

Bennett, Robert Russell, 1894–1981. *String quartet: To the memory of Hugo Grunwald* (1956). Unpublished. Source: *Bennett.* First performance Dec. 13, 1956, Brooklyn Academy of Music, Guilet String Quartet.

GUARNERI, GIUSEPPE ANTONIO, Italian luthier; b. Aug. 21, 1698; d. Oct. 17, 1744.

David, Johann Nepomuk, 1895–1977. "Giuseppe Guarneri del

Gesù in memoriam," in his *Vier Trios,* op. 33 (1928–1935). Trio for violin, viola, violoncello. Published *Breitkopf* 5598, 1948. CONTENTS: Nicola Amati in memoriam—Antonio Stradivario in memoriam—Giuseppe Guarneri del Gesù in memoriam—Jacobo Stainer in memoriam.

GUÉZEC, JEAN PIERRE, French composer; b. Aug. 29, 1934; d. Mar. 9, 1971.

Amy, Gilbert, 1936– . *D'un desastre obscur: À la mémoire de Jane-Pierre Guézec, mort le 9 mars 1971 à 36 ans* (1971). Mezzo-soprano and clarinet in A. Published *UE-L,* 1973. "The Alexandrine line used in this piece is taken from the poem 'Tombeau d'Edgar Poe' by Stéphane Mallarmé: Calme bloc isi bas chu d'un desastre obscur"—note in score.

Boucourechliev, André, 1925– . *Le tombeau* (1971). Clarinet and percussion (or piano). Published *Leduc* AL25161, 1974. "Tombeau, écrite an mars 1971, est dédié à la mémoire du compositeur français Jean-Pierre Guézec, mort à 37 ans"—composer's note in score.

Constant, Marius, 1925– . *9 mars 1971* (1971). Piccolo and glockenspiel. Published *Salabert* EAS17355: 1990. The title is the date of Guézec's death.

Darasse, Xavier, 1934–1992. *In memoriam Jean Pierre Guézec: Pour orgue et cinq instrumentistes* (1972). Organ with quintet for horn, trombone, trumpets (2), tuba. Published *Salabert* EAS17125, 1973.

Jolas, Betsy, 1926– . *Remember* (1971). English horn (or viola) and violoncello. Published *Heugel* H32215, 1972. First performed April 6, 1971, at the Festival de Royan as *Le tombeau de Jean-Pierre Guézec.*

Louvier, Alain, 1945– . *Etude pour agresseurs.* Performance medium unknown. Perhaps one of the *Etudes pour agresseurs,* book 3, for harpsichord (*Leduc,* 1971), though this publication does not identify a particular etude as memorializing Guézec. Source: *Mussat.* First performance April 6, 1971, at the Festival de Royan. A review of the premiere by R. Holhlweg, published in "Im Trauern war Royan diesmal am besten," *Melos* 38 (June 1971): 250, mentions this work and others performed in memoriam to Louvier at the festival.

Marie, Jean-Etienne, 1917– . *Hommage à Jean-Pierre Guézec* (1971). Electronic tape. Unpublished. Source: *NGrove.*

Messiaen, Olivier, 1908–1992. "Appel insterstellaire" (1971), in his

Des canyons aux étoiles . . .: Pour piano solo, cor, xylorimba, glock-enspiel, et orchestre. This movement (no. 6) is for horn solo. Published *Leduc* AL25314, 1978. First performed at Royan, April 6, 1971, as *Fanfares et signals: Le tombeau de Jean-Pierre Guézec.*

Xenakis, Iannis, 1922– . *Charisma: À Jean-Pierre Guézec* (Mar. 20, 1971). Clarinet and violoncello. Published *Salabert* MC587, 1971. Caption in score includes a quotation from the *Iliad:* "Then the soul like smoke moved into the earth, grinding."

GUILLAUME DE MACHAUT, French composer, poet; b. 1300?; d. 1377.

Andrieu, F[rançois?]. "Armes, amours, dames chevalerie," in *French secular compositions of the fourteenth century,* 3 vols., ed. by Willi Apel. Voices (4). Published *AIM,*1970–1972. vol. 1, p. 2–3. The composer is known only by this work, which is a setting of two ballades by Eustache Deschamps (1346?–1406), a pupil of Machaut in poetry. The refrain is "La mort Machaut, le noble rethoryque." Edited from Musée Condé (Chantilly, France), Ms. 1047. A facsimile of the folio from the manuscript containing this work is included in Friedrich Gennrich, *Abriss der Mensuralnotation des XIV. und der ersten Hälfte des XV. Jahrhunderts,* 2nd ed., Musikwissenschaftliche Studien-Bibliothek, vol. 3–4 (Langen bei Frankfurt, 1965), plate 16.

Thiele, Siegfried, 1934– . *Hommage à Machaut.* Solo voices (ABar) and orchestra. Published *Peters* 9215, 1979. Texts based in part on the *déploration* for Machaut by his pupil in poetry Eustache Deschampes, "Armes, amours, dames chevalerie."

GUILMANT, ALEXANDRE, French organist; b. Mar. 12, 1837; d. Mar. 29, 1911.

Migot, Georges, 1891–1976. "Douloureux, funèbre" (1937), in his *Premier livre d'orgue.* Organ. Published *Leduc* AL19641, 1938. No. 1 of 12 pieces.

Remondi, Roberto, 1851–1928. "Elégie: Sur la tombe d'Alexandre Guilmant," in *Les maitres contemporains de l'orgue,* vol. 3. Organ. Published Paris: M. Senart, 1912.

HÁBA, ALOIS, Czech composer, pedagogue; b. June 21, 1893; d. Nov. 18, 1973.

Pauer, Jiri, 1919– . *Iniciály = Initials* (1974). Orchestra. Published *Panton* 1830, 1979. "The symphonic movement INITIALS was inspired by the death-interrupted friendship between the author and his former teacher of composition, Professor Alois Hába. For this reason

the composition begins with the initials of the name A. Hába"—
introduction to score.

HADJIDAKIS (HADZIKAKIS), MANOS, Greek composer; b. June 23,
1925; d. June 15, 1994.

See: **CHATZIDAKES, MANOS.**

HALFFTER, RODOLFO, Spanish-Mexican composer; b. Oct. 20, 1900;
d. Oct. 14, 1987.

Lavista, Mario, 1943– . *Responsorio para fagot y percusiones: In
memoriam Rodolfo Halffter* (1988). Bassoon with percussionists (2
or 4). Published *Mexicanas* D64, 1991.

HANDEL, GEORGE FRIDERIC, German-born composer; b. Feb. 23,
1685; d. Apr. 14, 1759.

Söderstrom, Gunno, 1920– . *Sonatina for piano: Bach-Handel in
memoriam* (1984). Published *STIM*.

HANEY, LEWIS VAN, American trombonist; b. June 14, 1920; d. May
2, 1991.

Anderson, David, 1962– . *Elegy for Van* (1992). Bass trombone.
Unpublished. Source: *IUL*, recording of recital by trombonist Edwin
Anderson, May 3, 1992.

HANSON, HOWARD, American composer; b. Oct. 28, 1896; d. Oct. 28,
1981.

Hartley, Walter S., 1927– . *Centennial symphony: In memoriam
Howard Hanson* (1995). Concert band. Published *Ludwig* SWO367,
1998. Composed for the 100th anniversary of Hanson's birth.

Jones, Samuel, 1935– . *Symphonic requiem: Variations on a theme
of Howard Hanson* (1983). Orchestra. Published *CFischer*.

HARDER, PAUL O., American composer, pedagogue; b. Mar. 10, 1923;
d. Aug. 20, 1986.

Steinke, Greg A., 1942– . *Wind river country: In memory of Paul
Harder (1923–1986), teacher, friend, mentor* (1986). Woodwind
quintet. Unpublished. Source: *AMC.* Commissioned by the Fifteenth
Western Arts Festival for the New World Quintet. First performed
by them July 1, 1986, University of Wyoming, Laramie.

HARTMANN, GEORGES, French music publisher; d. Apr. 22, 1900.

Debussy, Claude, 1862–1918. *Pelléas et Mélisande: Drame lyrique*
(1902). Opera in 5 acts. Published *Durand* 7018, 1902. "À la mémoire de Georges Hartmann et en témoignage de profonde affection
à M. André Messager" —dedication in score.

HARTMANN, JOHAN PETER EMILIUS, Danish composer; b. May 14,
1805; d. Mar. 10, 1900.

Matthison-Hansen, Johann Gottfred, 1832–1909. *Trauermusik for organ,* op. 38: *In memoriam J. P. E. Hartmann.* Published *Hansen* 12775.

HARTOG, HOWARD, English artists agent; b. 1913; d. Nov. 27, 1991.

Birtwistle, Harrison, 1934– . *Antiphonies: To the memory of Howard Hartog* (1992). Piano and orchestra. Published *UE-L* 19780, 1992.

HAUPTMANN, MORITZ, German composer; b. Oct. 13, 1792; d. Jan. 3, 1868.

Kirchner, Theodor, 1823–1903. "Lento," in his *Gedenkblätter: Zwölf Musikstücke zur Erinnerung an die Einweihung des neuen Königl. Conservatoriums für Musik zu Leipzig,* op. 82 (1843–87). Piano. Published Leipzig: J. Rieter-Biedermann 1508, 1887. No. 5 of 12 short piano pieces memorializing Conrad Schleinitz, Felix Mendelssohn, Robert Schumann, Moritz Hauptmann, Ferdinand David, Ignaz Moscheles, Ernst Friedrich Richter, Carl Ferdinand Becker, Ernst Ferdinand Wenzel, and Louis Plaidy.

HAWKINS, COLEMAN, American jazz saxophonist; b. Nov. 21, 1904; d. May 19, 1969.

Karlins, M. William, 1932– . *Music for tenor saxophone and piano.* Published *Southern* SS978, 1972. Second movement (untitled) is captioned "To the memory of Coleman Hawkins."

HAYDN, JOSEPH, Austrian composer; b. Mar. 31, 1732; d. May 31, 1809.

Hommage à Haydn: Six pièces pour piano. Collection published as a musical supplement to the *Revue Société Internationale Musicale (S. I. M.)* (Jan. 15, 1910) for the centennial anniversary of the death of Haydn. All of the works are based on a theme on Haydn's name (B-A-D-D-G). CONTENTS: Hommage à Haydn / by Claude Debussy, 1862–1918—Prélude élégiac sur le nom de Haydn / by Paul Dukas, 1865–1935—Thème varié / by Reynaldo Hahn, 1874–1947— Menuet sur le nom d'Haydn / by Vincent d'Indy, 1851–1931— Menuet sur le nom d'Haydn / by Maurice Ravel, 1875–1937—Fugue sur le nom d'Haydn / by Charles-Marie Widor, 1844–1937.

Bolaffi, Michaele, 1768–1842. *Sonetto a voce sola con pianoforte in morte del celebre Haydn.* Song "Piangete o dive." Published London: s.n., 1809. Source: *CPM.*

Calegari, Antonio, 1757–1828. *Euterpe italica alla tomba dell'immortale Gius. Haydn* (1810). Chorus and orchestra. Unpublished. Source: *NGrove.* Manuscript at the Casa Erizzo, Venice.

Cherubini, Luigi, 1760–1842. *Chant sur la mort de Joseph Haydn* (1805). Vocal soloists (STT) and orchestra. Published Paris: Au Magazin de musique, 1809. Composed in Dec. 1805 when rumors of Haydn's death spread around Paris. The work was not performed once the rumors were proved false. The 1809 edition is of the vocal score; a modern edition based on the autograph in the Deutsche Staatsbibliothek, Berlin, is the first publication of the full score (*B&S* BS20, 1980).

Debussy, Claude, 1862–1918. *Hommage à Haydn: Pièce écrite pour le centenaire de Haydn* (1909). Piano. Published *Durand* 7582, 1910. First published in the collection *Hommage à Haydn* (q.v.).

Dukas, Paul, 1865–1935. *Prélude élégiaque pour le piano: Centenaire d'Haydn* (May 1909). Published *Durand*, 1910. Also published 1910 in the collection *Hommage à Haydn* (q.v.). For the centenary of Haydn's death.

Françaix, Jean, 1912–1997. *Symphony in G major: Ecrite à la mémoire de Joseph Haydn* (1953). Published *Schott-M* 7708, 1953.

Hummel, Johann Nepomuk, 1778–1837. *Vernahmest du gleich uns, O Orpheus: In memory of J. Haydn* (1813). Chorus (STB) and orchestra. Unpublished. Source: *BMms* Ms Add. 32194, f. 116, manuscript at the British Library.

Kalkbrenner, Friedrich Wilhelm Michael, 1785–1849. *Grand sonata for the piano forte, op. 56: Dedicated to the memory of Joseph Haydn by his pupil Frederick Kalkbrenner.* Published *Chappell* 1777; *Breitkopf*, 1821.

Kreutzer, Rodolphe, 1766–1831. *Concerto for violin and orchestra, no. 16 in E minor: Dédié au célèbre Haydn* (1805). Published Paris: Au Magazin de musique; Lyon: Garnier, 1806. Subsequent editions by *Costallat, Breitkopf* 355. Composed in 1805 upon receipt of a false report of Haydn's death. Incorporates themes from Haydn's works.

Lunssens, Martin, 1871–1944. *Symphony no. 4: En mémoire de Haydn.* Unpublished. Source: *Lunssens*.

Mayr, Giovanni Simone, 1763–1845. *Cantata in memory of Haydn's death* (1809). Tenor solo, chorus, orchestra. Unpublished. Source: *Mayr*, p. 185. Text by Mayr. Autograph score at Civico Istituto Musicale Gaetano Donizetti, Bergamo.

Neukomm, Sigismund, Ritter von, 1778–1858. *Messe solenelle de St. Joseph* (1853). Soloists (TTBB), chorus, organ. Published *Costallat*, 185–?

────. *Missa pro defunctis: Manibus parentum praeceptorumque meorum Josephi et Michaelis Haydn* (1813). Double chorus (SSAATTBB) unacc. Published *Peters*, 1815.

────. "Non omnis moriar: Canon enigmaticus 5 vocibus in tumulum Joseph Haydn" (1814). A puzzle canon inscribed on the gravestone of Haydn's first burial place at the Hundsturm Cemetery in Vienna. The canon and its resolution are published in *Neukomm*.

Ries, Ferdinand, 1784–1838. "Marche funebre," in *Symphony no. 1 in D major,* op. 23 (1809). Published *Simrock* 903, 1811. New edition in Ries, *Three symphonies,* ed. by Cecil Hill, The symphony, Ser. C, vol. 12 (New York: Garland, 1982). Suggestion that the funeral march might be a tribute to Haydn is by Cecil Hill in the Garland edition.

Takács, Jenö, 1902– . *Sinfonia breve,* op. 108*: Dem Andenken Joseph Haydns* (1981). Orchestra. Published *Doblinger*.

Verheyen, Pierre Emmanuel, 1750–1819. *Requiem* (1810). Unpublished. Source: *NGrove*. Commissioned by the Société des beaux-arts de Gand for a memorial service held for Haydn in 1810. Verheyen's manuscripts are held by the Rijksuniversiteit Centrale Bibliotheek, Ghent.

HAYDN, MICHAEL, Austrian composer; b. Sep. 14, 1737; d. Aug. 10, 1806.

Diabelli, Anton, 1781–1858. *Trauer Marsch auf den Todt des Herrn Michael Haydn* (1906). Guitar. Published Vienna: Chemische Druckerei am Graben 542, 1806. Reprint: *Trauermarsch auf den Tod des Herrn Michael Haydn,* ed. Gerhard Walterskirchen, Denkmäler der Musik in Salzburg, Faksimile-Ausgaben, vol. 7 (Salzburg: Selke Verlag, 1998).

Neukomm, Sigismund, Ritter von, 1778–1858. *Missa pro defunctis: Manibus parentum praeceptorumque meorum Josephi et Michaelis Haydn* (1813). Double chorus (SSAATTBB) unacc. Published *Peters,* 1815.

────. *Messe solenelle sous le titre distinctif de St. Michel: En mémoire de Michel Haydn* (1854). Vocal soloists (SSA), chorus, and organ. Published Paris: Richault, 185–?

HEATH, KENNETH RIPPINER, English violoncellist; b. 1919; d. Mar. 1, 1977.

Knussen, Oliver, 1952– . *Cantata,* op. 15*: In memory of Kenneth Heath* (1975–77). Oboe and string trio. Published *Faber* 0571506372, 1981. *Cantata* is the third panel of a triptych of chamber works comprised of *Autumnal* (violin and piano), *Sonya's lullaby* (piano) and *Cantata.* May be performed together or separately.

HEILLER, ANTON, Austrian organist; b. Sep. 25, 1923; d. Mar. 25, 1979.

Pfiffner, Ernst, 1922– . *Biblische Szene von der gekrümmten Frau: In memoriam Anton Heiller* (1979–81). Violin solo. Published *Müller* MS1126, 1991.

Planyavsky, Peter, 1947– . *Fantasia in memoriam A. H.* (1986). Organ. Published *Doblinger* 2390, 1990. Composed for the inauguration of the Heiler Memorial Organ in Collegedale, Tennessee.

HEINRICH, VON VELDEKE, German Minnesinger; d. 1210?

Meulemans, Arthur, 1884–1966. *Huldezang aan Hendrik van Veldeke* (1926). Bass reciter, chorus, orchestra (or piano). Published *CeBeDeM.*

HELLINCK, LUPUS, Netherlands composer; b. ca. 1496; d. Jan. 14, 1541.

Baston, Josquin, fl. 1542–1563. "Eheu dolor," in *Concentus octo, sex, quinqus et quator vocum, omnium iucuncisimi, nuspiam autea sic aediti.* Voices (6). Published Augsburg: Philipp Ulhard, 1545. *RISM-B1*: 1545/2. New edition in *Trésor musical*, ed. Robert Julien van Maldeghem (Brussels: Muquardt, 1865–93), vol. 12, p. 3. Includes quotation of the *Requiem aeternam* in canon.

HEMING, MICHAEL SAVAGE, English composer; b. Jan. 14, 1920; d. Nov. 3, 1942.

Collins, Anthony, 1893–1963. *Threnody for a soldier killed in action.* Orchestra. Published London: Keith Prowse, 1944. Based on a sketch left by Heming, who died at El Alamein during World War II.

HENSEL, FANNY MENDELSSOHN, German pianist, composer; b. Nov. 14, 1805; d. May 14, 1847.

Mendelssohn-Bartholdy, Felix, 1809–1847. *String quartet no. 6 in F minor,* op. 80 (1847). Published *Breitkopf* 8116, 1850? Composed during a period of mourning for his sister.

HENSELT, ADOLF VON, German pianist; b. May 9, 1814; d. Oct. 10, 1889.

Leschetizky, Theodor, 1830–1915. *Impromptu en souvenir de Henselt,* op. 46, no. 6. [Contes de jeunesse, piano, op. 46. Impromptu]. Published *Bote* 15344, 1902.

HESELTINE, PHILIP, English composer, writer; b. Oct. 30, 1894; d. Dec. 17, 1930.

See: **WARLOCK, PETER.**

HEUGEL, HANS, German Kapellmeister; d. 1563.
   Frisius, Johannes, 1505–1565. *Trauergesang* (1563?). Unpublished. Source: *EitnerQL.*
HEUSSER, HANS, Swiss composer; b. Aug. 8, 1892; d. Oct. 27, 1942.
   Jaeggi, Stephan, 1903–1957. *Trauermarsch: In memoriam Hans Heusser.* Band. Published *Euphonia.*
HIGGINS, JON B., American ethnomusicologist; b. 1939; d. Dec. 7, 1984.
   Lucier, Alvin, 1931– . *In memoriam Jon Higgins* (1987). Clarinet in A with slow-sweep pure wave oscillator. Unpublished. Recorded by Thomas Ridenour on *Crossings* (Lovely Music LCD101,: 1990); recorded by Jürg Frey on *Lucier, Wolff, Schlothauer, Frey* (Timescraper EWR9608, 1996).
HILDEGARD, SAINT, German composer, poet, mystic; b. 1098; d. Sep. 17, 1179.
   Magnar, Am, 1952– . *Unio mystica pro organo solo: In memoriam Hildegard von Bingen* (1998). Organ. Published *NMIC*, 1998.
HILDESHEIMER, WOLFGANG, German musicologist; b. Aug. 21, 1916; d. Aug. 21, 1991.
   Klebe, Giselher, 1925– . *Trauermusik for chamber orchestra, op. 106: In memoriam Wolfgang Hildesheimer* (1991). Published *Bärenreiter* BA7346, 1991.
HILL, RALPH, English music critic and editor; b. Oct. 8, 1900; d. Oct. 19, 1950.
   Collins, Anthony, 1893–1963 (transcriber). Liszt, Franz, 1811–1886. *Crucifixus: Passacaglia for piano and orchestra* [Variationen über das Motiv von Bach; arr.] (1951). Original for piano. Transcribed by Collins for piano and orchestra. Published London: Patterson's Publs., 1955. Variations on the basso continuo of the first movement of Bach's cantata *Weinen, Klagen,* and of the "Crucifixus" of the Mass in B minor. "This transcription is to the memory of Ralph Hill" —note in score.
HILSBERG, ALEXANDER, Polish-American violinist, conductor; b. Apr. 24, 1897; d. Aug. 10, 1961.
   Persichetti, Vincent, 1915– . *Sinfonia, Janiculum: Symphony no. 9* (1970). Published *E-V* 466-00021, 1972. Commissioned for the Philadelphia Orchestra under terms of the will of Mrs. Alexander Hilsberg in memory of her husband, who had been associate conductor of the orchestra 1945–1953.
   Schuman, William, 1910–1992. *Symphony IX: Le fosse Ardeatine*

(1968). Orchestra. Published *Merion*, 1971. Commissioned by the friends of Alexander Hilsberg in his memory. CONTENTS: Anteludium—Offertorium—Postludium.

HINDEMITH, PAUL, German composer; b. Nov. 16, 1895; d. Dec. 28, 1963.

Badings, Henk, 1907–1987. *Concerto for bassoon, contrabassoon and wind orchestra: In memoriam Paul Hindemith* (1964). Published *Peters*, 1964.

Baur, Jürg, 1918– . *Reminiszenzen: Ostinato und Trio: In memoriam Paul Hindemith* (1950; rev. 1980). Quintet for flute, oboe, clarinet, horn, bassoon. Published *Bosse* BE151, 1983.

Dello Joio, Norman, 1913– . *Antiphonal fantasy on a theme of Vincenzo Albrici: To the memory of Paul Hindemith* (1966). Organ solo with brasses, strings. Published *EBMarks* 14998, 1966.

Höller, Karl, 1907–1987. *Sonata for viola and piano in E, op. 62: In memoriam Paul Hindemith* (1967). Published *Schott-M* 5847, 1968.

Jeppsson, Kerstin, 1948– . *Hindemith in memoriam.* Clarinet and piano. Published *STIM.*

Lemeland, Aubert, 1932– . *Le tombeau de Paul Hindemith.* Tubas (6). Published *Billaudot* 3677.

Moran, Robert, 1937– . *Let's build a nut house* (1969). Memorial multimedia production. Unpublished. Source: *NGrove.* First performance at San Jose State College, April 19, 1969. The title parodies Hindemith's musical play for children *Let's build a town.*

Stahmer, Klaus, 1941– . *Threnos: In memoriam Paul Hindemith* (1964). Viola (or violoncello) and organ. Published *Simrock* 2981-2982, 1977.

Sutermeister, Heinrich, 1910–1995. *Poème funèbre: En mémoire de Paul Hindemith* (1965). String orchestra. Published *Schott-M.*

Takács, Jenö, 1902– . "Praeludium für Paul Hindemith," in his *Vier Epitaphe,* op. 79 (1964). Piano. Published *Doblinger* 681671, 1966. CONTENTS: Praeludium für Paul Hindemith—Elegie für Claude Debussy—Fragment für Alban Berg—Dialogue nocturne für Béla Bartók.

HINRICHSEN, WALTER, German music publisher; b. Sep. 23, 1907; d. July 21, 1969.

Pinkham, Daniel, 1923– . *Brass trio: To the memory of Walter Hinrichsen* (1970). Trio for trumpet, horn, trombone. Published *Peters* 66274a, 1970.

Tcherepnin, Alexander, 1899–1977. *Brass quintet,* op. 105: *For my dear friend Walter Hinrichsen* (1970). Quintet for trumpets (2), horn, trombone, tuba. Published *Peters* 6643, 1972.

HOFFMAN, CARL, German composer; b. 1847; d. Sep. 2, 1870.

Rheinberger, Josef, 1839–1901. "Einem Todten" (Nov. 3, 1870), in his *Vier deutsche Gesänge,* op. 48. Male voices (TTBB) unacc. Published *Forberg* VN969, 1871. Text by Hermann Lingg. CONTENTS: Schlachtgebet—Heerbannlied—Einem Todten—Mailied. The third of the four songs is dedicated "Dem Gedächtnis des jungen Vorstandes des akademischen Gesangvereins, Carl Hoffman, welcher bei Sedan den Heldentod starb." Hoffman died of wounds received at the Battle of Sedan, September 1, 1870.

HOFFNUNG, GERARD, British artist, illustrator, musician, humorist; b. Mar. 22, 1925; d. Sep. 28, 1959.

Josephs, Wilfred, 1927–1997. "In memoriam (to Gerard Hoffnung)," in his *Concerto a dodici: For wind instruments,* op. 21 (1959). Variations for 12 winds. Published *Weinberger* ENW134, 1974. Variation no. 14 is the memorial.

HOFMANNSTHAL, HUGO VON, Austrian poet, librettist; b. Feb. 1, 1874; d. July 15, 1929.

Henze, Hans Werner, 1926– . *Elegie für junge Liebende = Elegy for young lovers* (1960). Opera in three acts. Published *Schott-M* 5040, 1961. Libretto by W. H. Auden and Chester Kallman. "To the memory of Hugo von Hofmannsthal, Austrian, European and Master Librettist, this work is gratefully dedicated by its three makers"— note in score.

HOLIDAY, BILLIE, American jazz vocalist; b. Apr. 7, 1915; d. July 15, 1959.

Blake, Ran, 1935– . *No more: Dedicated to the memory of Billie Holiday* (1978). Song. Unpublished. Source: *BCP.* Composed after the work by Salvadore ("Toots") Camarata. A cassette recording by Wendy Shermet (voice) and Ran Blake (piano) is at the New England Conservatory Library.

HOLLINGSWORTH, JOHN, English conductor; b. Mar. 20, 1916; d. Dec. 29, 1963.

Bennett, Richard Rodney, 1936– . *Aubade: In memory of John Hollingsworth* (1964). Orchestra. Published *UE-L* 12981, 1965.

HOLLY, BUDDY, American rock musician; b. Sep. 7, 1936; d. Feb. 2, 1959.

McLean, Don, 1945– . *American pie* (1971). Pop song. Published

Miami, FL: Columbia Pictures Pubs., 1972. Recorded by the composer on *American pie* (United Artists Records UAS5535, 1971).

HOLST, GUSTAV, English composer; b. Sep. 21, 1874; d. May 25, 1934.

Alwyn, William, 1905–1985. *Overture in the form of a serenade: Men of Gloucester* (1946). Wordless chorus and orchestra. Unpublished. Source: *Alwyn.*

HONEGGER, ARTHUR, French composer; b. Mar. 10, 1892; d. Nov. 27, 1955.

Castérède, Jacques, 1926– . *Suite en trois mouvements: À la mémoire d'Arthur Honegger* (1957). Orchestra. Published *Salabert.*

DeGastyne, Serge, 1930– . *Hollin Hall: Ode in memory of Arthur Honegger.* Orchestra. Published *E-V.*

Jarre, Maurice, 1924– . *Passacaille: À la mémoire de Arthur Honegger* (1956). Orchestra. Published *Ricordi-P* 1571, 1957.

Milhaud, Darius, 1892–1974. *Quintet for strings no. 4,* op. 350*: À la mémoire d'Arthur Honegger* (1956). Quintet for violins (2), viola, violoncellos (2). Published *Heugel* H31570, 1956. CONTENTS: Déploration sur la mort d'un ami—Souvenirs de jeunesse—La douceur d'une longue amitié—Hymne de louanges.

Moeschinger, Albert, 1897–1985. *Symphony no. 4,* op. 80*: In memoriam A. H.* (1957). Published *Boosey,* 1958. Middle movement: "Adagio quasi marcia funebre."

Poulenc, Francis, 1899–1963. *Sonata for clarinet and piano: À la mémoire de Arthur Honegger* (1962). Published *Chester* 1618, 1963.

Sutermeister, Heinrich, 1910–1995. *Hommage à Arthur Honegger* (1956). Piano. Published *Schott-M* 5755, 1967.

HOWE, MARVIN CLARENCE, American hornist; b. Feb. 26, 1918; d. Aug. 3, 1994.

Presser, William, 1916– . *Elegy and caprice: In memory of Marvin C. Howe* (1994). Horn and piano. Published *Tenuto* 494-01952, 1997.

HOWELL, ALMONTE, American organist, musicologist; b. 1925; d. May 31, 1988.

Corina, John, 1928– . *Sonatina for oboe, bassoon, and harpsichord with handbells: In memoriam Almonte Howell* (1988). Unpublished. Source: *OCLC.*

HOWELLS, HERBERT, English composer; b. Oct. 17, 1892; d. Feb. 24, 1983.

Skarecky, Jana, 1957– . *Requiem: In memoriam Herbert Howells*

(1983). Chorus (SSATB) unacc. Unpublished. Source: *Canadian.*

Watson, Wilfred Ronald, 1936– . *Elegy: In memoriam Herbert Howells* (1983). Organ. Published *Oecumuse,* 1983. Based on Howells's hymn-tune "Michael."

HUGHES, EDWIN, American pianist, teacher; b. Aug. 15, 1884; d. July 17, 1965.

Hanson, Howard, 1896–1981. *Summer seascape II: To the memory of Edwin Hughes* (1965). Solo viola with string quartet (or string orchestra). Published *CFischer,* 1966.

HUNTLEY, DAVID, American music publishing executive; b. June 16, 1947; d. July 1, 1994. Huntley was a Vice President and Director of Promotions for Boosey & Hawkes, New York. The works listed below were composed for and performed at a memorial concert on October 13, 1994, in New York City, Merkin Concert Hall at Abraham Goodman House. Source of the following information is the program printed for the memorial concert (*A celebration of David Huntley*), and information supplied by *Boosey.* Although *Boosey* has not published these works, they are available for purchase on special order by contacting *Boosey* direct.

Andriessen, Louis, 1939– . *Base.* Piano. Unpublished.

Carter, Elliott, 1908– . *Fragment: David Huntley in memoriam.* String quartet. Published *Tempo* 192 (April 1995), musical supplement.

Ferrero, Lorenzo, 1951– . *Portrait for string quartet.* Unpublished.

Holloway, Robin, 1943– . *A free-association post-modernist casket of memories around D. H.* String quartet. Unpublished.

Kernis, Aaron Jay, 1960– . *Lullaby for string quartet.* Unpublished.

Kolb, Barbara, 1939– . *In memory of David Huntley.* String quartet. Unpublished.

Machover, Tod, 1953– . *Spirit quartet for string quartet.* Unpublished.

MacMillan, James, 1959– . *Memento for string quartet* (1994). Unpublished.

Mackey, Steven, 1956– . *Music, minus one, for string quartet with electric guitar.* Unpublished.

Pousseur, Henri, 1929– . *Sibyls.* String quartet. Unpublished.

Rouse, Christopher, 1949– . *Déploration.* String quartet. Unpublished.

Schwertsik, Kurt, 1935– . *Wake.* String quartet. Unpublished.

IBERT, JACQUES, French composer; b. Aug. 15, 1890; d. Feb. 5, 1962.

Lacour, Guy, 1932– . *Hommage à Jacques Ibert: Concertino* (1972). Alto saxophone and orchestra (or piano). Published *Billaudot*, 1972.

IRINO, YOSHIRO, Japanese composer; b. Nov. 14, 1921; d. June 28, 1980.

Yuasa, Joji, 1929– . *Clarinet solitude: A memorial for Yoshiro Irino* (1980). Clarinet solo. Published *Schott-J* SJ1015, 1983.

ISRAEL, BRIAN, American composer; b. Feb. 5, 1951; d. May 8, 1986.

Hartley, Walter S., 1927– . *Sonata elegiaca: For alto saxophone and piano* (1987). Published *Tenuto* 49401420, 1989. "*Sonata Elegiaca* . . . reflects the composer's feelings of loss on the recent departures from this life of several valued friends and companions in the art of music, including two considerably younger than himself: the composer-pianist Brian Israel and the saxophonist Kenneth Deans"—note in score.

IURLOV, ALEKSANDR ALEKSANDROVICH, Russian choral conductor; b. 1927; d. 1973.

Sviridov, Georgi, 1915–1998. "Kontsert pamiati A. A. IUrlova," in his *Sochineniia dlia khora: Bez soprovozhdeniia i v soprovozhdenii instrumentalnogo ansamblii.* Wordless unaccompanied chorus. Published *Muzyka* 13036, 1986. The published collection is of choral compositions by Sviridov for various vocal groups, with and without accompaniment by small instrumental ensemble.

IVES, CHARLES, American composer; b. Oct. 20, 1874; d. May 19, 1954.

Boehnlein, Frank, 1945– . *In memoriam Charles Ives: George and Teddy's all-American band.* Published Pendleton, OR: Manuscript Publications, 1975. CONTENTS: The old soldier's hymn (organ or brass choir)—The George and Teddy rag (piano and clarinets)—Lavender eyes and banana bouquet (wind and brass orchestra)—Forever true (marching band)—Bottled, aged and mellow (jazz-rock band).

Cyr, Gordon, 1925– . *Rhombohedra: In memoriam Charles Ives* (1974). Band. Unpublished. Recorded by the New England Conservatory Wind Ensemble, cond. by Frank Battisti on *Rhombohedra* (Society of Composers SCI10, 1989).

Finnissy, Michael, 1946– . *Ives: Piano solo for Charles Ives' 100th*

birthday, 20ᵗʰ October, 1974 (1974). Published *Modern* 1789, 1976.
Hamilton, David B., 1955– . *In memoriam Charles Ives* (1978). Orchestra. Unpublished. Source: *NZ.*
Harrison, Lou, 1917– . *At the tomb of Charles Ives* (1963). Small orchestra. Published *Peer-I* 60072-851, 1978.
Hidalgo, Juan, 1927– . *Tal vez = Perhaps: In memoriam Charles Ives* (1998). Orchestra. Published *EMEC*, 2000.

JACOB, GORDON, English composer; b. July 5, 1895; d. June 8, 1984.
Ridout, Alan, 1934–1996. *Until the breaking of the day: In memory of Gordon Jacob.* Wind quintet. Published *Emerson* 178, 2000.
JACOBS, PAUL, American pianist; b. June 22, 1930; d. Sep. 25, 1983.
Bennett, Richard Rodney, 1936– . *And death shall have no dominion* (1986). Motet for men's voices (TTBB) and solo French horn. Published *Novello.* Text by Dylan Thomas.
Bolcom, William, 1938– . "Adagio non troppo ma sostenuto," in his *Concerto in D for violin and orchestra* (1983; rev. 1986). Published *EBMarks* HL00841403, 1998. "The solemn 5/4 second movement is in memory of the great pianist Paul Jacobs, a close friend who died in 1982 [i.e., 1983]"—composer's note accompanying the recording by Sergiu Luca (violin), the American Composers Orchestra, cond. by Dennis Russell Davies (Argo 433 077-2, 1992). The concerto as a whole is a memorial to jazz violinist Joe Venuti.
Picker, Tobias, 1954– . *Bang!: In memory of Paul Jacobs* (1992). Piano and orchestra. Published *Helicon.* Commissioned and premiered by the New York Philharmonic for its 150ᵗʰ anniversary.
———. *Pianorama: In memory of Paul Jacobs* (1984). Pianos (2). Published *Helicon* EA562, 1984.
JAEGER, AUGUST JOHANNES, German musician; b. Mar. 18, 1860; d. May 18, 1909.
Holbrooke, Joseph Charles, 1878–1958. *Symphonic quartet no. 2, op. 21* (1898; rev. 1905). Published *Novello*, ca. 1910. Originated as the 3ʳᵈ piano trio (1898). Recast as a piano quartet in 1905. Not published until after Jaeger's death, when the memorial dedication was added.
JAHNN, HANS HENNY, German author, organ builder; b. Dec. 17, 1894; d. Nov. 29, 1959.
Zacher, Gerd, 1929– . *Trapez: In memoriam Hans Henny Jahnn* (1993). Organ. Unpublished. Source: *KdG.*

JANÁČEK, LEOŠ, Czech composer; b. July 6, 1854; d. Aug. 12, 1928.
Loudová, Ivana, 1941– . *Hukvaldy suite: In memory of Leoš Janáček* (1984). String quartet. Published *Cesky,* 1984.
Neumann, Veroslav, 1931– . "Na hrob Leosi Janackove = On the grave of Leoš Janáček," in his *Tri skladby = Three compositions.* Organ. Published *Panton* 1921, 1979. CONTENTS: Meditace = Meditation—Interludium = Interlude—Na hrobe Leosi Janackove = On the grave of Leoš Janáček.
Velden, Renier van der, 1910– . *Hulde aan Leoš Janáček: Drie korte stukken* (1973). Flute, oboe, string orchestra. Published *CeBeDeM,* 1973.
JARA, VICTOR, Chilean folksinger, composer, guitarist; b. Sep. 28, 1932; d. Sep. 14, 1973.
Osterling, Ulf, 1939– . *Epitaf for Victor Jara* (1979). String orchestra. Published *STIM.* Jara was a political activist arrested during the Sept. 11, 1973, coup d'état in Chile, and subsequently murdered while in custody.
JAROCINSKI, STEFAN, Polish musicologist; b. Aug. 16, 1912; d. May 8, 1980.
Lutoslawski, Witold, 1913–1994. *Grave: Metamorphoses in memoriam Stefan Jarocinski* (1981). Violoncello and piano. Published *Chester* 55413, 1982. Transcribed 1982 for violoncello and orchestra.
JAUBERT, MAURICE, French composer; b. Jan. 3, 1900; d. Jan. 3, 1940.
Barraud, Henry, 1900– . *Offrande à une ombre: À la mémoire de Maurice Jaubert* (1940–41). Orchestra. Published Paris: Lucien de Lacour, 1946. Also published *Billaudot,* 1959.
JELINEK, HANNS, Austrian composer; b. Dec. 5, 1901; d. Jan. 27, 1969.
Nobis, Herbert, 1941– . *Hommage à Jelinek: Fünf Klavierstücke mit einer Reihe* (1972). Piano. Published *Moeck* 5210, 1979. CONTENTS: Invention—English Waltz—Siciliano—Bolero—Epilog.
JOACHIM, JOSEPH, Austro-Hungarian violinist; b. June 28, 1831; d. Aug. 15, 1907.
Stanford, Sir Charles Villiers, 1852–1924. *String quartet no. 5,* op. 104*: In memoriam Joseph Joachim.* Published *Stainer,* 1908.
JOBST, MAX, German composer; b. Feb. 9, 1908; d. 1943.
Kaltenecker, Gertraud, 1915– . *Serenade for string orchestra,* op. 10*: In memoriam Max Jobst* (1950). Unpublished. Source: *Kal-*

tenecker. Manuscript copy located at the Manuskripte-Archiv des Deutschen Tonkünstlerverbandes, Munich.

JOHNSON, THOR, American conductor; b. June 10, 1913; d. Jan. 16, 1975.

Hailstork, Adolphus C., 1941– . *Spiritual: In memoriam Thor Johnson* (1974). Octet for trumpets (4), trombones (4). Published *Wimbledon* W1031, 1984.

JOLIVET, ANDRÉ, French composer; b. Aug. 8, 1905; d. Dec. 20, 1974.

Holstein, Jean-Paul, 1939– . *Le tombeau d'André Jolivet: Temple à la mémoire d'André Jolivet.* String orchestra. Published *Billaudot.*

Sauguet, Henri, 1901–1989. *Non morietur in aeternum: À André Jolivet in memoriam* (1979). Trumpet and organ. Published *Billaudot* MA117, 1982.

JOMMELLI, NICOLÒ, Italian composer; b. Sep. 10, 1714; d. Aug. 25, 1774.

Sabatini, Giovanni Andrea, ca. 1740–ca. 1808. *Funeral music* (1774). Double choir. Unpublished. Source: *Fétis.* Performed 1774 in Naples at Jommelli's funeral.

JONAS, MARYLA, Polish pianist; b. May 31, 1911; d. July 3, 1959.

Ley, Salvador, 1907– . *Semblanza: In memoriam Maryla Jonas* (1959). Piano. Unpublished. Source: *IUL.*

JONES, DAVID ROGER, Welsh music educator; b. 1898; d. May 10, 1965.

Violin music for young players: D. Roger Jones memorial volume. Published *Welsh,* 1972. Collection commissioned by the Guild in memory of Jones. Contains works (titles unknown) by Alun Hoddinott, 1929– ; Mervyn Burtch, 1929– ; Hubert Davies, 1893–1965; William Mathias, 1934–1992; David Harries, 1933– ; Ian Parrott, 1916– ; Bernard Rands, 1934– ; Mervyn Roberts, 1906– ; Robert Smith, 1922– ; Mansel Thomas, 1909– ; Gareth Walters, 1928– ; Grace Williams, 1906–1977; and David Wynn, 1900–1983.

JOPLIN, JANIS, American rock and blues vocalist; b. Jan. 19, 1943; d. Oct. 3, 1970.

Kolberg, Kare, 1936– . *Requiem for Janis Joplin: Music to the multimedia play by Paal-Helge Haugen* (1972). Electronic tape. Unpublished. Source: *NorO.* First performance, Henie-Onstad Art Center, 1972.

Konrad, Bernd, 1948– . *Burning flower: In memoriam Janis Joplin* (1997). Large orchestra with vocal, rock, and jazz soloists. Published *Gravis* EG577, 1998. Text by Awis Rosenthal and Bernd Konrad.

JOPLIN, SCOTT, American pianist, composer; b. Nov. 24, 1868; d. Apr. 1, 1917.

Hrabovskyi, Leonid Oleksandrovych, 1935– . "A little cake-walk: In memoriam Scott Joplin," in his *Homages: Seven pieces for guitar.* Published *Duma,* 1996. CONTENTS: Ciaccona: In memoriam Henry Purcell—Aria: In memoriam Johann Sebastian Bach—Impromptus: In memoriam Franz Schubert—Prelude: In memoriam Frédéric Chopin—A little cake-walk: In memoriam Scott Joplin—Chorale: In memoriam Johannes Brahms—Amoroso: In memoriam Sergei Prokofiev.

Kurtz, Eugene, 1923–1984. "Rag: À la mémoire de Scott Joplin," in his *Animations* (1968). Piano. Published *Jobert,* 1969. CONTENTS: Résonances—Rag. Movements may be performed separately.

JOSQUIN DES PREZ, Franco-Flemish composer; b. 1440?; d. Aug. 27, 1521.

Anonymous. *Absolve, quaesumus, Domine.* Voices (7). Four voice parts only survive in partbooks in Piacenza, Archivio del Duomo. *Picker,* pp. 256–57, prints the first 40 measures of the 4 surviving parts. Josquin is named in the text of this prayer for absolution that forms part of the Burial Service.

Appenzeller, Benedictus, fl. early 16th cent. "Musae Jovis ter maximi, nenia in mortem Judoci de Pretis," in *Septiesme livre contenant vingt et quatre chansons a cincq et a six parties . . . avecq troix epitaphes dudict Josquin, composez par divers aucteurs.* Voices (4). Published Antwerp: Tielman Susato, 1545. *RISM-B1:* 1545/15. Modern edition in *Klaagliederen op den dood van Josquin,* Werken van Josquin des Prés, vol. 1, ed. Albert Smijers (Leipzig: C. F. W. Siegel, 1922). Text by Gerard Avidus.

Becker, Günther, 1924– . *À la mémoire de Josquin* (1974). Organ. Published *Gerig* HG1169, 1975.

Borden, David, 1938– . *Le tombeau de Josquin: For two chamber groups.* Published Ann Arbor, MI: University Microfilms CMP 007-2-01, 1968. At head of title: MENC Contemporary Music Project for Creativity in Music Education.

Gombert, Nicolas, ca. 1495–ca. 1560. "Musae Jovis ter maximi," in *Septiesme livre contenant vingt et quatre chansons a cincq et a six parties . . . avecq troix epitaphes dudict Josquin, composez par divers aucteurs.* Voices (6). Published Antwerp: Tielman Susato, 1545. *RISM-B1:* 1545/15 Modern edition in *Klaagliederen op den dood van Josquin,* Werken van Josquin des Prés, vol. 1, ed. Albert

Smijers (Leipzig: C. F. W. Siegel, 1922). Text by Gerard Avidus.
Jacquet, of Mantua, 1483–1559. "Dum vastos Adriae. Josquini an-
tiquos," in *Motetti del Laberinto, a cinque voci libro quarto.* Voices
(5). Published Venice: Scotto: 1554. *RISM-B1*: 1554/16. Later edition: *Motetti de Jachet di Mantoa a cinque voci, libro primo de novo
ristampati* (Venice: Scotto, 1565). *RISM-A1*: J-8. New edition forth-
coming in: Jacquet, *Opera omnia,* ed. Philip Jackson and George
Nugent, Corpus mensurabilis musicae, vol. 54 (*AIM*, 1971–).
Richafort, Jean, d. 1548? "Requiem," in *Sextus liber duas missas
habet.* Voices (6). Published Paris: Attaingnant, 1532. *RISM-B1*:
1532/6, which also includes works by Nicolas Gombert. Modern edition in Richafort, *Collected works,* vol. 1, ed. by Harry Elzinga
(*AIM*, 1979). "The presence of a portion of 'Faulte d'argent' and the
canonic use of the chant melody, 'Circumdederunt me,' in the same
manner as employed by Josquin in three compositions . . . strongly
suggests that the Requiem was composed as a memorial after the
death of Josquin"—critical notes to new edition.
Vinders, Hieronymus, fl. 1540–1521. "O mors inevitabilis," in *Septiesme livre contenant vingt et quatre chansons a cincq et a six parties . . . avecq troix epitaphes dudict Josquin, composez par divers
aucteurs.* Voices (7). Published Antwerp: Tielman Susato: 1545.
RISM-B1: 1545/15. Modern edition in *Klaagliederen op den dood
van Josquin,* Werken van Josquin des Prés, vol. 1, ed. Albert Smijers
(Leipzig: C. F. W. Siegel, 1922).

KAFENDA, FRICO, Slovak composer; b. Nov. 2, 1883; d. Sep. 3, 1963.
Zimmer, Ján, 1926– . *String quartet no. 2,* op. 100*: In memoriam
Frico Kafenda.* Published *Hudobny,* 1984.
KAGAN, OLEG MOISEEVICH, Russian violinist; b. Nov. 21, 1946; d.
July 15, 1990.
Pärt, Arvo, 1935– (transcriber). Mozart, Wolfgang Amadeus,
1756–1791. *Mozart-Adagio: In memoriam Oleg Kagan* [Sonatas, pi-
ano, K. 280, F major. Adagio; arr.] (1992, rev. 1997). Piano trio.
Published *UE* 30456, 1997. Adapted from the second movement
Mozart's Piano sonata in F major, KV 189e (280).
Raskatov, Aleksandr. *Miserere: In memoriam Oleg Kagan* (1997).
Viola and violoncello soloists with orchestra. Published *Belaieff.*
Schnittke, Alfred, 1934–1998. "Madrigal in memoriam Oleg Ka-

gan," in his *Stücke* = *Pieces (Schnittke, Knaifel, Voostin, Mansuryan and Vasks).* Violoncello solo. Published *Sikorski* 1889, 1991. Version for violin solo: *Sikorski* 1914, 1997.

KALNINS, ALFRED, Latvian composer, organist; b. Aug. 23, 1879; d. Dec. 23, 1951.

Zilinskis, Arvids, 1905– . *Pieminot: In memoriam Alfred Kalnins* (1974). Organ. Unpublished. Source: *Beckmann.*

KAPELL, WILLIAM, American pianist; b. Sep. 20, 1922; d. Oct. 29, 1953.

Bernstein, Leonard, 1918–1990. "In memoriam William Kapell" (1981), in his *Thirteen anniversaries* (1964–88). Piano. Published *Jalni* PAB463, 1989.

Cameron-Wolfe, Richard. *Toccata: In memoriam William Kapell* (1983). Piano. Published s.l.: Cameron-Wolfe, 1983. Source: *IUL.* Commissioned by the William Kapell Foundation. Premiered in New York City at Symphony Space, Oct. 26, 1983, at a concert commemorating the 30th anniversary of Kapell's death.

Copland, Aaron, 1900–1990. *Piano fantasy* (1955–57). Published *Boosey* PIB173, 1957. "Commissioned by the Juilliard School of Music . . . on the occasion of its fiftieth anniversary celebration, and dedicated to the memory of William Kapell"—dedication in score.

KAPRÁL, VÁCLAV, Czech composer; b. Mar. 26, 1889; d. Apr. 6, 1947.

Martinu, Bohuslav, 1890–1959. "Adagio: Vzpominky" (1957), in his *Klavirni skaladby.* Piano. Published *Panton,* 1970. "Venováno vzpominkám na Václava Kaprála a Vitukla" (i.e., In memoriam Václav Kaprál and Vitulka [Kaprálová])—dedication in score.

KAPRÁLOVÁ, VITEZSLAVA, Czech composer; b. Jan. 24, 1915; d. June 16, 1940.

Martinu, Bohuslav, 1890–1959. "Adagio: Vzpominky" (1957), in his *Klavirni skaladby.* Piano. Published *Panton,* 1970. "Venováno vzpominkám na Václava Kaprála a Vitukla" (i.e., In memoriam Václav Kaprál and Vitulka [Kaprálová])—dedication in score.

KARLOWICZ, MIECZYSLAW, Polish composer; b. Dec. 11, 1876; d. Feb. 8, 1909.

Kilar, Wojciech, 1932– . *Koscielec 1909: Symphonic poem* (1976). Orchestra. Published *PWM,* 1977. The title and the headings "tema della montagna" and "tema dell'abisso chiamante" in the score refer to Karlowicz's death in an avalanche on mount Koscielec.

KAUFMANN, HARALD, Austrian musicologist; b. Oct. 1, 1927; d. July 6, 1970.

Dallapiccola, Luigi, 1904–1975. *Commiato: Harald Kaufmann in memoriam* (1972). Soprano with chamber orchestra. Published *Zerboni* 7526, 1973. Italian text attributed to Brunetto Latini.

KEE, COR, Dutch organist, composer; b. Nov. 24, 1900; d. 1997.

Wielenga, Gerrit. *6 variaties over de melodie van Psalm 23: In memoriam Cor Kee.* Organ. Unpublished. Source: *Beckmann.*

KHACHATURIAN, ARAM, Russian-Armenian composer; b. June 6, 1903; d. Aug. 28, 1978.

Babajanyan, Arno, 1921–1983. *Elegiia dlia fortepiano: Pamiati Arama Ilicha Khachaturiana* (1979). Piano. Published Moscow: Sov. Kompositor 5226, 1979.

Mirzoian, Eduard, 1921– . *Poem epitaph (Adagio): In memory of Aram Khachaturian* (1988). Chamber orchestra. Unpublished. Source: *ConCom.* Commissioned by conductor Aram Gharabekian for the SinfoNova Chamber Orchestra for the 10th anniversary of Khachaturian's death. Premiered by them in Boston on Mar. 4, 1988. Recorded by the St. Petersburg Chamber Ensemble, Roland Melia (cond) (ASV Records CDDCA916, 1994).

KINCAID, WILLIAM, American flutist; b. Apr. 26, 1895; d. Mar. 27, 1967.

Copland, Aaron, 1900–1990. *Duo for flute and piano: To the memory of William Kincaid* (1971). Published *Boosey* WFB19, 1971.

Yardumian, Richard, 1917– . *Epigram: William F. Kincaid* (1973). Flute with string quartet (or string orchestra). Published *E-V* 164-00119, 1976.

KINDLER, HANS, Dutch-American violoncellist, conductor; b. Jan. 8, 1892; d. Aug. 30, 1949.

Antoniou, Theodore, 1935– . "Threnos: In memory of Hans Kindler," in his *Lyrics* (1967). Violin and piano with optional recitation. Published *Bärenreiter* BA6103, 1968. Includes Greek text by Tassos Roussos, with English and German translations provided. "If these verses are not recited during the performance, they should be printed on the program"—program note in score. CONTENTS: Threnos: In memory of Hans Kindler—Epigram—Elegy—Nomos—Hymn—Ode—Skolion.

Martinu, Bohuslav, 1890–1959. *Sonata for violoncello and piano no. 3: À la mémoire de Hans Kindler* (1952). Published Prague: Státni Nakl. Krásné Literatury, Huidby, a Umeni, 1957.

Tansman, Alexandre, 1897–1986. *Fantaisie: In memoriam Hans Kindler* (1963). Violin and piano. Published *Eschig* ME8884, 1995.

CONTENTS: Divertimento—Elegie—Fuga—Improvisazione—Canon
—Finale-Scherzo.

Ward, Robert, 1917– . *Arioso and tarantelle* (1954). Violoncello
(or viola) and piano. Published *Highgate*, 1960. Composed for the
Kindler Foundation in memory of Kindler.

KLEIN, GIDEON, Czech composer, pianist; b. Dec. 6, 1919; d. Jan. 27,
1945.

Saudek, Vojtech, 1951– . *Concerto for piano and orchestra: In
memory of Gideon Klein* (1987). Published *Cesky.* Klein died in the
Theresienstadt Nazi concentration camp.

KLEMPERER, OTTO, German conductor; b. May 14, 1885; d. July 6,
1973.

Denniston, Donald Edwards, 1944– . *Six pieces for orchestra*
(1973). Unpublished. Source: *BCP.* The fourth piece is in memory of
Otto Klemperer.

KNEISEL, FRANZ, Austrian violinist; b. Jan. 26, 1865; d. Mar. 26,
1926.

Enesco, Georges, 1881–1955. *Sonata for violin and piano no. 3*, op.
25, in D minor*: À la mémoire de Franz Kneisel* (1926). Published
Enoch, 1933. Later edition: Bucurest: Editura de Stat pentru Litera-
tura si Arta, 1956. Subtitled "dans le caractère populaire roumain."

KOCHANSKI, PAUL, Polish violinist; b. Sep. 14, 1887; d. Jan. 12, 1934.

Szymanowski, Karol, 1882–1937. *Concerto for violin and orchestra no. 2*, op. 61. Published *Eschig* ME4465, 1934. "À la mémoire
du Grand musicien, mon cher et inoubliable ami Paul Kochanski"—
composer's note in score.

KODÁLY, ZOLTÁN, Hungarian composer; b. Dec. 16, 1882; d. Mar. 6,
1967.

Barrell, Bernard, 1919– . *Epitaph for Zoltán Kodály,* op. 49. Des-
cant recorder, percussion, strings. Published London: Performing
Rights Society Ltd.

Gárdonyi, Zoltán, 1906–1986. *Meditatio pro organo: In memoriam
Zoltán Kodály* (1982). Organ. Published *EMB* Z12421, 1983.

Jeney, Zoltán, 1943– . *Madárhivogató = Bird call: In memoriam
Zoltán Kodály* (1982). Four-part canon for high voices. Published
EMB Z12345, 1982? Hungarian text by Sándor Weöres.

Maros, Rudolf, 1917–1982. *Gemma: In memoriam Zoltán Kodály*
(1968). Chamber orchestra. Published *Peer-S* 60523-851, 1974.

Ránki, György, 1907– . *Kodály emlékezete* (1971). Soprano, mixed
chorus, cimbalom (or harpsichord or organ). Published *EMB*, 1973.

Szokolay, Sándor, 1931– . *Hommage à Kodály* (1975). Vocal soloists (SMz), chorus, organ, orchestra. Text by Gyula Illyés. Unpublished. Recorded by Julia Paszthy (soprano), Katalin Schulz (mezzo-soprano), Hungarian Radio and Television Chorus, Budapest Symphony Orchestra, cond. by the composer on *Hommage à Kodály* (Hungaroton SLPX12442, 1982).

Takács, Jenö, 1902– . "Erinnerung an Zoltán Kodály = Remembering Zoltán Kodály," in his *4 x 4: Klavierstücke für Klavier vier Händen = Piano pieces for 4 hands,* op. 106 (1980). Published *UE* 17419, 1981. No. 9 of 16 pieces.

KÖHLER, ERNESTO, Italian flutist; b. Dec. 4, 1849; d. May 17, 1907.

Lorenzo, Leonardo de, 1875–1962. *Pensiero elegiaco,* op. 7*: In memoria del compianto artista Ernesto Köhler* (1907). Flute and piano. Published *Zimmermann* 4616, 1908.

KOGAN, LEONID, Soviet violinist; b. Nov. 14, 1924; d. Dec. 17, 1982.

Mannino, Franco, 1924– . *Missa pro defunctis,* op. 233*: Alla memoria di Leonide Kogan* (1984). Solo voices (SATB), chorus (SATB), orchestra. Published *B&S* BSM10, 1987.

KOLDOFSKY, ADOLPH, Canadian violinist, conductor; b. Sep. 13, 1905; d. Apr. 8, 1951.

Schoenberg, Arnold, 1874–1951. *Phantasy for violin and piano,* op. 47*: In memory of Adolph Koldofsky* (1949). Published *Peters* 6060a, 1952. Schoenberg composed the Phantasy for Koldofsky in 1949; the memorial dedication is a later addition.

KOMITAS, SOGOMON, Armenian composer; b. Oct. 8, 1869; d. Oct. 22, 1935.

Eghiazaryan, Grigor Eghiziari, 1908–1989. *Pamiati Komitasa = In memory of Komitas* (1936). Piano. Unpublished. Source: *NGrove.*

Hovanessian, Simon, 1940– . *Requiem on the memory of Komitas* (1966). Voices and orchestra. Unpublished. Source: *ConCom.*

———. *Symphonic poem on the memory of Komitas* (1969). Orchestra. Unpublished. Source: *ConCom.*

KOSTELANETZ, ANDRÉ, Russian conductor; b. Dec. 22, 1901; d. Dec. 22, 1980.

Bernstein, Leonard, 1918–1990. *A musical toast: Fondly dedicated to the memory of André Kostelanetz* (1980). Orchestra. Published *Jalni* HPS976, 1980.

KOUSSEVITZKY, SERGE, Russian-born conductor; b. July 26, 1874; d. June 4, 1951.

The Koussevitzky Music Foundation was established by Koussevitzky in 1942 as a memorial to his wife. In 1949 the parent foundation permanently endowed the Serge Koussevitzky Music Foundation in the Library of Congress to carry on the work of commissioning new works by composers, and encouraging their dissemination through performances. Manuscripts of commissioned works are deposited in the Music Division of the Library of Congress. These scores commonly include pro forma dedications to the memory of Serge and Natalia Koussevitzky. A catalog of commissions by both foundations may be found in *The Koussevitzky Music Foundations, 1942–1967: 1967 Edition of the Catalog of Works Commissioned* (Lenox, MA: The Koussevitzky Music Foundation, Inc.; Washington, DC: The Serge Koussevitzky Music Foundation, 1967). A listing of works through 1984 is found in *The New Grove Dictionary of American Music*, s.v. "Koussevitzky Foundations," by Jane Gottlieb. The following is a selection of Koussevitzky commissions not appearing in either of those lists. Works memorializing Koussevitzky but not originating from the Foundation program are indentified by the inclusion of a memorial statement in the entry.

Adams, John, 1947– . *Eros piano* (1989; rev. 1990). Piano and chamber orchestra. Published *Hendon*, 1989. "Eros Piano began as an elegy on the death of Morton Feldman. . . . [It] became an homage to both [Feldman and Toru Takemitsu]"—notes accompanying the recording by Paul Cossley (piano), Orchestra of St. Lukes, cond. by John Adams (Elektra/Nonesuch 792349).

Adler, Samuel, 1928– . *Symphony no. 6* (1984–85). Published *Presser*.

Albright, William, 1944–1998. *Chasm: Symphonic fragment* (1985–89). Orchestra. Published *Peters*.

Alexander, Peter, 1959– . *Ferrafunx: For drum set and brass quintet* (1998). Quintet for trumpets (2), horn, trombone, tuba. Unpublished. Source: *OCLC*.

Anderson, Allen Louis, 1951– . *String quartet* (1990). Unpublished. Source: *OCLC*. Recorded by the Lydian String Quartet on *Drawn from life: Music of Allen Anderson* (CRI CD727, 1996).

Andriessen, Louis, 1939– . *Zilver* (1994). Septet for flute, clarinet, violin, violoncello, vibraphone, marimba, piano. Published *Boosey*.

Asia, Daniel, 1953– . *Piano quartet* (1989). Published *Merion* 144-40204, 1992. Library of Congress cataloging for the manuscript (*OCLC* 23654118) incorrectly identifies the composer as "David" Asia. Program notes about the piece are found at the Daniel Asia web site: http://www.danielasia.com.

Babbitt, Milton, 1916– . *Septet, but equal* (1992). Septet for 3 clarinets (1 doubling on bass clarinet), violin, viola, violoncello, piano. Published *Peters* 67773.

Bassett, Leslie, 1923– . *Concerto for orchestra* (1991). Published *Peters*, 1991.

Bauer, Ross, 1951– . *Halcyon birds* (1993). Orchestra. Unpublished. Source: *OCLC*.

Bazelon, Irwin, 1922–1995. *Fusions: For chamber ensemble* (1983). Ensemble of flute/piccolo, oboe/English horn, clarinet, bass clarinet, bassoon/contrabassoon, horn, trumpets (2), trombone, viola, double bass, piano, percussion. Published *Novello* 890149, 1988.

Bennett, Richard Rodney, 1936– . *Wind quintet* (1967–68). Quintet for flute, oboe, clarinet, horn, bassoon. Published *UE-L* 14623, 1968.

Bolcom, William, 1938– . *Lyric concerto for flute and orchestra* (1992–93). Published *EBMarks*, 1993.

Boykan, Martin, 1931– . *Symphony* (1989). Orchestra. Unpublished. Source: *OCLC*.

Brant, Henry, 1913– . *Plowshares & swords: Spatial announcements for 74 musicians* (1995). Orchestra. Published *CFischer*.

Bresnick, Martin, 1946– . *Pontoosuc* (1989). Orchestra. Published New Haven, CT: CommonMuse Music, 1989.

Brief, Todd, 1953– . *Idols* (1986–87). Sextet for flute/piccolo/alto flute, clarinet/bass clarinet, percussion, piano, violin, violoncello. Published *UE* 19055, 1988.

Chou, Lung, 1953– . *The ineffable* (1994). Sextet for flute, percussion, pipa, zheng, violin, violoncello. Published *Presser* 114-40885, 1997.

Currier, Sebastian. *Broken consort* (1996). Sextet for flute, oboe, violin, violoncello, guitars (2). Unpublished. Source: *AMC*. Recorded by Cygnus Ensemble on *Broken consort* (CRI CD834, 2000).

Davidovsky, Mario, 1934– . *Divertimento for violoncello and orchestra* (1984). Published *Peters*, 1984.

Diesendruck, Tamas. *Such stuff* (1988). String quartet. Unpublished. Source: *AMC*.

Dobbins, Lori Ellen, 1958– . *Tres recuerdos del cielo* (1990). Soprano with chamber ensemble. Published University of California, Berkeley (Ph.D. thesis), 1990. Text by Rafael Alberti.

Drummond, Dean, 1949– . *Dance of the seven veils* (1992). Sextet for flute, violoncello, keyboard player (chromelodeon I and Yamaha DX7 II synthesizer), percussion (3 players). Unpublished. Microtonal music. Recorded by musical group Newband on *Dance of the seven veils* (Music & Arts CD931, 1996).

Felder, David, 1953– . *Inner sky* (1994). Flute, percussion (2), piano, strings, computer-processed flute sounds on tape (or disc), optional sound reinforcement processing. Published *Merion*, 1996.

Fennelly, Brian, 1937– . *Fantasy variations for orchestra* (1985). Published *ACE*, 1985.

Festinger, Richard, 1948– . *Tapestries* (1997). Piano trio. Published *Peters* 67895, 1997.

Fine, Vivian, 1913–2000. *Poetic fires: From the Greeks* (1984). Piano and orchestra. Published Shaftsburt, VT: Catamount Facsimile Editions, 1984.

Fontyn, Jacqueline, 1930– . *Reverie and turbulence* (1990?). Orchestra. Unpublished. Source: *OCLC*.

Froom, David, 1951– . *Emerson songs* (1996). Soprano with octet for flute/piccolo/alto flute, oboe/English horn, clarinet/bass clarinet, bassoon, piano, violin, viola, violoncello. Unpublished. Source: *OCLC*. Texts by Ralph Waldo Emerson. CONTENTS: Cloud upon cloud—The snow storm—I cannot find.

Gandolfi, Michael James, 1956– . *Caution to the wind* (1992). Concerto for flute with percussion, harp, violins (2), viola, violoncello, double bass. Published Beverly, MA: Gateway Music, 1992. Also at *AMC*.

Goehr, Alexander, 1932– . *Colossos or panic: Symphonic fragment after Goya,* op. 55 (1991–92). Published *Schott-L* 12444, 1994.

Greenberg, Robert, 1954– . *Among friends: String quartet no. 3* (1995). Unpublished. Source: *OCLC*.

Gustavson, Mark. *String quartet* (1989). Published Columbia University (D.M.A. thesis), 1990. Distributed by Bell & Howell Information and Learning Company (formerly University Microfilms).

Hanson, Howard, 1896–1981. *Elegy,* op. 44: *To the memory of my friend Serge Koussevitsky* (1956). Orchestra. Published *CFischer*, 1957. For the 75th anniversary of the Boston Symphony Orchestra.

Hartke, Stephen Paul, 1952– . *Concerto for violin and orchestra: Auld Swaara* (1992). Published *MMB*, 1993.

Harvey, Jonathan, 1939– . *Timepieces: For orchestra with two conductors* (1987). Published *Faber*, 1987.

Holloway, Robin, 1943– . *Double concerto for clarinet and saxophone with two chamber orchestras,* op. 67 (1987–88). Published *Boosey.*

Husa, Karel, 1921– . *Five poems: For wind quintet* (1994). Quintet for flute, oboe, clarinet, horn, bassoon. Published *AMP* 8144, 1999. CONTENTS: Walking birds—Happy bird—Interlude: Lamenting bird—With a dead bird—Fighting birds—Bird flying high above.

Hyla, Lee, 1952– . *The dream of Innocent III* (1987). Amplified violoncello, piano, percussion. Unpublished. Source: *AMC*. Recorded by Rhonda Rider (violoncello), Lee Hyla (piano), James Pugliesi (percussion) on *Works of Arthur Berger, Lee Hyla, Steven Mackey, Donald Martino, and Anton von Webern* (CRI CD-564, 1988).

Ince, Kamran. *Waves of Talya* (1988). Sextet for flute/piccolo, clarinet, piano, percussion, violin, violoncello. Unpublished. Recorded by musical group Present Music, Kevin Stalheim (artistic director) (Northeastern Records NR254-CD, 1993).

Jarvinen, Arthur. *The modulus of elasticity* (1992). Viola with chamber ensemble. Published *LeisureP*, 1992.

Kernis, Aaron Jay, 1960– . *Songs of innocents, book 1* (1989). High voice and piano. Published *AMP*.

Kirchner, Leon, 1919– . *Of things exactly as they are* (1996). Soprano and baritone soloists, chorus (SATB), orchestra. Published *AMP*, 1996.

Korf, Anthony, 1947– . *Cantata* (1992). Chorus (SATB divisi, with solos), piano, synthesizer, "percussion sounds," double bass. Unpublished. Source: *OCLC*. Text from Edna St. Vincent Millay, E. E. Cummings, and "a friend."

Koutzen, Boris, 1901–1966. *Elegiac rhapsody: In memory of Serge Koussevitzky* (1961). Orchestra. Published *General*.

Kraft, William, 1923– . *Encounters X: Duologue* (1992). Violin and marimba. Published *NewWest*, 1992.

Lee, Thomas Oboe, 1945– . *Waltzes for wind quintet,* op. 26 (1984; rev. 1994). Quintet for flute, oboe, clarinet, horn, bassoon. Unpublished. Source: *AMC*.

Levinson, Gerald, 1951– . *Symphony no. 2: For large orchestra* (1994; rev. 1996). Published *Merion*, 1995.

Lindroth, Scott, 1958– . *Duo for violins* (1990). Published *Davidge*, 1990?

Lister, J. Rodney, 1951– . *Where I say hours* (1985). Quintet for clarinet and strings. Unpublished. Source: *OCLC*.

Machover, Tod, 1953– . *Nature's breath: For large chamber ensemble* (1984–85) Ensemble of winds, percussion, strings. Published *Ricordi* 2373, 1985.

Mackey, Steven, 1956– . *Moebius band* (1988). Soprano, instrumental ensemble, electronic tape. Unpublished. Recorded on *Indigenous instruments: The music of Steven Mackey* (Newport Classics NPD85541, 1993).

Mamlock, Ursula, 1928– . *Girasol* (1990). Sextet for flute, clarinet, violin, viola, violoncello, piano. Published *Peters* 67480, 1995.

Martino, Donald, 1931– . *Serenata concertante* (1999). Octet for flute/alto flute/piccolo, clarinet/bass clarinet, flugel horn/cornet, horn, percussion, piano, violin, violoncello. Published *Dantalian* DSE517e, 1999.

Maw, Nicholas, 1935– . *Piano trio* (1990–91). Published *Faber* 0571515533, 1995.

Moe, Eric. *Up & at 'em* (1988). Quintet for alto flute, English horn, bass clarinet, viola, piano. Unpublished. Source: *AMC*. First performance August 3, 1989, Wellesley, MA, Jewett Arts Center, Wellesley Composers Conference.

Murail, Tristan, 1947– . *De terre et de ciel* (1986). Orchestra. Published *Salabert*.

Olan, David, 1948– . *String quartet no. 2* (1991). Unpublished. Source: *OCLC*.

Osborne, Nigel, 1948– . *Zansa* (1985). Orchestra. Published *UE*.

Perle, George, 1915– . *Concerto for piano and orchestra no. 2* (1992). Published *ECS*.

Peterson, Wayne, 1927– . *Diptych* (1992). Sextet for flute/alto flute/piccolo, clarinet/bass clarinet, viola (or violin), violoncello, percussion, piano. Published *Henmar* 67608, 1996. CONTENTS: Aubade—Odyssey.

Primosch, James, 1956– . *Five meditations* (1993). Orchestra. Published *Merion*, 1993. CONTENTS: Victimae paschali laudes—Corde natus ex parentis—Pange lingua gloriosi—Caelestis formam gloriae—Exsultet.

Rakowski, David, 1958– . *Sesso e violenza* (1996). Chamber concerto for flutes (2) and small ensemble. Published *Peters*.

Rands, Bernard, 1934– . *Canzoni per orchestra* (1995). Published *Helicon*, 1995.

———. "Suite no. 2," in his *Le tambourin: Suites 1 and 2* (1984). Orchestra. Published *UE-L* 17930, 1989.

Reich, Steve, 1936– . *Three movements for orchestra* (1986). Published *Hendon* HPS1215, 1986.

Riley, Terry, 1935– . *June Buddhas: The Mexico City blues* (1991).

Chorus and orchestra. Unpublished. Source: *OCLC*. Based on three choruses from Jack Kerouac's poetic manifesto *Mexico City Blues*. First performed Nov. 1991 at the Brooklyn Academy of Music by the Voices Saintpaulia and the Brooklyn Philharmonic Orchestra. Recorded by the same forces, cond. by Dennis Russell Davies (MusicMasters Classics 67089-2).

Rosenzweig, Morris, 1952– . *String quartet* (1997). Unpublished. Source: *OCLC*. Recorded by the Abramayan Quartet on the collection of Rosenzweig's *Chamber music 1992-1997* (CRI 787, 1997).

Rouse, Christopher, 1949– . *Compline* (1996). Septet for flute, clarinet, harp, string quartet. Published *Boosey* HPS1343, 1996. "Unlike the majority of other works I composed in the half dozen years before it, *Compline* does not concern itself with death but rather with light. In this it perhaps augurs a change in my musical outlook"—composer's note in score.

Ruders, Poul, 1949– . *Symfoni no. 2: Symfoni og forvandling = Symphony and transformation* (1995–96). Published *Hansen*, 1996.

Selig, Robert, 1939–1984. *Concerto for two pianos* (1983). Without orchestra. Published *Margun* MP7154, 1979. The holograph in the Library of Congress is subtitled "Sketch of Symphony no. 3." The second movement of the published edition has the title "Symphony #3 (2 piano)."

Sheinfeld, David, 1906– . *Dear Theo: For baritone voice and 9 instrumentalists* (1996). Baritone with nonet for flute, clarinet, trumpet, trombone, piano, percussion, violin, viola, double bass. Unpublished. Source: *OCLC*.

Shinohara, Makoto, 1931– . *Cooperation: For 8 Japanese and 8 Western instrumentalists* (1990). Unpublished. Recorded on *Portrait of Makoto Shinohara: Toward musical fusions of Japan and the West* (Camerata 30CM-375, 1994).

Soley, David B., 1962– . *—de cámara* (1992). Chamber ensemble of flute/alto flute, clarinet/bass clarinet, horn, trumpet, percussion (2 players), harp, piano, string quartet. Unpublished. Source: *OCLC*. Score also located at *AMC*.

Spratlan, Lewis, 1940– . *Sojourner: For ten players* (1999). Flute/piccolo, clarinet, bass clarinet, horn, piano, percussion, violin, viola, violoncello, double bass. Unpublished. Source: *OCLC*. "Sojourner" refers to the rover sent to Mars in July 1997.

Stock, David, 1939– . *Parallel worlds* (1984). Ensemble of flute/alto flute, oboe/English horn, clarinet/bass clarinet, bassoon, horn, trumpet, harp, marimba, suspended cymbals, violoncello, double bass. Unpublished. Source: *OCLC*.

Stucky, Steven, 1949– . *Four poems of A. R. Ammons* (1992). Baritone voice with sextet of flute/alto flute/piccolo, clarinet, horn, viola, violoncello, double bass. Published *Merion*, 1992. CONTENTS: Consignee—Mansion—Songlet—Some months ago.

Takemitsu, Toru, 1930–1996. *Fantasma: Cantos II* (1994). Trombone and orchestra. Published *Schott-J* SJ1117, 1999.

Tenzer, Michael. *Sources of current.* Quintet for flute/alto flute/piccolo, oboe, harp, viola, violoncello. Published Hamden, CT: Bridge of Monkeys Music, 1995.

Thorne, Francis, 1922– . *Rhapsodic variations no. 5* (1987). Violin and piano. Published *Merion* 144-40327, 1998.

Thorne, Nicholas C. K., 1953– . *Three tales, book 2: The great silences,* op. 11b (1983). Chamber ensemble. Published *Margun.*

Torke, Michael, 1961– . *Chalk* (1992). String quartet. Published *Hendon,* 1992.

Tower, Joan, 1938– . *Music for violoncello and orchestra* (1984). Published *AMP* 8006, 1984.

Ung, Chinary, 1942– . *Spiral VII: For wind quintet* (1994). Quintet of alto flute, English horn, bass clarinet, horn, bassoon. Published *Peters.*

Walker, George, 1922– . *Sinfonia no. 2* (1990). Orchestra. Published *MMB*, 1990.

————. *Wind set: Woodwind quintet* (1999). Published *MMB*, 1999.

Wernick, Richard, 1934– . *Piano trio* (1996). Published *Presser* 114-40884, 1998.

Wheeler, Scott, 1952– . *Northern lights: Symphony in three movements* (1987). Unpublished. Source: *OCLC*. Score also located at *AMC*.

Wilson, Olly, 1937– . *Expansions II* (1987). Orchestra. Unpublished. Source: *OCLC*. Score also located at *AMC*.

Wilson, Richard, 1941– . *Triple concerto: For horn, bass clarinet, marimba, and orchestra* (1998). Unpublished. Source: *OCLC*.

Wood, Hugh, 1932– . *Trio for horn, violin, and piano,* op. 29 (1987–89). Published *Chester* 55919, 1992.

Wuorinen, Charles, 1938– . *Concertino for orchestra or for 15 solo instruments* (1984). Soli: flutes (2), oboes (2), clarinets (2), bass clarinet, double bass, bassoon, contrabassoon, horns (4), double bass; string acc. Published *Peters* 67017.

————. *Symphony six* (1996–97). Unpublished. Source: *OCLC*.

Wyner, Yehudi, 1929– . *Intermedio.* Ballet with wordless vocalises for soprano and string orchestra. Published *ACA,* 1974.

Yun, Isang, 1917–1995. *Concerto for oboe (doubling oboe d'amore) and orchestra in one movement* (1990). Published *Bote* 23411, 1993.

KRUMPHOLZ, WENZEL, Bohemian violinist; b. 1750; d. May 2, 1817.

Beethoven, Ludwig van, 1770–1827. "Gesang der Mönche aus Schillers Wilhelm Tell" (May 3, 1817), in *Sammlung von Musikstücken alter und neuer Zeit als Zulage zur neuen Zeitschrift für Musik,* vol. 6. Voices (TTB) unacc. Published Leipzig: A. H. Friese, 1839. WoO 104. "Zur Erinnerung an den schnellen unberhaften Tod unseres Krumpholz"—note in autograph. Later edition in Beethoven, *Lieder und Gesänge mit Begleitung des Pianoforte,* Beethovens Werke, Ser. 23 (*Breitkopf,* 18—). Also edited by Karl Etti: *Doblinger* D13377, 1969. Text incipit "Rasch tritt der Tod den Menschen an."

KRZANOWSKI, ANDRZEJ, Polish composer; b. 1951; d. Oct. 1, 1991.

Pstrokonska-Nawratil, Grazyna, 1947– . *String quartet no. 2: Andrzej Krzanowski in memoriam* (1991). Unpublished. Source: *No/Gro.*

KUHLAU, FRIEDRICH, German composer; b. Sep. 11, 1786; d. Mar. 12, 1832.

Siebert, Wilhelm Dieter, 1931– . *Exercitium: In memoriam Friedrich Kuhlau* (1970). Orchestra. Published *Bote,* 1970.

Sollberger, Harvey, 1938– . *Grand quartet for flutes: In memoriam Friedrich Kuhlau* (1962). Published *McGinnis* 80, 1966.

Weyse, Christoph Ernst Friedrich, 1774–1842. *Ved Friddrich Kuhlaus Grav* (1832). Men's voices and piano. Published Copenhagen: C. C. Lose, 1832? Text by Chr. Winther.

LAMAS, JOSÉ ANGEL, Venezuelan composer; b. Aug. 2, 1775; d. Dec. 9, 1814.

Plaza, Juan Bautista, 1898–1965. *Popule meus: A la memoria de José Angel Lamas* (1937). Voices (TTB) and orchestra. Published Montevideo: Instituto Interamericano de Musicologia, 1943.

LAMBERT, JOHN, English composer; b. July 15, 1926; d. Mar. 7, 1995.

Bainbridge, Simon, 1952– . *Ad ora incerta: Four orchestral songs from Primo Levi: In memory of John Lambert* (1994).

Mezzo-soprano, solo bassoon, orchestra. Published *Novello* 890183, 1994 [sic]. CONTENTS: Il canto del corvo—Lunedi—Il tramonto di Fossoli—Buna. Received the 1997 Grawemeyer Award for musical composition.

LANE, LEWIS, American composer, music librarian; b. Aug. 3, 1901; d. Jan. 24, 1977.

Helps, Robert, 1928– . "Valse mirage: To the memory of Lewis Lane and Ignaz Friedman" (1977), in *Waltzes by 25 contemporary composers.* Piano. Published *Peters* 66735, 1978.

LANGGAARD, RUED, Danish composer, organist; b. July 28, 1893; d. July 10, 1952.

Nielsen, Tage, 1929– . *Lamento: In memoriam Rued Langgaard* (1993). Organ. Published *SUDM,* 1996? Published in series Contemporary Danish organ, no. G001, together with Nielsen's *Chorale fantasy* (1995) for organ. "*Lamento* has the subtitle *In memoriam Rued Langgaard,* and is inspired by the love of the absurd one finds in many places in the work of that composer, especially in his works from the 1940s, such as the symphonies No. 11 and No. 15, and the piano sonata *Le béguinage.* The inspiration is particularly evident in the form of the piece, which thanks to numerous repetitions must be said to be—if not actually absurd—at least rather 'different'"—composer's note in score.

LANGLAIS, JEAN, French organist, composer; b. Feb. 15, 1907; d. May 8, 1991.

Hakim, Naji, 1955– . *Mariales: À la mémoire de mon maitre et amie Jean Langlais* (1993). Organ. Published *UMP,* 1993. CONTENTS: Incantation—Pastorale—Antienne—Hymne—Danse.

LASSO, ROLAND DE, Netherlands composer; b. 1532; d. June 14, 1594.

Genzmer, Harald, 1909– . *Triptychon: In memoriam Orlando di Lasso* (1983). Organ. Published *Peters* 8884, 1996.

Leduc, Jacques, 1932– . *Intrada et dancerie,* op. 75*: In memorium Orlando di Lasso: 1594–1994* (1994). String quartet. Published *CeBeDeM* D199456514, 1994. Composed in the 400th anniversary year of Lasso's death.

Loos, Armin, 1904–1971. *Canon: In memory of Orlando di Lasso.* Piano. Unpublished. Source: *Loos.*

Schickele, Peter, 1935– . *Epitaphs for piano.* Published *E-V* 160-00202, 1981. "*Epitaphs* is a set of tributes written over a period of thirteen years; the composers to whom homage is paid represent each century from the 16th through the 20th"—composer's note in

score. CONTENTS: Orlando di Lasso—Michael Praetorius—
Domenico Scarlatti—Frédéric Chopin—Igor Stravinsky.
LAUB, FERDINAND, Austrian violinist; b. Jan. 19, 1832; d. Mar. 17,
1875.
    Tchaikovsky, Piotr Ilych, 1840–1893. *String quartet no. 3,* op. 30,
E-flat minor: *À la mémoire de F. Laube* (1876). Published Moscow:
Jurgenson, 1876. New edition in Tchaikovsky, *Kamernye ansambli,*
Polnoe sobranie sochinenii [Works], vol. 31 (Moscow: Gos.
muzykalnoe izd-vo, 1955).
LAURO, ANTONIO, Venezuelan guitarist, composer; b. Aug. 3, 1909; d.
Apr. 17, 1986.
    Carreño, Inocente, 1919– . "Merengue: En hommage a Antonio
Lauro" (1989?), in *Les cahiers de la guitare* (1989, no. 2). Guitar.
Published Kremlin-Bicêtre, France: Danielle Ribouillault, 1982.
    Ore, Osted. "Hommage to Antonio Lauro," published in the journal
Classical guitar (Oct. 1989).
LAVISTA, RAUL, Mexican composer, conductor; b. 1914; d. 1980.
    Lavista, Mario, 1943– . *Lamento: A la muerte de Raul Lavista*
(1981). Bass flute solo. Published *Mexicanas,* 1984.
LAWES, WILLIAM, English composer; b. May 1, 1602; d. 1645.
    *Choice Psalmes put into musick for three voices: The most of which
may properly enough be sung by any three, with a thorough base:
Compos'd by Henry and William Lawes, brothers and servants to
His Majestie; with divers elegies, set in musick by sev'rall friends,
upon the death of William Lawes; and at the end of the thorough
base are added nine canons of three and foure voices made by William Lawes.* Vocal trios and quartets. Published London: Printed by
James Young for Humphrey Moseley . . . and for Richard Wodeno-
the. . . , 1648. *RISM-A1*: L-1164, also *RISM-B1*: 1648/4. Microform
reprint available from Bell & Howell Information and Learning
Company (formerly University Microfilms) in the series *Early English books, 1641–1700,* 461:34. ELEGIES: Deare Will is dead / by
John Cobb, fl. 1638–1667—Lament and mourne / by Simon Ives,
1600–1662—O doe not now lament and cry / by John Wilson, 1595–
1674—Brave spirit, art thou fled / by Captain Edmund Foster—
Bound by the neare conjunction of our soules / by John Hilton,
1599–1657—Not well, o no; draw back you cloud / by John Jenkins,
1592–1678—Cease, o cease, ye jolly shepherds / by Henry Lawes,
1596–1662—But that, lov'd friend, we have been taught / by John
Taylor, fl. 1637–1645.

LEBOEUF, HENRI, Belgian musicologist; d. Jan. 29, 1935.

Roussel, Albert, 1869–1937. *Aeneas,* op. 54: *À la mémoire de Henry LeBoeuf* (1935). Ballet in 1 act and 2 tableaux. Published *Durand* 12608, 1936.

LECAINE, HUGH, Canadian acoustician; b. May 27, 1914; d. July 3, 1977.

Keane, David, 1943– . *In memoriam Hugh LeCaine.* Synthesizer. Unpublished. Recorded on the album *Lyra* (Music Galery Editions MGE29, 1979).

LECLAIR, JEAN MARIE, French violinist, composer; b. May 10, 1697; d. Oct. 22, 1764.

Dupont, Guillaume-Pierre, 1718–after 1778 (transcriber). Leclair, Jean Marie, 1697–1764. *Sonata for violin and continuo "Le tombeau"* [Sonatas, violin, continuo, op. 5, no. 6; arr.]. Orchestra. Unpublished. Source: *NGrove.* Dupont arranged Leclair's sonata known as "Le tombeau" for orchestra to be performed at Leclair's memorial service, planned for December 1765, but never realized; on Nov. 25, 1765, *l'Avant-coureur* announced a Mass to memorialize Leclair, "mis en grande symphonie par Dupont, de l'Académie royal de musique, son élève."

LEDUC, EMILE ALPHONSE III, French music publisher; b. Nov. 14, 1878; d. May 24, 1951.

Migot, Georges, 1891–1976. "O Tristan, chevalier d'Amour pur: À Alphonse Leduc in memoriam," in his *Dix quatuors vocaux ou choeurs mixtes* (1949). Vocal quartet or chorus unacc. Published *Leduc,* 1952. Text by the composer. Dedication added for publication.

LEDUC, GILBERT ALPHONSE, French music publisher; b. Oct. 17, 1911; d. 1985.

Charpentier, Jacques, 1933– . *Dona Ei: In memoriam Gilbert Leduc* (1986). Organ. Published *Leduc* AL27275, 1986.

LEIBNITZ, JOHANN GEORG, German clergyman, composer; d. Mar. 3, 1671.

Leibnitz, Johann Georg, d. 1671. *Eckel, Ob der eitlen Welt empfangen . . . des . . . H. Iohann-Georg Leibnitz . . . Anfangs von ihm selbst eigenhändig aufgestezet: Jetzo aber, nach seinem den 3. Martii dieses 1671sten Iahres . . . Ableiben zum Druck befördert.* Voices (4). Published Nuremberg: W. E. Felssecker, 1671. *RISM-A1*: L-1650. Composed by Leibnitz for performance at his own funeral.

LEIBOWITZ, RENÉ, Polish-French composer; b. Feb. 17, 1913; d. Aug. 28, 1972.

Engelmann, Hanns Ulrich, 1921– . *Mémoires: À René Leibowitz* (1997). Guitar. Published *Breitkopf* 9113, 1998.

LEIFS, JÓN, Icelandic composer; b. May 1, 1899; d. July 30, 1968.

Pálsson, Páll Pampichler, 1928– . *Requiem in memoriam Jón Leifs* (1968). Mixed chorus unacc. Published *IMIC*, 1968.

LEIGHTON, KENNETH, English composer; b. Oct. 2, 1929; d. Aug. 24, 1988.

Kenneth Leighton memorial album for organ. Published *Banks* 14025, 1998. CONTENTS: Elegy / by Philip Moore, 1943——Epicedium / by Richard Lloyd, 1935——Saraband for a wake / by Stanley Vann, 1910——Pavane / by Gary Sieling—To Orpheus / by Alan Ridout, 1934–1966—Interlude / by Francis Jackson, 1917——Valediction: Drop, drop slow tears / by Arthur Wills, 1926——Recessional / by John Joubert, 1927——Carillon de Wakefield / by Jonathan Bielby, 1944– .

Harper, Edward, 1941– . *In memoriam Kenneth Leighton* (1990). Violoncello and orchestra. Published *OUP* N6897, 1990. Opening motive is based on Leighton's name (E-B [**H** in German]-**G**).

LEJEUNE, CLAUDE, French composer; b. 1528; d. Sep. 25, 1600.

Vercken, François, 1928– . *Fanfare: En mémoire de Claude Lejeune* (1975). Octet for trumpets (4), trombones (4). Published *Durand* 14098, 1983.

LEKEU, GUILLAUME, Belgian composer; b. Jan. 20, 1870; d. Jan. 21, 1894.

Hoérée, Arthur, 1897–1986. *Trois fanfares.* Piano. Unpublished. Source: *Rownd.* One of the three is in memory of Lekeu.

LENNON, JOHN, British rock musician; b. Oct. 9, 1940; d. Dec. 8, 1980.

Dumond, Arnaud, 1950– . *John Lennon lay not* (1984). Guitars (4). Published *Doberman* DO259, 1999.

Foss, Lukas, 1922– . *Night music for John Lennon: Prelude, fugue, and chorale* (1980). Large or small orchestra with brass quintet concertante. Published *Pembroke* PCB121, 1982. "Lukas Foss began the composition of this work the morning of the day that John Lennon was killed"—note in score.

Kernis, Aaron Jay, 1960– . *Meditation: In Memory of John Lennon* (1981). Violoncello and piano. Published *AMP.*

Kolb, Barbara, 1939– . *Point that divides the wind: Dedicated to the memory of John Lennon* (1982). Male voices (3), organ, percussion. Published *Boosey* ONB405, 1985.

Maiben, William, 1953– . "Lennon extract: The martyrdom of Saint John: A tombeau for John Lennon 1940–1980," in *Perspectives* 19 (1980–1981): 532–535. Song with rhythm, lead, and bass guitars and drums. Text by the composer, John Lennon, and Paul McCartney.

Russo, Frank L. *Hommage: To John Lennon* (1981). Flute solo. Unpublished. Source: *OCLC.*

LENO, DAN, English music-hall performer; b. Dec. 20, 1860; d. Oct. 31, 1904.

Hamilton, Iain, 1922–2000. *1912: A light overture,* op. 38: *To the memory of Dan Leno of Drury Lane* (1958). Orchestra. Published *Schott-L* 6552, 1968.

LIATOSHYNSKYI, BORYS MYKOLAIOVYCH, Ukrainian composer; b. Jan. 3, 1895; d. Apr. 15, 1968.

Sylvestrov, Valentyn Vasylovych, 1937– . *Poema: In memoriam B. N. Ljatoschinsky* (1968). Orchestra. Published *Sikorski.*

LIBERACE (WLADZIU VALENTINO LIBERACE), American popular pianist, entertainer; b. May 16, 1919; d. Feb. 4, 1987.

Daugherty, Michael, 1954– . *Tombeau de Liberace* (1996). Piano and orchestra. Published *Peermusic.* CONTENTS: Rhinestone kick-step—How do I love thee?—Sequin music—Candelabra rhumba.

LIEBERSON, GODDARD, English-American recording executive; b. Apr. 5, 1911; d. May 29, 1977.

Bernstein, Leonard, 1918–1990. "In memoriam, Goddard Lieberson" (1981), in his *Thirteen anniversaries* (1964–1988). Piano. Published *Jalni* PAB463, 1989.

LIER, BERTUS VAN, Dutch composer, conductor; b. Sep. 10, 1906; d. Feb. 14, 1972.

Franco, Johan, 1906– . *Le tombeau de Bertus van Lier.* Carillon. Published *Donemus,* 1973. Published with *The Bells,* by Wim Thijsse.

LILJE, PEETER, Estonian conductor; b. Oct. 13, 1950; d. 1993.

Tüür, Erkki-Sven, 1959– . *Requiem: In memoriam Peeter Lilje* (1994). Chamber chorus, piano, strings. Published *Litolff* 8886, 1996.

LIND, JENNY, Swedish soprano; b. Oct. 6, 1820; d. Nov. 2, 1887.

Popp, Wilhelm, 1828–1903. *Erinnerungen an Jenny Lind: Introduction und grosser Concert-Walzer,* op. 169. Soprano with orchestra (or piano). Published Nuremberg: Schmid WS84.

LINDSAY, ALEX, New Zealand violinist, conductor; b. May 28, 1919; d. Dec. 5, 1974.

Rimmer, John Francis, 1939– . *Epitaphium* (1975). Violin solo. Published Auckland, NZ: Catena Press, 1985.

LINNAVALLI, ESKO, Finnish jazz musician; b. Sep. 4, 1941; d. after 1995.

Lintinen, Kirmo, 1967– . *Spring poem: Esko Linnavalli in memoriam* (199–). For big band. Unpublished. Source: *RLIN*. Score located at the Harvard University Music Library.

LIST, EUGENE, American pianist; b. July 6, 1918; d. Feb. 28, 1985.

Adler, Samuel, 1928– . *Double portrait.* Violin and piano. Published *Southern* ST785, 1989. "Commissioned by Carey Lewis and Ronald Nead to honor the memory of two great artists and two beautiful people, Carroll Glenn and Eugene List"—note in score. Glenn was the wife of List.

LISZT, FRANZ, Hungarian composer, pianist; b. Oct. 22, 1811; d. July 31, 1886.

Garrido Vargas, Pablo, 1905–1982. *Sonata for piano in A major: A la memoria de Franz Liszt* (1948). Piano. Unpublished. Source: *Chile.*

Glazunov, Aleksandr Konstantinovich, 1865–1936. *Élégie,* op. 17: *à la mémoire de François Liszt* (1887). Violoncello and piano. Published *Belaieff* 177, 1889. Reprint: *Belaieff,* 1978.

————. *Symphony no. 2,* op. 16, in F-sharp minor: *À la mémoire de François Liszt* (1886). Published *Belaieff* 469, 1899.

Gut, Serge. *In memoriam Franz Liszt.* Piano. Published *Zurfluh* AZ1383, 1992.

Kodály, Zoltán, 1882–1967. *An Franz Liszt: Liszt ferenchez* [Liszt Ferenchez] (1936). Mixed voices unacc. Published *UE-L* 10862a, 1937. Composed for the 50th anniversary of Liszt's death. Text by Mihaly Vörösmarty.

Liapunov, Sergei Mikhailovich, 1859–1924. *Douze études d'execution transcendante,* op. 11 (1905). Piano. Published *Zimmermann* 1172–1175, 1905? Later edition: *Peters* 9578, 1982. The dedication "à le mémoire de François Liszt" is at the head of the collection; the 12th etude in addition is titled "Elégie in mémoire de François Liszt."

Niehaus, Manfred, 1933– . *Le tombeau de Liszt* (1985). Orchestra. Published *Gravis* EG60, 1985.

Rimsky-Korsakov, Nikolay, 1844–1908. *Concerto for piano and orchestra,* op. 30, C-sharp minor (1882–83). Published *Belaieff* 28, 1886. New edition: *Belaieff* 403, 1980. Although the 1886 publication is dedicated "à la mémoire de François Liszt," the concerto was composed 1882–83 prior to Liszt's death.

Saint-Saëns, Camille, 1835–1921. *Symphony no. 3,* op. 78, in C minor: *À la mémoire de Franz Liszt* (1886). Published *Durand* 3700, 1886.

Soler, Josep, 1935– . "Pour le tombeau de Ferenc Liszt" (1995), in his *Album para piano.* Unpublished. Source: *Soler.*

Stevenson, Ronald, 1928– . *Symphonic elegy for Liszt* (1986). Piano. Published *Bardic,* 1987.

Takács, Jenö, 1902– . *Le tombeau de Franz Liszt = Am Grabe von Franz Liszt,* op. 100 (1977). Piano. Published *Doblinger* 1596, 1979. CONTENTS: Lacrimosa—Dies irae (Totentanz).

LITAIZE, GASTON, French organist, composer; b. Aug. 11, 1909; d. Aug. 5, 1991.

Weinhart, Christoph, 1958– . *Epitaphe pour Gaston Litaize* (1991). Organ. Published *ProOrgano* 1057, 1992.

LITTLE, BOOKER, American jazz trumpeter; b. Apr. 2, 1938; d. Oct. 5, 1961.

Hubbard, Freddie, 1938– . "Lament for Booker" (1962), recorded on *Hub-tones*: Blue Note Records BST84115, 1963? Jazz quintet. Reissued on *Freddie Hubbard Ballads* (Blue Note CDP-724385669125, 1997).

LLOYD WEBBER, WILLIAM, English composer, music educator; b. 1914; d. Oct. 29, 1982.

Lloyd Webber, Lord Andrew, 1948– . *Requiem for soprano, tenor, treble, chorus, and orchestra* (1984). Published *Novello* 07046600, 1985. Inspired in part by the death of the composer's father.

LOCKE, MATTHEW, English composer; b. 1630?; d. Aug. 1677.

Purcell, Henry, ca. 1659–1695. "What hope for us remains now he is gone?" (1677), in *Choice ayres and songs to sing to the theorbo-lute or bass-viol . . . the second book.* Soprano solo, chorus (SB), and continuo. Published London: Printed by Anne Godbid, sold by John Playford, 1679. *RISM-B1*: 1679/7. "On the death of his worthy friend Mr. Matthew Lock, musick-composer to his majesty, and organist of her majestie's chapel, who dyed in August 1677"— dedication in score. Modern edition in Purcell, *Secular songs and cantatas for a single* voice, Works of Henry Purcell, vol. 25, ed. under the supervision of the Purcell Society (*Novello,* 1928).

LOKSHIN, ALEKSANDRE, Soviet composer; b. Sep. 19, 1920; d. June 11, 1987.

Tishchenko, Boris Ivanovich, 1939– (transcriber). Grieg, Edvard, 1843–1907. *Songs: Orchestrated by Tishchenko* [Songs. Selections; arr.]. Unpublished. Tishchenko's orchestral accompaniments to songs by Grieg are dedicated to the memory of Lokshin. Recorded by the Northern Crown Soloists Ensemble, cond. by Igor Zaidenshnir with various soloists on *Works by Alexander Lokshin and Edvard Grieg* (MK Records 417124, 1993).

LOPATNIKOFF, NICOLAI, Estonian-American composer; b. Mar. 16, 1903; d. Oct. 7, 1976.

    McKinley, William Thomas, 1939– . *Symphony no. 1: To the memory of Nikolai Lopatnikoff* (1977). Published *Margun*.

LOUIS FERDINAND, PRINCE OF PRUSSIA, German prince, composer; b. Nov. 18, 1772; d. Oct. 10, 1806.

    Dussek, Johann Ladislaus, 1760–1812. *Élégie harmonique sur la mort de son altesse royale le Prince Louis Ferdinand de Prusse,* op. 61. Sonata for piano. Published *Breitkopf* 6010, 1808? Later edition: *Peters*, 1949.

LUCCA, FRANCESCO, Italian music publisher; b. 1802; d. Nov. 20, 1872.

    Bernardi, Enrico, 1838–1900. *Alla memoria di Francesco Lucca: Preludio funebre.* Band. Published Milan: Francesco Lucca 21386, 1873.

    Ponchielli, Amilcare, 1834–1886. *Marcia funebre per i funerali di Francesco Lucca,* op. 112a (Nov. 23, 1872*).* Orchestra or band. Published Milan: Francesco Lucca 21084, 1873. Various later editions and arrangements. Performed in 1872 at Lucca's funeral.

LUENING, OTTO, American composer, teacher, conductor; b. June 15, 1900; d. Sep. 2, 1996.

    Kraft, Leo, 1922– . *A single voice: In remembrance of Otto Luening* (2000). Alto flute solo. Published *Seesaw*, 2000.

LUKASHEVSKII, ILIA AVSEEVICH, Soviet violinist; b. Aug. 20, 1892; d. June 11, 1967.

    Finko, David, 1936– . *Mourning music: String quartet without the first violinist* (1968*).* Trio for violin, viola, violoncello. Published Philadelphia: Dako, 1996. "In memory of Elijah Lukashevsky (1892–1967), the first violinist of the Glazunov Quartet"—note in score.

LULLY, JEAN BAPTISTE, Italian-born French composer; b. Nov. 26, 1632; d. Mar. 22, 1687.

    Anonymous. *Le triomphe des Mélophilètes.* An "Idyll in music."

Unpublished. Text by Pierre Bouret. The work is lost, but a description survives in the *Mercure de France* (December, 1725). Marc Pincherle, in *Corelli: His life and work* (New York: Norton, 1956), conjectures a connection between this work and the *Apothéoses* by Couperin for Corelli and Lully: either that Bouret and his collaborator reworked and expanded the works by Couperin, or that Couperin composed the music of the *Triomphe*, and then retained only the instrumental parts for publication, and from them formed the *Apothéose* for Lully.

Couperin, François, 1668–1733. *Concert instrumental sous le titre D'apothéose, composé à la mémoire immortelle de l'incomparable Monsieur de Lully.* Treble instruments (2 and 3) with continuo, and for violins (2) solo. Published Paris: L'autheur, Boivin, Le Clerc, 1725. *RISM-A1*: C-4276. Facsimile reprint: *Minkoff* 2826606964, 1979. New edition in *Oeuvres complètes de François Couperin*, ed. Maurice Cauchie, vol. 10 (*Oiseau-L*, 1932–1933).

Kiesewetter, Peter, 1945– . *Le tombeau de Lully.* Quintet for flute, oboe, clarinet, horn, bassoon. Published *Gerig* HG1358, 1980.

Marais, Marin, 1656–1728. "Le tombeau pour Mons. de Lully," in his *Pièces de violes: Composées par M. Marais, ordinaire de la musique de la Chambre du Roy [livre 2]* [Pièces de violes, 2e livre]. Viols (1 and 2) and continuo. Published Paris: L'autheur, Marais le fils, Hurel, Foucault, 1701. *RISM-A1*: M-389. New edition in Marais, *The instrumental works*, ed. by John Hsu (*Broude*, 1986).

Rebel, Jean Féry, 1667–1747. "Tombeau de M. de Lully" (ca. 1695), in his *Recueil de douze sonates à II et à III parties avec la basse chifrée.* Violins (2) and continuo. Published Paris: Christoph Ballard, 1712. *RISM-A1*: R-506. Modern edition in Rebel, *Le tombeau de Monsieur de Lully,* ed. Charles Medlam (Ottawa: Dovehouse Editions, 1985).

LUTHER, MARTIN, German church reformer, hymnodist; b. Nov. 10, 1483; d. Feb. 18, 1546.

Othmayr, Caspar, 1515–1553. "Per quiem salvifici," in *Epitaphium D. Martini Lutheri a Gaspare Othmaier musicis elegiis redditum.* Voices (5). Published Nuremberg: Berg & Neuber, 1546. *RISM-A1*: O-259. New edition in Othmayr, *Abteilung ausgewahlter Werke einzilner Meister,* Ausgewahlte Werke, vol. 4, ed. Hans Albrecht, Das Erbe deutscher Musik, vol. 26 (*Peters,* 1956).

Petsch, Johann Friedrich, fl. 1546. *Seid from ihr lieben Christen Leut: Ein schön christlich Lied von dem ehrwirdigen Herren D:*

Mart. Luth. und seiner Lere (1546). Song. Published Wittenberg: G. Rhaw, 1546. *RISM-A1*: P-1658. Text by Luther.

LUTOSLAWSKI, WITOLD, Polish composer; b. Jan. 25, 1913; d. Feb. 7, 1994.

Denisov, Edisson Vasilevich, 1929–1996. *Postludio: In memoriam Witold Lutoslawski* (1994). Orchestra. Published *DVfM* 1753, 1996.

Frank, Gabriela Lena. *String quartet no. 4* (1995). Published *Hildegard* 02029, 2000.

Godár, Vladimir, 1956– . *Déploration sur la mort de Lutoslawski* (1994). Piano and string quartet. Unpublished. Source: *KdG*.

Lindberg, Magnus, 1958– . *Aura: In memoriam Witold Lutoslawski* (1994). Orchestra. Published *Chester*, 1994.

Stucky, Steven, 1949– . *Concerto for two flutes and orchestra: In memoriam Witold Lutoslawski* (1995). Published *Merion* 144-40261, 1995.

Takemitsu, Toru, 1930–1996. *Paths: In memoriam Witold Lutoslawski* (1994). Trumpet unaccompanied. Published *Schott-J* SJ1085, 1994.

Xenakis, Iannis, 1922– . *Mnamas xapin Witoldowi Lutlslawskiemu* (1994). Quartet for trumpets (2), horns (2). Published *Salabert* EAS19253, 1994.

Zechlin, Ruth, 1926– . *In memoriam Witold Lutoslawski* (1995). Viola solo. Published *Ries* 11018, 1996.

Zielinski, Maciej, 1971– . *Lutoslawski in memoriam* (1999). Oboe and piano. Published *PWM* 9959, 2000. CONTENTS: Hesitant—Direct.

MAAS, WALTER ALFRED FRIEDRICH, German-Dutch music administrator; b. July 18, 1909; d. Dec. 1, 1992.

Raxach, Enrique, 1932– . *Twelve preludes for piano: In memoriam Walter Maas* (1993). Published *Donemus*, 1995. Maas founded the Gaudeaumus Foundation.

MACHAUT, GUILLAUME DE, French composer, poet; b. 1300?; d. 1377.
See: **GUILLAUME DE MACHAUT**

MACIUNAS, GEORGE, Lithuanian-American composer, performance artist; b. Nov. 8, 1931; d. May 9, 1978.

Shiomi, Mieko, 1938– . *Requiem for George Maciunas.* Electronic tape. Unpublished. Source: *No/Gro*. Maciunas was founder of the performance group Fluxus.

MADERNA, BRUNO, Italian composer, conductor; b. Mar. 21, 1920; d. Nov. 13, 1973.

Berio, Luciano, 1925– . *Calmo: A Bruno Maderna in memoriam* (1974; rev. 1988–89). Soprano with octet for flute, oboe, clarinets (2), bassoon, horn, trumpet, trombone. Published *UE* 19478, 1989. Revised 1988–89 for soprano with chamber orchestra. Text from various sources.

Boulez, Pierre, 1925– . *Rituel: In memoriam Bruno Maderna* (1974–75). Orchestra in 8 groups. Published *UE-L* 15941, 1975.

Donatoni, Franco, 1927– . *Duo pour Bruno: Per orchestra* (1974–75). Published *Zerboni* 7819, 1975.

Druckman, Jacob, 1928–1996. *Delizie contente che l'alme beate* (1973). Wind quintet and electronic tape. Published *Boosey* ENB118, 1978. Recorded by the Dorian Woodwind Quintet, for which it was written, on *The avant garde woodwind quintet in the USA* (Vox Box SVBX5307, 1977). Based on an aria from Francesco Cavalli's opera *Il Giasone* (1649). "It was Bruno Maderna, great and inspiring musician and my dear friend, who first interested me in the music of Cavalli. *Delizie contente* was written during Maderna's last few months, he in Italy and Germany and I in France. His premature ending was constantly with me as I worked on the piece. *Delizie contente* is dedicated to his memory"—composer's note in score.

Méfano, Paul, 1937– . *A Bruno Maderna* (1974). Electronic music. Unpublished. Source: *Méfano.* "Réalisée peu après la disparition d'un ami irremplaçable, cette musique est une déploration confiée à une texture électroacoustique résolument quadriphonique."

Olive, Vivienne, 1950– . *Tomba di Bruno* (1975). Flute and orchestra. Published *Furore* 2501, 1994.

Pablo, Luis de, 1930– . *Trimalchio: In memoriam Bruno Maderna* (1997–98). Duo for bassoon/contrabassoon and horn. Published *Zerboni* 11313, 1998.

Pousseur, Henri, 1929– . *Vue sur les jardins interdits: In memoriam Bruno Maderna* (1973). Saxophones (4). Published *Zerboni* 7809, 1974.

Wittinger, Róbert, 1945– . *Omaggio for string sextet,* op. 26: *Musica in memoria di Bruno Madern* (1974). Published *Breitkopf* PB4876, 1974.

MADURA, ROBERT, American violoncellist; b. July 11, 1933; d. Feb. 1980.

Ott, David, 1947– . *Symphony no. 2* (1990). Published *MMB*, 1990.

Recorded by the Grand Rapids Symphony, which commissioned the work in memory of its late principal violoncellist (Koss Classics KC3301, 1992).

MAGNARD, ALBERIC, French composer; b. June 9, 1865; d. Sep. 3, 1914.

Milhaud, Darius, 1892–1974. *Suite symphonique no. 2: À la mémoire d'Alberic Magnard* (1919). Orchestra. Published *Durand* 10504, 1921.

MAHLER, GUSTAV, Austrian composer, conductor; b. July 7, 1860; d. May 18, 1911.

Ali-Sade, Frangis, 1947– . *Zu den Kindertotenlieder: To the memory of Gustav Mahler* (1977). Trio for violin, clarinet, percussion. Published *Sikorski*, 1977.

Hamilton, Iain, 1922–2000. *Alastor: In memory of Gustav Mahler* (1970). Orchestra. Published *Presser* 416-41087, 1974. Additional dedication in score: "In honour of those who died young."

Menotti, Gian Carlo, 1911– . *La donna immobile* (1972). Unfinished "opera buffa" without music, dedicated to the memory of Mahler. Unpublished. Source: *Menotti*. Improvised by Menotti during the summer of 1972.

Pousseur, Henri, 1929– . *Ballade berlinoise: À la mémoire de Brahms, Mahler, Schoenberg et . . . J. S. Bach* (1974–77). Piano. Published *Zerboni* 8373, 1979.

Schoenberg, Arnold, 1874–1951. "Sehr langsam" (1911), in his *Sechs kleine Klavierstücke,* op. 19. Piano. Published *UE* 5069, 1913. The last of the six pieces. "Mahler died on 18 May. . . . A few weeks later, on 17 June 1911, Schoenberg wrote the last of his Little Piano Pieces, op. 19, and later said that it was written in memory of Mahler's death"—*Schoenberg*, p. 108.

MALAWSKI, ARTUR, Polish violinist, composer; b. July 4, 1904; d. Dec. 26, 1957.

Penderecki, Krzysztof, 1933– . *Epitafium Artur Malawski in memoriam* (1958). String orchestra with timpani. Unpublished. Source: *Penderecki*. First performance September 1958, Krakow Philharmonic, cond. by Michal Baranowski.

MALIBRAN, MARIA FELICITA, French contralto; b. Mar. 24, 1808; d. Sep. 23, 1836.

In morte di M. F. Malibran De Bériot (1837). Cantata. Published *Ricordi* 10037-10044, 1837. Text by Antonio Piazza. CONTENTS: Sinfonia / by Gaetano Donizetti, 1797–1848—Il cippo di Manches-

ter [Vocal quintet with orchestra] / by Giovanni Pacini, 1796–
1867—L'inaugurazioni [3 soloists, chorus and orchestra] / by
Saverio Mercadante, 1795–1870—La Corona [Bass and soprano soloists, chorus and orchestra] / by Pietro Antonio Coppola, 1793–
1877—Il monumento di Milano [Vocal sextet, chorus and orchestra]
/ by Nicola Vaccai, 1790–1848. Each movement also published
separately by *Ricordi* in 1837. For more about this cantata, see Alexander Weatherson, "Lament for a dead nightingale," *Donizetti
Society journal* 5 (1984): 155–168.

Moja, Leonardo, 1811–1888. *Note lugubri della Malibran:
Sull'aria finale della Giuletta e Romeo de Vaccai.* Variations for
violoncello and piano. Published *Ricordi* 9490, 1836. Based on a
theme from Nicola Vaccai's opera *Giulettta e Romeo* after Shakespeare. Malibran had sung the role of Romeo in this opera.

Moscheles, Ignaz, 1794–1870. *Hommage caractéristique à la mémoire de Madame Malibran de Bériot, en forme de fantaisie,* op.
94b. Piano. Published *Kistner* 10380, 1838? Later edition: *Ricordi,*
1936.

Neumann, Antonio. *Anacreontica in memoria della celebre Malibran* (1836). Voice and piano. Published *Ricordi* 9125, 1836.

Wesley, Samuel, 1766–1837. *Eyes long unmoisten'd: Elegy on the
death of Malibran* (1836). Voice and piano. Published London: s.n.,
1836. Source: *NGrove.*

MALTOT, French guitarist, theorbist; d. 1703?

Campion, François, ca. 1686–ca. 1748. "Le tombeau de Mr. de
Maltor" [sic], in his *Nouvelles découvertes sur la guitarre: Con-
tenantes plusieurs suittes de pièces sur huit manières différentes
d'accorder.* Guitar. Published Paris: Brunet, 1705. *RISM-A1*: C-621.
Facsimile reprint: *Minkoff* 2826606417, 1977. Campion succeeded
Maltot in 1703 at the Academie royale de musique, Paris.

MAMMOT, ISAAC, Canadian violoncellist; b. 1907; d. Apr. 5, 1964.

Glick, Srul Irving, 1934– . *Elegy for orchestra* (1964). Published
Canadian. In memory of three Toronto violoncellists who died in
1964: John Adaskin, Isaac Mammot, and Rowland Pack.

MANGEOT, ANDRÉ, French-British violinist; b. Aug. 25, 1883; d. Sep.
11, 1970.

Jeffreys, John, 1927– . *Elegy for André Mangeot.* String orchestra.
Unpublished. Recorded by the Orchestra de Camera of Birmingham,
England, cond. by Kenneth Page (Meridian Records CDE84331,
1996).

MARAIS, MARIN, French gambist; b. May 31, 1656; d. Aug. 15, 1728.
   Bartholomée, Pierre, 1937– . *Le tombeau de Marin Marais* (1967).
   Quartet for violin, violas da gamba (2), harpsichord. Published *UE*
   15628, 1967?
   Dollé, Charles, fl. 1735–1740. "Le tombeau de Marais le père," in
   his *Pièces de viole avec la basse continue, oeuvre IIe* [Pièces, viol,
   continuo, op. 2]. Published Paris: L'autheur, 1737. *RISM-A1*:
   D-3354. Facsimile edition: *Minkoff* 2826606980, 1979.
   Pinchard, Max, 1928– . *Le tombeau de Marin Marais.* Viola da
   gamba (or violoncello) solo with trio for flute, violin, harpsichord (or
   piano). Published *EMT* TRPA1010, 1968.
MARBÉ, MYRIAM, Romanian composer; b. Jan. 9, 1931; d. Dec. 25,
1997.
   Vieru, Anatol, 1926–1998. *Elegia I: In memoriam Myriam Marbé*
   (1998). Alto saxophone and organ. Unpublished. Source: *Beckmann.*
MARCUS, ADELE, American pianist, teacher; b. 1906; d. May 3, 1995.
   Liebermann, Lowell, 1961– . *Nocturne no. 5 for piano* (1995). Pub-
   lished *Presser* 110-40724, 2000. Commissioned by the Adele
   Marcus Foundation in memory of Adele Marcus.
MARIANI, ANGELO, Italian conductor, composer; b. Oct. 11, 1821; d.
June 13, 1873.
   Petrella, Errico, 1813–1877. *Messa funèbre per la morte di Angelo
   Mariani* (June 1874). Unpublished. Source: *NGrove.* Composed for
   the first anniversary of Mariani's death.
MARLIAVE, JOSEPH DE, French musicologist; b. Nov. 16, 1873; d.
Aug. 24, 1914.
   Ravel, Maurice, 1875–1937. "Toccata: À la mémoire du capitaine
   Joseph de Marliave," in his *Le tombeau de Couperin: Suite pour pi-
   ano* (1914–17). Published *Durand* 9569, 1918. CONTENTS:
   Prélude—Fugue—Forlane—Rigaudon—Menuet—Toccata. The
   Toccata is omitted from the orchestral version.
MARLOWE, SYLVIA, American harpsichordist; b. Sep. 26, 1908; d.
Dec. 11, 1981.
   Rieti, Vittorio, 1898–1994. *Trittico* (1982). Harpsichords (2). Un-
   published. Source: *Bedford.* Commissioned by The Harpsichord
   Society and dedicated to the memory of Sylvia Marlowe. First per-
   formance December 10, 1985, New York, Carnegie Recital Hall, by
   Kenneth Cooper and Wendy Young.
MARTIN, FRANK, Swiss composer; b. Sep. 15, 1890; d. Nov. 21, 1974.
   Samama, Leo, 1951– . *Tombeau concertant: Pour Frank Martin*

(1975). Violins concertante (2) and small string orchestra. Published *Donemus*, 1978.

MARTINELLI, CATERINA, Italian vocalist; b. 1589?; d. Mar. 1608.

Monteverdi, Claudio, 1567–1643. "Lagrime d'amante al sepolcro dell'amata," in his *Sesto libro de madrigali a cinque voci: Con un dialogo a sette, con il suo basso continuo per poterli concertare nel clavacembano, et altri stromenti* [Madrigals, book 6]. Madrigal for voices (5). Published Venice: Ricciardo Amadino, 1614. *RISM-A1*: M-3490. Modern edition in Monteverdi, *Madrigali a 5 voci: Libro sesto*, ed. Antonio Delfino, Opera Omnia, vol. 10 (Cremona: Fondazione Claudio Monteverdi, 1991). Martinelli's premature death prevented her scheduled performance of the role of Arianna in 1608. Duke Vincenzo commissioned Count Scipione Agnelli to write a poem to memorialize her; two years later Vincenzo had Monteverdi set the text to music.

MARTINI, GIOVANNI BATTISTA, Italian composer, pedagogue; b. Apr. 24, 1706; d. Aug. 3, 1784.

Mozart, Wolfgang Amadeus, 1756–1791. "Kleiner Trauermarsch in c: Marche funebre del Sigr. Maestro Contrapunto" (1784) [Kleiner Trauermarsch, piano, K. 453a, C minor], in *Einzelstücke für Klavier*, ed. Wolfgang Plath, Neue Ausgabe sämtlicher Werke, Ser. IX, Wg. 27, vol. 2 , p. 35. Published *Bärenreiter* BA4584, 1982. The suggestion that the work might have been intended as a memorial for Martini is by *Burke*, p. 48. Martini was a teacher of Mozart.

MARTINU, BOHUSLAV, Czech composer; b. Dec. 8, 1890; d. Aug. 28, 1956.

Moyse, Louis, 1912– . *Quintet for winds: To Bohuslav Martinu in memoriam* (1961). Quintet for flute, oboe, clarinet, horn, bassoon. Published *McGinnis* 53a–e, 1966.

Randalls, Jeremy Stuart. *Le tombeau de Martinu* (1990). Flute and piano. Unpublished. Source: *OCLC*.

MARTIRANO, SALVATORE, American composer; b. Jan. 12, 1927; d. Nov. 17, 1995.

In memoriam Salvatore Martirano. A collection of remembrances and compositions by various contributors. Published in *Perspectives* 34 (Winter 1996): 162–241. MUSICAL CONTENTS: L. V. for solo trumpet: In memoriam Sal Martirano / by John Fonville—Quietness: In memory of Salvatore Martirano [Solo voice spoken on pitch, and string quartet] / by Ben Johnson, 1926– —For Salvatore [Brass choir] / by Henry Weinberg, 1931– .

MARX, JOSEF, German-American oboist, publisher; b. Sep. 9, 1913; d. Dec. 21, 1978.

Sollberger, Harvey, 1938– . *Three or four things I know about the oboe: To the memory of Josef Marx* (1985–86). Concerto for oboe and chamber ensemble. Published *McGinnis,* 1988.

MATAMOROS, MIGUEL, Cuban guitarist, composer; b. May 8, 1894; d. Apr. 15, 1971.

Chaviano, Flores, 1946– . *Requiem a un sonero: Homenaje a Miguel Matamoros* (1975). Guitar. Published Havana: Editora musical de Cuba 10772, 1979.

MATHIAS, WILLIAM, Welsh composer, teacher; b. Nov. 1, 1934; d. July 29, 1992.

Lewis, Geraint, 1958– . *The souls of the righteous: Iustorum animae* (1992). Chorus (SATB) and organ. Published *Aureus* AP55, 1995.

MATTEINI, IVO, Italian clarinetist; d. Dec. 1968.

Bucchi, Valentino, 1916–1976. *Concerto for clarinet solo: Carte fiorentine n. 2* (1969). Clarinet unaccompanied. Published *Ricordi* 131531, 1969. "Il concerto è dedicato alla memoria del mio amico Ivo Matteini, insegnante de clarinetto presso il Conservatorio di Musica 'Morlacchi' di Perugia, sino al dicembre del 1968"—note in score.

MAYNARD, PAUL, American harpsichordist, organist; b. Oct. 31, 1923; d. June 14, 1998.

Kraft, Leo, 1922– . *Garden of memory: In memory of Paul Maynard* (1998). Harpsichord. Published *Seesaw,* 1998.

MAZZEO, ROSARIO, American clarinetist; b. Apr. 5, 1911; d. July 19, 1997.

LeSiege, Annette, 1942– . *Serenade: In memory of Rosario Mazzeo* (1997). Clarinet and piano. Published *Seesaw,* 1997.

MEEROVITCH, JULIETTE, French pianist; b. 1896; d. 1920.

Poulenc, Francis, 1899–1963. *Napoli* (1922–25). Suite for piano. Published Paris: Rouart, Lerolle, 1926. CONTENTS: Barcarolle—Nocturne—Caprice italien.

MÉHUL, ÉTIENNE-NICOLAS, French composer; b. June 22, 1763; d. Oct. 18, 1817.

Poissl, Johann Nepomuk, 1783–1865. *Méhuls Gedächtnisfeyer* (1817). Chorus. Unpublished. Source: *NGrove.* Text by J. Sendtner. Performed in Munich, Dec. 22, 1817. Manuscript is in the Bayerische Staatsbibliothek, Munich.

MELANCHTON, PHILIPPE, German theologian, music scholar; b. Feb. 16, 1497; d. Apr. 19, 1560.

Mauverus, Thomas, fl. 1561. *Melodia Epicedii in doitum reverendi et clarissimi viro . . . D. Philippi Melanthonis . . . 4 vocibus composita.* Voices (4). Published Wittenberg: G. Rhaw, 1561. *RISM-A1*: M-1453. Text incipit "Plangite leucarides ululantes."

Praetorius, Christoph, d. 1609. *De obitu viri, pietate, eruditione et virtute praesantis, praeceptoris et patris omnium studiosorum charissimi, Dui Philippi Melanthonis, studiorum summi & felicissimi gubernatoris in Academia Vuitebergensi.* Voices (4). Published Wittenberg: G. Rhaw, 1560. *RISM-A1*: P-5323. Text incipit "Plangite leuconides musae."

MELITON, French lutenist, composer; d. 17th cent.

Marais, Marin, 1656–1728. "Le tombeau de Meliton," in his *Pièces a une et a deux violes* [Pièces de violes, 1er livre]. Viols (1 or 2). Published Paris: L'autheur, 1686. *RISM-A1*: M-383. New edition in Marais, *The instrumental works*, ed. by John Hsu (*Broude, 1986*).

MENDELSSOHN-BARTHOLDY, FELIX, German composer; b. Feb. 3, 1809; d. Nov. 4, 1847.

Berlinski, Herman, 1910– . *Variationen über das Lied Allnächtlich im Traume,* op. 86, no. 4 (1997). Piano trio. Published *Peters 8929,* 1999. Commissioned by the Internationale Mendelssohn-Stiftung, Leipzig, and first performed on the 150th anniversary of Mendelssohn's death. Variations on Mendelssohn's song *Allnächtlich im Traume.*

Gambini, Carlo Andrea, 1819–1965. *Un fiore sulla tomba di Felice Mendelssohn-Bartholdy: Pensiero elegiaco per pianoforte* (1847). Published *Ricordi 20234,* 1847.

Heinrich, Anthony Philip, 1781–1861. *Tomb of genius: To the memory of Mendelssohn-Bartholdy: Sinfonia sacra.* Orchestra. Unpublished. Source: *Heinrich.* Undated autograph score is at the Library of Congress.

————. *The laurel and the cypress: Petit impromptu for the pianoforte, suggested by pleasing recollections of the departed Felix Mendelssohn-Bartholdy* (1847). Published New York: C. Holt Jr., 1847.

Kirchner, Theodor, 1823–1903. "Marsch," and "Lento melancolico," in his *Gedenkblätter: Zwölf Musikstücke zur Erinnerung an die Einweihung des neuen Königl. Conservatoriums für Musik zu Leipzig,* op. 82 (1843–87). Piano. Published Leipzig: J. Rieter-Biedermann 1508, 1887. No. 1–2 of 12 short piano pieces memorializing Conrad Schleinitz, Felix Mendelssohn, Robert Schumann, Moritz Hauptmann, Ferdinand David, Ignaz Moscheles, Ernst Friedrich Richter, Carl Ferdinand Becker, Ernst Ferdinand Wenzel, and Louis Plaidy.

Levy, Maurice. *Una lagrima sulla tomba del celebre maestro Felice Mendelssohn-Bartoldy: Adagio per pianoforte,* op. 5. Published *Ricordi* 20235, 1847.

Pitsch, Karl Franz (Karel Frantisek), 1786–1859. *Fantasie und Fuge an den Tod Felix Mendelssohn.* Organ. Published Prague: Hoffmann. New edition in *Varhanni skladby starych ceskych mistru = Orgelkompositionen alter böhmischer Meister,* ed. Bohumil Geist and Miroslav Kampelsheimer, Musica viva historica, vol. 21 (Prague: Supraphon H4506, 1970).

Schumann, Robert, 1810–1856. "Erinnerung, 4. Nov. 1847" (1848), in his *40 Clavierstücke für die Jugend* [Album für die Jugend. Erinnerung]. Published *Schuberth,* 1848. Numerous modern editions. The date in the title is the date of Mendelssohn's death.

MENGELBERG, KAREL, Dutch composer, conductor; b. July 18, 1902; d. July 11, 1984.

Straesser, Joep, 1934– . *Gran trio: Per sassofono contralto, arpa e percussione* (1984). Trio for alto saxophone, harp, percussionist (marimba and glockenspiel). Published *Donemus,* 1986. The third of three untitled movements is captioned "Tombeau: Karel Mengelberg in memoriam."

MERCADANTE, SAVERIO, Italian composer; b. Sep. 17, 1795; d. Dec. 17, 1870.

Pisani, Bartolomeo, 1811–1876. *Una lacrima sulla tomba di Mercadante: Canto funebre* (1870?). Mezzo-soprano (or baritone) and piano. Published *Ricordi* 42227, 1871. Text by E. Lifonti.

Rossi, Lauro, 1812–1885. *Elegia in morte di Mercadante* (1876). Voice and orchestra. Unpublished. Source: *MGG.*

Serrao, Paolo, 1830–1907. *Omaggio a Mercadante* (1871). Orchestra. Unpublished. Source: *NGrove.*

MERCURI, AGOSTINO, Italian composer; b. Aug. 2, 1839; d. Feb. 1, 1892.

Belati, Tito, 1865–1941. *Sulla tomba di Agostino Mercuri: Marcia funebre* (1892). Band. Published Florence: A. Lapini, 1892.

MERIKANTO, AARRE, Finnish composer; b. June 29, 1893; d. Sep. 29, 1958.

Kuusisto, Ilkka, 1933– . *In memoriam Aarre Merikanto.* Organ. Published *FIMIC.*

MERIKANTO, OSCAR, Finnish composer; b. Aug. 5, 1868; d. Feb. 17, 1924.

Maasalo, Armas, 1885–1960. *In memoriam Oskar Merikanto,* op. 26, no. 1. Organ. Published *Fazer.*

MERRITT, THOMAS, British composer; b. Oct. 26, 1863; d. Apr. 17, 1908.

Arnold, Sir Malcolm, 1921– . *Salute to Thomas Merritt,* op. 98 (1967). Brass bands (2) and orchestra. Unpublished. Source: *Arnold.* Written to honor the 60ᵗʰ anniversary of the death of Thomas Merritt. First performance March 16, 1968, by the St. Dennis Silver Band, the St. Agnes Silver Band, Penzance Orchestral Society, Cornwall Symphony Orchestra, cond. by Malcolm Arnold at the Truro Cathedral. Autograph score at the Royal College of Music, London.

MESANGEAU, RENÉ, French lutenist; d. 1638?

Anonymous. *Le tombeau de M. Messangior.* Viola-baryton. Unpublished. Source: *Mesangeau,* p. xv. Manuscript source: Murhardsche und Landesbibliothek, Kassel, Ms. 61-L1.

Gaultier, Enemond, ca. 1575–1651. "Allemande, Tombeau de Mesangeau," in *Pieces de luth: En musique avec des regles pour les toucher parfaitem sur le luth et sur le clavessin.* Lute. Published Paris: L'autheur, 1680. *RISM-B1:* 1680/6. Modern edition in Enemond Gaultier, *Oeuvres du vieux Gaultier,* ed. André Souris (Paris: CNRS, 1966).

MESSIAEN, OLIVIER, French composer; b. Dec. 10, 1908; d. Apr. 27, 1992.

Benjamin, George, 1960– . *Three inventions* (1993–95). Chamber orchestra. Published *Faber* 0571517021, 1997. The first invention (untitled), composed 1993 and originally titled "Tribute," is dedicated "In memory of Olivier Messiaen."

Finnissy, Michael, 1946– . *A solis ortus cardine: In memory of Olivier Messiaen* (1992). Piano. Published *OUP,* 1992.

Goehr, Alexander, 1932– . *In memoriam Olivier Messiaen* (1998). Instrumental ensemble. Published *Schott-M,* 1998.

Hakim, Naji, 1955– . *Le tombeau d'Olivier Messiaen* (1993). Organ. Published *UMP,* 1994, in the Organ repertoire series, no. 25. CONTENTS: Par ma vie, par ma mort—Je rends grâce à mon Dieu—Christ avec le Saint-Esprit, dans la gloire du Père.

Hambraeus, Bengt, 1928– . *Missa pro organo: In memoriam Oliv-*

ier Messiaen (1992). Organ. Published *Canadian*. CONTENTS: Introitus—Meditatio super canticum credo—Offertorium—Meditatio sub communione—Postludium.

Harvey, Jonathan, 1939– . *Le tombeau de Messiaen* (1994). Piano and electronic tape. Published *Faber* 0571516262, 1996. Recorded by Philip Mead (SDC Sound Distribution Channel 28029, 1999).

Hummel, Bertold, 1925– . *Trio for flute, oboe, and piano,* op. 95c: *In memoriam Olivier Messiaen*. Published *Zimmermann* 31290, 1995.

Miroglio, Francis, 1924– . *Et les bleu-violets sont dans le si . . .: À la mémoire d'Olivier Messiaen* (1992). Piano. Published *UE* 30158, 1994.

Takemitsu, Toru, 1930–1996. *Rain tree sketch II: In memoriam Olivier Messiaen* (1992). Piano. Published *Schott-J* SJ1072, 1992.

Terényi, Ede, 1935– . *In solemnitate corporis Christi: In memoriam Messiaen* (1993). Organ. Unpublished. Source: *Beckmann.*

Tower, Joan, 1938– . *Très lent: Hommage à Messiaen* (1994). Violoncello and piano. Published *AMP* 8080, 1995. "*Très lent* is written as an hommage to Olivier Messiaen, particularly to his *Quartet for the end of time,* which had a special influence on my work"—caption in score.

MEWTON-WOOD, NOËL, Australian pianist; b. Nov. 20, 1922; d. Dec. 5, 1953.

Bliss, Sir Arthur, 1891–1975. *Elegiac sonnet: In memoriam Noel Mewton-Wood* (1954). Tenor with string quartet, piano. Published *Novello,* 1955. Text by Cecil Day Lewis.

Britten, Lord Benjamin, 1913–1976. *Canticle III: Still falls the rain: To the memory of Noel Mewton-Wood* (1954). Tenor, horn, piano. Published *Boosey* VAB159, 1956. Text by Edith Sitwell.

MEYER, WOLFGANG SEBASTIAN, German organist; b. 1936; d. Jan. 10, 1966.

Stockhausen, Karlheinz, 1928– . *Adieu für Wolfgang Sebastian Meyer* (1966). Woodwind quintet. Published *UE,* 1969.

MEYERBEER, GIACOMO, German composer; b. Sep. 5, 1791; d. May 2, 1864.

Audran, Edmond, 1840–1901. *Funeral march on the death of Meyerbeer* (1864). Orchestra? Unpublished. Source: *NGrove.*

Branzoli, Giuseppe, 1835–1909. *Una lagrima sulla tomba di Giacomo Meyerbeer: Elegia,* op. 18. Violin and piano. Published Milan: Paolo De Giorgi 247.

Galli, Raffaele, 1824–1889. *Alla memoria di Meyerbeer: Tre capricci.* Flute and piano. Published Milan: Giovanni Canti 6321–6323.

Litolff, Henry, 1818–1891. *À la mémoire de Meyerbeer: Marche funèbre,* op. 116. Orchestra. Published *Litolff*; Ricordi, 1864. Also arr. for piano solo (or 4-hands). Manuscript score of the orchestral version located in the Bibliothèque et Musée de l'Opéra, Paris.

Platania, Pietro, 1828–1907. *Bellini e Meyerbeer: Sinfonia caratteristica a grande orchestra* (July 31, 1864). Vocal soloists (SMzTB) with orchestra. Unpublished. Source: *NGrove*. Text by Luigi de Brun ("Salvete o divi geni del canto"). Manuscript at the Conservatorio Santa Cecilia, Rome.

Rossini, Gioachino, 1792–1868. "Chant funèbre" (May 6, 1864), in his *Cori a voci pari o dispari.* Men's chorus and bass drum. Published Pesaro: Fondazioni Rossini, 1958, in the series Quaderni Rossiniani, vol. 7. Text by Emilien Pacini. The manuscript, in the Liceo musicale in Pesaro, has the inscription "Quelques mésures de chant funèbre à mon pauvre ami Meyerbeer. 8 heurs du matin, Paris, 6 mai 1864." Meyerbeer's death also provoked wry comment from Rossini. "Verdi told Italo Pizzi that a young nephew of Meyerbeer composed a funeral march for the dead man, and then went to play it on the piano for Rossini, soliciting his approval. . . . [Rossini responded] 'Very good, very good! But, truthfully, wouldn't it have been better if *you* had died and your poor uncle had composed the march?'"—*Rossini*, p. 327.

Zeni, Antonio. *Canto affettuoso sulla tomba di Meyerbeer.* Piano. Published Milan: Albini 333, 187– .

MIASKOVSKY, NICOLAI, Russian composer; b. Aug. 20, 1881; d. Aug. 8, 1950.

Eshpai, Andrei, 1925– . *Passacaglia: In memory of N. Ia. Miaskovsky* (1951). Organ. Unpublished. Source: *Eshpai*.

———. *Concerto for violin and orchestra no. 2: Pamiati N. IA. Miaskovskogo* (1977). Published Moscow: Sov. Kompozitor, 1979.

Khachaturian, Aram, 1903–1978. *Sonata for piano: In memory of Nicolay Miaskowsky my teacher* (1961). Published *Muzyka*, 1964. Rev. edition published *Muzyka*, 1976. Also in Khachaturian, *Sochineniia dlia fortepiano,* Sobranie sochinenii [Works], vol. 21 (Moscow: Izdatelstvo Muzyka; *Sikorski*, 1983).

MICHAEL, TOBIAS, German composer; b. June 13, 1592; d. June 26, 1657.

Michael, Tobias, 1592–1657. *Christliche Gedancken über den müh-seligen Lebenslauf Hrn. Tobias Michael . . . welche er . . . bey seiner Beerdigung zu musiciren begehret, welches geschehen den 30 Iuni 1657.* Voices (5). Published Leipzig: I. E. Hahn, 1657. *RISM-A1*: M-2640. Composed by Michael for his own funeral.

MIKHASHOFF, YVAR, American pianist, composer; b. Mar. 8, 1941; d. Oct. 11, 1993.

Finnissy, Michael, 1946– . *Yvaroperas: In memory of Yvar Mik-hashoff* (1993–94). Piano. Published *OUP*, 1994.

MILÁN, LUIS DE, Spanish musician, courtier, poet; b. 1500 (ca.); d. after 1561.

Lerich, Pierre, 1937– . *Le tombeau de Luys Milan.* Guitar. Published *Billaudot* 3742, 1983.

MILHAUD, DARIUS, French composer; b. Sep. 4, 1892; d. June 22, 1974.

Andriessen, Louis, 1939– . *Hymne: To the memory of Darius Mil-haud, juni 1974* (1978). Orchestra. Published *Donemus*, 1978.

Armer, Elinor, 1939– . *Mirror, mirror: In memory of Darius Mil-haud* (1995). Piano 4-hands. Published Berkeley, CA: Fallen Leaf Press FLPCM60, 1995.

Harrison, Lou, 1917– . "Homage to Milhaud" (1978), in *12 x 11: Piano music in twentieth century America,* compiled and ed. by Maurice Hinson. Published *Hinshaw*, 1979.

Rands, Bernard, 1934– . *Scherzi: To the memory of Darius Mil-haud* (1974). Quartet for clarinet/bass clarinet, violin, violoncello, piano. Published *UE-L* 16048, 1978.

Tansman, Alexandre, 1897–1986. *Elégie: À la mémoire de Darius Milhaud* (1976). Orchestra. Published *Eschig*, 1976.

MILLER, GLENN, American trombonist, band leader; b. Mar. 1, 1904; d. Dec. 16, 1944.

Schanke, David. *Five mellow winds: To the memory of Glenn Miller.* Solo woodwind quintet (or clarinet, saxophones (4)) with concert band. Published *Chappell*, 1959.

MILLER, ROBERT, American pianist; b. Dec. 5, 1930; d. Nov. 30, 1981.

Sollberger, Harvey, 1938– . *Angel and stone: To the memory of Robert Miller* (1981; rev. 1983). Flute and piano. Published *ACA*, 1983.

MITROPOULOS, DIMITRI, Greek-born American conductor, composer; b. Mar. 1, 1896; d. Mar. 1, 1960.

Cordero, Roque, 1917– . *Mensaje fúnebre: In memoriam Dmitri Mitropoulos* (1961). Clarinet and string orchestra. Published *Peer-I*, 1961.

Schuller, Gunther, 1925– . *Threnos: In memoriam Dimitri Mitropoulos* (1963). Oboe and orchestra. Published *AMP*.

MOMPOU, FEDERICO, Spanish composer; b. Apr. 16, 1893; d. June 30, 1987.

Halffter, Cristobal, 1930– . *Cancion callada: In memoriam Federico Mompou* (1988). Piano trio. Unpublished. Source: *ConCom*.

Mairants, Ivor, 1908–1998. *Hommage à Mompou.* Guitar solo. Published *UMP*, 1989

Pablo, Luis de, 1930– . *Federico Mompou in memoriam: Da caligrafías* (1988). Piano trio. Published *Zerboni* 9845, 1993.

MONK, THELONIOUS, American jazz pianist, composer; b. Oct. 10, 1918; d. Feb. 17, 1982.

Amram, David, 1930– . *Blues and variations for Monk* (1982). Horn solo. Published *Peters* 67130, 1991. "In memory of Thelonious Monk for his friendship and inspiration"—dedication in score.

Castérède, Jacques, 1926– . *Hommage à Thélonious Monk* (1983). Piano. Published *Leduc* AL26232, 1983. CONTENTS: Portrait—Apocalypsis rock.

MONTEUX, PIERRE, French conductor; b. Apr. 4, 1875; d. July 1, 1964.

Creston, Paul, 1906–1985. *Introit for orchestra,* op. 87: *Hommage à Pierre Monteux* (1965). Orchestra. Published *Schirmer*.

Milhaud, Darius, 1892–1974. *Elégie pour Pierre: En mémoire de mon cher Pierre Monteux* (1965). Viola, percussion (2 players), timpani. Unpublished. Source: *OCLC*. Holograph score is at the Library of Congress.

Schuller, Gunther, 1925– . *Four soundscapes: Dedicated to the memory of Pierre Monteux* (1974). Orchestra. Published *AMP* 7738, 1978.

Stravinsky, Igor, 1882–1971. *Canon: For concert introduction or encore* (1965). Orchestra. Published *Boosey* FSB414, 1973. Theme is from the finale of Stravinsky's *L'oiseau de feu.* Also known as *Canon on a Russian popular theme.* Memorial dedication is according to *Caesar*, though no dedication appears in the published score.

MONTEVERDI, CLAUDIO, Italian composer; b. May 15, 1567; d. Nov. 29, 1643.

Poulenc, Francis, 1899–1963. *Dialogues des Carmelites* (1956).

Opera in 3 acts. Published *Ricordi-P* R1471, 1957. "À la mémoire de ma mère, qui m'a révélé la musique, de Claude Debussy, qui m'a donné le goût d'en écrire, de Claudio Monteverdi, Giuseppe Verdi, Modeste Moussorgski, qui m'ont servi ici de modèles"—dedication in score. Text by Georges Bernanos.

MONTGOMERY, WES, American jazz guitarist; b. Mar. 6, 1923; d. June 15, 1968.

Duarte, John W., 1919– . *Sua cosa,* op. 52: *To the memory of Wes Montgomery and to Angelo Gilardino, whose idea this was* (1972). Published *Berben* 2043, 1975. "In one of his last recordings Wes Montgomery played a piece of his own which he called 'Mi Cosa' ('My Thing') (sic) and I have taken some phrases from this in building the central part (A major) of this piece; it also explains the title I have given it"—composer's note in score.

MORLEY, THOMAS, English composer; b. 1557; d. Oct. 1602.

Weelkes, Thomas, ca. 1575–1623. "Death hath deprived me," in his *Ayeres or phantasticke spirites for three voices.* Published London: William Barley, 1608. *RISM-A1:* W-487. Modern edition in *Airs, or fantastic spirits,* 2 vols., ed. G. E. P. Arkwright (London: J. Williams, 1895–1896). This, the final work in the collection, is for six voices, composed "as a remembrance for my friend Mr. Thomas Morley."

MORONDO, LUIS, Spanish choral conductor; d. 1983.

González Acilu, Agustin, 1929– . *Pater noster: A Luis Morondo in memoriam* (1983). Chorus (SSSAAATTTBBB) unacc. Published *Tripharia* MV1, 1984.

MORRISON, JIM, American rock musician; b. Dec. 8, 1943; d. July 3, 1971.

Huber, Hans. "Prelude 8: In memoriam Jim Morrison," in his *Ten preludes for piano.* Published *ConBrio* CD1104, 1998. CONTENTS: Prelude 1: Von D7'9 bis Ab—Prelude 2: Für Angie—Prelude 3: Begegnungen—Prelude 4: Lavendelfelder in der Provence—Prelude 5: Quartendialog—Prelude 6: Für Jasmin—Prelude 7: Berceuse—Prelude 8: In memoriam Jim Morrison—Prelude 9: Der Clown tritt auf—Prelude 10: Das verlorene Lachen.

MOSCHELES, IGNAZ, Czech-born pianist, composer; b. May 23, 1794; d. Mar. 10, 1870.

Kirchner, Theodor, 1823–1903. "Vivace," in his *Gedenkblätter: Zwölf Musikstücke zur Erinnerung an die Einweihung des neuen Königl. Conservatoriums für Musik zu Leipzig,* op. 82 (1843–87).

Piano. Published Leipzig: J. Rieter-Biedermann 1508, 1887. No. 7 of 12 short piano pieces memorializing Conrad Schleinitz, Felix Mendelssohn, Robert Schumann, Moritz Hauptmann, Ferdinand David, Ignaz Moscheles, Ernst Friedrich Richter, Carl Ferdinand Becker, Ernst Ferdinand Wenzel, and Louis Plaidy.

MOSONYI, MIHALY, Hungarian composer; b. Sep. 4, 1814; d. Oct. 31, 1870.

Liszt, Franz, 1811–1886. *Mosonyi gaszmenete = Mosonyis Grabgeleit* (Nov. 1870). Piano. Published Pest: Taborszky & Parsch T&P200, 1871. New edition in Liszt, *Hungarian and late piano works*, Liszt Society publications, vol. 3 (*Schott-L* 5805, 1954).

MOSSMAN, SHEILA, English choral conductor; b. 1923; d. Aug. 17, 1971.

Bliss, Sir Arthur, 1891–1975. *Prayer of Saint Francis of Assisi: In memoriam Sheila Mossman* (1972). Chorus (SSAA) unacc. Published *Novello*, 1973. Also published as a musical supplement in the journal *Musical times* 1568 (1973).

MOTTA, JOSÉ VIANNA DA, Portuguese pianist; b. Apr. 22, 1868; d. May 31, 1948.

Santos, Joly Braga, 1924–1988. *Elegia a Vianna da Motta* (1948). Orchestra. Unpublished. Recorded by the Orquestra Clássica do Porto, cond. by Meir Minsky (Koch-Schwann 3-1510-2, 1993).

MOUTON, CHARLES, French lutenist; b. 1626; d. 1699?

Visée, Robert de, ca. 1650–ca. 1725. "Le tombeau de Mr. Mouton, allemande," in *Manuscrit Vaudry de Saizenay: Tablature de luth et de théorbe de divers auteurs* (1699). Lute. Published *Minkoff* 2826606859, 1980, which is a facsimile of the manuscript source, Besançon, Bibliothèque de la ville, Ms. 279.152, 279.153.

MOZART, WOLFGANG AMADEUS, Austrian composer; b. Jan. 27, 1756; d. Dec. 5, 1791.

Argento, Dominick, 1927– . *Bravo Mozart!: An imaginary biography for orchestra: Dedicated to the memory of W. A. M.* (1969). Published *Boosey* HPS940, 1978. Incorporates quotations from Mozart's piano works K. 1, 3, 355, 574, 399, and 236.

Boone, Charles, 1939– . *Oblique formation* (1965). Flute and piano. Published *Salabert*, 1970. "For Benjamin Borson, Günter Grass and the memory of W. A. Mozart"—dedication in score.

Cannabich, Carl, 1771–1806. *Feyert! Feyert! . . . Mozarts Gedaechtnis Feyer seinen Manen gewidmet.* Soloists, chorus, orchestra. Published Munich: Macario Falter, 1797. *RISM-A1*: C-848.

Danzi, Franz, 1763–1826. *Cantate am Jahrestage von Mozarts Tod zu singen.* Voice and piano. Published *Schott-M* 360, 179–? *RISM-A1*: D-922.

Eberl, Anton, 1765–1807. *Cantate bey Mozarts Grab* (1791). Cantata. Unpublished. Source: *NGrove.* Manuscript of piano reduction is at the library of Karl-Marx-Universität Leipzig.

Françaix, Jean, 1912–1997. *Elégie pour 10 instruments à vent: Pour commémorer le bicentenaire de la mort de W. A. Mozart* (1990). Ensemble of flute, alto flute, oboe, English horn, basset horn, bass clarinet, bassoon, contrabassoon, French horns (2). Published *Schott-M*, 1991.

Franzen, Olov, 1946– . *In memoriam 1791 sopra Requiem di W. A. Mozart* (1991). Winds. Unpublished. Source: *Stoneham.*

Haydn, Joseph, 1732–1809. "Adagio cantabile," in his *Sinfonie à grand orchestre, Oe. 80, Livre 2* [Symphonies, H. I, 98, B-flat major. Adagio cantabile] (1791). Published Offenbach: André 911, 1796. *RISM-A1*: H-3194. Various later editions. The fourth "London" symphony. According to Donald Tovey in *Essays in Musical Analysis*, vol. 1, p. 153 (*OUP*, 1935), "The slow movement might almost be called his Requiem for Mozart, the news of whose death had so deeply shocked him during his London visit."

Kraus, Joseph Martin, 1756–1792. "Ofver Mozarts död," in his *Skalde-stycken satte i musik.* Song. Published Stockholm: s.n., 1794. Source: *Kraus.* Autograph manuscript (Kungliga Biblioteket, Stockholm, MS Vf.37) bears the memorial dedication to Mozart. The published version has a different text.

Lodi, Joseph Ludwig, fl. 1796–1800. *La morte di Mozart: Sinfonia per il pianoforte,* op. 27. Published *Breitkopf* 27, 1795. "Luigi" Lodi in *CPM.*

Martin, Frank, 1890–1974. *Ouverture en hommage à Mozart* (1956). Orchestra. Published *UE*, 1962. Commissioned by Radio Geneva for a broadcast concert in memory of Mozart on the bicentennial of his birth.

Mettraux, Laurent, 1970– . *Lacrimosa: In memoriam W. A. M.: 5. 12. 1791.* (1990). Orchestra. Published *Mettraux* M458, 1990.

Mozart, Franz Xaver Wolfgang, 1791–1844. *Festchor mit Pianoforte-Begleitung,* op. 30: *Zur Enthüllung des Mozart- Denkmales in Salzburg.* Vocal soloists with chorus, orchestra. Published Vienna: T. Haslinger, 1842. Composed for the unveiling of the Mozart memorial in Salzburg. Based on motives from Wolfgang Amadeus's opera *La clemenza di Tito*, with text by Franz Xaver Mozart. Published edition is a piano reduction.

Rosetti (Rössler), Anton, ca. 1750–1792. *Requiem* (1791). Music is lost. Composed for a memorial service for Mozart in Prague. According to *NGrove* and *MGG*, only the title page survives in the Schwerin Landesbibliothek.

Schneider, George Abraham, 1770–1839. *Trois quintetti: Dédiéz aux mânes de Mozart.* Quintet for violins (2), violas (2), violoncello. Published Paris: chez Cardon 10–12; chez Salomon, between 1795–1803?

Stracke, Hans Richard, 1932– . *Mozart-Epitaph: Fantasie for organ* (1985–89). Unpublished. Source: *Beckmann*.

Tiensuu, Jukka, 1948– . *Le tombeau de Mozart* (1990). Trio for violin, clarinet, piano. Published *SMT* 11043, 1992.

Torres-Santos, Raymond, 1958– . *Danza: From "Variaciones puertorriqueñas sobre un tema de Mozart"* (1991). Orchestra. Published San Juan, PR: RTS Music, 1991. Commissioned by the Casals Festival in honor of the bicentennial of Mozart's death.

Villa-Lobos, Heitor, 1887–1959. *Sinfonietta no. 1: A memoria de Mozart* (1916). Small orchestra. Published *Peer-S* 61119-851, 1955.

Webbe, Samuel, 1770–1843. *Father of Heav'n: Quartett from the epicedium on Mozart . . . the translation (from the German) & the music adapted by S. Webbe Junr.* Voices (SATB) with piano. Published London: R. Birchall, 1795?

Wessely, Carl Bernhard, 1768–1826. *Mozarts Urne* (1791). Cantata. Published Berlin: s.n., 1791. Source: *NGrove*. Text by Gottlob Wilhelm Burmann. Announced in the *Musikalisches Wochenblatt* of December 10, 1791.

MUENCH, GERHART, German-Mexican pianist, composer; b. Mar. 23, 1907; d. Nov. 9, 1988.

Lavista, Mario, 1943– . *Lacrymosa: A la memoria de Gerhart Muench* (1992). Orchestra. Published *Mexicanas* E39, 1993.

MUL, JAN, Dutch composer; b. Sep. 20, 1911; d. Dec. 30, 1971.

Strategier, Herman, 1912–1988. *Mors responsura: In memoriam fratris spiritualis Jan Mul* (1972). Vocal soloists (SA), chorus (SATB), orchestra. Published *Donemus*, 1972.

MÜLLER, HEINRICH I., German theologian, composer; b. 1631; d. Sep. 17, 1675.

Barclaius, L., fl. 1675. *Klagstimmen über den Tod Henr. Müllers* (1675). Unpublished. Source: *EitnerQL*. The composer apparently is known only for this work. *EitnerQL* gives as source the "Kat. Stargard," not identified in Eitner's sigla, but probably refers to a library at or near Stargard Szczecinski, Poland.

MUNCH, CHARLES, French conductor; b. Sep. 26, 1891; d. Nov. 6, 1968.

> **Dutilleux, Henry, 1916– .** *Timbres, espace, mouvement, ou, La nuit étoilée: À la mémoire de Charles Munch* (1978). Orchestra. Published *Heugel* PH307, 1980.

> **Landowski, Marcel, 1915–2000.** *Messe de l'aurore: À la mémoire de Charles Munch* (1977). Solo voices (STB), chorus (SATBSATB), and orchestra. Published *Salabert* EAS17287, 1977. Text by Pierre Emmanuel.

MUNROW, DAVID, English recorder player; b. Aug. 12, 1942; d. May 15, 1976.

> **Crosse, Gordon, 1937– .** *Verses: In memoriam David Munrow* (1979). Countertenor with trio of recorder, violoncello, harpsichord. Published *OUP* R5278, 1979.

> **Dickinson, Peter, 1934– .** *A Memory of David Munrow* (1977). Countertenors (2) with recorders (2), viola da gamba, harpsichord. Unpublished. Source: *ConCom.* Wordless.

MURESIANU, IACOB, Romanian composer; b. June 29, 1857; d. May 25, 1917.

> **Popovici, Doru, 1932– .** *In memoriam Iacob Muresianu.* Chorus (SSAA). Published in *Muzica* 33/3 (March 1983): 25–28. Text by Martha Popovici.

MUSSORGSKY, MODEST, Russian composer; b. Mar. 21, 1839; d. Mar. 28, 1881.

> **Poulenc, Francis, 1899–1963.** *Dialogues des Carmelites* (1956). Opera in 3 acts. Published *Ricordi-P* R1471, 1957. "À la mémoire de ma mère, qui m'a révélé la musique, de Claude Debussy, qui m'a donné le goût d'en écrire, de Claudio Monteverdi, Giuseppe Verdi, Modeste Moussorgski, qui m'ont servi ici de modèles"—dedication in score. Text by Georges Bernanos.

> **Rimsky-Korsakov, Nikolay, 1844–1908.** *Svetlyi prazdnik vskresnaia uvertiura = Ouverture "La grande Pâque Russe": À la mémoire de Moussorgski et de Borodine* (1888). Orchestra. Published *Belaieff* 245, 1890. New edition in Rimsky-Korsakov, *Sochineniia dlia orkestra*, Polnoie sobranie sochineni [Works], vol. 21 (*Muzyka*, 1958). Popularly known in English as the *Russian Easter overture.*

NABOKOV, NICOLAS, Russian composer; b. Apr. 17, 1903; d. Apr. 6, 1978.

Reimann, Aribert, 1936– . *Lear: In memory of Nicolas Nabokov* (1976–78). Opera after Shakespeare. Published *Schott-M* 6857, 1978.

NANNY, ÉDOUARD, French double bassist; b. Mar. 24, 1872; d. Dec. 12, 1942.

Bozza, Eugène, 1905–1991. *Pièce sur le nom d'Édouard Nanny* (1946). Double bass and piano. Published *Leduc* AA20469, 1956.

NAUMANN, JOHANN GOTTLIEB, German composer; b. Apr. 17, 1741; d. Oct. 23, 1801.

Berger, Ludwig, 1777–1839. *Trauercantata auf Naumanns Tod* (1801). Vocal soloists, chorus, orchestra. Unpublished. Source: *Berger*. Manuscript score in the Deutsche Staatsbibliothek, Berlin.

Tag, Christian Gotthilf, 1735–1811. *Naumann: Ein Todtenopfer* (1803). Voice and piano. Unpublished. Source: *Tag*. Cited in *NGrove* as *Todtenopfer unserm vollendeten Naumann*.

NELSON, OLIVER EDWARD, American saxophonist, composer; b. June 4, 1932; d. Oct. 27, 1975.

Wykes, Robert, 1926– . *In memoriam Oliver Nelson: Two short pieces*. Flute and piano. Published Berkeley, CA: Fallen Leaf Press FLPCM46, 1990.

NERUDA, FRANZ XAVER, Bohemian violoncellist; b. Dec. 3, 1843; d. Mar. 20, 1915.

Nielsen, Carl, 1865–1931. *Prologue: In memoriam Franz Neruda* (1915). Narrator and orchestra. Unpublished. Source: *Nielsen*. Text by Julius Clausen. First performance in Copenhagen October 11, 1915, the composer conducting. Manuscript in the Royal Library, Copenhagen.

NEWTON, FRANKIE, American swing trumpeter; b. Jan. 4, 1906; d. Mar. 11, 1954.

Mailman, Martin, 1932– . *In memoriam Frankie Newton,* op. 50 (1970). Stage band or concert band. Published *Southern* O17, 1971.

NIELSEN, CARL, Danish composer; b. June 9, 1865; d. Oct. 3, 1931.

Langgaard, Rued, 1893–1952. *Carl Nielsen: Vor store Komponist!* = *Carl Nielsen: Our great composer!* (1948). Chorus (SATB) and organ (or orchestra). Published *SUDM*. This work is included for the sake of ironic counterpoint. It is one of Langgaard's "most desperate—and sarcastic—utterances. In a foreword to the piece (the whole text of which is identical to the title) Langgaard complains at having had to live and breathe in a musical Denmark 'infested' by Carl Nielsen. Langgaard was highly critical of Nielsen . . . and his music, even though the latter was one of Langgaard's most important sources of inspiration around 1920. . . . The work comprises thirty-two bars, and after the last bar Langgaard dictates that the work is to be 'repeated to eternity!'"—note by Bendt Viinholt Nielsen accompanying the premiere recording by the Danish National Radio Symphony Orchestra, the Danish National Radio Choir, cond. by Gennady Rozhdestvensky, together with other works by Langgaard on *The end of time* (Chandos CHAN 9786, 2000).

NIKOLAYEV, LEONID, Russian pianist, pedagogue; b. Aug. 13, 1878; d. Oct. 11, 1942.

Shostakovich, Dmitri, 1906–1975. *Sonata for piano no. 2, op. 61, B minor: Dedicated to the memory of Leonid Nikolaev* (Feb.–Mar. 1943). Published Moscow: Muzgiz 17846, 1943. Subsequent editions by *MCA*, *Peters*, and *Muzyka*.

NOBLE, T. TERTIUS, English organist, composer; b. May 5, 1867; d. May 4, 1953.

Schuller, Gunther, 1925– . *Triptych* (1976). Organ. Published *AMP* 7806, 1981. "*Triptych* is dedicated to [the memory of] T. Tertius Noble, my first 'master' and harmony/counterpoint teacher"—composer's note in score.

NOEL, HENRY, English court musician; fl. 1592.

Weelkes, Thomas, ca. 1575–1623. "Noel, adieu thou court's delight," in his *Madrigals of 5 and 6 parts, apt for the viols and voices.* Voices (6). Published London: Thomas Este, 1600. *RISM-A1*: W-486. Modern edition in Weelkes, *Madrigals of six parts*, The English madrigal school, vol. 12 (*Stainer*, 1916).

NONO, LUIGI, Italian composer; b. Jan. 29, 1924; d. May 8, 1990.

Kancheli, Giia, 1935– . *Lament: Music of mourning in memory of Luigi Nono* (1994). Violin and soprano soloists with orchestra. Published *Schirmer*. Text from Hans Sahl's *Strophen.*

Klebe, Giselher, 1925– . *Glockentürme, op. 103: Komponiert im Andenken an Luigi Nono, gest. 8. Mai 1990* (1990). Piano 4-hands. Published *Bärenreiter* BA7225, 1997.

Rihm, Wolfgang, 1952– . *Cantus firmus: Musik in memoriam Luigi Nono: 1. Versuch* (1990). Ensemble of 14 instruments. Published *UE*, 1990.

————. *Ricercare: Musik in memoriam Luigi Nono: 2. Versuch* (1990). Ensemble of 14 instruments. Published *UE*, 1990.

————. *Abgewandt II: Musik in memoriam Luigi Nono: 3. Versuch* (1990). Ensemble of 14 instruments. Published *UE*, 1990.

————. *Umfassung: Musik in memoriam Luigi Nono: 4. Versuch* (1990). Orchestra in two groups. Published *UE*, 1990.

————. *La lugubre gondola: Das Eismeer: Musik in memoriam Luigi Nono: 5. Versuch* (1990–92). Orchestra in two groups and piano. Published *UE*, 1992

Tarnopolskii, Vladimir, 1955– . *La crimoso: In memoriam Luigi Nono* (1990). Percussion ensemble. Unpublished. Source: *ConCom.*

NORDRAAK, RIKARD, Norwegian composer; b. June 12, 1842; d. Mar. 20, 1866.

Grieg, Edvard, 1843–1907. *Sorgemarsch over Rikard Nordraak* (1866). Piano. Published Copenhagen: Chr. E. Hornemans Forlag, 1866. Other editions: *Trauermarsch zum Andenken zu Richard Nordraak* (*Peters* 7376, 1899); reprinted in vol. 3 of Grieg's *Werke für Klavier zu 2 Händen* (*Peters* 10038). Nordraak was the composer of the Norwegian national anthem, and a friend of Grieg in his youth. For a brief study of Grieg's 1899 arrangement of this work for band, see John Jay Hilfiger, "Edvard Grieg's funeral march in memory of Rikard Nordraak for military band," *Journal of band research* 24/2 (Spring 1989): 12–16.

NOTORIOUS B. I. G. (BIGGIE SMALLS), American rap musician.; b. 1972; d. Mar. 9, 1997.

Puff Daddy (Sean "Puffy" Combs) with Faith Evans. *Tribute to the Notorious B. I. G.* (1997). Collection of rap songs recorded by the composers (Bad Boy Records 78612-79097-2, 1997). CONTENTS: I'll be missing you—We'll always love Big Poppa—Cry on—I'll be missing you (instrumental)—We'll always love Big Poppa (instrumental). Dedicatee's real name: Chris Wallace. Faith Evans was married to B. I. G. The lead song "I'll be missing you," which was also issued as a single, borrows heavily from "Every breath you take" by the musical group Police. For more on the death of this rap musician, see Cathy Scott, *The murder of Biggie Smalls* (New York: St. Martin's Press, 2000).

OCKEGHEM, JOHANNES, Flemish composer; b. 1410?; d. Feb. 6, 1496.
Busnois, Antoine, ca. 1430–1492. "In hydraulis" (between 1465–

67?), in *Sechs Trienter Codices: Geistliche und weltliche Compositionen des XV Jahrhunderts,* 1. Auswahl, p. 105, Denkmäler der Tonkunst in Österreich, vol. 14, ed. By Guido Adler. Voices (4). Published Vienna: Artaria, 1900. New edition in Busnois, *The Latin-texted works,* Collected works, vol. 2, ed. Richard Taruskin, Masters and monuments of the Renaissance, vol. 5 (*Broude,* 1990). Text by Busnois. Manuscript source: Bayerische Staatsbibliothek, Mus. Ms. 3154 ("Chorbuch des Nikolaus Leopold"). Though composed in tribute to Ockeghem before his death, the work is included in the study of laments by *Geary,* and thus is cited here as well.

Hanard, Martin, fl. 1465–1500. A lament for Ockeghem by Hanard is lost. Source: *Brenet.*

Josquin des Prez, ca. 1440–1521. "Nymphes des bois, la déploration de Johan Okeghem," in *Septiesme livre contenant vingt et quatre chansons a cincq et a six parties . . . avecq troix epitaphes dudict Josquin, composez par divers aucteurs.* Voices (5). Published Antwerp: Tielman Susato, 1545. *RISM-B1*: 1545/15. Text by Jean Molinet. The music was published earlier without the French text in the collection *Motetti a cinque, libro primo* (Venice: Petrucci, 1508), *RISM-B1*: 1508/1. Another version was copied in the Medici Codex and is published in facsimile and modern transcription in *The Medici codex of 1518,* ed. Edward Lowinsky, Monuments of Renaissance music, vol. 3–5 (Chicago: University of Chicago Press, 1968). Lowinsky considers the Medici codex version superior to Petrucci's textless and Susato's "adulterated" versions; see notes in his edition for particulars.

Károlyi, Pál, 1934– . *Ad Lydiam: In memoriam Jean de Ockeghem* (1967). Chorus unacc. Unpublished. Source: *NGrove.* Text from Horace.

Lupus, fl. 1518–1530. "Ergo ne conticuit, in Joa Okegi musicorum principem, Naenia," in *Liber tertius sacrum cantionum, quatuor vocum.* Voices (4). Published Antwerp: Tielman Susato, 1547. *RISM-B1*: 1547/5. Text by Erasmus.

Obrecht, Jacob, 1450?–1505. "Missa Sicut spina rosam," in *New Obrecht edition,* vol. 11, ed. by Barton Hudson. Voices (4). Published *VNM,* 1990. Manuscript source: Universitätsbibliothek Jena, Manuscript 22 (ca. 1500). The memorial intent is the editor's conjecture; see *Hudson.*

Parik, Ivan, 1936– . *In memoriam Ockeghem* (1972). Electronic tape. Unpublished. Source: *NGrove.*

OGDON, JOHN, English pianist; b. Jan. 27, 1937; d. Aug. 1, 1989.

Rumson, Gordon, 1960– . *Threnody for John Ogdon: In the form of chorale variations with introduction and finale* (1990). Piano. Published *Sikesdi*, 1991.

ONNOU, ALPHONSE, Belgian violinist; b. 1893; d. Nov. 19, 1940.

Stravinsky, Igor, 1882–1971. *Elegie* (1944). Violin (or viola) solo. Published *Schott-L* 4477, 1945. Later edition: *Boosey* SVB11, 1972. "Composée à l'intention de Germain Prevost pour être jouée à la mémoire de Alphonse Onnou, fondateur de Quatuor Pro Arte"— dedication in score.

ORDZHONIKIDZE, GIVI, Russian musicologist; b. June 9, 1929; d. 1984.

Kancheli, Giia, 1935– . *Vom Winde beweint: Liturgie in memoriam Giwi Ordschonikidse = Mourned by the wind: Liturgy in memory of Givi Ordzhonikidze* (1989). Solo viola and orchestra. Published *Sikorski* 1832, 1996.

O RIADA, SEÁN (JOHN RIEDY), Irish composer; b. Aug. 1, 1931; d. Oct. 3, 1971.

Bodley, Seóirse, 1933– . *In memory of Seán O Riada* (1971). Flute and piano. Unpublished. Source: *Irish-82*.

Kinsella, John, 1932– . *A selected life: In memoriam Seán O Riada* (1973). Tenor solo, speaker, chorus, orchestra. Unpublished. Source: *Irish-82*.

ORLOWSKI, ANTONI, Polish violinist, pianist, conductor, composer; b. 1811; d. Feb. 11, 1861.

Moniuszko, Stanislaw, 1819–1872. "Marsz zalobny Antoniego Orlowskiego = Trauermarsch Antoni Orlowskis," in his *Muzyka instrumentalna I = Instrumentalmusik I,* Dziela = Werke [Works], vol. 32. Orchestra. Published *PWM*, 1993. May be an arrangement or transcription of a work by Orlowski. Autograph is in the Warszawskie Towarzystwo Muzyczne (Warsaw), sig. 315/M.

OSBORNE, RICHARD, English composer; d. 1737.

Carey, Henry, 1687?–1743. *Where is my soul's chief comfort flown: The muse's tears . . . an elegiac ode to the memory of that sober ingenious youth Mr. Richard Osborne.* Song? Published London: ca. 1737. *RISM-A1*: C-1215. Text by the composer.

OTHMAYR, CASPAR, German composer; b. Mar. 12, 1515; d. Feb. 4, 1553.

In epitaphiis Gasparis Othmari. Voices. Published Nuremberg: Berg & Neuber?, 1554. *RISM-B1*: 1554/30. Only the bass part is ex-

tant in the British Library. CONTENTS: Justi praeripiuntur; Mit Fried
und Freud / by Caspar Othmayr, 1515–1553—E vaevo Gaspar / by
Nicolaus Puls, fl. 1553—Harmonicae decus / by Conrad Praetorius,
ca. 1515–1555—Grande decus musis / by Andraeas Schwartz, fl.
1553—Grande decus musis / by Hans Buchner, 1483–1538—Prae
reliquis / by Andraeas Schwartz, fl. 1553—Est locus elysium / by
Georg Forster, 1510?–1568.

OVERTON, HALL, American composer; b. Feb. 23, 1920; d. Nov. 24,
1972.

> **Moore, Carman, 1936– .** *Gospel fuse: To the memory of Hall Over-
> ton.* Gospel quartet (SSAA) and orchestra. Published *Peer-S,* 1978.
> Text by the composer.

PACINI, GIOVANNI, Italian composer; b. Feb. 17, 1796; d. Dec. 6,
1867.

> **Mercadante, Saverio, 1795–1870.** *Omaggio a Pacini: Fantasia in
> quattro parte* (1868). Orchestra. Published *Ricordi,* 1868. Published
> version is for piano solo. Orchestral manuscript located in Naples,
> Conservatorio de Musica S. Pietro a Majella.

> **Platania, Pietro, 1828–1907.** *Sinfonia: Scritta in occasione della
> pompa funebre celebrata in onore dell'illustre maestro G. Pacini.*
> Orchestra. Published Milan: Francesco Lucca 17643, 1868?

PACK, ROWLAND, Canadian violoncellist, conductor; b. July 15, 1927;
d. Jan. 3, 1964.

> **Glick, Srul Irving, 1934– .** *Elegy for orchestra* (1964). Published
> *Canadian.* In memory of three Toronto violoncellists who died in
> 1964: John Adaskin, Isaac Mammot, and Rowland Pack.

PADEREWSKI, IGNACY JAN, Polish pianist, composer; b. Nov. 6, 1860;
d. June 29, 1941.

> *Homage to Paderewski.* Piano. Published *Boosey,* 1942. CONTENTS:
> Three Hungarian folk-tunes / by Béla Bartók, 1881–1945—Elegiac
> mazurka / by Arthur Benjamin, 1893–1960—Hommage a Pad-
> erewski / by Mario Castelnuovo-Tedesco, 1895–1968—Aftermath /
> by Theodore Chanler, 1902–1961—Homage / by Eugene Goossens,
> 1893–1962—Dance / by Richard Hammond, 1896– —Threnody / by
> Felix Roderick Labunski, 1895–1974—Mazurka / by Bohuslav Mar-
> tinu, 1890–1959—Choral / by Darius Milhaud, 1892–1974—In
> memoriam Paderewski / by Joaquin Nin-Culmell, 1908– —
> Kujawiak / by Karol Rathaus, 1895–1954—Allegro danzante / by

Vittorio Rieti, 1898–1994—[Untitled] / by Ernst Schelling, 1876–1939—Cradle song / by Sigismond Stojowski, 1869–1946—Etude in G major / by Jaromir Weinberger, 1896–1967—Hommage / by Emerson Whithorn, 1884–1958. "Because two copies are required for performance, Mr. Benjamin Britten's contribution to this album [Mazurka elegiaca] . . . has been issued in separate form"—note in score.

Britten, Lord Benjamin, 1913–1976. *Mazurka elegiaca,* op. 23 (1941). Pianos (2). Published *Boosey* PFB101, 1942. Composed for the collection *Homage to Paderewski* (q.v.). "Because two copies are required for performance, Mr. Benjamin Britten's contribution to this album . . . has been issued in separate form" —note in score.

PAGANINI, NICCOLÒ, Italian violinist, composer; b. Oct. 27, 1782; d. May 27, 1840.

Bentzon, Niels Viggo, 1919–2000. *Paganini variations,* op. 241: *Niccolò Paganini in memoriam* (1968). Piano. Published *Hansen* 4198, 1968.

Ruggieri, Pietro, 1801–1866. *Il 28 settembre 1853, giorno della tumulazione della salma di Nicolò Paganini: Marcia funebre* (1853). Band. Published *Ricordi,* 1853. Composed for the reburial of Paganini's remains, Sept. 28, 1853.

Vieuxtemps, Henry, 1820–1881. *Hommage à Paganini: Caprice pour le violon avec acc. de piano,* op. 9. Violin and orchestra (or piano). Published *Peters,* 1846.

PAISIELLO, GIOVANNI, Italian composer; b. May 9, 1740; d. June 5, 1816.

Platania, Pietro, 1828–1907. *A Giovanni Paisiello: Elegia* (1891). Strings, organ (or harmonium), harp, timpani. Unpublished. Source: *SBN.* First performance Dec. 9, 1891, Chiesa di Donnalbina, Naples, on the occasion of the moving of Paisiello's remains. Manuscript is at the Biblioteca Civica Pietro Acclavio, Taranto, Italy.

PANUFNIK, ANDRZEJ, Polish-English composer, conductor; b. Sep. 24, 1914; d. Oct. 27, 1991.

Knussen, Oliver, 1952– . *Elegiac arabesques,* op. 26a: *In memory of Andrzej Panufnik* (1991). Duo for English horn and clarinet. Published *Faber* 0571514812, 1994.

Osborne, Nigel, 1948– . *Homage à Panufnik* (1993). String orchestra. Published *UE-L* 19798, 1993.

PARAS, JASON, American gambist; b. 1953; d. July 14, 1982.

Strizich, Robert, 1945– . *Tombeau: Dedicated to the memory of vi-*

ola da gamba player Jason Paras (1982). Baroque flute and harpsichord. Published Berkeley, CA: Fallen Leaf Press FLPCM81, 1996.

PARKER, CHARLIE, American jazz saxophonist; b. Aug. 29, 1920; d. Mar. 12, 1955.

> **Baker, David, 1931– .** *Bird: To the memory of Charlie Parker* (1970). Jazz band. Published Chicago: Music Workshop Publications, 1970.
>
> ————. *C C P: Charles Christopher Parker.* Jazz ensemble. Published Bowie, MD: Bow Bel Music; dist. Creative Jazz Composers, 1978.
>
> **Feather, Leonard, 1914–1994.** *I remember Bird* (1967?). Jazz band. Published *Kendor*, 1967. Published ed. arr. by Oliver Nelson. Recorded by various artists.
>
> **Swafford, Jan, 1946– .** *In time of fear* (1984; rev. 1985). Flute and harpsichord. Unpublished. Source: *Bedford.* First performance April 1, 1984, Deerfield, Mass., Akal Dev Khalsa (flute) and Miriam Whaples (harpsichord).

PARKER, HORATIO WILLIAM, American composer; b. Sep. 15, 1863; d. Dec. 18, 1919.

> **Chadwick, George Whitefield, 1854–1931.** *Elegy: In memoriam Horatio Parker* (1920). Organ. Published *Gray* 6489, 1920, in St. Cecilia Series, no. 250. Version for orchestra is unpublished; holograph score at the Library of Congress.

PARLOW, KATHLEEN, Canadian violinist; b. Sep. 20, 1890; d. Aug. 19, 1963.

> **Buczynski, Walter J., 1933– .** *Elegy: In memoriam to Kathleen Parlow* (1963). Violin and piano. Published *Canadian.*

PARRY, SIR CHARLES HUBERT HASTINGS, English composer; b. Feb. 27, 1848; d. Oct. 7, 1918.

> ***Little organ book: In memory of Hubert Parry.*** Published London: A. & C. Black; Boston: C. C. Birchard, 1924. "At Sir Hubert Parry's funeral in St. Paul's Cathedral on October 16th 1918, a few of his friends made a small wreath of melodies, which were woven together and played. The pieces in this Book have been written and given by these friends and a few besides, as a rather larger wreath, in loving memory of him"—preface to score. CONTENTS: [Untitled] / by C. Hubert H. Parry, 1848–1918—Chorale prelude on song "Why does azure deck the sky" / by C. V. Stanford, 1852–1924—Carillon / by A. Herbert Brewer, 1865–1928—[Untitled] / by Alan Gray, 1855–1935—[Untitled] / by Charles Macpherson, 1870–1927—

Chorale prelude on the tune "Worcester" / by Ivor Atkins, 1869–1953—Lento: In memoriam C. H. H. P. / by Frank Bridge, 1879–1941—[Untitled] / by Harold E. Darke, 1888–1976—[Untitled] / by Charles Wood, 1866–1926—[Untitled] / by Walter G. Alcock, 1861–1947—Elegy / by George Thomas Thalben Ball, 1896–1987—Improvisation / by Henry G. Ley, 1887–1962—Jesu dulcis memoria / by Walford Davies, 1869–1941.

Vaughan Williams, Ralph, 1872–1958. *Prayer to the Father of Heaven: Motet* (1948). Chorus (SATB) unacc. Published *OUP* 1883, 1942. Text by John Skelton. "To the memory of my master Hubert Parry, not as an attempt palely to reflect his incomparable art, but in the hope that he would have found in this motet (to use his own words) something characteristic"—composer's note in score.

PARTCH, HARRY, American composer; b. June 25, 1901; d. Sep. 3, 1974.

Johnston, Ben, 1926– . *In memory* (1975). Strings, percussionists (8), electronic tape, slides. Unpublished. Source: *Johnston*. Composed in memory of Partch and of Margaret Erlanger, formerly head of the dance department at the University of Illinois. Premiered Oct. 5, 1975, at dedication of the Erlanger House, Urbana, Illinois.

PARTOS, OEDOEN, Israeli composer; b. Oct. 1, 1907; d. July 6, 1977.

Dorati, Antal, 1906–1988. *Threnos: In memory of Oedoen Partos.* Strings. Published *Israeli*.

PASTA, GIUDITTA, Italian soprano; b. Oct. 28, 1797; d. Apr. 1, 1865.

Spadina, Antonio, b. 1822. *Omaggio alla memoria de Giudita Pasta: Duetto concertante sopra motivi dell'opera Norma.* Clarinet and piano. Published *Ricordi*, 186–? Pasta created the role of Bellini's Norma in 1831. Recorded by Colin Bradbury on *The art of the clarinettist* (Clarinet Classics Records CC0008, 1994); recorded by Bernhard Röthlisberger on *Il clarinetto all'opera* (Gallo Records CD916, 1996).

PASTORIUS, JACO, American electric bass guitarist; b. Dec. 1, 1951; d. Sep. 21, 1987.

Karpman, Laura, 1959– . *Portrait of Jaco* (1988). String quartet and piano. Published *MMB*, 1996. Fantasy based on themes of Pastorius. CONTENTS: Portrait—Rondo a la teen—Three views of an opus.

Raaff, Robin de, 1968– . *Athomus: In memoriam Jaco Pastorius* (1992–93). String quartet. Published *Donemus*, 1995.

PAUMANN, CONRAD, German organist, composer; b. 141–; d. Jan. 24, 1473.

Beck, Jochen, 1941– . *Hommage à M. C. P.: Zum 500. Todestag des Magisters Conrad Paumann* (1973). Organ. Published *Möseler* 19402, 1973. For the 500th anniversary of Paumann's death.

PAUWELS, JEAN-ENGELBERT, Belgian composer; b. Nov. 24, 1768; d. June 4, 1804.

Suremont, Pierre Jean, 1762–1831. *Requiem* (1804). Unpublished. Source: *EitnerQL.* Composed for Pauwels's memorial service.

PAZ, JUAN CARLOS, Argentine composer; b. Aug. 5, 1901; d. Aug. 25, 1972.

Moretto, Nelly, 1925–1978. *Composition no. 13: In memoriam Juan Carlos Paz* (1972). Trumpet and electronic tape. Unpublished. Source: *No/Gro.*

PEAKER, CHARLES, Canadian organist; b. Dec. 6, 1899; d. Aug. 11, 1978.

Sursum corda: A book of organ voluntaries in memory of Charles Peaker. Published *Thompson,* 1981. CONTENTS: Offertory on "Slane" / by William France, 1912–1985—Elegy / by Keith Bissell, 1912–1992—Prelude and fugue in C minor / by Margaret Drynan, 1915–1999—Soliloquy / by Gordon Atkinson, 1928– —Passacharlia [sic] / by John Cook, 1918–1984—Prelude in the lydian mode / by Barrie Cabena, 1933– —Pastorale on "Capetown" / by Gerald Bales, 1919– —Prelude on "Ave Virgo Virginum" / by Derek Holman, 1931– —Laus Deo / by George Fox, 1911–1990.

PEARSON, WILLIAM, American bass-baritone; b. 1934; d. June 18, 1995.

Ruck, Jürgen, 1961– (transcriber). Henze, Hans Werner, 1926– *Memorias de El Cimarron* (1995). Guitars (2). Published *Schott-M* GA239. Arrangement done at Henze's suggestion of themes from his opera *El Cimarron.* Though Henze's music is arranged by another composer, the work is listed in *Henze.* Pearson created one of the roles in the opera.

PEDRELL, FELIPE, Spanish composer, musicologist; b. Feb. 19, 1841; d. Aug. 19, 1922.

Falla, Manuel de, 1876–1946. "Pedrelliana," in his *Homenajes* (1938–39). Orchestra. Published *Ricordi* PR667; *Chester,* 1953. CONTENTS: Fanfare sobre el nombre E. P. Arbós—À Claude Debussy (Elegia de la guitarra)—À P. Dukas (Spes vitae)—Pedrelliana. Based on themes from Pedrell's opera *La Celestina.* The second movement "À Claude Debussy" is an orchestral transcription of the guitar work originally composed 1920 as a memorial for Debussy.

PERGOLESI, GIOVANNI BATTISTA, Italian composer; b. Jan. 4, 1710; d. Mar. 16, 1736.

Vogel, Wladimir, 1896–1984. *Alla memoria di Giovanni Battista Pergolesi: Recitativo ed epitafio* (1958). Cantata for tenor and strings. Published *Ricordi* 129897, 1959. Text by Guido Lorenzo Brezzo.

PERLEA, JONEL, Romanian conductor, composer; b. Dec. 13, 1900; d. July 30, 1970.

Grigoriu, Theodor, 1926– . *Tristia: In memoriam Ionel Perlea* (1974). Orchestra of violins, violas, trumpets, trombones, and percussion. Published *EditMuz*, 1983. Based on a theme from Perlea's symphonic poem *Don Quichotte*.

PERSICHETTI, VINCENT, American composer; b. June 6, 1915; d. Aug. 14, 1987.

Druckman, Jacob, 1928–1996. *In memoriam Vincent Persichetti* (1987). Orchestra. Published *Boosey* HPS1181, 1987. Also a version for symphonic winds: *Boosey*. Based on the opening theme of Persichetti's Symphony for strings, op. 61.

Schuman, William, 1910–1992. *String quartet no. 5: To the memory of Vincent Persichetti* (1987). Published *Merion* 144-40161, 1989.

PETRI, EGON, German pianist; b. Mar. 23, 1881; d. May 27, 1962.

Sitsky, Larry, 1934– . *Fantasia: In memory of Egon Petri* (1962). Piano. Published *Ricordi*, 1972. Orchestrated in 1973 as *Symphonic elegy*, which also may be performed as No. 3 of *Four orchestral pieces*.

PIAF, EDITH, French chanteuse; b. Dec. 19, 1915; d. Oct. 11, 1963.

Blake, Ran, 1935– . *Death of Edith Piaf* (1977). Piano. Publication "in preparation" according to 1996 catalog of *Margun*; no subsequent reference found. Recorded by the composer on *Realization of a dream* (Owl Records OWL012, 1978).

PIATIGORSKY, GREGOR, Russian violoncellist; b. Apr. 17, 1903; d. Aug. 6, 1976.

Rózsa, Miklós, 1907–1995. *Toccata capricciosa*, op. 36: *Gregor Piatigorsky in memoriam* (1977). Violoncello solo. Published *Breitkopf* 8062, 1979.

PIAZZOLLA, ASTOR, Argentine composer; b. Mar. 11, 1921; d. July 5, 1992.

Engel, Claude, 1948– . *Fuego!: Hommage à Astor Piazzolla* (1992). Tango for guitar. Published *Oz* DZ275, 2000.

Mollberg, Jonas. *Prelude and waltz: Homage to Astor Piazzolla.* Guitars (2). Published *Mollberg*, 1999?

Núñez Allauca, Alejandro, 1943– . *Omaggio a Piazzolla* (1998). Piano. Published *Pizzicato* PVH453, 1998.

Pujol, Máximo Diego, 1957– . *Elegia por la muerte de un tanguero: Homenaje a Astor Piazzolla* (1994). Guitar. Published *Lemoine* 26175, 1994. CONTENTS: Confuseta—Melancolia—Epilogo.

PIJPER, WILLEM, Dutch composer; b. Sep. 8, 1894; d. Mar. 18, 1947.

Hommage à Willem Pijper: 10 compositions. Principally piano. Published *Broekmans*, 1950. Edited by Marius Flothuis. "[The editors chose] to give this publication a special character: that of a posthumous homage to the composer to whom all of us, whether we were his pupils or not, owe so much: Willem Pijper. . . . We have given the composers as much freedom as possible concerning the character of the pieces: It was not intended that every contribution should be an In memoriam, and this is the case in only a small minority of the pieces"—preface to score. CONTENTS (composition dates added to identify those composed prior to Pijper's death): Ad lucem aeternam "in memoriam Willem Pijper" (1948) / by Henri Zagwijn, 1878–1954—Hor ai dolor (1950) / by Sem Dresden, 1881– 1957—Vieille chanson (1948) / by Henriette Bosmans, 1895– 1952—Toccata (1950) / by Karel Mengelberg, 1902–1984— Sonatina "in memoriam Willem Pijper" (1948) / by Kees Van Baaren, 1906–1970—Dans (1943) / by Bertus Van Lier, 1906– 1972—Sonatine (1946) / by Wolfgang Wijdeveld, 1910–1985—Due voci (1949) / by Rudolf Escher, 1912–1980—Epilogue per flauto e pianoforte (1947) / by Hans Henkmans, 1913–1995 —Sonatina no. 3 (1949) / by Jan Van Dijk, 1918– .

Leeuw, Ton de, 1926–1996. *Treurmuziek: In memoriam Willem Pijper* (1948). Chamber orchestra. Published *Donemus*, 1949.

Straesser, Joep, 1934– . *Sonatine: Hommage à Willem Pijper* (1957; rev. 1964). Piano. Published *Donemus*, 1964.

PISTON, WALTER, American composer; b. Jan. 20, 1894; d. Nov. 12, 1976.

Pinkham, Daniel, 1923– . *Serenades: Dedicated to the memory of Walter Piston* (1979). Trumpet with wind ensemble. Published *Ione* ECS262, 1981.

PLAIDY, LOUIS, German pianist; b. Nov. 28, 1810; d. Mar. 3, 1874.

Kirchner, Theodor, 1823–1903. "Vivace," in his *Gedenkblätter: Zwölf Musikstücke zur Erinnerung an die Einweihung des neuen*

Königl. Conservatoriums für Musik zu Leipzig, op. 82 (1843–87). Piano. Published Leipzig: J. Rieter-Biedermann 1508, 1887. No. 11 of 12 short piano pieces memorializing Conrad Schleinitz, Felix Mendelssohn, Robert Schumann, Moritz Hauptmann, Ferdinand David, Ignaz Moscheles, Ernst Friedrich Richter, Carl Ferdinand Becker, Ernst Ferdinand Wenzel, and Louis Plaidy.

PLAYFORD, JOHN, English music publisher; b. 1623; d. Nov. 1686.

Purcell, Henry, ca. 1659–1695. *Gentle shepherds, you that know: Pastoral elegy on the death of Mr. John Playford.* Soprano solo, chorus (SB), continuo. Published London: Printed for Henry Playford, 1687. *RISM-A1:* P-6038. Later edition in *Orpheus britannicus* (London: J. Heptinstall, 1698). *RISM-B1:* P-5979. Facsimile reprint: *Broude,* 1965. Text by Nahum Tate.

PLEYEL, IGNAZ, Austro-French composer, pianist, music publisher; b. June 18, 1757; d. Nov. 14, 1831.

Louvier, Alain, 1945– . *Pleyel in memoriam: For harpsichord.* Unpublished. Recorded by an unidentified performer on *Le clavecin bien improvisé* (Royer Musique Editions RME001, 196–?).

POLLIKOFF, MAX, American violinist, conductor; b. Mar. 30, 1904; d. May 13, 1984.

Luening, Otto, 1900–1996. *Fantasia and dance: In memoriam Max Pollikoff* (1984). Solo violin. Published Rhinebeck, NY: Phantom Press 8966, 1989.

Thomas, Andrew, 1929– . *Elegy: In memory of Max Pollikoff* (1985). Trio for clarinet, English horn, violoncello. Published *ACA,* 1985.

PONCE, MANUEL MARIA, Mexican composer; b. Dec. 8, 1882; d. Apr. 24, 1948.

Domeniconi, Carlo, 1947– . *Sonata in tre movimenti,* op. 14: *Dedicata alla memoria de Manuel Maria Ponce.* Guitars (2). Published *Margaux* EM2042, 1990.

Mitéran, Alain, 1941– . *Le tombeau de Manuel Ponce.* Guitar. Published *Billaudot* 5343, 1992.

Siccardi, Honorio, 1897–1963. *Por la muerte de Manuel Ponce* (1948). Piano. Unpublished. Source: *CompAmer,* vol. 2.

Usher, Terry, 1909–1969. *Epitaph for Manuel M. Ponce.* Guitar. Published in the journal *Guitar review* 8 (1949).

PONCHIELLI, AMILCARE, Italian composer; b. Aug. 31, 1834; d. Jan. 17, 1886.

Barberis, Pier Luigi. *Compianto: Marchia funebre ad Amilcare*

Ponchielli. Band. Published *Ricordi* 53593, 1889.

Pizzi, Emilio, 1861–1940. *Sulla tomba di Amilcare Ponchielli: Elegia per pianoforte composta su rimembranze delle opere del grand Maestro* (1886). Piano. Published *Ricordi* 50424, 1886.

Ponchielli, Amilcare, 1834–1886. *Marcia funebre per Amilcare Ponchielli,* op. 121 (1865). Band. Unpublished. Source: *Ponchielli.* Ponchielli composed this work for performance at his own funeral. The autograph manuscript, at the Museo Civico in Cremona, has the inscription "Dedicato all'anima dell'Autore quando creperà!"

PORADOWSKI, STEFAN BOLESLAW, Polish composer; b. Aug. 16, 1902; d. July 9, 1967.

Wysocki, Zdzislaw, 1944– . *Elegia for orchestra,* op. 9: *In memoriam S. B. Poradowsky* (1967–1968). Orchestra. Unpublished. Source: *OZOK.*

PORTER, QUINCY, American composer; b. Feb. 7, 1897; d. Nov. 12, 1966.

Stevens, Halsey, 1908–1989. *Threnos: In memoriam Quincy Porter* (1968). Orchestra. Published *CFE,* 1968.

POTTER, A. J. (ARCHIBALD JAMES), Irish composer; b. Sep. 22, 1918; d. July 5, 1981.

De Bromhead, Jerome, 1945– . *Magister* (1982). Octet for flute, oboe, clarinet, bassoon, string quartet. Unpublished. Source: *Irish-96.*

POULENC, FRANCIS, French composer; b. Jan. 7, 1899; d. Jan. 30, 1963.

Berkeley, Sir Lennox, 1903–1989. "Automne, op. 60, no. 3: In memory of Francis Poulenc" (1963), in his *The complete French songs: Solo voice and piano.* Published *Chester* 55985, 1992. Text by Guillaume Apollinaire.

———. *Four Ronsard sonnets, Set 2,* op. 62: *In affectionate memory of Francis Poulenc* (1963). Tenor and orchestra. Published *Chester* 130, 1964. Texts from *Sonnets pour Helène* by Pierre de Ronsard, 1524–1585. CONTENTS: Ce premier jour de mai—Je sens une douceur—Ma fiévere croist tousjours—Yeux, qui versez en l'ame.

Bush, Geoffrey, 1920–1998. *Venus and Adonis: To the memory of Francis Poulenc, songwriter* (1985). Voice and piano. Published *Novello* 17032010, 1985. Text from *Never too late* (1590) by Robert Greene.

Dijk, Rudi van, 1932– . *Le tombeau de Francis Poulenc* (1965). Piano 4-hands (or 2 pianos). Published *Donemus,* 1999.

Dubois, Pierre Max, 1930– . *Hommage à Poulenc* (1963). Piano. Published *Leduc* AL23361, 1963.

Haieff, Alexei, 1914–1994. *Sonata for violoncello and piano: In memory of Francis Poulenc* (1963). Published *Chappell*, 1965.

Josephs, Wilfred, 1927–1997. "In fond memory of Francis Poulenc" (1982), in *Modern English flute studies*. Published *Pan*, 1982. No. 1 of "Two studies" by Josephs in this collection of studies by nine composers.

McLeod, John, 1934– . *Le tombeau de Poulenc.* Flute with harp and strings. Published *Scotus*.

Madsen, Trygve, 1940– . *Sonate for bassoon and piano,* op. 25*: À la mémoire de Francis Poulenc.* Published *MusHuset* 2418, 1987.

Milhaud, Darius, 1892–1974. *Suite de sonnets: Cantate sur des vers du XVIe siècle: À la chere mémoire de Francis Poulenc* (1963). Soprano and countertenor with sextet of bass flute, oboe, viola, bassoon, trombone, harpsichord. Published *Eschig* ME8807, 1988. CONTENTS: Prélude I—Jeux rustiques d'un vanneur de blé aux vents / text by Joachim du Bellay—Prélude II—J'aime de vert laurier / text by Etienne Jodelle—Prélude III—Bienheureux est celui / text by Olivier de Magny—Prélude IV—À Venus pour la paix / text by Amadis Jamyn.

————. *Preparatif à la mort et allegorie maritime,* op. 403*: À la memoire de Francis Poulenc* (1963). Voice and piano. Unpublished. Source: *Milhaud.* First performance January 13, 1964, Carnegie Hall, by Alice Esty.

Rorem, Ned, 1923– . *For Poulenc* (June 23, 1963). Voice and piano. Published *ECS* 2032, 1968. Text by Frank O'Hara.

————. *Lift up your heads (The Ascension): To Francis Poulenc, in memoriam* (1963). Mixed chorus and organ. Published *Boosey* LCB80, 1964. Also arranged for chorus with trumpets (2), trombones (2), timpani, and organ. Text by John Beaumont.

Sauguet, Henri, 1901–1989. *Celui qui dort: À la mémoire de Francis Poulenc* (July 1963). Voice and piano. Unpublished. Source: *Sauguet.* Text by Paul Eluard.

Szokolay, Sándor, 1931– . *Déploration: À la mémoire de Francis Poulenc* (1964). Piano solo, mixed chorus, organ, chamber orchestra. Published *Leduc* AL24426, 1982. Text from the Latin Requiem

Tailleferre, Germaine, 1892–1983. *L'adieu du cavalier: Hommage à Francis Poulenc* (1963). Voice and piano. Unpublished. Source: *Tailleferre.* First performance New York City, Carnegie Hall, Janu-

ary 13, 1964, by Alice Esty, in a recital titled "Hommage à Poulenc."
POZO, CHANO, Afro-Cuban percussionist; b. June 7, 1915; d. Dec. 2, 1948.

Amram, David, 1930– . *En memoria de Chano Pozo.* Jazz trio (flute, electric bass, piano) and orchestra. Published *Peters* 66752, 1978. Also arranged by the composer for band: *Peters*, 1980.

PRAETORIUS, MICHAEL, German theorist, composer; b. Feb. 15, 1571; d. Feb. 15, 1621.

Schickele, Peter, 1935– . *Epitaphs for piano.* Published *E-V* 160-00202, 1981. "*Epitaphs* is a set of tributes written over a period of thirteen years; the composers to whom homage is paid represent each century from the 16th through the 20th"—composer's note in score. CONTENTS: Orlando di Lasso—Michael Praetorius—Domenico Scarlatti—Frédéric Chopin—Igor Stravinsky.

PREMRU, RAYMOND EUGENE, American trombonist, conductor, composer; b. June 6, 1934; d. May 8, 1998.

Hartley, Walter S., 1927– . *Memorial music* (1998). Duo for tenor and bass trombones. Published *Nichols* 084, 1999. "Ray Premru and Reginald Fink were distinguished trombonists. Premru also a composer and Fink the author of a much-used instrumental manual. Both were fellow students with me at Eastman over 40 years ago, and both died recently of cancer"—introduction in score.

PRESLEY, ELVIS, American rock music icon; b. Jan. 8, 1935; d. Aug. 16, 1977.

Daugherty, Michael, 1954– . *Dead Elvis: For bassoon-playing Elvis impersonator and chamber ensemble* (1993). Bassoon solo with sextet for clarinet, trumpet, trombone, percussion, violin, double bass. Published *Peermusic* 620097910, 1999. Recorded by Charles Ullery (bassoon) and ensemble on *American icons* (Argo 458 145-2, 1998). "It is more than a coincidence that *Dead Elvis* is scored for the same instrumentation as Stravinsky's *Histoire du soldat* (1918), in which a soldier sells his violin, and his soul, to the devil for a magic book"—composer's notes on the recording. Incorporates the *Dies irae* chant in the instrumental accompaniment.

Harbin, Juanita. *In memory of Elvis Presley* (1977). Song. Published Gulf Breeze, FL: Sky High Productions, 1977. Words by Alma Paradise

McDowell, Ronnie, 1950– . "The king is gone," recorded two days after Presley's death for *The king is gone* (Scorpion GRT 8021, 1977). Pop song. CONTENTS: The king is gone—Dixie—You and me—Naturally—If not for the love of Jesus—Only the lonely / by R. Orbison and J. Melson—When it comes to you—What a way to go—Walking through Georgia in the rain—Heartbreak hotel / by M. Axton, T. Durden, E. Presley.

PRESTI, IDA, French guitarist; b. May 31, 1924; d. Apr. 24, 1967.

Castelnuovo-Tedesco, Mario, 1895–1968. *Fuga elegiaca: To the memory of Ida Presti* (1967). Guitars (2). Published *Chanterelle*, 1993. First published in the journal *Guitar review* 31 (May 1969).

Rodrigo, Joaquin, 1901–1999. *Concierto madrigal: A la memoria de Ida Presti* (1966). Guitars (2) with orchestra. Published *Schott-M* 7391, 1983.

Sanchez, Blas, 1935– . *Complainte funèbre: Fantaisie pour guitare: À la mémoire de Ida Presti* (1967). Guitar. Published *EMT* TR001044, 1969. "Paris 2 Mai 1967. Jour de son enterrement"— score caption [i.e. played at her burial].

PREUSENSIN (PREISS), GERHARD, German organist; d. May 22, 1672.

Knüpfer, Sebastian, 1633–1676. "Was sind wir Menschen doch?" in his *Das vierstimmte Orgel-Werck des menschlichen Lebens, Welches Bey de . . . Leichenbestattung des . . . Herrn Gerhard Preusensins . . . dieses 1672. Iahres . . . in einer Trauer-Ode dargestelled Das Collegium Musicum.* Voices (4). Published Leipzig: Johann Bauer, 1672. *RISM-A1*: K-1004.

PROKOFIEV, SERGEY, Russian composer; b. Apr. 23, 1891; d. Mar. 5, 1953.

Baervoets, Raymond, 1930– . *Hommage à Serge Prokofieff* (1958). Piano. Published Antwerp: Editions Metropolis, 1958?

Barraine, Elsa, 1910– . *Hommage à Prokofiev* (1953). Harpsichord and orchestra. Unpublished. Source: *No/Gro.*

Goehr, Alexander, 1932– . *Sonata for piano in one movement,* op. 2: *In memory of Serge Prokoviev.* Published *Schott-L* 10417, 1955.

Hrabovskyi, Leonid Oleksandrovych, 1935– . "Amoroso: In memoriam Sergei Prokofiev," in his *Homages: Seven pieces for guitar.* Published *Duma*, 1996. CONTENTS: Ciaccona: In memoriam Henry Purcell—Aria: In memoriam Johann Sebastian Bach—Impromptus: In memoriam Franz Schubert—Prelude: In memoriam Frédéric Chopin—A little cake-walk: In memoriam Scott Joplin—Chorale: In memoriam Johannes Brahms—Amoroso: In memoriam Sergei Prokofiev.

Kabalevsky, Dmitri Borisovich, 1904–1987. *Rondo pamiati Prokof'eva = Rondo in memory of Prokofiev,* op. 79. Violoncello and piano. Published *Muzyka* 8753; *Schirmer* 3358, 1975.

Ledenev, Roman Semenovich, 1930– . *Sonata for piano,* op. 4: *In memory of Sergei Prokofiev* (1957). Unpublished. Source: *ConCom.* First performance, Moscow, 1958.

Maillard-Verger, Pierre, 1930– . *Hommage à Prokofieff.* Piano. Published *Salabert* EAS15768, 1954.

Poulenc, Francis, 1899–1963. *Sonata for oboe and piano: À la mémoire de Serge Prokofieff* (1962). Published *Chester* 1617, 1963.

Yagling, Victoria. *Sonata for violoncello and piano no. 3: In memory of Prokofiev* (1980). Published Moscow: House of Composers. Source: *Homuth.*

PRUDEN, LARRY, New Zealand composer; b. July 28, 1925; d. Oct. 1, 1982.

Burch, Robert William, 1929– . "Threnody," in *Three by four* (1984). Orchestra. Unpublished. Source: *NZ,* 3rd ed. Second movement of a three-movement work jointly composed by Burch, David Farquhar, and Edwin Carr.

Carr, Edwin, 1926– . *In memoriam: Paraphrase on "Kiwi"* (1984). Clarinet and strings. Published Taupo, New Zealand: Edwin Carr, 1984? Tribute to Larry Pruden based on his film score for *Kiwi.*

Farquhar, David, 1928– . "March," in *Three by four* (1984). Clarinet and string orchestra. Unpublished. Source: *NZ,* 3rd ed. Third movement of a three-movement work jointly composed by Farquhar, Robert Burch, and Edwin Carr.

PUCCINI, GIACOMO, Italian composer.; b. Dec. 22, 1858; d. Nov. 29, 1924.

Manente, Giuseppe, 1867–1941. *In memoriam G. Puccini: Marcia funebre.* Band. Published Florence: A. Lapini, 192–?

PUCCINI, MICHELE, Italian composer; b. Nov. 27, 1813; d. Jan. 23, 1864.

Pacini, Giovanni, 1796–1867. *Requiem* (1864). Unpublished. Source: *NGrove.* Michele Puccini was the father of Giacomo.

PUGNO, RAOUL, French pianist; b. June 23, 1852; d. Jan. 3, 1914.

LeBoucher, Maurice, 1882–1964 (transcriber). Chabrier, Emmanuel, 1841–1894. *Capriccio: À la mémoire de Raoul Pugno* (1914). Piano. Published *Billaudot* 1949, 1914. Reprint: *Masters* M1949, 1991. Left unfinished at Chabrier's death. The dedication is apparently by Maurice LeBoucher, who completed the work.

PURCELL, DANIEL, English composer; b. 1660?; d. Nov. 26, 1717.

Bosco, Gilberto, 1946– . *Le tombeau d'Angleterre: Omaggio a*

Daniel Purcell. Sextet for recorders (SATB), viola, harpsichord. Published *Impero* 9036, 1977.

PURCELL, HENRY, English composer; b. 1659?; d. Nov. 21, 1695.

Blow, John, d. 1708. *Ode on the death of Mr. Henry Purcell.* Countertenors (2) with treble instruments (2), continuo. Published London: Printed by J. Heptinstall for Henry Playford, 1696. *RISM-A1*: B-3002. Facsimile reprint: Huntingdon, UK: King's Music, 1987? Another edition by Walter Bergmann (*Schott-L,* 1962). Text by John Dryden ("Hark how the lark and linnet sing").

Clarke, Jeremiah, 1669–1707. *Come, come along, for a dance and a song* (1695?). Soloists (SAB), chorus (SAATB) with ensemble of trumpets (2), recorders (2), oboes (2), strings, timpani, harpsichord. Published *Purcell.* Also published separately: *Schott-L,* 1961. Edited from British Library Ms. Add. 30934.

Eben, Petr, 1929– . *Hommage à Henry Purcell* (1995). Organ. Published *Schott-M* 8442, 1995. "The celebrations of the 300th anniversary of the death of Henry Purcell have inspired me to compose this music"—composer's note in score. Incorporates thematic quotations from Purcell's opera *Dido and Aeneas.*

Finger, Godfrey, ca. 1660–1730. *Suite in G minor, "Farewell."* Oboes (2), bassoon, strings, and continuo. Unpublished. These instrumental movements appear to be part of Finger's setting, now mostly lost, of James Talbot's ode on the death of Purcell, performed as "Mr. Purcell's Farewell" at York Buildings on January 13, 1696. The instrumental movements preserved in the manuscript source at the Royal College of Music, Ms 1172, are titled simply "Farewell." Recorded by The Parley of Instruments Baroque Ensemble, cond. by Peter Holman on *Odes on the death of Henry Purcell* (Hyperion Records CDA66578, 1992).

Hall, Henry, 1655–1707. *Yes my Aminta 'tis too true: A peace of musicke upon ye death of Mr. Henry Purcell.* Voices (SB) with recorders (2), continuo. Unpublished. Manuscript source: St. Michael's College, Tenbury, MS 1232. Text by the composer. Recorded by The Parley of Instruments Baroque Ensemble, cond. by Peter Holman on *Odes on the death of Henry Purcell* (Hyperion Records CDA66578, 1992). "This was composed by the ingenious Mr. H. Hall, organist at Hereford, upon the death of Mr. H. Purcell, who was educated with him in the Chapell Royall in the reign of K. Charles the Second"—quote from the manuscript source in *Purcell.*

Hrabovskyi, Leonid Oleksandrovych, 1935– . "Ciaconna: In memoriam Henry Purcell," in his *Homages: Seven pieces for guitar.* Published *Duma*, 1996. CONTENTS: Ciaccona: In memoriam Henry Purcell—Aria: In memoriam Johann Sebastian Bach—Impromptus: In memoriam Franz Schubert—Prelude: In memoriam Frederic Chopin—A little cake-walk: In memoriam Scott Joplin—Chorale: In memoriam Johannes Brahms—Amoroso: In memoriam Sergei Prokofiev.

Jenkins, Joseph Willcox, 1928– . *Rounds and sounds,* op. 35: *In memory of Messrs. Purcell and Byrd.* Men's chorus (TTBB), strings, percussion. Published by the composer (c/o *ASCAP*). Source: *ASCAP.*

Morgan, Thomas, fl. 1691–1699. *Mr. Purcell's farewell tune.* Ensemble of oboes (2), bassoon, strings, continuo. Unpublished. Source: *Purcell.* Composed for performance in Aphra Behn's play *The younger brother*, produced at Drury Lane in late 1695 or early 1696. Recorded by The Parley of Instruments Baroque Ensemble, cond. by Roy Goodman on *Odes on the death of Henry Purcell* (Hyperion Records CDA66578, 1992).

Purcell, Daniel, ca. 1660–1717. "Lamentation for the death of Mr. Henry Purcell, sett to musick by his brother, Mr. Daniel Purcell. The words by N[ahum] Tate, esq.", in *Orpheus britannicus: A collection of all the choicest songs for one, two, and three voices: Together with such symphonies for violins or flutes as were by him designed for any of them, and a through-bass to each song, figures for the organ, harpsichord, or theorbo-lute.* Published London: J. Heptinstall, 1698. The text only ("A gloomy mist o'er spreads the plains") is printed in *Orpheus Britannicus.* The music for the work apparently is lost.

Ruders, Poul, 1949– . *Concerto in pieces: Purcell variations for orchestra* (1994–95). Published *Hansen* WH30261, 1995. Commissioned by the BBC for the tercentenary of Purcell's death. Incorporates thematic material from the witches' chorus in Purcell's opera *Dido and Aeneas*

Terényi, Ede, 1935– . *Concerto for organ and orchestra no. 1: Purcell-Epitaph* (1997). Unpublished. Source: *Beckmann.*

RACHMANINOFF, SERGEI, Russian pianist, composer; b. Apr. 1, 1873; d. Mar. 28, 1943.

Drozdoff, Vladimir. *Au tombeau de Rachmaninoff: Dies irae, epi-*

taphe, psalmodie du printemps (March 28, 1943). Piano. Published New York: Omega Music Edition, 1951. "Composed March 28, 1943—the day Sergei Rachmaninoff passed away"—note in score.

Goldenveizer, Aleksandr Borisovich, 1875–1962. *Piano trio,* op. 31*: Posviashaemsia S. V. Rakhmaninova* (1953). Published Moscow: Gosudarstvennoe Muzykalnoe Izdatelstvo 25595, 1956.

Ovchinnikov, Viacheslav Aleksandrovich, 1936– . "Elegia pamiati S. V. Rakhmaninova = Elegy in memory of Sergei Rachmaninov" (1973), in *Proizvedeniia dlia solistov, khora i simfonicheskogo orkestra = Works for soloists, chorus, and symphony orchestra.* Vocal soloists, chorus, orchestra. Published *Muzyka* 11954, 1983.

RACQUET, CHARLES, French organist; b. 1597; d. Jan. 1, 1664.

Gaultier, Denis, d. 1672. "Pavanne, ou le tombeau de Mr. Raquette," in his *Pièces de luth de Denis Gaultier sur trois differens modes nouveaux.* Lute. Published Paris: L'autheur, ca. 1669. *RISM-A1*: G-588. Facsimile and modern edition in *Rhétorique.*

RAFF, JOSEPH JOACHIM, German composer; b. Apr. 11, 1822; d. June 24, 1882.

MacDowell, Edward, 1860–1908. *Sonata for piano no. 1,* op. 45, G minor*: Sonata tragica* (1893). Piano. Published *Breitkopf* 19801, 1893. MacDowell's memorial intent is reported in multiple biographies, though no dedication is printed in the score.

RAMEAU, JEAN-PHILIPPE, French composer, theorist; b. Sep. 25, 1683; d. Sep. 12, 1764.

Philidor, François-André Danican, 1726–1795. *Requiem* (1764). Unpublished. Source: *NGrove,* which declares the work lost. Performed October 11, 1764, at the Carmelite Church, Paris.

RAMOVS, PRIMOZ, Slovenian composer; b. Mar. 20, 1921; d. Jan. 1999.

Petric, Ivo, 1931– . *Fantasia for trumpet and organ* (1997–98). Published *Pizzicato* PVH406, 1999.

RAPIER, LEON, American trumpeter; d. Jan. 15, 1988 at 65.

Taggart, Mark Alan, 1956– . *Song at sunset: In memoriam Leon Rapier.* Trumpet and string quartet. Published U.S.: Sound Ideas, 1988.

RATH, FELIX VON, German composer; b. June 17, 1866; d. Aug. 25, 1905.

Thuille, Ludwig, 1861–1907. "Threnodie: Zum Andenken an den früh verstorbenen Komponisten Felix von Rath," in his *Zwei Klavierstücke,* op. 37 (1906). Piano. Published *Kistner,* 1906.

RATHAUS, KAROL, Polish composer; b. Sep. 16, 1895; d. Nov. 21, 1954.

Kraft, Leo, 1922– . *Larghetto: In memory of Karol Rathaus* (1955). Timpani and string orchestra. Published *Presser.*

Rosenman, Leonard, 1924– . *Threnody on a song of Karol Rathaus* (1971). Orchestra. Published *Peer-S.*

Turok, Paul, 1929– . *Elegy,* op. 23*: In memory of Karol Rathaus* (1963). Ensemble of trumpets (3), horns (2), trombones (3), baritone horn, tuba. Published *MusicaRara,* 1971.

RAVEL, MAURICE, French composer; b. Mar. 7, 1875; d. Dec. 28, 1937.

Amengual Astaburuaga, René, 1911–1954. *Homenaje a Ravel* (1939). Piano. Unpublished. Source: *Chile.*

Barrell, Bernard, 1919– . *Suite,* op. 1a*: Homage à Ravel* (1938). Piano. Unpublished. Source: *BMIC.*

Benjamin, Arthur, 1893–1960. *Le tombeau de Ravel: Valse-caprices* (1949). Viola (or clarinet) and piano. Published *Boosey* WCB91, 1958.

Bourdin, Roger, 1923–1976. *À la mémoire de Maurice Ravel.* Trio for flute, double bass, organ. Published Paris: R. Bourdin.

Casella, Alfredo, 1883–1947. *Sei studi,* op. 70. Piano. Published *Curci* 4020, 1944? "La presente collana di 'studi' vuol essere un umile omaggio di ammirazione e di gratitudine verso le memorie di F. F. Chopin e di M. Ravel"—note in score.

Diamond, David, 1915– . *Elegy in memory of Maurice Ravel* (1938). Ensemble of horns (4), trumpets (3), trombones (3), tuba, harps (2), percussion. Published *Peer-S* 60398-766, 1969. A second version for string orchestra, composed 1939, is published by *Southern.*

Doppelbauer, Josef Friedrich, 1918–1989. *Toccata und Fuge: In memoriam Maurice Ravel* (1959). Organ. Published *Doblinger* 9902, 1959.

Dupriez, Christian Léon Charles, 1922– . *Tambourin pour servir de thrène à Maurice Ravel* (1945). Piano. Published Brussels: Musica nova, 1951. Also a version for orchestra.

Escher, Rudolf, 1912–1980. *Sinfonia in memoriam Maurice Ravel* (1940). Orchestra. Published *Donemus,* 1981.

―――. *Le tombeau de Ravel,* op. 24 (1952). Sextet for flute, oboe, violin, viola, violoncello, harpsichord. Published *Donemus,* 1952.

Eshpai, Andrei, 1925– . *Concerto for piano and orchestra no. 1: To* *the memory of Maurice Ravel* (1954). Published Moscow: Sov. Kompozitor, 1957.

————. *Sonata for violoncello (or violin) and piano: In memory of Maurice Ravel* (1990). Published Moscow: Sov. Kompozitor 9433, 1992. Version for violin is arranged by L. Dmiterko.

Forst, Rudolf, 1900–1977. *Hommage to Ravel.* Flute and piano. Published *Musicus*, 1944. Also available in versions for violin, viola, violoncello, and harp.

Françaix, Jean, 1912–1997. *Pavane pour un génie vivant: À la mémoire de Maurice Ravel, si présent parmi nous . . .* (1987). Orchestra. Published *Eschig*.

Giazotto, Remo, 1910– . *Au tombeau de Ravel* (1959). Suite for piano. Published *Ricordi* 129762, 1959. CONTENTS: Introduzione, alla gavotta—Minuetto e trio—Valzer lento—Toccata.

Halffter, Ernesto, 1905–1989. *Rapsodia portuguesa: À Maurice Ravel in memoriam* (1940; rev. 1951). Piano and orchestra. Published *Eschig* ME6242, 1951.

Kahn, Erich Itor, 1905–1956. "Hommage à Ravel," in his *Huit inventions,* op. 7 (1937). Piano. Published *ACA*, 1960. No. 6 in the set of 8 inventions.

Montsalvatge, Xavier, 1912– . *Elegia a Maurice Ravel* (1945). Piano. Published *UME* 22459, 1993.

Moran, Robert, 1937– . "Waltz (In memoriam Maurice Ravel)," in *Waltzes by 25 contemporary composers.* Piano. Published *Peters* 66735, 1978.

Münz, Harald, 1965– . *Idée s'augmentanté: In memoriam Maurice Ravel* (1980). Sextet for flute, clarinet, percussion, violin, violoncello, piano. Published *Bosse* BE158, 1982.

Stehman, Jacques, 1912–1975. *Le tombeau de Ravel* (1949). Suite for piano. Published *CeBeDeM*, 1972. CONTENTS: Prelude—Menuet—Habañera—Toccata.

Velden, Renier van der, 1910– . *Symphonische suite: Homage à Ravel* (1938). Orchestra. Published *Elkan*

Xenakis, Iannis, 1922– . *À R.: Hommage à Maurice Ravel* (1987). Piano. Published *Salabert* EAS18568, 1989. Commissioned by the Radio-France International Festival at Montpellier as part of the commemoration of the 50th anniversary of Ravel's death.

RAWSTHORNE, ALAN, English composer; b. May 2, 1905; d. July 24, 1971.

Hoddinott, Alun, 1929– . *Sonata for piano no. 6, op. 78, no. 3: In* *memory of Alan Rawsthorne* (1972). Published *OUP* 3728370, 1974.

REGER, MAX, German composer; b. Mar. 19, 1873; d. May 11, 1916.

> **Hambraeus, Bengt, 1928– .** "Toccata: Monumentum per Max Reger," in his *Five organ pieces* (1969–75). Published *Hansen* NMS10384, 1979. No. 2 of the 5 pieces.
>
> **Schilling, Hans Ludwig, 1927– .** *Adagio: In memoriam Max Reger* (1973). String orchestra. Unpublished. Source: *NGrove*.

REHER, SVEN, American violist; b. Sep. 6, 1911; d. Jan. 31, 1991.

> **MacLean, John Torry, 1933– .** *Elegy: In memory of Sven Reher.* Violas (4). Published *Castle* CE031, 2000.

REINHARDT, DJANGO, Belgian jazz guitarist; b. Jan. 23, 1910; d. May 16, 1953.

> **Arnold, Sir Malcolm, 1921– .** "Lento," in his *Concerto for guitar and chamber orchestra,* op. 67 (1959). Published London: Patterson's Publs., 1961. CONTENTS: Allegro—Lento—Con brio. The memorial dedication of the slow movement is according to *Arnold,* but does not appear in the printed score.
>
> **Blyton, Carey, 1932– .** *In memoriam Django Reinhardt: Two variations and a theme,* op. 64a. Guitar. Published *Berben,* 1973. CONTENTS: Prelude—Elegy—Django Reinhardt's Stomp.
>
> **Grappelli, Stéphane, 1908–1997.** *I remember Django* (1969?). Jazz quintet. Unpublished. Recorded by the New Hot Club Quintet featuring Stéphane Grappelli (violin) and Barney Kessel (guitar) on *I remember Django* (Black Lion Records BL-105, 1969).
>
> **Lewis, John Aaron, 1920– .** *Django: For the Jazztet* (1954?). Jazz sextet for trumpet, tenor saxophone, trombone, piano, drums, double bass. Published New York: MJQ Music, 1955. Recorded 1954 by the Modern Jazz Quartet on *The Modern Jazz Quartet* (Prestige PRLP170, 1955); and subsequently by other artists.
>
> **Wright, Brian A.** *In memoriam Django Reinhardt.* Guitar. Published *Hampton,* 1983.

REIZENSTEIN, FRANZ, German pianist, composer; b. June 7, 1911; d. Oct. 15, 1968.

> **Martin, Philip, 1947– .** *Aubade* (1969). String orchestra. Unpublished. Source: *Irish-82.*

REMINGTON, EMORY, American trombonist; b. 1893; d. Dec. 10, 1972.

> **Benson, Warren, 1924– .** *Largo tah: To the memory of Emory Remington* (1978). Bass trombone and marimba. Published *Presser* 114-40772, 1995.

Hartley, Walter S., 1927– . *Concerto breve for bass trombone and small orchestra: In memory of Emory Remington* (1995). Published *Masters* M2640, 1996.

White, Donald H., 1921– . "In memory of 'The Chief'," in his *Tetra ergon: Four pieces* (1972). Bass trombone and piano. Published Nashville, TN: Brass Music Press, 1975. CONTENTS: For Van [Haney]—In memory of "The Boss" [i.e. Donald H. White]—In memory of "The Chief"—In memory of "Dottie" [i.e. Dorothy Ziegler].

REUBKE, JULIUS, German pianist, composer; b. Mar. 23, 1834; d. June 3, 1858.

Stör, Carl, 1814–1889. "Trauermarsch nach dem Verscheiden von Julius Reubke," in *Das Pianoforte: Ausgewählte Sammlung älterer und neuerer Original-Compositionen*, ed. by Franz Liszt, Jahrgang 2, Heft 9. Published Stuttgart: E. Hallberger, 1858.

RHAW, GEORG, German composer, music publisher; b. 1488; d. Aug. 6, 1548.

Reusch, Johannes, ca. 1525–1582. *Epitaphia Rhauorum.* Voices (5). Published Wittenberg: G. Rhaws Erben, 1550. *RISM-A1*: R-1207.

RHEINBERGER, JOSEPH, German organist, composer; b. Mar. 17, 1839; d. Nov. 25, 1901.

Terrabugio, Giuseppe, 1842–1933. *In memoria del suo maestro l'Illustre prof. Giuseppe v. Rheinberger: Requiem aeternam: Adagio funebre* (1908). Organ. Unpublished. Source: *SBN*. Manuscript located at the Conservatorio di Musica Giuseppe Verdi, Milan.

RIADIS, EMILIOS, Greek composer; b. May 13, 1855; d. July 17, 1935.

Papaioannou, Giannes Andreou, 1911–1989. *Fantasia for violin and piano: In memory of Em. Riadis* (1936). Unpublished. Source: *Papaioannou.* First performance Sept. 4, 1938. Manuscript located at the Historical Archives Dept. of the Benaki Museum in Athens. *Papaioannou* states that the memorial dedication appeared on the program of the premiere performance, but is crossed off the manuscript.

RICHARD I, COEUR DE LEON, English monarch, poet and composer; b. Sep. 1157; d. Apr. 11, 1199.

Gaucelm Faidit, fl. 1156–1209. "Fortz chauza es que tot lo major dan," in *La musique des troubadours*, by Jean Baptiste Beck. Monophonic song. Published Paris: Laurens, 1910. Edited from Biblioteca Ambrosiana ms. R.71 sup., and other manuscript sources.

RICHARDSON, ALAN, Scottish composer, pianist; b. Feb. 29, 1904; d. Nov. 29, 1978.

Lutoslawski, Witold, 1913–1994. *Epitafium: Alan Richardson in memoriam* (1979). Oboe and piano. Published *PWM* 8382, 1980. Another edition: *Chester* 55256, 1981.

RICHTER, ERNST FRIEDRICH, German composer, theorist; b. Oct. 24, 1808; d. Apr. 9, 1879.

Kirchner, Theodor, 1823–1903. "Beharre!" in his *Gedenkblätter: Zwölf Musikstücke zur Erinnerung an die Einweihung des neuen Königl. Conservatoriums für Musik zu Leipzig*, op. 82 (1843–87). Vocal quartet. Published Leipzig: J. Rieter-Biedermann 1508, 1887. No. 8 of 12 short piano pieces memorializing Conrad Schleinitz, Felix Mendelssohn, Robert Schumann, Moritz Hauptmann, Ferdinand David, Ignaz Moscheles, Ernst Friedrich Richter, Carl Ferdinand Becker, Ernst Ferdinand Wenzel, and Louis Plaidy.

RICORDI, GIOVANNI, Italian music publisher; b. 1785; d. Mar. 15, 1853.

Pappalardo, Salvatore, 1817–1884. *Un pensiero sulla tomba di Giovanni Ricordi: Romanza senza parole per pianoforte*, op. 24. Published *Ricordi* 25681, 1853?

Perny, Pietro, 1822–1908. *Una lagrima sulla tomba di Giovanni Ricordi: Pensiero funebre per pianoforte*, op. 51, no. 1. Published *Ricordi* 25020, 1853.

Toja, Giovanni. *Lamento sulla tomba di Giovanni Ricordi: Per voce soprano o tenore*, op. 21. Soprano (or tenor) and piano. Published *Ricordi* 25486, 1853?

RIEDY, JOHN, Irish composer; b. Aug. 1, 1931; d. Oct. 3, 1971.

See: O RIADA, SEÁN

RIEGGER, WALLINGFORD, American composer; b. Apr. 29, 1885; d. Apr. 2, 1961.

Smith, Hale, 1925– . *Contours: In memory of my two friends Dr. Clarence Cameron White and Dr. Wallingford Riegger* (1961). Orchestra. Published *Peters* 6503, 1962.

Thorarinsson, Leifur, 1934– . *Epitaph: Wallingford Riegger in memoriam* (1961). Orchestra. Published *IMIC*.

RIMSKY-KORSAKOV, NIKOLAI, Russian composer; b. Mar. 18, 1844; d. June 21, 1908.

Glazunov, Aleksandr Konstantinovich, 1865–1936. "À la mémoire de N. Rimsky-Korssakow," in his *Two preludes for orchestra*, op. 85. Published *Belaieff*, 1911. CONTENTS: À la mémoire de Wladimir Stassoff—À la mémoire de N. Rimsky-Korssakow.

Gnesin, Mikhail Fabianovich, 1883–1957. *Requiem for piano quintet,* op. 11 (1913–14). Published Moscow: Jurgenson 37921, 1918.

Stravinsky, Igor, 1882–1971. *Chant funèbre for winds,* op. 5: *Sur la morte de Rimsky-Korsakov* (1908). Unpublished. Source: *Stravinsky.* The work is presumed lost. First performance February 13, 1909, Grand hall of the St. Petersburg Conservatory, cond. by Felix Blumenfeld.

RIST, JOHANN, German theologian, composer; b. Mar. 8, 1607; d. Aug. 31, 1667.

Bernhard, Christoph, 1628–1692. *Letzter Schwanen-Gesang, so bei christlicher Beerdigung des . . . Johann Risten, gewesenen XXXII. Jährigen . . . am 12ten Tage Septembris dieses 1667 Jahres.* Voices (4), violins (2), viols (3), continuo. Published Hamburg: Georg Rebenlein, 1667. *RISM-A1:* B-2081.

ROLLAND, ROMAIN, French author, musicologist; b. Jan. 29, 1866; d. Dec. 30, 1944.

Arma, Paul, 1905– . "Pour Romain Rolland," in his *Trois epitaphes* (1945). Piano. Published *EMT* TR001082, 1969. CONTENTS: Pour Romain Rolland—Pour ceux qui ne sont jamais revenus: Mes amis torturés, massacrés—Pour Béla Bartók.

ROMAIN, LOUIS DE, French musicologist; b. 1845; d. 1912.

Ollone, Max d', 1875–1959. *Ode à la musique: Choeur composé pour l'érection du buste de Louis de Romain à Angers.* Chorus and orchestra. Unpublished. Source: *Ollone.* Composed for the installation of a bust of Romaine at Angers. A manuscript score was announced for sale in catalogue no. 12 of music antiquarian Lisa Cox of Devon, England.

ROMAN, JOHAN HELMICH, Swedish composer; b. Oct. 26, 1694; d. Nov. 20, 1758.

Söderholm, Valdemar, 1909–1990. *Concerto in ancient style for organ and string orchestra: To the memory of Roman* (1947). Unpublished. Source: *Satorius.* Photocopy available from *STIM.*

ROMANN, JACK, American pianist, director of the concert artist department of the Baldwin Piano Company; b. Feb. 13, 1928; d. May 5, 1987.

Corigliano, John, 1938– . "Tarantella," in his *Symphony no. 1: Dedicated to the memory of Sheldon Shkolnik* (1990). Published *Schirmer* HL50481774, 1990. "[The AIDS quilt] made me want to memorialize in music those I have lost, and reflect on those I am losing. I decided to relate the first three movements of the Symphony to three lifelong musician-friends. In the third movement, still other friends are recalled in a quilt-like interweaving of motivic melodies"—composer's program note in the score. The "friends" are not named in the published score, though Corigliano's note states that the "Tarantella" movement memorializes the dedicatee of the "Tarantella" of his *Gazebo dances* for band who was a friend in the music industry [i.e. Jack Romann]. CONTENTS: Apologue: Of rage and remembrance—Tarantella—Chaconne: Giulio's song—Epilogue.

RONNEFELD, PETER, German composer, conductor; b. Jan. 26, 1935; d. Aug. 6, 1965.

> **Reimann, Aribert, 1936– .** *Verrà la morte = Death shall come* (1966). Cantata for soloists (STBar), two mixed choruses, orchestra. Published *Schott-M.* Text by Cesare Pavese.

ROSENBERG, HILDING, Swedish composer; b. June 21, 1892; d. May 19, 1985.

> **Lidholm, Ingvar, 1921– .** *Tre elegier = Three elegies: A Hilding Rosenberg con reverenza* (1986). String quartet. Unpublished. Source: *KdG*. Recorded by the Tale Quartet on *Songs and chamber music of Ingvar Lidholm* (Caprice Records CAP21499, 1996).

ROSSINI, GIOACHINO, Italian composer; b. Feb. 29, 1792; d. Nov. 13, 1868.

> *Messa per Rossini* (1869). Soloists (SATBarB), chorus (4–6 voices), orchestra. Published *StudiVerdi*, 1988. A composite Requiem mass, with contributions by 13 composers, written at the suggestion of Verdi and intended to be performed on the first anniversary of Rossini's death. The contributions were completed, and the libretto published in 1869 by *Ricordi* as *Messa da Requiem . . . in onore di Gioachino Rossini*, but not performed until September 11, 1988, in Stuttgart at the European Music Festival. CONTENTS: Requiem and Kyrie / by Antonio Buzolla, 1815–1871—Dies irae / by Antonio Bazzini, 1818–1897—Tuba mirum / by Carlo Pedrotti, 1817–1893—Quid sum miser / by Antonio Cagnoni, 1828–1896—Recordare Jesu / by Federico Ricci, 1809–1877—Ingemisco / by Alessandro Nini, 1805–1880—Confutatis / by Raimondo Boucheron, 1800–1876—Lacrimosa / by Carlo Coccia, 1782–1873—Offertorium / by Gaetano Gaspari, 1808–1881—Sanctus / by Pietro Platania, 1828–1907—Agnus Dei / by Lauro Rossi, 1812–1885—Communio / by Teodulo

Mabellini, 1817–1897—Libera me / by Giuseppe Verdi, 1813–1901 [later used by Verdi in his Requiem for Manzoni]. Publication is a facsimile only of Verdi's autograph of the Libera me. An extensive study of this work is found in *Messa per Rossini: La storia, il testo, la musica*, ed. Michele Girardi and Pierluigi Petrobelli (*StudiVerdi*, 1988).

Androet, Cesare, 1827–1889. *Sinfonia funebre* (1868). Band. Unpublished. Source: *Rehrig*. Performed in Florence at the funeral memorial for Rossini.

Bussi, Alessandro, 1833–1895. *Pensieri di Rossini: Elegia* (1868). Orchestra. Published Bologna: Trebbi, 1868. Composed for the memorial in honor of Rossini held at the Accademia Filarmonica, Bologna, Dec. 1868.

Cavallini, Ernesto, 1807–1874. *Una lagrima sulla tomba dell'immortale Rossini.* Clarinet and piano. Published *Ricordi*, 1868? Recorded by Colin Bradbury on *The art of the clarinettist* (Clarinet Classics Records CC 0008).

Filippa, Giuseppe. *Marcia funebre per il trasporto delle ceneri di G. Rossini da Parigi al Tempio ai S. Croce di Firenze* (1887). Band. Published Northridge, CA: W.I.N.D.S., 199–? Composed for the transfer of Rossini's remains from Paris to Florence.

Giner, Salvador, 1832–1911. *Elegia a Rossini.* Orchestra. Unpublished. Source: *NGrove*.

Mercadante, Saverio, 1795–1870. *Omaggio all'immortale Rossini: Fantasia* (1868). Orchestral fantasia on themes by Rossini. Published *Ricordi*, 1870. Written for Rossini's memorial service in Naples Dec. 22, 1868. Published version is for piano 4-hands. Orchestra manuscript located at the conservatory in Naples.

Perolini, Eugenio, 1829–1907. *A Rossini: Marcia funebre.* Band. Published Florence: E. Paoletti, 186–?

Platania, Pietro, 1828–1907. *Sinfonia funebre per la morte di Rossini.* Orchestra. Unpublished. Source: *NGrove*.

ROTA, NINO, Italian composer; b. Dec. 3, 1911; d. Apr. 10, 1979.

Challulau, Patrice, 1959– . *Le tombeau de Nino Rota* (1982). Harpsichord. Unpublished. Source: *Bedford,* who states "available from the composer." Composed for the short film *Le cratère*, by Gérard Fabre. First performance by the composer 1982, Vitrolles, France, Festival of Sound and Images.

ROTH, ERNST, English music publisher; b. June 1, 1896; d. July 17, 1971.

Einem, Gottfried von, 1918–1996. *Bruckner dialog,* op. 39: *To the memory of Ernst Roth* (1971). Orchestra. Published *Boosey* HPS892, 1974.

RUBINSTEIN, ARTUR, Polish-born American pianist; b. Jan. 28, 1887; d. Dec. 20, 1982.

    Homs, Joaquin, 1906– . *In memoriam Rubinstein* (1987). Piano. Unpublished. Source: *Homs.*

RUBINSTEIN, BERYL, American pianist, composer; b. Oct. 26, 1898; d. Dec. 29, 1952.

    Nowak, Lionel, 1911–1995. *Piano trio: To the memory of Beryl Rubinstein.* Published *ACA,* 1954.

    Smith, Hale, 1925– . *In memoriam Beryl Rubinstein* (1953). Mixed chorus with chamber orchestra (or piano). Published *Galaxy* HP46, 1959. Words by Langston Hughes and Russell Atkins.

RUBINSTEIN, NIKOLAI, Russian pianist, conductor; b. June 14, 1835; d. Mar. 23, 1881.

    Sauer, Emil von, 1862–1942. *Concerto for piano and orchestra no. 1 in E minor: À la mémoire de mon grand maître Nicolas Rubinstein.* Published *Schott-M* 26810, 1900.

    Taneev, Sergei Ivanovich, 1856–1915. *Johannes Damaskusest: Kantate = John of Damascus: Cantata,* op. 1 (1884). Chorus and orchestra. Published Moscow: Jurgenson, 1886. Modern editions by *Sikorski,* 1969; *Muzyka,* 1971. Text by Alexei Tolstoy.

    Tchaikovsky, Piotr Ilych, 1840–1893. *Piano trio,* op. 50, A minor: *À la mémoire d'un grand artiste.* Published Moscow: Jurgenson; Hamburg: Rahter, 1882. New edition in Tchaikovsky, *Kamernye ansambli,* Polnoe sobranie sochinenii [Works], vol. 32a (Moscow: Gos. muzykalnoe izd-vo, 1951).

RUGGLES, CARL, American composer; b. Mar. 11, 1876; d. Oct. 24, 1971.

    Burt, Warren, 1949– . *Aardvarks II: Mr. Natural encounters Flakey Foont!: In memoriam Carl Ruggles* (1971). Piano. Published *Lingua,* 1977.

    Melby, John, 1941– . *Epitaph for winds and percussion: In memoriam Carl Ruggles* (1974–75). Ensemble of flutes (2), oboes (2), English horn, clarinets (2), bass clarinet, bassoons (2), contrabassoon, trumpets (2), horns (2), trombones (2), tuba, percussion (4 players). Published *Margun,* 1975.

    Tenney, James, 1934– . "Quintext III: A choir of angels for Carl Ruggles" (1972), in his *Quintext: Five textures.* String quartet with double bass. Published *SmithPubs*, 1988.

RUTKOWSKI, BRONISLAW, Polish organist, composer; b. Feb. 27, 1898; d. June 1, 1964.

Penderecki, Krzysztof, 1933– . *Piesn zalobna ku czci B. Rutkowskiego = Funeral song in memory of Rutkowski* (1964). Chorus. Unpublished. Source: *NGrove*. This work is not listed in *Penderecki*.

SACCHINI, ANTONIO, Italian composer; b. June 14, 1730; d. Oct. 6, 1786.

Désaugiers, Marc-Antoine, 1742–1793. *Requiem* (1786). Chorus. Unpublished. Source: *NGrove*. Manuscript is at the Bibliothèque nationale (France).

Lesueur, Jean François, 1760–1837. *L'ombre de Sacchini* (1786). Cantata. Unpublished. Source: *Pierre*, p. 333. Text by De Moline. Performed at the Concert Spirituel, in Paris on December 8, 1786, at a memorial concert for Sacchini. The work is not listed in *Lesueur*.

SACHER, PAUL, Swiss conductor, philanthropist; b. Apr. 28, 1906; d. May 26, 1999.

Rochberg, George, 1918– . *Three elegiac pieces for piano: In memoriam Paul Sacher* (1998). Published *Presser* 110-40735, 2000. Memorial dedication added for publication. The first two of the untitled pieces are revisions of earlier works: no.1 is dated 1947–1998; no. 2 is dated 1945–1998; no.3 is dated 1998.

SAINTE-COLOMBE, SIEUR DE (PÈRE), French gambist; d. 17th cent.

Marais, Marin, 1656–1728. "Le tombeau pour M. Sainte-Colombe," in his *Pièces de violes: Composées par M. Marais, ordinaire de la musique de la Chambre du Roy [livre 2]* [Pièces de violes, 2e livre] Violes (1 and 2) and continuo. Published Paris: L'autheur, Marais le fils, Hurel, Foucault, 1701. *RISM-A1*: M-389. New edition in Marais, *The instrumental works*, ed. by John Hsu (*Broude, 1986*).

Sainte-Colombe, Sieur de (fils), fl. 1703. *Le tombeau for Le Sieur de Sainte-Colombe (le père).* Bass viol and keyboard. Published Ottawa, Canada: Dove House, 1990. Edited by Margaret Sampson from a manuscript at Durham Cathedral.

SALMOND, FELIX, American violoncellist; b. Nov. 19, 1888; d. Feb. 19, 1952.

Shulman, Alan, 1915– . *Elegy: In memoriam Felix Salmond* (1971). Eight-part violoncello ensemble. Unpublished. Source: *ASCAP*.

SALZEDO, CARLOS, French harpist; b. Apr. 6, 1885; d. Aug. 17, 1961.
> **Petric, Ivo, 1931– .** *Elégie sur le nom de Carlos Salzedo* (1962).
> Harp. Published *Slovensk*, 1962.
> **Von Wurtzler, Aristid, 1925–1998.** *Memory of Salzedo.* Harp. Published *Lyra*.

SAMINSKY, LAZARE, Russian-American composer, conductor; b. Nov. 8, 1882; d. June 30, 1959.
> **Adler, Samuel, 1928– .** *Toccata, recitation, and postlude: In memory of Lazare Saminsky* (1962). Organ. Published *OUP* 93P105, 1962.

SAMUEL, HAROLD, English pianist; b. May 23, 1879; d. Jan. 15, 1937.
> **Ferguson, Howard, 1908–1999.** *Sonata for piano*, op. 8, F minor: *To the memory of Harold Samuel* (1938–40). Published *Boosey* PIB455, 1940.

SAN MIGUEL, MARIANO, Spanish clarinetist, composer; b. 1880; d. Oct. 1935.
> **Luna, Pablo, 1880–1942.** *A la memoria de Mariano San Miguel.* Funeral march for band. Unpublished. Source: *Rehrig*.

SANTOS, JOLY BRAGA, Portuguese composer, conductor.; b. May 14, 1924; d. July 18, 1988.
> **Capedeville, Constança, 1937– .** *Di lonatan fa specchio il mare: Joly Santos Braga in memoriam* (1989). Instrumental ensemble. Unpublished. Source: *No/Gro*.

SARASATE, PABLO DE, Spanish violinist; b. Mar. 10, 1844; d. Sep. 20, 1908.
> **Bretón, Tomás, 1850–1923.** *Concierto: Dedicado a la memoria de Pablo Sarasate* (1909). Violin and orchestra. Published Madrid: Santiago de Compostela 8460536521, 1995, in series Cuadernos de "Musica en Compostela," no. 9. The published edition is a reproduction of the composer's manuscript piano reduction.
> **Vanecek, Jaroslav.** *Spanish rhapsody: To the memory of Pablo de Sarasate.* Violin solo. Published *Roberton* 95501, 1946.

SARTO, JOHANNES DE, Franco-Flemish composer; fl. 1458–1464.
> **Compère, Loyset, d. 1518.** "Omnium, bonorum plenum," in his *Opera omnia*, vol. 4, ed. Ludwig Finscher, Corpus Mensurabilis Musicae, vol. 15, p. 32–38. Voices (4). Published *AIM*, 1958. Known as the "singers prayer." Concludes with prayers for a number of "magistri cantilenarum" and "cantores," most still living at the time of composition (ca. 1470–1474): Dufay, Johann Dussart (i.e. Johannes de Sarto), Busnois, Caron, Georget de Brelles, Tinctoris,

Ockeghem, Josquin Corbet, Hemart (i.e. Martin Hanard), Fauges, and the poet Jehan Molinet. From Trent codices, Tr. 91, fol. 33b.

SATIE, ERIK, French composer; b. May 17, 1866; d. July 1, 1925.

    Cerha, Friedrich, 1926– . *Double concerto for violin and violoncello and orchestra* (1976). Published *UE* 15025, 1976. "Eric Satie zum 50. Todestag und mir zum 50. Geburtstag"—note in score.

    Cliquet-Pleyel, Henri, 1894–1963. *Le tombeau de Satie.* Piano. Published *RevueMus* (Apr. 1, 1928): supplément musical.

    Farren, Martin, 1942– . "Canticle: In memoriam Eric Satie," in his *Passage of three times* (1975). String orchestra. Unpublished. Source: *BCP.* CONTENTS: On paths to other places—Among celestial plains—Canticle: In memoriam Eric Satie. First performance by the MIT Symphony, cond. by David Epstein, December 11, 1976.

    Johnston, Ben, 1926– . *Ci-git Satie* (1996). Mixed voices, double bass, drum set. Published *SmithPubs*, 1996. Text of scat syllables. The title is a tombstone phrase meaning "Here lies Satie."

    Louvier, Alain, 1945– . *Trois gymnopédies automatiques.* Piano. Published *Leduc* AL25355, 1976. "These short pieces were written thanks to . . . the title and the pianistic writing of the 'Gymnopédies' by Mr. Eric Satie to whom these pieces are obviously dedicated"—composer's note in score.

    Sauguet, Henri, 1901–1989. *Les forains: Ballet à la mémoire d'Erik Satie* (1945). Orchestra. Published Paris: Rouart, Lerolle, 1946.

SAUBERT, JOHANN, German composer, clergyman; b. 1592; d. Nov. 2, 1646.

    Dretzel, Valentin, 1578–1658. "Über dich, du theurer Mann," in *Christliche Trauer- und Leichpredigt . . . bey . . . Leichbestattung . . . Johannis Sauberti . . . gehlaten den VI. Nov. 1646.* Voices (4). Published Nuremberg: W. Endter, 1647. *RISM-A1:* D-3544.

SAUGUET, HENRI, French composer; b. May 18, 1901; d. June 22, 1989.

    Ancelin, Pierre, 1934– . *Lamento: In memoriam Henri Sauguet.* Violoncello solo. Published *Eschig* ME8790, 1990.

SAX, ADOLPHE, Belgian inventor of the saxophone; b. Nov. 6, 1814; d. Feb. 4, 1894.

    Lancen, Serge, 1922– . *Dedicace: À la mémoire d'Adolphe Sax* (1974). Saxophone and band. Published *Molenaar* 01.1682.10, 1985.

SCARLATTI, DOMENICO, Italian composer; b. Oct. 26, 1685; d. July 23, 1757.

Gladd, Neil Laurence, 1955– . *Le tombeau de Scarlatti* (1977). Harpsichord. Published *AMC*, 1977.

Huzella, Elek, 1915– . *Három tánc gitárra = Three dances for guitar: In memoriam Domenico Scarlatti*. Published *EMB* Z8529, 1978.

Jonás, Alberto, 1868–1943. *In memoriam Domenico Scarlatti,* op. 19. Piano. Published *CFischer*, 1932.

Schickele, Peter, 1935– . *Epitaphs for piano.* Published *E-V* 160-00202, 1981. "*Epitaphs* is a set of tributes written over a period of thirteen years; the composers to whom homage is paid represent each century from the 16th through the 20th"—composer's note in score. CONTENTS: Orlando di Lasso—Michael Praetorius—Domenico Scarlatti—Frédéric Chopin—Igor Stravinsky.

SCHAEFFER, PIERRE, French acoustician, composer.; b. Aug. 14, 1910; d. Aug. 19, 1995.

Le tombeau de Pierre Schaeffer. Unpublished. Source: "Synthèse 96: The 26th International Festival of Electroacoustic Music, Bourges, France, 31 May–9 June 1996," *Computer music journal* 21/2 (Summer 1997): 90–92. "Among the highlights of the evening performances were the 150 pieces composed for the Tombeau de Schaeffer—a memorial to the recently deceased French pioneer (some say inventor) of electroacoustic music, Pierre Schaeffer. These 3–5 min. pieces, collected from almost all of the significant composers active in the field, were mostly 'sprinkled in' with the full-length pieces on the program, and ranged from Schaeffer-esque musique concrète studies (a few of which even used his pieces as source materials), to intimate statements about loss and mortality"—festival review in *Computer music journal*, which does not name individual composers or works.

SCHAUB, FABIO, German conductor; b. 1948; d. Sep. 18, 1975.

Hoch, Francesco, 1943– . *Arcano: Alla memoria di Fabio Schaub* (1975–76). Chorus (SSSSSSMzMzATTTBarBB). Published *Zerboni* 8190, 1976. Text adapted from *Das Kapital* by Karl Marx.

SCHEIDT, SAMUEL, German organist, composer; b. 1587; d. Mar. 24, 1654.

Froidebise, Pierre, 1914–1962. "In memoriam Samuel Scheidt," in his *Sonatine for organ* (1939). Published *CeBeDeM*, 1958. CONTENTS: In memoriam Samuel Scheidt—In memoriam Louis Vierne—In memoriam Dietrich Buxtehude.

SCHEIN, JOHANN HERMANN, German composer; b. Jan. 20, 1586; d. Nov. 19, 1630.

Dietrich, Marcus, fl. 1630. "Ode discolos tetrastrophos," in *Leich-predigt . . . bey der Leichbestattung des . . . Johann Herman Scheins . . . welcher . . . den 19. Nov. anno 1630 . . . entschlaffen.* Published Leipzig: Gregor Ritssch, 1630. *RISM-A1*: D-3013.

Schütz, Heinrich, 1585–1672. *Verba d. Pauli, ex Epist. ad Timotheum Cap. 1, v. 15: Das ist je gewisslich wahr* [Das ist je gewisslich wahr]. Voices (SSATTB) with continuo. Published Dresden: Gottfried Seyffert, 1631. *RISM-A1*: SS-2287a. Modern edition in Schütz, *Trauermusiken*, ed. Werner Breig, Neue Ausgabe sämtlicher Werke, vol. 31 (*Bärenreiter* BA4483, 1970). SWV 277. Text from Timothy I, verses 1, 15–17.

SCHERCHEN, HERMANN, German conductor; b. June 21, 1891; d. June 12, 1966.

Malipiero, Gian Francesco, 1882–1973. *Symphony no. 10: Atropo: In memoria di Hermann Scherchen* (1967). Published *Ricordi 1042*, 1967.

Schidlowsky, León, 1931– . *Epitafio: A la memoria de Hermann Scherchen.* Orchestra. Unpublished. Source: *Chile*.

SCHINDLER, KURT, German conductor; b. Feb. 17, 1882; d. Nov. 16, 1935.

Chávez, Carlos, 1899–1978. *Tree of sorrow: Arbolucu, te sequeste* (1942). Chorus (SATB). Published *Mercury*, 1949. The archaic Spanish text and the melody are from Schindler's study of *Folk music and poetry of Spain and Portugal* (New York: Hispanic Institute, 1941).

SCHIPPERS, THOMAS, American conductor; b. Mar. 9, 1930; d. Dec. 16, 1977.

Rorem, Ned, 1923– . *Remembering Tommy: Double concerto in ten movements: To the memory of Thomas Schippers* (1978). Piano and violoncello soloists with orchestra. Published *Boosey*.

SCHISKE, KARL, Austrian composer; b. Feb. 12, 1916; d. June 16, 1969.

Johns, Donald, 1926– . *Three bagatelles: In memoriam Karl Schiske* (1989). Clarinet solo. Published *Doblinger* 5327, 1994.

SCHITTLER, LUDWIG, German music editor; d. Feb. 19, 1916.

Haas, Joseph, 1879–1960. *Alte, unnennbare Tage: Elegien, op. 42: Dem Andenken meines geliebten Freundes Ludwig Schittler* (1916). Piano. Published *Schott-M* 2632, 1937.

SCHLEINITZ, HEINRICH CONRAD, German composer; b. 1803; d. May 13, 1881.

Kirchner, Theodor, 1823–1903. "Marsch," in his *Gedenkblätter: Zwölf Musikstücke zur Erinnerung an die Einweihung des neuen Königl. Conservatoriums für Musik zu Leipzig,* op. 82 (1843–87). Piano. Published Leipzig: J. Rieter-Biedermann 1508, 1887. No. 1 of 12 short piano pieces memorializing Conrad Schleinitz, Felix Mendelssohn, Robert Schumann, Moritz Hauptmann, Ferdinand David, Ignaz Moscheles, Ernst Friedrich Richter, Carl Ferdinand Becker, Ernst Ferdinand Wenzel, and Louis Plaidy.

SCHLESINGER, DANIEL, German-American pianist, conductor; b. Dec. 15, 1799; d. Jan. 8, 1838.

Heinrich, Anthony Philip, 1781–1861. *Elegiac impromptu fantasia: A tribute to the memory of Daniel Schlesinger, late conductor and pianist to the German society The Concordia.* Piano. Published New York: For the author by C. G. Christman, 1840.

SCHOEMAKER, MAURICE, Belgian composer; b. Dec. 17, 1890; d. Aug. 24, 1964.

Veremans, Renaat, 1894–1969. *In memoriam Maurice Schoemaker* (1965). Voice and piano. Published *CeBeDeM,* 1965.

SCHOENBERG, ARNOLD, Austrian-born American composer; b. Sep. 13, 1874; d. July 13, 1951.

Coppens, Claude-Albert, 1936– . *Konzertstück: In memoriam Arnold Schoenberg* (1974). Piano; also for band. Published *CeBeDeM,* 1974.

Keller, Alfred, 1907–1987. *Epitaph für Arnold Schoenberg* (1956). Piano. Unpublished. Source: *SKZ.*

Moroi, Makoto, 1930– . *Schönberg sho = Ode to Schoenberg* (1961). Orchestra. Unpublished. Source: *NGrove.*

Pousseur, Henri, 1929– . *Ballade berlinoise: À la mémoire de Brahms, Mahler, Schoenberg et . . . J. S. Bach* (1974–77). Piano. Published *Zerboni* 8373, 1979.

Przybylski, Bronislaw Kazimierz, 1941– . *ArnolD SCHönBErg [sic] in memoriam* (1977). String quartet. Published *PWM* 8322416113, 1981.

Spies, Claudio, 1925– . *Animula vagula, blandula: Memoriae Arnold Schoenberg ante XC annos nati D. D.* (1964). Chorus (SATB) unacc. Published *Boosey* OCTB5689, 1969. In honor of Schoenberg's 90th birthday.

SCHUBERT, FRANZ, Austrian composer; b. Jan. 31, 1797; d. Nov. 19, 1828.

Hommage à Franz Schubert. Piano. Published *Schott-M* 6916,

1980, in series Journal für das Pianoforte, Heft 1. CONTENTS: Fuge in c "Dem Andenken des zu früh verblichenen Franz Schubert" / by Simon Sechter, 1788–1867—Nachruf an Schubert in Trauertönen am Pianoforte / by Anselm Hüttenbrenner, 1794–1868—Variationen über den beliebten Wiener Trauerwalzer von Franz Schubert / by Carl Czerny, 1791–1857.

Baur, Jürg, 1918– . *Frammenti: Sinfonische Erinnerungen an Schubert* (1996). Orchestra. Published *Breitkopf*, 1996. CONTENTS: Wetterfahne—Stürmischer Morgen—Die weite Himmel—Ende der Reise—Rückblick.

Bondon, Jacques, 1927– . *Le tombeau de Schubert* (1980). Piano quintet. Published *Eschig* ME8387, 1980.

Fine, Vivian, 1913–2000. *Momenti: In honor of the 150th anniversary of Schubert's death* (1978). Piano. Published *GunMar*, 1983. Also published in the memorial collection *In memoriam Roger Sessions*, 1896–1985 (q.v.).

Françaix, Jean, 1912–1997. *Octet for winds and strings: À la mémoire vénérée de Franz Schubert* (1972). Octet for clarinet, horn, bassoon, string quartet, double bass. Published *Schott-M* 6155; *Eschig*, 1974.

Harbison, John, 1938– . *November 19, 1828* (1988). Piano with string trio. Published *AMP*, 1989. The date constituting the title is the date of Schubert's death.

Holbrooke, Joseph Charles, 1878–1958. *Symphony no. 4 in B minor,* op. 95: *The little one: Homage to Schubert* (1928?). Unpublished. Source: *Holbrooke*. Possibly intended as a 100th anniversary memorial for Schubert's death. First performance March 7, 1929, Bournemouth Municipal Orchestra.

Hrabovskyi, Leonid Oleksandrovych, 1935– . "Impromptus: In memoriam Franz Schubert," in his *Homages: Seven pieces for guitar.* Published *Duma*, 1996. CONTENTS: Ciaccona: In memoriam Henry Purcell—Aria: In memoriam Johann Sebastian Bach—Impromptus: In memoriam Franz Schubert—Prelude: In memoriam Frédéric Chopin—A little cake-walk: In memoriam Scott Joplin—Chorale: In memoriam Johannes Brahms—Amoroso: In memoriam Sergei Prokofiev.

Hüttenbrenner, Anselm, 1794–1868. *Nachruf an Schubert in Trauertönen am Pianoforte* (1829). Piano. Published Vienna: T. Haslinger, 1829? Facsimile reprint in Otto Erich Deutsch, *Franz Schubert: Die Dokumente seines Lebens und Schaffens*, vol. 3, *Sein*

Leben in Bildern (Munich, 1913). New edition in *Hommage à Franz Schubert* (q.v.).

Lasne, George, 1905–1972. *Deux esquisses: À la mémoire de Schubert* (1946). Saxophone and piano (or organ). Unpublished. Source: *Londeix*.

Orrego Salas, Juan, 1919– . *Encuentros*, op. 115: *For string quartet and piano* (1997). Published *MMB* X505003, 2000. Dedicated to Schubert on the 200th anniversary of his birth.

Reger, Max, 1873–1916. *Fünf Lieder*, op. 12: *Den Manen Franz Schuberts* (1893). Voice and piano. Published London: Augener, 1894. New edition in Reger, *Sologesänge mit Klavier*, ed. Fritz Stein, Max Reger sämtliche Werke, vol. 31 (*Breitkopf* MR31, ca. 1955). CONTENTS: Friedhofsgang—Das arme Vögelein—Wenn ich's nur wüsst—Gruss—Um Dich.

Schubert, Ferdinand, 1794–1859. *Requiem*, op. 9, in G minor: *Componirt und dem Andenken des verblichenen Tonsetzers Franz Schubert geweiht von seinem Bruder*. Soloists (STB), chorus (SATB), violins (2), trombones or horns (2), trumpets (2), timpani, violoncello, double bass, organ. Published Vienna: A. Diabelli 3721, 1831. Modern ed. by Otto Biba (Altötting: A. Coppenrath, 1978). Ferdinand Schubert was Franz's brother.

Sechter, Simon, 1788–1867. *Fuge in C-Moll: Dem Andenken des zu früh verblichenen Franz Schubert* (Nov. 28,1828). Organ (or piano). Published Vienna: A. Diabelli, 1829. Facsimile reprint in Otto Erich Deutsch, *Franz Schubert: die Dokumente seines Lebens und Schaffens*, vol. 3, *Sein Leben in Bildern* (Munich, 1913). Reprinted in Sechter, *Drei Fugen für Orgel*, ed. Otto Biba (*Doblinger*, 1972). Also published in *Hommage à Franz Schubert* (q.v.).

Stadler, Maximilian, Abbé, 1748–1833. *Fuge für die Orgel oder das Pianoforte, über den Nahmen des zu früh'verblichenen Tonsetzers Franz Schubert* (1828). Organ or piano. Published Vienna: A. Diabelli 3207, 1829. Facsimile reproduction in Otto Erich Deutsch, *Franz Schubert: Die Dokumente seines Lebens und Schaffens*, vol. 3, *Sein Leben in Bildern* (Munich, 1913).

SCHUMANN, ROBERT, German composer; b. June 8, 1810; d. July 29, 1856.

Kirchner, Theodor, 1823–1903. "Lento," in his *Gedenkblätter: Zwölf Musikstücke zur Erinnerung an die Einweihung des neuen Königl. Conservatoriums für Musik zu Leipzig*, op. 82 (1843–87). Piano. Published Leipzig: J. Rieter-Biedermann 1508, 1887. No. 4 of

12 short piano pieces memorializing Conrad Schleinitz, Felix Mendelssohn, Robert Schumann, Moritz Hauptmann, Ferdinand David, Ignaz Moscheles, Ernst Friedrich Richter, Carl Ferdinand Becker, Ernst Ferdinand Wenzel, and Louis Plaidy.

Nicodé, Jean Louis, 1853–1919. *Andenken an Robert Schumann: 6 Phantasiestücke,* op. 6. Piano. Published *Breitkopf* 14312, 1876. New edition: London: Augener, 1934

Reimann, Aribert, 1936– . *Sieben Fragmente: In memoriam Robert Schumann* (1988). Orchestra. Published *Schott-M* 46632, 1988.

Schafer, R. Murray, 1933– . *Adieu Robert Schumann* (1976). Contralto and orchestra. Published *UE* 16520a, 1980. Words, principally English, freely adapted from the diaries of Clara Schumann. Includes musical quotations from Robert Schumann's musical works.

SCHWEITZER, ALBERT, Alsatian missionary, organist, musicologist; b. Jan. 14, 1875; d. Jan. 14, 1965.

Krol, Bernhard, 1920– . *Pas de deux supra B–A–C–H,* op. 59: *In memoriam Albert Schweitzer* (1974). Organs (2). Published *Bote.*

Lohmann, Heinz, 1934– . *Fantasia for organ: In memoriam Albert Schweitzer.* Unpublished. Source: *Beckmann.*

SCIONTI, SILVIO, Italian-American pianist, teacher; b. Nov. 20, 1882; d. May 22, 1973.

Mailman, Martin, 1932– . *In memoriam Silvio Scionti* (1974). Prepared piano. Unpublished. Source: *AMC.*

SCOTT, FRANCIS GEORGE, Scottish composer; b. Jan. 25, 1880; d. Nov. 6, 1958.

Stevenson, Ronald, 1928– . *A Keening sang for a Makar: In memoriam Francis George Scott* (1959). Piano. Published London: Performing Rights Society Ltd. (orchestral version). Based on a motive on Scott's initials (F. G. S. = F–G–E flat). Arranged in 1963 for orchestra.

SCRIABIN, ALEXANDER, Russian composer; b. Jan. 6, 1872; d. Apr. 27, 1915.

Achron, Joseph, 1886–1943. *Epitaph,* op. 38: *In memory of Scriabin* (1915). Orchestra. Unpublished. Source: *Achron.*

Kelkel, Manfred, 1929– . *Le tombeau de Scriabine,* op. 22 (1972). Piano. Unpublished. Source: Recorded by Peter-Jürgen Hofer on *Rarities of piano music: Live recordings from the 1992 Festival at Schloss vor Husum* (Danacord DACOCD399, 1993)

Yasser, Joseph, 1893–1981. *Epitaphe: À la mémoire de A. Scriabine.* Piano. Unpublished. Source: *OCLC.*

SEGOVIA, ANDRÉS, Spanish guitarist; b. Feb. 21, 1893; d. June 3, 1987.

Behrend, Siegfried, 1933–1990. *Conserere: In memoriam Andrés Segovia* (1987). Sextet for guitar with quintet of violins (2), viola, violoncello, double bass; or for guitars (2) with mandola, mandolins (2), double bass. Published *Zimmermann* 2717, 1987.

Fernández, José Manuel. *Zul: Homenaje a Andrés Segovia* (1990). Guitar. Published Madrid: Opera tres ediciones musicales 009, 1990. "Zul ha sido escrita en elogio a la figra de Andrés Segovia"— composer's note in score. Thematic material taken from "Estudio sin luz" by Segovia.

Hurley, Donal, 1950– . *Sonata for guitar: Homage to Segovia* (1993). Published *CMC*, 1993.

Tomasi, François, 1943– . *Le tombeau de Segovia.* Guitar. Published in journal *Les cahiers de la guitare* (1988, no. 1)

Tucker, Robert E. *Elegy: Homage to Andrés Segovia.* Guitar. Published in journal *Guitar international* 17/9 (April 1988).

SEIBER, MÁTYÁS, Hungarian composer; b. May 3, 1905; d. Sep. 24, 1960.

Fricker, Peter Racine, 1920–1990. *Symphony no. 4, op. 43: Dedicated to the memory of Mátyás Seiber* (1966). Published Hollywood, CA: Alpheus Music, 1979.

Kodály, Zoltán, 1882–1967. *Media vita in morte sumus: In memoriam Mathias Seiber* (1960). Chorus (SATB) unacc. Published *Boosey* OCTB5463, 1963. "We are in the hand of death in the middle of our life"—note in score. Also known as *Homo perpende fragilis*, which is the text incipit.

Ligeti, György, 1923– . *Atmosphères: In memoriam Mátyás Sieber* (1961). Large orchestra without percussion. Published *UE* 11418, 1963.

Schat, Peter, 1935– . *Improvisations and symphonies for wind quintet: To the memory of Mátyás Seiber* (1960). Quintet for flute, oboe, clarinet, horn, bassoon. Published *Donemus*, 1960.

SELL, STEPHEN, American orchestra executive; b. 1942; d. May 26, 1989.

Bolcom, William, 1939– . *Symphony no. 5.* Unpublished. Source: Recording by the American Composers Orchestra, cond. by Dennis Russell Davies (Argo 433 077-2, 1992). "When the time came to give the Philadelphia Orchestra its expected commission, I took the onus off by deciding not to write a symphony after all, only to find that the piece was becoming a symphony anyway! (The dedicatee was the Philadelphia's manager Stephen Sell, whom I had known since his early days with the Saint Paul Chamber Orchestra; Steve died during the work's composition, and I have to note that a great deal of the music on this disc is eulogistic in one sense or another)"—composer's note accompanying the recording

Hodkinson, Sydney, 1934– . *Two poems: In memory of Stephen Sell.* Violoncello and piano, with optional percussion. Published *Merion* 144-40258, 1997. CONTENTS: Where light is stone—The unsinging fields.

SENN, KURT WOLFGANG, Swiss organist; b. Mar. 11, 1905; d. June 25, 1965.

Huber, Klaus, 1924– . *Ausgespannt: Geistliche Musik in memoriam Kurt Wolfgang Senn* (1972). High baritone voice, 5 instrumental groups, percussion, organ, loudspeaker, electronic tape. Published *Schott-M*, 1972. Text derived by the composer from various sources.

SERMISY, CLAUDE DE, French composer; b. 1490?; d. Oct. 13, 1562.

Certon, Pierre, ca. 1510–1572. "Musiciens, chantres melodieux: Déploration sur la mort de Claudin de Sermisy," in *Les meslanges . . . esquelles sont quatre vingtz dix-huict tant cantiques que chansons spirituelles.* Voices (6). Published Paris: du Chemin, 1570. *RISM-A1*: C-1718. Quinta pars is lost. Modern reconstructed edition in Eric Rice, "Tradition and imitation in Pierre Certon's déploration for Claudin de Sermisy," *Revue de musicologie* 85/1 (1999): 29–62.

SEROCKI, KAZIMIERZ, Polish composer; b. Mar. 3, 1922; d. Jan. 9, 1981.

Lorentzen, Bent, 1935– . *Paradiesvogel for seven instruments: Homage to Kazimierz Serocki* (1983). Septet for flute/piccolo, clarinet, violin, violoncello, guitar, percussion, piano. Published *Hansen* 4440, 1985.

SESSIONS, ROGER, American composer; b. Dec. 28, 1896; d. Mar. 16, 1985.

In memoriam Roger Sessions, 1896–1985. A collection of remembrances and compositions by various contributors. Published in *Perspectives* 23 (Spring/Summer 1985): 110–165. MUSICAL CONTENTS: Another page from a diary (to the memory of Roger Sessions): Piano (June 1985) / by Edward T. Cone, 1917– —Momenti: Piano (In honor of the 150th anniversary of Schubert's death, and dedicated to Roger Sessions) [composed 1978] / by Vivian Fine, 1913–2000 —Praeludium: Piano (In memoriam Roger Sessions) / by

Harold Schiffman, 1928– —Roger Sessions in memoriam: Clarinet / by William O. Smith, 1926– .

Beeler, C. Alan, 1939– . *Homage to Roger Sessions* (1986). Orchestra. Unpublished. Source: *Koshgarian.*

Harbison, John, 1938– . *Sonata for piano no. 1: Roger Sessions in memoriam* (1985). Published *AMP* 8071, 1994.

Shackelford, Rudy, 1944– . *Paradise on the rooftops* (1985). Song cycle for soprano, flute/alto flute/piccolo, harpsichord/celesta. Published *AMC*, 1985. Text in Italian by Cesare Pavese. CONTENTS: Mattino = Morning—Paesaggio VIII = Landscape VIII—Il paradiso sui tetti = Paradise on the rooftops.

SHAND, ERNEST, English guitarist, composer; b. Jan. 31, 1868; d. Nov. 30, 1924.

McConnell, David Edward. "Marche funebre: En mémoire d'Ernest Shand, 1868–1924" (1993), in journal *Classical guitar* 12/6 (Feb. 1994). Guitar. Shand (born Ernest Watson) was best known to the British public as an actor and comedian, but also was a prolific composer for the guitar.

SHIFRIN, SEYMOUR J., American composer; b. Feb. 28, 1926; d. Sep. 26, 1979.

Barkin, Elaine, 1932– . ". . . *in its surrendering . . . find its continuing . . .":* In memoriam Seymour Shifrin. Tuba solo. Published *APNM*, 1982. The title is a line in Marianne Moore's poem "What are years?"

Spies, Claudio, 1925– . "Verschieden (26–IX–1979): A lament for Seymour Shifrin" in *Perspectives* 17 (Spring/Summer 1979): 1–8. Piano.

SHIRINSKY, VASILI PEOTROVICH, Russian violinist, composer; b. Jan. 17, 1901; d. Aug. 16, 1965.

Shostakovich, Dmitri, 1906–1975. *String quartet no. 11,* op. 122, F minor: *To the memory of Vasily Shirinsky* (1966). Published *Sikorski* 2264, 1966. Also published by Sovetskii Kompositor, *Boosey,* and others.

SHKOLNIK, SHELDON, American pianist; b. 1937; d. Mar. 24, 1990.

Corigliano, John, 1938– . *Symphony no. 1: Dedicated to the memory of Sheldon Shkolnik* (1990). Published *Schirmer* HL50481774, 1990. "[The AIDS quilt] made me want to memorialize in music those I have lost, and reflect on those I am losing. I decided to relate the first three movements of the Symphony to three lifelong musician-friends. In the third movement, still other friends are recalled in a quilt-like interweaving of motivic melodies"—composer's program note in the score. The "friends" are not named in the published score, though Corigliano's note states that the "Tarantella" movement memorializes the dedicatee of the "Tarantella" of his *Gazebo dances* for band who was a friend in the music industry, Jack Romann. CONTENTS: Apologue: Of rage and remembrance—Tarantella—Chaconne: Giulio's song—Epilogue.

SHOSTAKOVICH, DMITRI, Russian composer; b. Sep. 25, 1906; d. Aug. 9, 1975. For a survey of additional musical tributes to Shostakovich, see the Appendix "DSCH—The composer's monogram, compositions based on DSCH by other hands, and tributes" in *Hulme*. DSCH in German musical orthography is the motive D–E-flat–C–B.

    D. Shostakovich: Statti i materialy, ed. by Grigorii Shneerson. Published Moscow: Sov. Kompozitor, 1976. Contains a musical appendix of short piano pieces on the theme "DSCH" by 13 composers. Originally conceived as a musical tribute for Shostakovich's 70th birthday, the project was reconceived as a memorial when the composer died prior to its completion. MUSICAL CONTENTS: DSCH / by Kara Karayev, 1918–1982—Preliudiia (DSCH) / by Miroslav Skorik, 1938– —DSCH / by Sergei Slonimskii, 1932– —DSCH / by Boris Tishchenko, 1939– —DSCH / by Andrei Eshpai, 1925– —Pismo-Galiaria, op. 79 / by Alan Dudley Bush, 1900–1995—Für D. Sch. / by Giunter Kokhan, 1930– —Kolybelnaia / by Daniel Lesur, 1908– —Preliudiia DSCH / by Ernst Meyer, 1905–1988—DSCH / by Siegfried Matthus, 1934– —DSCH / by Carlos Palacio, 1911– —D. S. C. H.—B. A. C. H. (25 September 1976) / by Nicolas Slonimsky, 1894–1995—Rechitativ i ariia / by Ronald Stevenson, 1928– .

Abeliovich, Lev, 1912–1985. *Vokaliz: Pamiati D. D. Shostakovicha.* Voice and orchestra. Unpublished. Recorded by Tamara Pechinskaia (mezzo-soprano), the Gosudarstvennyi simfonicheskii orkestr BSSR, cond. by Iurii Efimov (Melodiia S10-12705/6, 1979).

Babajanian, Arno, 1921–1983. *String quartet no. 3: In memory of D. Shostakovich* (1975). Published Moscow: Sov. Kompozitor 4939, 1979.

Banshchikov, Gennadii Ivanovich, 1943– . *Sonata for flute and piano* (1975). Published Moscow: Sov. Kompozitor, 1981.

Bibik, Valentin, 1940– . *Symphony no. 4,* op. 29: *Pamiati D. D. Shostakovycha* (1976). Chamber orchestra, with solo viola in the 3rd movement. Published *Ukraina,* 1984.

Boer, Ed de, 1957– . *Hommage aan Dimitri Schostakowitsch,* op. 4

(1978; rev. 1983). Orchestra. Published *Donemus*, 1979.

Bronner, Mikhail, 1952– . *Pridanoe = The dowry: Dramaticheskaia legenda.* Soloists (STB) with chamber ensemble. Unpublished. Text by Dmitri Kedrin. Recorded by Lidia Davydova (soprano), Aleksei Martynov (tenor), IAn Kratov (baritone), unspecified instrumental ensemble, cond. by Aleksandr Korneev (Melodiia C10-13247-8, 1980).

Brotons, Salvador, 1959– . "Elegia per la mort d'en Shostakovich" (1975), in *Llibre per a piano.* Piano. Published *ACC*, 1980. The *Llibre* contains piano music by several contemporary Catalan composers.

Burch, Robert William, 1929– . *Essay: To the memory of Dmitri Shostakovich* (1975). Violoncello and piano. Unpublished. Source: *NZ.*

Dorfmann, Joseph, 1940– . *Piano trio: In memory of Dmitri Shostakovich* (1975). Published *Israeli*, 1979.

Englund, Einar, 1916–1999. *Symphony no. 4* (1976). Strings and percussion. Published *Fazer* 06882-5, 1984. The memorial intent is according to *Hulme*. No dedication is in the published score.

Falik, IUrii Aleksandrovich, 1936– . *String quartet no. 3* (1976). Published Moscow: Sov. Kompozitor 413, 1977. Reprinted 1988. Attribution as a memorial to Shostakovich is by *Hulme*.

Franceschini, Romulus, 1929–1994. *String quartet: Ommagio a Shostakovich* (1980). Unpublished. Source: *OCLC.*

Freidlin, IAn Mikhailovich, 1944– . *Epitaph.* Orchestra. Unpublished. Source: *Hulme.*

Fridlender, Aleksandr, 1906– . *Poem: In memoriam Dmitri Shostakowitsch* (1976). Orchestra. Published *Sikorski.*

Gabichvadze, Revaz, 1913– . *Chamber symphony no. 4: Pamiati D. D. Shostakovicha* (1975). Unpublished. Recorded by the Chamber Orchestra of Georgia, cond. by Shavleg Shilakadze (Melodiia C10-13235/6). Incorporates the DSCH motive.

Josephs, Wilfred, 1927–1997. *Testimony: Toccata for organ,* op. 122: *In memoriam DSCH* (1981). Published *Ramsey*, 1981? "In memory of a great man"—additional dedication in score.

Joubert, John, 1927– . "Adagio: In memoriam DSCH," in his *String quartet no. 2,* op. 91 (1977). Published *Novello* 12053900, 1982. CONTENTS: Moderato: Poco lento—Allegro vivace—Adagio: In memoriam DSCH—Allegretto.

Kalinkovich, Grigorii, 1917–1992. *Elegiu pamiati Dmitriia Shos-*

takovicha = *Elegia zur Erinnerung an Dmitri Schostakowitsch.*
Trombone and piano. Published *Parow'sche* PM14006, 1993.
Khalmamedov, Nury, 1940– . *String quartet* (1976). Published
Muzyka, 1978. Incorporates the DSCH theme.
Levitin, IUrii, 1912– . *Epigrafiia*, op. 89 (1976). Soprano with quin-
tet of clarinet, string quartet. Unpublished. Source: *Hulme*. Text by
Ana Akhmatova. Recorded by Liudmila Belogragina (soprano), Ivan
Mozgovovenko (clarinet), and the Borodin String Quartet on *Pa-
miati Shostakovicha* (Melodiia S10-21425-005, 1984).
————. *Prelude (D–Es–H) for organ*, op. 105 (1984). Unpublished.
Source: *Hulme*. Recorded by Oleg IAnchenko on *Pamiati
Shostakovicha* (Melodiia S10-21425-005, 1984).
————. *Preludes (24) for violin solo*, op. 84 (1976). Unpublished.
Source: *Hulme*. Recorded by Irina Medvedeva on *Pamiati
Shostakovicha* (Melodiia S10-21425-005, 1984).
Lokshin, Aleksandre, 1920–1987. *Quintet for 2 violins, 2 violas
and violoncello: In memory of Dmitry Shostakovich* (1978). Pub-
lished Moscow: Sov. Kompozitor 6203, 1982.
Lucky, Stepan, 1919– . *Concerto for orchestra* (1976). Published
Cesky. Dedication is according to *Hulme*.
Malovec, Jozef, 1933– . "Poéma pre sólové husle: In memoriam
Dmitrij D. Sostakovic," in *Slovenská musl'ová tvorba = Slowakische
Kompositionen*. Poem for violin solo. Published *Opus*, 1981. The
collection includes also non-memorial works for solo violin by Jozef
Sixta, Juraj Benes, Tadeás Salva, and Ivan Hrusovsky.
Mansurian, Tigran, 1939– . *Concerto for violoncello and orchestra
no. 1: In memoriam Dmitri Shostakovich* (1976). Published Moscow:
Sov. Kompozitor 5151, 1980.
Martin, Frederick, 1921– . *Le tombeau de DSCH.* String quartet.
Published *Billaudot* 5612.
Miller, Karl Frederick, 1947– . *Variations for orchestra on a
theme by Shostakovich* (1978). Published North Texas State Univer-
sity (thesis), 1978. Theme is taken from Shostakovich's Symphony
no. 15, final movement, meas. 14–35. According to *Hulme* the work
is "intended to be something of an orchestral requiem."
Minor, Eugene, 1940– . *Requiem*, op. 24: *In memoriam Dimitri
Shostakovich.* Chorus (SATB), soloists, children's chorus, organ, pi-
ano, orchestra. Published *Kalmus* 6329, 1986.
Nikolaev, Aleksei Aleksandrovich, 1931– . *String quartet no. 3:
Pamiati D. D. Shostakovtscha.* Published *Muzyka* 13189, 1986.

Nordgren, Pehr Henrik, 1944– . *Concerto for viola and orchestra no. 2* (1979). Unpublished. Source: *Hulme.* Second of two movements ("Testimony") is a memorial to Shostakovich. First performance December 7, 1979, Jarmo Ahvenainen (viola), Helsinki Philharmonic, cond. by Pekka Helasvuo.

Nosyrev, Mikhail Iosifovich, 1924– . *Symphony no. 2* (1976). Unpublished. Source: *Hulme.*

Prigozhin, Liutsian Abramovich, 1926– . *Soltse i kamni = Sun and stone: Pamiats D. D. Shchostakovtscha.* Cantata for mezzo-soprano, flute, string quartet, piano. Published Moscow: Sov. Kompozitor 562, 1978. Text by Mira Aleckovic.

Raaff, Robin de, 1968– . *In memoriam Dimitri Shostakovich* (1994). Solo trumpets (2) and horns (2) with orchestra. Published *Donemus*, 1996.

Sarkisian, Ruben, 1945– . *Music in memory of Shostakovich* (1975). Trio for flute, violoncello, piano. Unpublished. Source: *Hulme.* First performance Nov. 1975, Yerevan, Armenia.

Schnittke, Alfred, 1934–1998. *Praeludium: In memoriam Dmitri Schostakowitsch* (1975). Violins (2), or violin with pre-recorded electronic tape. First published in *Noviye sochineniya sovetskikh kompozitorov dlia skripki solo = New works by Soviet composers for solo violin*: Published Moscow: Sov. Kompozitor, 1976. Later editions by *Sikorski* 2255; *Schirmer*, 1978.

Schnittke, Alfred, 1934–1998. *Hommage à Strawinsky, Prokofjew und Schostakowitsch* (1979). Piano 6-hands. Published *Sikorski* 1818, 1998.

Smirnova, Tatiana Georgievna, 1940– . *Adagio for string orchestra,* op. 25, no. 1 (Sep. 25, 1975). Published *Muzyka*, 1978.

Susskind, Walter, 1913–1980. *Passacaglia: In memoriam D. Shostakovich* (1976). Chamber orchestra with timpani. Published *MMB* X073003, 1976.

Sylvestrov, Valentyn Vasylovych, 1937– . *Postludium D–S–C–H* (1981–82). Soprano, violin, violoncello, piano. Published Moscow: VAAP; *Schirmer*.

Tarnopolskii, Vladimir, 1955– . *In memoriam Dmitri Shostakovich: A musical collage* (1983). Narrator and chamber orchestra. Unpublished. Source: *ConCom.*

Tichy, Vladimir, 1946– . *Concerto for violoncello and orchestra* (1976–77). Published *Panton* 2065, 1982.

Tishchenko, Boris Ivanovich, 1939– . *Symphony no. 5: Dedicated* *to Dmitry Dmitrievich Shostakovich* (1976). Published Moscow: Sov. Kompozitor 766, 1980. Incorporates the DSCH motive and quotations from Shostakovich works, notably from the 8th and 10th symphonies in the Scherzo movement.

Tsintsadze, Sulkhan, 1925– . *String quartet no. 9: Pamiati D. D. Shostakovicha* (1975). Published Moscow: Sov. Kompozitor 6809, 1984. First movement incorporates the DSCH motive.

Vainberg, Moisei Samuilovich, 1919–1996. *Symphony no. 12, op. 114: Pamiamu Dmitriia Dmitrievicha Shostakovicha = In memory of Dmitry Shostakovich* (1976). Published *Muzyka* 12017, 1983.

Vartazarian, Martin Tsolakovich, 1938– . *Concerto for violoncello and orchestra.* Unpublished. Source: *Hulme.* Recorded by Karine Georgian (violoncello), the Armenian State Symphony Orchestra, cond. by D. Khandzhian (Melodiia C10-11381-2).

Voigtländer, Lothar, 1943– . *Memento: Hommage à D. Schostakowitsch* (1976). Orchestra. Published *Peters* 5529, 1981.

Wheeler, Tony, 1958– . *Movement for string orchestra: In memoriam Dmitri Shostakovich* (1981). Published *Australia*, 1981?

Zivkovic, Nebojsa, 1962– . *CTPAX: STRAH, op. 12: To [the memory of] Dmitri Shostakovich* (1987). Multipercussion with optional electronic tape. Published *Moeck.* Tape includes Shostakovich's voice.

SIBELIUS, JEAN, Finnish composer; b. Dec. 8, 1865; d. Sep. 20, 1957.

Meriläinen, Usko, 1930– . *Hommage à Jean Sibelius* (1965). Violin and piano. Unpublished. Source: *FIMIC.*

Rak, Stepán, 1945– . "Elegy: Hommage a Sibelius," in his *Guitar music of Stepán Rak*, vol. 1. Published *MelBay* MB967830, 1999.

Rudin, Rolf, 1961– . *Legende for string orchestra, op. 21: In memoriam Jean Sibelius.* Published *Bote.*

Still, William Grant, 1895–1978. *Threnody: In memory of Jan Sibelius* (1965). Orchestral tone poem. Published *Still.*

SICOTTE, LUCIEN, Canadian violinist; b. Sep. 22, 1902; d. Sep. 23, 1943.

Papineau-Couture, Jean, 1916– . *Sonata for violin and piano in G: À la mémoire de Lucienn Sicotte* (1944; rev. 1953). Unpublished. Source: *Canadian.*

SIKORSKI, TOMASZ, Polish composer, pianist; b. May 19, 1939; d. 1988.

Montague, Stephen, 1943– . *In memoriam: Barry Anderson and Tomasz Sikorski* (1989–91). Ensemble of string quartet, percussion

(2), electronics, tape. Published *UMP*, 1991. A revision of the composer's String quartet, 1989. "In memoriam . . . was inspired by my close friendship with these two men, and uses short thematic and harmonic material from their works"—note in score.

SILBERMAN, AARON, American clarinet aficionado and patron of the arts; b. Jan. 8, 1916; d. Aug. 30, 1993.

Stock, David, 1939– . *For cl-Aaron-et: In memory of Aaron Silberman* (1993). Solo clarinet. Published *MMB* X130013, 2000. Silberman, a clarinet student of Simeon Bellison in his youth, made his fortune as founder of the American Thermoplastic Company of Pittsburgh. He served on the boards of several orchestras and chamber music societies, and for many years was Vice President of Finance for ClariNetwork International Inc. In 1990 he endowed the principal clarinet chair of the Pittsburgh Symphony Orchestra.

SILVER, ANNON LEE, Canadian soprano; b. 1939; d. July 28, 1971.

Tavener, John, 1944– . *Responsorium: In memoriam Annon Lee Silver* (1971). Solo trebles (2) or mezzo-sopranos (2), with mixed chorus (SATB) unacc. Published Chester 60997, 1993. Text for soloists is from the funeral service ("Suscipiat te Christus"), with the accompanying chorus repeating "Annon Lee."

SIMMONS, CALVIN, American conductor; b. Apr. 27, 1950; d. Aug. 21, 1982.

Harrison, Lou, 1917– . *Elegy: To the memory of Calvin Simmons* (1982). Ensemble of oboe, celesta, vibraphone, harp, percussion, strings. Published *FrogPeak* HAR18, 1993.

Tippett, Michael, 1905–1998. *The blue guitar: Sonata for solo guitar: Dedicated to the memory of the conductor Calvin Simmons* (1982–83). Published *Schott-L* 12218, 1985.

SIMPSON, ROBERT, British composer; b. Mar. 2, 1921; d. Nov. 21, 1997.

Taylor, Matthew. *Adagio: In memory of Robert Simpson.* String quartet. Unpublished. Source: *Tempo* 207 (Dec. 1998): 54. First performance by the Delmé String Quartet, Sept. 19, 1998, London.

SJÖGREN, JOHANN GUSTAV EMIL, Swedish composer; b. June 16, 1853; d. Mar. 1, 1918.

Alfvén, Hugo, 1872–1960. *Elégie,* op. 38: *Vid Emil Sjögrens bar* (1918). Orchestral tone poem. Published *Lundquist.* Performed at Sjögren's funeral.

SKALKOTTAS, NIKOS, Greek composer; b. Mar. 21, 1904; d. Sep. 19, 1949.

Goehr, Rudolph, 1910– . *Concerto cancrizante: In memoriam Niko Skalkottas.* Violins (2), or a choir of violins. Published New York: Rongwen Music RM2006, 1956.

Papaioannou, Giannes Andreou, 1911–1989. *Meteorissi: Fantasy in memoriam Nikos Skalkottas* (1979). Violoncello and orchestra. Published Athens: Edition Nomos EN138, 1983.

Varvoglis, Mario, 1885–1967. *Dedication to Nikos Skalkottas* (1957–1964). String quartet. Unpublished. Source: *NGrove.*

SMETANA, BEDRICH, Bohemian composer; b. Mar. 2, 1824; d. May 12, 1884.

Husa, Karel, 1921– . *Smetana fanfare* (1984). Wind ensemble. Published *AMP* 7984, 1989. Composed for the centennial of Smetana's death.

Jirák, Karel Boleslav, 1891–1972. *Tri poetické polky = Three poetical polkas,* op. 48 (1944). Piano. Published Prague: Melantrich M246, 1948. Written in memory of Smetana in the jublilee year 1944.

Loudová, Ivana, 1941– . *String quartet no. 2: Pamatce Bedricha Smetany* (1976). Published *Panton* P1962, 1981.

SMOLENSKY, STEPAN VASSILIEVICH, Russian musicologist; b. Oct. 20, 1848; d. Aug. 2, 1909.

Rachmaninoff, Sergei, 1873–1943. *Vsenoshchnoe bdenie = Vesper mass,* op. 37: *Pamiati Stepana Vasilevicha Smolenskovo* (1915). Chorus (SATB) unacc. Published Moscow; Petrograd: Rossiiskago muzikalnoe Izd-vo, 1915. Also published by *Boosey* and others.

SMYTHE, PATRICK, British jazz pianist; b. 1923; d. May 6, 1983.

Bennett, Richard Rodney, 1936– . *Memento: In memory of Pat Smythe, May 7 [sic], 1983* (May 28, 1983). Flute and strings. Published *Novello* 360015, 1991. CONTENTS: Canto—Intermezzo—Elegiac blues.

SOKOLOV, NICOLAI, Russian composer, pedagogue; b. Mar. 26, 1859; d. Mar. 27, 1922.

Shostakovich, Dmitri, 1906–1975. *Variations for orchestra,* op. 3, B-flat major (1922), in his *Sochineniia dlia orkestra,* Sobranie sochinenii [Works], vol. 10. Published *Muzyka,* 1984. "Svetloi Pamiati Nikolaia Aleksandrovicha Sokolova = To the bright memory of Nikolai Alexandrovitch Sokolov" —caption in score. Shostakovich also transcribed this work for solo piano.

SOLER, ANTONIO, Spanish composer; b. Dec. 3, 1729; d. Dec. 20, 1783.

Castillo, Manuel, 1930– . *Suite mediterranea: In memoriam P. Antonio Soler* (1979). Octet for flute, oboe, clarinet, horn, vibraphone, violoncello, double bass, harpsichord. Published *Alpuerto*, 198–?

SOLLERTINSKY, IVAN, Russian musicologist; b. Nov. 20, 1902; d. Feb. 11, 1944.

Shostakovich, Dmitri, 1906–1975. *Piano trio no. 2,* op. 67, E minor*: Pamiati I. I. Sollertinskogo* (Feb.–Aug. 1944). Published Moscow: Gosudarstvennoe Muzykalnoe Izdatelstvo, 1945. Subsequent editions by *UE, Peters, Sikorski,* and others.

SONIUS, KARL-HEINZ, German flutist; b. 1955; d. 1976.

Denhoff, Michael, 1955– . *Epitaph für Karl-Heinz Sonius* (1977). Flute solo. Published *Gerig* HG1314, 1977.

SOUSA, JOHN PHILLIP, American bandmaster, composer; b. Nov. 6, 1854; d. Mar. 6, 1932.

Goldman, Edwin Franko, 1878–1956. "Tribute to Sousa" (1933), in his *Marches for piano.* Published *Schirmer,* 1933.

SPIER, ROSA, Dutch harpist; b. Nov. 7, 1891; d. July 8, 1967.

Andriessen, Jurriaan, 1925–1996. *In memoriam Rosa Spier* (1967). Harp. Published *Donemus,* 1967.

SPILLING, WILLY (KARL WILHELM), German composer; b. Sep. 18, 1909; d. Aug. 14, 1965.

Jacob, Werner, 1938– . *Requiem,* op. 11*: Epitaph auf Willy Spilling* (1966). Soloists (SBar), mixed chorus (SATB), orchestra. Published *Bärenreiter* BA6005, 1966.

SPORER, THOMAS, German composer; b. 1490?; d. 1534.

Dietrich, Sixt, ca. 1492–1548. *Epicedion Thomae Sporeri musicorum principis, modulis musica a Sixto Dittricho illustratum.* Voices (5). Published Strassburg: Peter Schöffer & Mathias Apiarius, 1534. *RISM-A1:* D-3014. Survives incomplete only in the Staats-, Kreis-, und Stadtbibliothek, Augsburg.

STAINER, JAKOB, Austrian luthier; b. July 14, 1621; d. 1683.

David, Johann Nepomuk, 1895–1977. "Jacobo Stainer in memoriam," in his *Vier Trios,* op. 33 (1928–1935). Trio for violin, viola, violoncello. Published *Breitkopf* 5598, 1948. CONTENTS: Nicola Amati in memoriam—Antonio Stradivario in memoriam—Giuseppe Guarneri del Gesù in memoriam—Jacobo Stainer in memoriam.

STANFORD, SIR CHARLES VILLIERS, English composer; b. Sep. 30, 1852; d. Mar. 29, 1924.

Vaughan Williams, Ralph, 1872–1958. *Silence and music: To the memory of Charles Villiers Stanford, and his Blue Bird* (1953). Chorus (SATB) unacc. Published *OUP* 56809, 1953. Text by Ursula Wood Vaughan Williams. No. 4 in *A Garland for the Queen*, a cycle of songs for mixed voices by ten British composers and ten British poets to mark the occasion of the coronation of H. M. Queen Elizabeth II.

STASOV, VLADIMIR, Russian musicologist; b. Jan. 14, 1824; d. Oct. 1, 1906.

Glazunov, Aleksandr Konstantinovich, 1865–1936. "À la mémoire de Wladimir Stassoff," in his *Two préludes for orchestra,* op. 85. Published *Belaieff*, 1911. CONTENTS: À la mémoire de Wladimir Stassoff—À la mémoire de N. Rimsky Korssakow.

STEIN, ERWIN, Austrian conductor, editor; b. Nov. 7, 1885; d. July 19, 1958.

Williamson, Sir Malcolm, 1931– . *English eccentrics: Chamber opera in 2 acts: In memory of Erwin Stein* (1963–64). Published *Chappell*. Text by Geoffrey Dunn after the book by Edith Sitwell.

STEINFIRST, DONALD, American music critic; b. July 26, 1904; d. Aug. 22, 1972.

Rochberg, George, 1918– . *Concerto for violin and orchestra* (1974). Published *Presser* 414-41111, 1977. "Commissioned by the Pittsburgh Symphony Orchestra, William Steinberg, Music Director, in memory of Donald Steinfirst, for Isaac Stern"—dedication in score. Donald Steinfirst was music critic for the Pittsburgh *Post-Gazette*.

STEVENS, BERNARD, English composer; b. Mar. 2, 1916; d. Jan. 2, 1983.

Finnissy, Michael, 1946– . *B. S.: In memory of Bernard Stevens* (1985–86). Piano. Published *OUP*, 1986.

STEWART, SIR ROBERT PRESCOTT, Irish organist, conductor, composer; b. Dec. 16, 1825; d. Mar. 24, 1894.

Culwick, James Cooksey, 1845–1907. *Elegy composed in loving memory of Sir Robert Stewart, who fell asleep 24th March, 1894.* Song? Published Archibald: Hull, 1894.

STOBAEUS, JOHANN, German composer; b. July 6, 1580; d. Sep. 11, 1646.

Colb, Georg, 1630–1649. *Schuldiges Danck- und Denck-Mahl welches dem Johanni Stobaeo, Capellm. nunmehr Seligen, meinem Lehr-Meistern . . . mit 5 Stimmen ausgefertiget von mir.* Voices (5). Published Konigsberg: Reusner, 1646. Text incipit: "Wer wird in der Engel Chor."

STOESSEL, ALBERT, American conductor, composer; b. Oct. 11, 1894; d. May 12, 1943.

Bauer, Marion, 1887–1955. *Sonata for viola (or clarinet) and piano,* op. 22: *To the memory of Albert Stoessel.* Published *Schirmer,* 1951. Reprint edition: New York: Da Capo, 1986.

STRADIVARI, ANTONIO, Italian luthier; b. 1644; d. Dec. 18, 1737.

David, Johann Nepomuk, 1895–1977. "Antonio Stradivario in memoriam," in his *Vier Trios,* op. 33 (1928–1935). Trio for violin, viola, violoncello. Published *Breitkopf* 5598, 1948. CONTENTS: Nicola Amati in memoriam—Antonio Stradivario in memoriam—Giuseppe Guarneri del Gesù in memoriam—Jacobo Stainer in memoriam.

STRAUSS, JOHANN, Austrian composer; b. Oct. 25, 1825; d. June 3, 1899.

Busoni, Ferruccio, 1866–1924. *Tanz-Walzer* = *Dance-waltz,* op. 53: *Dem Andenken Johann Strauss* (1920). Orchestra. Published Vienna: Wiener Philharmonischer Verlag, 1922.

STRAUSS, RICHARD, German composer; b. June 11, 1864; d. Sep. 8, 1949.

Cruz, Ivo, 1901– . "A Richard Strauss," in his *Homenagens* = *Hommages* (1955). Piano. Published Lisbon: Sassetti; *Mercury,* 1958. CONTENTS: A Richard Strauss—A Manuel de Falla—A Oscar da Silva.

STRAVINSKY, IGOR, Russian-born composer; b. June 17, 1882; d. Apr. 6, 1971.

***In memoriam Igor Fedorovich Stravinsky: Canons and epitaphs,* Set I.** Published in *Tempo* 97 (1971): musical supplement. "Each piece [in Set I] uses some or all of the instruments required for two brief commemorative works composed by Stravinsky in 1959: the Epitaphium for flute, clarinet and harp; and the Double Canon (in memory of Dufy) for string quartet." CONTENTS: Kanon pamiati I. F. Stravinskogo [Trio for flute, clarinet, harp] / by Edisson Denisov, 1929–1996—Canon in memory of Igor Stravinsky [Duo for violin, violoncello] / by Boris Blacher, 1903–1975—Canon in mem. I. S. [Unspecified instruments] / by Peter Maxwell Davies, 1934– — Canon in memoriam Igor Stravinsky [Trio for flute, clarinet, harp] / by Hugh Wood, 1932– —In memoriam Igor Stravinsky: Canon [String quartet] / by Lennox Berkeley, 1903–1989—Epitaph-canon in memory of Igor Stravinsky [Trio for flute, clarinet, harp] / by Nicholas Maw, 1935– —In memoriam magister [Sextet for flute,

clarinet, string quartet] / by Michael Tippett, 1905–1998—Shall we
all die? [Septet for flute, clarinet, harp, string quartet] / by Harrison
Birtwistle, 1934– —Autre fois [Trio for flute, clarinet, harp] / by
Luciana Berio, 1925– —Kanon pamiati I. F. Stravinskogo [String
quartet] / by Alfred Schnittke, 1934–1998.

—————, **Set II.** Published in *Tempo* 98 (1972): musical supplement.
"Except for Carter's Canon for 3 (muted trumpets) each piece [in Set
II] uses some or all of the instruments required for two brief commemorative works composed by Stravinsky in 1959: the Epitaphium
for flute, clarinet, and harp: and the Double Canon (in memory of
Dufy) for string quartet." CONTENTS: Requiescat [Soprano with violin, viola, violoncello; text from William Blake's "Couch of death"] /
by Elisabeth Lutyens, 1906–1983—Threnody: Igor Stravinsky in
memoriam [Quartet for flute, violin, viola, violoncello] / by Aaron
Copland, 1900–1990—Canon for 3 [Muted trumpets (3)] / by Elliott
Carter, 1908– —Canons to the memory of Igor Stravinsky [String
quartet] / by Roger Sessions, 1896–1985—In memoriam I. S. [String
quartet] / by Darius Milhaud, 1892–1974—Canonic chorale for Igor
Stravinsky [String quartet] / by Alexander Goehr, 1932– —
Explosante-fixe [Suggested instrumentation: violins (2), flutes (2),
clarinets (2), harp] / by Pierre Boulez, 1925– .

Stravinsky au futur: ou, L'apothéose d'Orphée (1972). Chance music for voice, instrumental ensemble, electronics. Unpublished. A
collaborative work by Henri Pousseur, 1929– ; Pierre Bartholomée,
1937– ; Philippe Boesmans, 1936– ; René César, and Sigiswald Kui-
jken, 1944– . First performance 1972, Liège, by the Ensemble
Musiques Nouvelles, which also recorded the work on *Stravinsky au
futur* (Harmonia Mundi 20-21554-7, 1974). CONTENTS: Hier ou les
adieux—Aujourd'hui ou l'absence—Demain ou le retour.

Stravinskii: A composer's memorial. A collection of remembrances
and compositions by various contributors. Published in *Perspectives*
9/2–10/1 (1971): special double issue. MUSICAL CONTENTS: In memoriam Igor Stravinsky [Graphic notation for unspecified per-
former] / by Roman Haubenstock-Ramati, 1919– —Sarabande: In
memoriam Igor Stravinsky [Violoncello solo] / by Peter Racine
Fricker, 1920–1990—Birthday canon for Igor Stravinsky (1961)
[Violas. "This little gift for Stravinsky's 79th birthday turns out to
fall symmetrically between the two death years, 1951 and 1971"] /
by Claudio Spies, 1925– —An Alleluia from and to Igor Stravinsky
[Melody for unspecified solo instrument] / by Vincent Persichetti,

1915–   —Dirge (Antiphonae) ["The linguistic compositions given here (4 from a set of 12), are formed from the text used by Stravinsky in his *Symphony of psalms*, second section, the 2nd, 3rd, and 4th verses of the 39th Psalm. Each group of 4 in the set utilizes the total available phonetic structure of these verses in some manner"] / by Kenneth Gaburo, 1926–1993 —Elegy for Igor Stravinsky [Trio for flute, violoncello, piano] / by Harvey Sollberger, 1938– .

Antoniou, Theodore, 1935– . *Threnos: The memory of Igor Stravinsky* (1972). Ensemble of winds, piano, double bass, percussion. Published *Bärenreiter* BA6287, 1972.

Arapov, Boris Alexandrovich, 1905– . *Concerto for violin, piano, and percussions with chamber orchestra: In memory of Igor Feodorovich Stravinsky* (1973). Published Moscow: Sov. Kompozitor 488, 1975.

Baker, David, 1931– . *Five pieces: Igor Stravinsky in memoriam.* Piano. Published Hamilton, OH: Composers Autograph Publications, 1973.

Balassa, Sándor, 1935– . *Lupercalia: Concerto in memory of Stravinsky for woodwind and brass,* op. 24 (1971). Ensemble of piccolo, flute, alto flute, oboes (2), English horn, clarinets (3), bass clarinet, saxophones (2), bassoons (2), contrabassoon, trumpets (2), horns (2), trombones (2), tuba. Published *EMB* Z10154, 1976.

Benton, Daniel, 1945– . *Dirge: In memoriam Igor Stravinsky* (1977). Soprano with octet of violin, flute, alto flute, trumpet, violoncello, bassoon, bass trombone, percussion. Published *Seesaw,* 1977. Syllabic text.

Bentzon, Niels Viggo, 1919–2000. *Epitaph for Igor Stravinsky: Stravinsky compendium no. 1,* op. 272 (1971). Orchestra. Published *Hansen,* 1971.

Berio, Luciano, 1925– . *Autre fois: Berceuse canonique pour Igor Stravinsky* (1971). Trio for flute, clarinet, harp. Published Milan: Universal Edition, 1979. Also published in *In memoriam Igor Fedorovich Stravinsky: Canons and epitaphs, Set I* (q.v.).

Birtwistle, Harrison, 1934– . *Tombeau: In memoriam Igor Stravinsky: 1971.* Septet for flute, clarinet, harp, string quartet. Published *UE-L* 16045, 1998. First published as "Shall we all die?" (1971), in *In memoriam Igor Fedorovich Stravinsky: Canons and epitaphs, Set I* (q.v.).

Bornefeld, Helmut, 1906–1990. *Barcarolle* (1972–73). Organ, harpsichord, celesta. Unpublished. Source: *NGrove.*

Boulez, Pierre, 1925– . "Explosante-fixe. . . ," in *In memoriam Igor Fedorovich Stravinsky: Canons and epitaphs, Set II* (q.v.). Suggested instrumentation: Septet for violins (2), flutes (2), clarinets (2), harp. Boulez reworked this material several times, incorporating instrumental and electronic adjustments in *Memoriale (. . . explosante-fixe . . . originel)* for flute solo and 8 instruments (1985), dedicated in memory of flutist Lawrence Beauregard (q.v.); in *Anthemes* (1992) for violin solo; and in a version for solo flute with two accompanying flutes with computer transformation recorded on *Boulez dirigiert Boulez* (Deutsche Grammophon 445 833-2, 1995), which includes the score printed "in its original form" in the accompanying notes.

Brandmüller, Theo, 1948– . *Venezianische Schatten: Tango für kleines Orchester: Epitaph auf Igor Strawinsky* (1981). Chamber orchestra. Published *Bote*.

Broege, Timothy, 1947– . "Le tombeau de Igor Stravinsky" (1972), in his *Partita no. 2 "Le lardon."* Harpsichord. Published Arlington, VA: Plucked Strings Editions, 198–? CONTENTS: Le tombeau de Igor Stravinsky—Death dance: Yasuari Kawabata—Death dance: John Berryman—Death dance: Yukio Mishima—Le tombeau de Louis Armstrong.

Burton, Stephen Douglas, 1943– . *Stravinskiana: Concertino* (1971). Flute and chamber orchestra (or piano). Published *Salabert*, 1975.

Carpenter, Kurt, 1948– . *Marlboro concerto "alla Stravinsky"* (1971–72). Alto saxophone and string orchestra (or piano). Unpublished. Source: *Londeix*.

Carter, Elliott, 1908– . *Canon for 3* (1971). Muted trumpets (3); or trio for oboe, clarinet, trumpet. Published *AMP* 7203, 1972. First published in *In memoriam Igor Fedorovich Stravinsky: Canons and epitaphs, Set II* (q.v.).

Copland, Aaron, 1900–1990. *Threnodies I and II* (1971). Quartet for flute, violin, viola, violoncello. Published *Boosey* ENB149, 1977. First published in *In memoriam Igor Fedorovich Stravinsky: Canons and epitaphs, Set II* (q.v.).

Csemiczky, Miklós, 1954– . *Capriccios, epitaphs and choral: In memoriam Igor Stravinsky* (1983). Wind quintet no. 2 for flute, oboe, clarinet, horn, bassoon. Published *EMB* Z12367, 1984.

Davies, Peter Maxwell, 1934– . "Canon in mem. I. S.," in *In memoriam Igor Fedorovich Stravinsky: Canons and epitaphs, Set I* (q.v.). Performance medium not specified.   The canon is resolved in

Tempo 100 (Spring 1972) as a quintet for flute, clarinet, viola, violoncello, and harp.

Delancey, Charles, 1959– . *The love of L'histoire* (1973). Multipercussion solo. Published *Peters*, 1973. "To the memory of Igor Stravinsky, and to all percussionists who love playing the 'Batterie' in *L'histoire du soldat*"—note in score.

Denisov, Edisson Vasilevich, 1929–1996. *Canon en mémoire d'Igor Strawinsky* (1971). Trio for flute, clarinet, harp. Published *Gerig*, 1979. Originally published in *In memoriam Igor Fedorovich Stravinsky: Canons and epitaphs, Set I* (q.v.).

Dondeyne, Désiré, 1921– . *In memoriam Igor Stravinsky* (1971). Band. Published *Molenaar*, 1988.

Falik, IUrii Aleksandrovich, 1936– . *Elegicheskaiia muzyka: Pamiati I. Stravinskogo = Elegiac music: In memoriam Igor Stravinsky* (1975). String orchestra with trombones (4). Published *Sikorski*; *Muzyka* 2238, 1978.

Farren, Martin, 1942– . *InMIS: In Paradisum: In memoriam Igor Stravinsky* (1971). Handbell and viola. Unpublished. Source: *BCP*. First performance by William Parsons (chimes) and unidentified violist at University of Iowa Composers Symposium Concert, spring 1971.

Finnissy, Michael, 1946– . *Untitled piece to honor Igor Stravinsky: On the death of Igor Stravinsky* (1971). Trio for flute, harp, viola. Unpublished. Source: *Finnissy*. Available from the composer through the British Music Information Centre. An earlier version (1967) for solo flute was composed "For Igor Stravinsky's 85th birthday."

Firsova, Elena, 1950– . *Misterioso: In memoriam Igor Strawinsky* (1980). String quartet no. 3. Published *Sikorski* 895, 1982.

Fox, Erika, 1936– . *In memoriam Igor Stravinsky* (1971). Wind quintet with piano, percussion. Published London: Erika Fox, 1971. Source: *ConCom.*

———. *On visiting Stravinsky's grave at San Michele* (1988). Piano. Published London: Erika Fox, 1988. Source: *ConCom.*

Heider, Werner, 1930– . *Pyramide für Igor Stravinsky* (May 15, 1971). Ensemble of piccolo, oboe, clarinet, bassoon, horn, trumpet, trombone, percussion, harp, piano, harpsichord, string quartet, double bass. Published *Litolff* 8161, 1974.

Helmschrott, Robert M., 1939– . *Drei Stücke: In memoriam I. S.* Organ. Published *Kistner*, 1972, in series Die Orgel, Reihe I, no. 25.

Iturriaga, Enrique, 1918– . *Homenaje a Strawinsky* (1971). Orchestra and cajon (a traditional Peruvian percussion instrument). Unpublished. Source: *NGrove*.

Jeney, Zoltán, 1943– . *Monody: In memory of Igor Stravinsky* (1974–77). Soprano and piano. Published *EMB* Z12491, 1983. Poem by Herman Melville. Also a version for mixed chorus.

Kern, Matthias, 1928– . *Herr, höre doch auf meine Rede: Partita im Gedenken an Igor Strawinsky* = *Hear my cry, O Lord: Partita in memory of Igor Strawinsky* (1991). Organ. Published *Möseler* 19417, 1974.

Ketting, Otto, 1935– . *In memoriam Igor Stravinsky* (1971). Orchestra. Unpublished. Source: *ConCom*. Commissioned by the Hague Philharmonic Orchestra.

Klebe, Giselher, 1925– . *Tomba di Igor Strawinsky,* op. 81 (1978). Oboe/oboe d'amore/English horn, piano, strings. Published *Bärenreiter* BA6760, 1978.

Kont, Paul, 1920– . *Pavane auf den Tod von Igor Strawinsky* (1971). Orchestra. Published *Doblinger*.

Kraft, William, 1923– . *In memoriam Igor Stravinsky* (1972–74). Violin and piano. Published *NewWest*, 1974.

Kurtág, György, 1926– . "Antiphona no. 3 in D: In memoriam Igor Strawinsky" (1971), in *In memoriam Igor Strawinsky*. Two groups of violoncellos (3 each) and cimbaloms (1 each). Published *EMB*, 1972. This is the sole musical work in this memorial volume.

Mansurian, Tigran, 1939– . *Da ich nicht hoffe: In memoriam Igor Stravinsky* (1983). Solo instrumentalists (14). Published *Sikorski*.

————. *Commemorating Stravinsky* (1981). Solo instrumentalists (15). Unpublished. Source: *ConCom*.

Moryl, Richard, 1929– . *De morte cantoris: In memoriam Igor Stravinsky* (1973–74). Soprano and mezzo-soprano soloists with quintet for oboe, electronic piano (celeste), harp, percussion (2). Published Hastings-on-Hudson, NY: Joshua Music, 1974. Settings of Kyrie eleison, Dies irae, Requiem (libera me), the Act of contrition, and poems from James Joyce's *Portrait of the artist as a young man*.

Moss, Lawrence, 1927– . *Auditions: Dedicated to the memory of Igor Stravinsky* (Dec. 4, 1971; rev. 1973). Woodwind quintet and electronic tape. Published *CFischer*, 1973. Recorded by the Dorian Wind Quintet on *Modern music played by the Dorian Woodwind Quintet* (CRI SD-318, 1974).

Pironkov, Simeon, 1927– . *Baletna muzika v pamet na Igor Stravinski* = *Ballet music in memory of Igor Stravinsky* (1972). Orchestra. Published *Breitkopf.*

Rasmussen, Karl Aage, 1947– . *Le tombeau de père Igor* (1977). Trio for clarinet, violoncello, piano. Published *Hansen*, 1977.

Rhodes, Philip, 1940– . *Ad honorem Stravinsky* (1981). Chorus (SATB) unacc. Published *Peters* 66985, 1986. Latin text by Jackson Bryce based on four English pentameter verses from John Milton's "On the death of a fair infant dying of a cough." Composed for the centennial of Stravinsky's birth.

Robison, John, 1949– . "In memoriam Igor Stravinsky," in his *Three dirges* (1975). Vocalist with trio for bass trombones (2), piano. Unpublished. Source: *Everett.* CONTENTS: In memoriam Igor Stravinsky—In memoriam George Szell—In memoriam Dagmar Godowsky.

Sáry, László, 1940– . *In memoriam Igor Stravinsky: For 24 wind instruments.* Ensemble of flute, piccolo clarinet, clarinets (4), alto saxophones (2), tenor saxophone, horns (3), flugelhorns (4), trumpets (4), alto trombones (2), tenor trombones (2). Published *EMB* Z12454, 1982.

Saxton, Robert, 1953– . *Canzona: In memoriam Igor Stravinsky* (1978). Octet for flute, oboe, clarinet, horn, harp, violin, viola, violoncello. Published *Chester*, 1978.

Schickele, Peter, 1935– . *Epitaphs for piano.* Published *E-V* 160-00202, 1981. "*Epitaphs* is a set of tributes written over a period of thirteen years; the composers to whom homage is paid represent each century from the 16th through the 20th." CONTENTS: Orlando di Lasso—Michael Praetorius—Domenico Scarlatti—Frédéric Chopin—Igor Stravinsky.

Schnittke, Alfred, 1934–1998. *Hommage à Strawinsky, Prokofjew und Schostakowitsch* (1979). Piano 6-hands. Published *Sikorski* 1818, 1998.

———. *Kanon in memoriam I. Strawinsky* (1971). String quartet. Published *Sikorski* 2250; *Schirmer*, 1977. Initially published in *In memoriam Igor Fedorovich Stravinsky: Canons and epitaphs, Set I* (q.v.).

Shackelford, Rudy, 1944– . *Le tombeau de Stravinsky* (Dec. 1971; rev. 1976). Harpsichord. Published *Jerona*, 1977.

Smirnov, Dmitrii, 1948– . *Dirge-canons*, op. 33: *In memoriam Igor Stravinsky* (1981). Ensemble of flute, oboe, clarinet, bassoon, horn, trumpet, trombone, tuba, percussion, violin, viola, violoncello, double bass. Published *Sikorski.*

Stravinsky, Soulima, 1910–1994. *Three preludes and fugues for piano: In memoriam Igor Stravinsky* (1982). Published *Peters* 66933, 1985. Composed on the centennial of Igor Stravinsky's birth by his son.

Szunyogh, Balázs, 1954– . *Hommage à Stravinsky: Tétel zongorára = Movement for piano.* Published *EMB* Z8723, 1979.

Tansman, Alexandre, 1897–1986. *Stèle: In memoriam d'Igor Strawinsky* (1972). Suite for orchestra. Published *Eschig* ME8054, 1973. CONTENTS: Elegia—Studio ritmico—Lamento.

Tavener, John, 1944– . *In memoriam Igor Stravinsky* (1971). Alto flutes (2), organ, hand bells. Published *Chester*, 1999.

Trombly, Preston, 1945– . *In memoriam Igor Stravinsky* (1971–72). Viola and double bass with woodwind quartet. Published *ACA*, 1974.

Vajda, János, 1949– . *Stabat Mater: In memoriam Igor Stravinsky.* Vocal soloists (SMz), women's chorus, instrumental ensemble. Unpublished. Recorded by Mária Zádori (soprano), Anna Bogdány (mezzo-soprano), women of the Hungarian Radio and Television Chorus, instrumental ensemble cond. by Géza Török (Hungaroton SLPX12263, 1982).

Wuorinen, Charles, 1938– . *Canzona: To the memory of Igor Stravinsky* (1971). Ensemble of flute, oboe/English horn, clarinet/bass clarinet, bassoon, trumpet, violin, viola, violoncello, contrabass, vibraphone, harp, piano. Published *Peters* 66451.

————. *Reliquary for Igor Stravinsky* (1975). Orchestra. Published *Peters* 66631, 1978. Based on Stravinsky's last sketches and drafts.

Zamecnik, Evzen, 1939– . *In memoriam Igor Stravinskij* (1971). Orchestra. Published *Panton* 3500680, 1980.

Zanettovich, Daniele, 1950– . *In memoria di Igor Stravinski: Suite su temi populari Russi* (1983). Duo for flute and bassoon. Published *Pizzicato* 8877360046.

STRECKER, WILHELM, English music publisher; b. July 4, 1884; d. Mar. 1, 1958.

Françaix, Jean, 1912–1997. *Scuola di ballo: Sur des thèmes di Boccherini* (1966). Published *Schott-M*, 1984. Music by Boccherini, arranged for orchestra by Françaix for a ballet choreographed by Massine. Published score is a reduction for two pianos. "À la mémoire de mon cher Willy Strecker sans qui cette oeuvre n'existerait pas"—note in score.

SULLIVAN, SIR ARTHUR SEYMOUR, English composer; b. May 13, 1842; d. Nov. 22, 1900.

MacKenzie, Alexander Campbell, Sir, 1847–1935. "The singers: In memoriam Arthur Sullivan" (1901), in *Novello's part-song book,* Second series, no. 870. Voices (SATB). Published *Novello,* 1901. Text by Longfellow.

SULLIVAN, THOMAS, English bandmaster; b. 1805; d. Sep. 22, 1866.

Sullivan, Sir Arthur Seymour, 1842–1900. *Overture in C: In memoriam.* Orchestra. Published *Novello,* 1867? Dedicated to the memory of Sir Arthur Sullivan's father, who was master of the band at the Royal Military College, Sandhurst, and later professor of brass band at Kneller Hall (Royal Military School of Music).

SUMSION, HERBERT, English organist, composer; b. Jan. 14, 1899; d. Aug. 11, 1995.

Beechey, Gwilym, 1938– . *Elegy: In memory of Herbert Sumsion* (1995). Organ. Published *Oecumuse,* 1995.

SURDIN, MORRIS, Canadian composer; b. May 8, 1914; d. June 19, 1979.

Kulesha, Gary, 1954– . *A dream of dark and troubling things: In memoriam Morris Surdin* (1982). Brass quintet with piano, percussion, electronic tape. Unpublished. Source: *Canadian.*

SWEELINCK, JAN PIETERSZOON, Dutch organist, composer; b. 1562; d. Oct. 16, 1621.

Bull, John, ca. 1562–1628. "Fantasia on a theme by Sweelinck" (December 15, 1621), in *Musica Britannica,* vol. 14, p. 12. Harpsichord. Published *Stainer,* 1960. Edited from British Library Ms. Add. 23623, f. 52.

SZABÓ, FERENC, Hungarian composer; b. Dec. 27, 1902; d. Nov. 4, 1969.

Sárai, Tibor, 1919–1995. *Sirfelirat: Szabó Ferenc Emlékére = Epitaffio: In memoriam Szabó Ferenc* (1974). Symphonic poem. Published *EMB* Z10197, 1975.

SZELIGOWSKI, TADEUSZ, Polish composer; b. Sep. 15, 1896; d. Jan. 10, 1963.

Slowinski, Wladyslaw, 1930– . *Quartetto piccolo: In memoriam Tadeusz Szeligowski* (1980). String quartet. Published *WMAA,* 1985.

SZELL, GEORGE, Hungarian-born conductor; b. June 7, 1897; d. July 30, 1970.

Robison, John, 1949– . "In memoriam George Szell," in his *Three dirges* (1975). Vocalist with trio for bass trombones (2), piano. Unpublished. Source: *Everett.* CONTENTS: In memoriam Igor Stravinsky—In memoriam George Szell—In memoriam Dagmar Godowsky.

Walton, Sir William, 1902–1983. *Symphony no. 2* (1960). Published *OUP*, 1960. Originally dedicated to the Royal Liverpool Philharmonic Society; later amended to "Commissioned by the Royal Liverpool Philharmonic Society, and rededicated to the memory of George Szell"—note in score.

SZERVÁNSZKY, ENDRE, Hungarian composer; b. Dec. 27, 1911; d. June 25, 1977.

Kurtág, György, 1926– . *Officium breve,* op. 28: *In memoriam Andreae Szervánszky* (1988–89). String quartet. Published *EMB* Z13959, 1995.

Sáry, László, 1940– . *Musica per 24 archi e 24 fiati: Hommage à Szervánszky* (1977). Strings (24), winds (24). Published *EMB* Z10231, 1980. "The string and wind parts may be performed simultaneously, in succession, or—independently from each other—separately as well"—note in score.

SZYMANOWSKI, KAROL, Polish composer; b. Oct. 6, 1882; d. Mar. 29, 1937.

Baird, Tadeusz, 1928–1981. *Glosy z oddali = Voices from afar* (1981). Songs (3) for baritone and orchestra. Published *PWM* 8584, 1984. German texts by Jaroslaw Iwaszkiewicz. Commissioned by the Committee for the Celebration of Karol Szymanowski's Birth Centenary. CONTENTS: An einem ewigen See stehe ich—Die Nacht—In der Kirche.

Bloch, Augustyn, 1929– . *Variations for piano: Karol Szymanowski in memoriam* (1953). Published *PWM* 6058, 1962.

Huber, Klaus, 1924– . *Fragmente aus Frühling: In memoriam Karol Szymanowski und Bruno Schulz* (1987). Mezzo-soprano with viola, piano. Published *Ricordi*, 1987. Text by Bruno Schulz.

Koprowski, Peter Paul, 1947– . *In memoriam Karol Szymanowski* (1966). Orchestra. Published *Canadian*, 1987. CONTENTS: Chorale—Interlude—Elegy—Finale: Funèbre.

Lenot, Jacques, 1945– . *Le tombeau de Szymanowski* (1987) Unpublished. Source: *Mussat.* Medium of performance not identified.

Mycielski, Zygmunt, 1907–1987. *Lamento di Tristano: In memory of Szymanowski* (1937). Small orchestra. Published *PWM*.

Perkowski, Piotr, 1901– . *Karolowi Szymanowskiemu* (1952). Violin and piano. Published *PWM*, 1955.

Przybylski, Bronislaw Kazimierz, 1941– . *In memoriam: 4 songs for voice and chamber ensemble to verses of Polish poets: Devoted to the memory of Karol Szymanowski* (1982). High voice with flute, oboe, piano, percussion. Published *WMAA*, 1983. Composed for the 100th anniversary of the Szymanowski's birth.

Szeligowski, Tadeusz, 1896–1963. *Epitaphium na smierc Karola Szymanowskiego* (1937). String orchestra. Published *PWM* 262, 1948.

TABUTEAU, MARCEL, French oboist, pedagogue; b. July 2, 1887; d. Jan. 4, 1966.

Amram, David, 1930– . *Trail of beauty: Based on poetry, prayers, and speeches of native American peoples.* Mezzo-soprano, solo oboe, orchestra. Published *Peters* 66704, 1977. "Marcel Tabuteau gave all musicians who knew him a higher sense of what music was about. . . . The oldest and first Americans have a tradition in their making of music that best expresses the feeling all of us in music have when we honor a musician. Leonard Crowdog, Sioux Medicine Man, said this to Richard Erdos in 1970: 'When you have grown old, when you are dead and gone, the younger ones among us will remember you. At a pow-wow somebody will give a donation to the drummers, go to the announcer, stand and tell the people—they'll sing a song for you.' This is for Marcel Tabuteau"—dedication in score.

TAFFANEL, PAUL, French flutist, conductor; b. Sep. 16, 1844; d. Nov. 22, 1908.

Gaubert, Philippe, 1879–1941. *Sonata for flute and piano no. 1: À la mémoire de mon cher maître Paul Taffanel* (1918). Published *Durand* 9572, 1918.

TAKEMITSU, TORU, Japanese composer; b. Oct. 8, 1930; d. Feb. 20, 1996.

Brouwer, Leo, 1939– . *Hika: In memoriam Toru Takemitsu* (1996). Guitar. Published *Gendai* GG207, 1997. "The title 'HIKA' is the same as Takemitsu's 1966 composition for violin, however there is no connection aside from the use of the title to denote a dirge = elegy = mourning song"—note in score by editor Shin-ichi Fukuda, who also premiered and recorded the work on *In memoriam: Guitar works of Toru Takemitsu* (Denon COCO80447).

Foss, Lukas, 1922– . *For Toru* (1997). Flute and string orchestra (or string quartet). Published *Pembroke* PCB134, 1999. "Toru Takemitsu is a much admired composer. He was a great friend. *For Toru* was composed in his memory"—composer's note in score.

Hosokawa, Toshio, 1955– . *Concerto for violoncello and orchestra: In memory of Toru Takemitsu* (1997). Published *Schott-J*, 1997. —
———. *Singing trees: Requiem for Toru Takemitsu* (1997). Children's chorus. Published *Schott-J*.

Ichiyanagi, Toshi, 1933– . *Still time IV: In memory of Toru Takemitsu* (1996). Flute solo. Published *Schott-J* SJ1112, 1998.

Knussen, Oliver, 1952– . *Prayer bell sketch*, op. 29 (1997). Piano. Published *Faber*, 1997. Commissioned by Masako Okamura and Motoyuki Nakagawa in memory of Takemitsu.

Lieberson, Peter, 1946– . *The ocean that has no west and no east: Elegy in memory of Toru Takemitsu* (1997). Piano. Published *AMP*, 1997.

Rogg, Lionel, 1936– . *Hommage à Takemitsu: La terre, l'eau, le feu, l'air* (1997). Organ. Published *Lemoine* 26719, 1997.

Tan, Dun, 1957– . *Concerto for water percussion and orchestra: In memory of Toru Takemitsu* (1998). Published *Schirmer*.

Yuasa, Joji, 1929– . *Concerto for violin and orchestra: In memory of Toru Takemitsu* (1996). Published *Schott-J* SJ1111, 1998.
———. *Solitude: In memoriam T. T.* (1997). Piano trio. Published *Schott-J* SJ1106, 1997.

TALLIS, THOMAS, English composer, organist; b. 1505?; d. Nov. 23, 1585.

Byrd, William, 1543–1623. "Ye sacred muses: An elegy on the death of Thomas Tallis" (1585), in his *Songs,* ed. by Edmund H. Fellowes, Collected vocal works of William Byrd, vol. 15. Voice and strings. Published *Stainer*, 1948. Another edition in *Consort songs for voice and viols*, ed. Philip Brett, The collected works of William Byrd, vol. 15 (*Stainer*, 1970).

TALVELA, MARTTI, Finnish bass; b. Feb. 4, 1935; d. June 22, 1989.

Segerstam, Leif, 1944– . *Monumental thoughts: Martti Talvela in memoriam* (1989). Orchestra. Published *SFC*, 1989. Composed within three days after Segerstam received word of Talvela's death.

TANENBAUM, YADIN, Israeli flutist; b. 1954; d. 1973.

Bernstein, Leonard, 1918–1990. *Halil: Nocturne* (1981). Solo flute with string orchestra, percussion. Published *Jalni*, 1981. "To the Spirit of Yadin, and to his Fallen Brothers. . . . I never knew Yadin Tanenbaum, but I know his spirit"—composer's note in score.

TANSMAN, ALEXANDRE, Polish composer; b. June 12, 1897; d. Nov. 15, 1986.

> **Moss, Piotr, 1949– .** *Elegia: Alexandre Tansman in memoriam* (1986). Violoncellos (2). Published *Eschig* ME8678, 1989.

TÁRREGA, FRANCISCO, Spanish guitarist; b. Nov. 29, 1852; d. Feb. 26, 1909.

> **Fortea, Daniel, 1882–1953 .** *Elegía for guitar,* op. 15: *A la memoria del maestro Francisco Tárrega.* Published Madrid: Biblioteca Fortea 309.

TATUM, ART, American jazz pianist; b. Oct. 13, 1910; d. Nov. 5, 1956.

> **Eklund, Hans, 1927–1999.** "Mesto (marcia funebre)," in his *Musica da camera,* op. 10 (1956). Trumpet, piano, percussion, strings. Published *Suecia,* 1963. The second movement is a memorial to Tatum according to *NGrove,* although there is no dedication in the published score.

TCHAIKOVSKY, PIOTR ILYICH, Russian composer; b. May 7, 1840; d. Nov. 6, 1893.

> **Bax, Arnold, 1883–1953.** *Funeral march: In mem. P. I. T.* (1900). Piano. Unpublished. Source: *Bax.* Quotes the Tsarist national anthem, which also is quoted in Tchaikovsky's overture *1812.*
>
> **Holbrooke, Joseph Charles, 1878–1958.** "Introduction and Russian dance: Hommage à Tchaikovsky," in his *Hommages: Grand suite no. 3* (1905). Orchestra. Published *Novello,* 1910. CONTENTS: Festival: Hommage à Wagner—Serenata: Hommage à Grieg—Elegia e poem: Hommage à Dvorak—Introduction and Russian dance: Hommage à Tchaikovsky.
>
> **Rachmaninoff, Sergei, 1873–1943.** *Muzyka,* op. 34, no. 8 (1912). Song for mezzo-soprano and piano. Published Moscow: Gutheil; *Breitkopf,* 1913. Dedicated to "P. Ch." as a memorial. Text by Yakov Polonsky. Various later editions, including in Rachmaninoff, *Songs (Boosey* VAB179, 1973).
>
> ———. *Trio élégiaque,* op. 9: *À la mémoire d'un grand artiste* (1893). Piano trio. Published Moscow: Gutheil A6784G, 1894. Later edition: *Boosey* 17308, 1947.
>
> **Stravinsky, Igor, 1882–1971.** *Baiser de la fée: Ballet-allégorie en 4 tableaux inspiré par la muse de Tchaikowsky* (1928; rev. 1950). Published Berlin; New York: Editions Russe de Musique, 1928. "Je dédie ce ballet à la mémoire de Pierre Tschaikowsky"—composer's note in score. Revised version published: *Boosey,* 1954.
>
> ———. *Mavra: Opéra bouffe: À la mémoire de Pouchkine, Glinka*

et Tschaikovsky (1922; rev. 1947). Opera in one act. Published Paris; New York: Editions Russe de Musique, 1925. Revised edition: *Boosey* HPS843, 1947. Libretto by Boris Kochno after Pushkin's *The little house of Kolomma.*

TCHEREPNIN, ALEXANDER, Russian composer, pianist; b. Jan. 21, 1899; d. Sep. 29, 1977.

    Caltabiano, Ronald, 1959– . *Sonata for violoncello solo* (1982). Published *Merion* 144-40133, 1986. Commissioned by the Tcherepnin Society to commemorate the 5th anniversary of the death of Alexander Tcherepnin.

    Ramey, Phillip, 1939– . *Memorial: In memoriam Alexander Tcherepnin* (1977). Piano. Published *Henmar* 66773, 1981. Uses material from Tcherepnin's 4th symphony.

    Tcherepnin, Ivan, 1943–1998. *La va et le vient = The coming and going: Based on an instrumental-electronic realization of "Set, hold, clear and squelch": In 5 parts* (1978). Orchestra. Published *Belaieff,* 1978. To the memory of Alexander Tcherepnin, and the newborn Stefan Tcherepnin. Based on an earlier version (1976) for oboe, frequency follower, synthesizer (Serge), titled "Set, hold, squelch and clear."

TEAGARDEN, JACK, American jazz trombonist, vocalist; b. Aug. 29, 1905; d. Jan. 15, 1964.

    Kalitzke, Johannes, 1959– . *Bericht über den Tod des Musikers Jack Tiergarten [sic] = Report on the death of the musician Jack Tiergarten* (1991–92). Scenic broadside ballad for 2 actors, soprano, baritone, and chamber orchestra. Published *Gravis* EG266, 1992.

TERTIS, LIONEL, English violist; b. Dec. 29, 1876; d. Feb. 22, 1975.

    Josephs, Wilfred, 1927–1997. *Concerto for viola and small orchestra,* op. 131: *In memory of Lionel Tertis* (1983). Published *Ramsey,* 1983? Commissioned by the Lionel Tertis International Viola Competition.

THALBERG, SIGISMOND, Swiss pianist, composer; b. Jan. 8, 1812; d. Apr. 27, 1871.

    Leonardo, Luisa, 1859–1926. *Prière à la mémoire de Thalberg.* Piano. Published Rio de Janeiro: Bevilaqua, 187–? Source: *No/Gro,* which cites composition date of 1869!

THOMSON, CÉSAR, Belgian violinist; b. 1857; d. Aug. 21, 1931.

    Lunssens, Martin, 1871–1944. *Concerto for violin and orchestra no. 2 in B minor: À la mémoire de César Thomson.* Published *CeBeDeM.*

THURSTON, FREDERICK, English clarinettist; b. Sep. 21, 1901; d. Dec. 12, 1953.

Howells, Herbert, 1892–1983. *Sonata for clarinet and piano: In remembrance of Frederick Thurston* (1946). Published *Boosey* WCB88, 1954. The sonata was written for Thurston, who premiered it in January 1947. The memorial dedication added at publication.

TIETJENS, THERESE, German soprano; b. 1831; d. Oct. 3, 1877.

Roeckel, Joseph Leopold, 1838–1906. *In memoriam Therese Tietjens, obit Oct. 3, 1877.* Partsong. Published in journal *Musical times* 418 (1877). Later edition: *Novello,* 1884.

TIPPETT, MICHAEL, English composer; b. Jan. 2, 1905; d. Jan. 8, 1998.

Birtwistle, Harrison, 1934– . *Exody "23:59:59": Dedicated to the memory of Michael Tippett* (1997). Orchestra. Published *Boosey* HPS1338, 1998. "The subtitle '23:59:59' is the second before midnight, the moment before time stops temporarily when 24:00 becomes 0:00, which carries increased significance and expectation on New Year's Eve at the turn of a century or millennium"— composer's note in score.

TITELOUZE, JEHAN, French organist, composer; b. 1563; d. Oct. 25, 1633.

Dupré, Marcel, 1886–1971. *Le tombeau de Titelouze: Sixteen chorales for organ based on liturgical hymns* (1942). Published *Bornemann* SB5331, 1942.

TOMKINS, JOHN, English organist; b. 1586?; d. Sep. 27, 1638.

Lawes, William, 1602–1645. "Musick, musick, the master of thy art is dead," in *Choice psalmes put into musick for three voices . . . with a thorough bass: Composed by Henry and William Lawes.* Voices (3) and continuo. Published London: Printed by J. Young for H. Moseley, 1648. *RISM-A1*: L-1164; also *RISM-B1*: 1648/4. Microfilm reprint available from Bell & Howell Information and Learning Company (formerly University Microfilms) in the series *Early English books, 1641–1700,* 461:34. An excerpt is included in Murray Lefkowitz, *William Lawes* (London: Routledge & Kegan Paul, 1960), p. 179–80.

TORRES, EDUARDO, Spanish composer; b. 1872; d. Dec. 23, 1934.

Benavente, José Maria. *Toccata for organ: In memoriam Eduardo Torres* (1984). Published *Monge* 8489057001, 1994.

TOSCANINI, ARTURO, Italian conductor; b. Mar. 25, 1867; d. Jan. 16, 1957.

Kodály, Zoltán, 1882–1967. *Symphony: In memoriam Arturo Toscanini* (1961). Published *Boosey* 18943; *EMB*, 1962.

Leibowitz, René, 1913–1972. *Introduction, funeral march, and fanfare,* op. 57: *Arturo Toscanini in memoriam* (1961). Brass and percussion. Published *Mobart*, 1978.

TOUCHE, JEAN-CLAUDE, French organist; d. Aug. 29, 1944.

Dupré, Marcel, 1886–1971. "Mater dolorosa: À la mémoire de Jean-Claude Touche," in his *Offrande à la Vierge,* op. 40 (1944). Organ. Published *Bornemann* SB5338, 1945. CONTENTS: Virgo Mater—Mater dolorosa—Virgo mediatrix.

TOURNEMIRE, CHARLES, French organist, composer; b. Jan. 22, 1870; d. Nov. 3, 1939.

Duruflé, Maurice, 1902–1986 (transcriber). Tournemire, Charles, 1870–1939. *Cinq improvisations: En souvenir de mon maître Charles Tournemire pour orgue.* Published *Durand* 13863, 1958. Duruflé's reconstruction of improvisations by Tournemire, based on a recording made in 1930. CONTENTS: Petite rapsodie improvisée—Cantilène improvisée—Improvisation sur le Te Deum—Fantaisie-improvisation sur l'Ave Maris Stella—Choral-improvisation sur le Victimae Paschali.

Langlais, Jean, 1907–1991. *In memoriam: À la mémoire de mon maître, Charles Tournemire* (1986). Organ. Published *Combre* 5061, 1986.

TULDER, LOUIS VAN, Dutch tenor; b. May 22, 1892; d. Oct. 1969.

Andriessen, Jurriaan, 1925–1996. *Epitaph voor Louis van Tulder* (1970). High voice, clarinet, piano. Published *Donemus*, 1970. Latin text.

TUNNELL, JOHN, British violinist; d. Sep., 1988 at 52.

Davies, Peter Maxwell, 1934– . *Symphony no. 4: To the memory of John Tunnell* (1989). Published *Boosey* HPS1203, 1992.

TURINA, JOAQUIN, Spanish composer; b. Dec. 9, 1882; d. Jan. 14, 1949.

Garcia Roman, José, 1945– . *Contra est y aquello: In memoriam Joaquin Turina.* Instrumental ensemble. Published *Alpuerto*, 1982.

Homs, Joaquin, 1906– . "In memoriam Turina" (1982), in *Libro-homenaje en el I centenario del nacimiento de Joaquin Turina: 1882–1949.* Piano. Published Barcelona: Ministerio de Cultura, Dirección General de Música y Teatro, 1983. For the centennial of Turina's birth.

Montsalvatge, Xavier, 1912– . *Alegoria: Homenaje a Joaquin*

Turina: A la memoria de Joaquin Turina (1988). Piano. Published
UMEsp 22426, 1989.

UNINSKY, ALEXANDER, Russian-American pianist; b. Feb. 2, 1910; d.
Dec. 19, 1972.
Mather, Bruce, 1939– . *In memoriam Alexandre Uninsky* (1974).
Piano. Unpublished. Source: *Canadian.* Mather studied piano with
Uninsky.

VAET, JACOBUS, Flemish composer; b. 1529; d. Jan. 8, 1567.
Regnart, Jacob, ca. 1540–1599. "Defunctum charitates Vaetem," in
his *Novus thesaurus musicus, liber 5.* Voices (7). Published Venice:
A. Gardano, 1568. *RISM-B1:* 1568/6. Modern edition in Vaet,
Hymns and Chansons, Complete works, vol. 7, ed. Milton Steinhardt
(*DTÖ,* vol. 118, 1968). Poet unknown.
VALEN, FARTEIN, Norwegian composer; b. Aug. 25, 1887; d. Dec. 14,
1952.
Evensen, Bernt Kasberg, 1944– . *Sonata for piano no. 2: In me-
moriam Fartein Valen* (1968). Unpublished. Source: *NorP.*
Thoresen, Lasse, 1949– . *Four pieces for piano: In memory of
Fartein Valen* (1967–1968). Unpublished. Source: *NorP.*
VALLS, MANUEL, Catalonian composer.; b. 1920; d. Sep. 9, 1984.
Lewin Richter, Andrés, 1937–. *In memoriam Manuel Valls* (1984).
Voice and electronic tape. Unpublished. Source: *Catalan.* First per-
formed December 1984 in Barcelona.
VAN HULSE, CAMIL, Belgian-American organist, composer; b. Aug. 1,
1897; d. July 16, 1986.
Muczynski, Robert, 1929– . *Duos for flute and clarinet,* op. 24: *To
the memory of Camil Van Hulse.* Published *Schirmer* 3840, 1991.
Also in a version for 2 flutes.
VARÈSE, EDGARD, French composer; b. Dec. 22, 1883; d. Nov. 6,
1965.
Bentzon, Niels Viggo, 1919–2000. *Formula,* op. 261: *Edgard
Varèse in memoriam* (1970). Orchestra. Published *Hansen,* 1970.
Bergeijk, Gilius van, 1945– . *Tussen twee werelden: In memoriam
Edgard Varèse* (1985–86). Instrumental ensemble with electronic
tape. Published *Donemus,* 1985. Joint composer: Huib Emmer,
1951– .

Erb, Donald, 1927– . *Cenotaph for Edgar Varèse* (1979). Symphonic band. Published *Presser*.

Franceschini, Romulus, 1929–1994. *Metamusic 1: In memoriam Edgard Varèse* (1966). Eight players. Unpublished. Source: *ASCAP*.

Jolivet, André, 1905–1974. *Cérémonial: Hommage à Varèse* (1968). Percussionists (6). Published *Billaudot*, 1970.

Porcelijn, David, 1947– . *Requiem: Ter nagedachtenis aan Edgard Varèse* (1970). Percussionists (7). Published *Donemus*, 1973.

VAUGHAN, SARAH, American jazz vocalist, pianist; b. Mar. 27, 1924; d. Apr. 3, 1990.

Blake, Ran, 1935– . "Sarah" (1994), recorded on *Unmarked van: A tribute to Sarah Vaughan* (Soul Note SN121227-2, 1997). The entire disc is intended as a tribute to Vaughan.

VAUGHAN WILLIAMS, RALPH, English composer; b. Oct. 12, 1872; d. Aug. 26, 1958.

Howells, Herbert, 1892–1983. *Stabat Mater: In affectionate memory of Ralph Vaughan Williams* (1963). Tenor solo, chorus, orchestra. Published *Novello* 19252, 1964.

Whear, Paul W., 1925– . *In memoriam R. V. W.: From Symphony no. 2 "The bridge"* [Symphonies, no. 2. In memoriam R. V. W.] (1970). Orchestra. Published *Ludwig*, 1972. This movement of the symphony is published separately.

VENUTI, JOE, Italian-born American jazz violinist; b. Sep. 1, 1903; d. Aug. 14, 1978.

Bolcom, William, 1938– . *Concerto in D for violin and orchestra* (1983; rev. 1986). Published *EBMarks* HL00841403, 1998. CONTENTS: Quasi una Fantasia—Adagio non troppo ma sostenuto—Rondo–Finale. "The solemn second movement, in 5/4, is in memory of a close friend [pianist Paul Jacobs]; the long adagio line includes a ghostly discourse between the soloist and an offstage D trumpet. This leads without pause into the Rondo–Finale, in which the influence of the late jazz violinist Joe Venuti is most apparent"—note in score. The concerto as a whole is a memorial to Venuti.

Smart, Gary, 1943– . *Fancy: In memoriam Joe Venuti.* Violin and piano. Published *Margun* MM47, 1983.

VERDI, GIUSEPPE, Italian composer; b. Oct. 9, 1813; d. Jan. 27, 1901.

Manente, Giuseppe, 1867–1941. *Alla memoria di G. Verdi: Marcia funebre.* Band. Published Florence: A. Lapini, 190–?

Nevi, Pio Carlo, 1848–1930. *In memoria di G. Verdi: Melodia verdiane trascritte in forma di marcie funebri.* Band. Published *Ricordi*.

Poulenc, Francis, 1899–1963. *Dialogues des Carmelites* (1956). Opera in 3 acts. Published *Ricordi-P* R1471, 1957. "À la mémoire de ma mère, qui m'a révélé la musique, de Claude Debussy, qui m'a donné le goût d'en écrire, de Claudio Monteverdi, Giuseppe Verdi, Modeste Moussorgski, qui m'ont servi ici de modèles"—dedication in score. Text by Georges Bernanos.

Puccini, Giacomo, 1858–1924. *Requiem* (1905). Chorus (STB), viola, organ (or harmonium). Published *Ricordi* 132301, 1974. Another edition by Pietro Spada (*E-V* 362-03209, 1976). Composed for the celebrations held in Milan in 1905 to mark the fourth anniversary of Verdi's death. It was performed on January 27, 1905, at the Casa di Riposo, a charitable institution sponsored by Verdi to help retired and elderly musicians.

Silvestri, Giuseppe, 1841–1921. *Omaggio alla memoria di G. Verdi: Otto fantasie sopra motivi delle sue opere* (1901). Mandolin (or violin) and piano. Published *Ricordi* 104500-104507, 1901. Eight fantasies on motives from Verdi's operas.

Vanni, Giovanni. *Cantata elegiaca: In memoria di Giuseppe Verdi.* Soprano (or tenor) with piano. Published Milan: Giudici & Strada 22496.

VERESS, SÁNDOR, Hungarian-Swiss composer; b. Feb. 1, 1907; d. Mar. 6, 1992.

Holliger, Heinz, 1939– . *(S)irato: Monodie für grosses Orchester: In memoriam Sándor Veress* (1993). Orchestra. Published *Schott-M* 8439, 1993.

Holliger, Heinz, 1939– . *Tombeau for violin and piano* (1993). Unpublished. Source: *Tempo* 185 (June 1993): 62.

VERHULST, EDU, Dutch musicologist; d. 1987 at 46.

Yun, Isang, 1917–1995. *Concerto for violin and small orchestra no. 3: In memoriam Edu Verhulst* (1992). Published *Bote* 23626, 1995.

VIERNE, LOUIS, French organist, composer; b. Oct. 8, 1870; d. June 2, 1937.

Cochereau, Pierre, 1924–1984. *Berceuse: À la mémoire de Louis Vierne* (1973). Organ. Published *Chantraine* EC119, 1997.

Froidebise, Pierre, 1914–1962. "In memoriam Louis Vierne," in his *Sonatine for organ* (1939). Published *CeBeDeM*, 1958. CONTENTS: In memoriam Samuel Scheidt—In memoriam Louis Vierne—In memoriam Dietrich Buxtehude.

Grimm, Heinrich, 1951– . *Hommage à Louis Vierne: Zum 50. Todestag am 2. 6. 1987* (1987). Organ. Unpublished. Source: *Beck-*

mann. Paraphrase on the Prelude from Vierne's Organ symphony no. 1, op. 14. For the 50th anniversary of Vierne's death.

Hesse, Lutz-Werner, 1955– . *Symphony no. 3 for large orchestra and organ,* op. 35: *Le tombeau de Vierne.* Unpublished. Source: *NZfM* (July-Aug. 2000): 92, announcing the first performance on Aug. 19, 2000, at the Stadthalle Wuppertal by the Sinfonieorchester Wuppertal, Dame Gillian Weir (organ), cond. by George Hanson.

Joulain, Jeanne, 1920– . *In memoriam* (1962; rev. 1994). Organ. Published *Chantraine* EC86, 1995. "Composé en 1962 pour le 25e anniversaire de la mort de Louis Vierne. Version révisée par le compositeur en 1994"—caption in score.

VIERNE, RENÉ, French organist, composer; b. 1876; d. May 29, 1918.

Dupré, Marcel, 1886–1971. *Trois préludes et fugues pour grand orgue* [Préludes et fugues, organ, op. 7. No. 1] (1912). Published *Leduc* AL16405, 1920. The first of the preludes and fugues was dedicated post-composition "à la mémoire de René Vierne, organiste de Notre-Dame-des-Champs, mort pour la France"—dedication in score.

VILLA LOBOS, HEITOR, Brazilian composer; b. Mar. 5, 1887; d. Nov. 17, 1959.

Bentzon, Niels Viggo, 1919–2000. *Chorus daniensis no. 2: In stila Brasiliero-Danico: Maestro Heitor Villa-Lobos in memoriam* (1969). Orchestra with solo piano. Published *Hansen.*

Campos Parsi, Héctor, 1922– . *Rapsodia elegiaca: In memoriam Heitor Villa-Lobos* (1960). String orchestra. Published *Peer-S,* 1960.

Coeck, Armand, 1941– . *Le tombeau de Villa Lobos.* Guitar. Published *EMC* 90710120.

Guarnieri, Camargo, 1907-1993. *Homenagem a Villa-Lobos* (1966). Wind ensemble with percussion, piano, celeste, harp. Published *Peters,* 1979. CONTENTS: Tempo de coco—Tempo de toada—Tempo de baião. Performed without interruption.

Lerich, Pierre, 1937– . *Hommage à Villa-Lobos.* Guitar. Published *Eschig* ME7667, 1966.

Rosauro, Ney Gabriel, 1952– . "Prelude in A major: To the memory of Heitor Villa Lobos" (1986), in his *Three preludes for solo marimba* (1983–87). Published *Southern* ST796, 1990. CONTENTS: Prelude in E minor: To Rose Braunstein—Prelude in A major: To the memory of Heitor Villa Lobos—Prelude in C major: To Luiz Anunciação.

Sapieyevski, Jerzy, 1945– . *Toada: In memory of Heitor Villa-*

Lobos (1981). Clarinet and piano. Published *Mercury* 454-40008, 1982.

Sierra, Roberto, 1953– . *Toccata y lamento: A la memoria de Heitor Villa-Lobos* (1987). Guitar. Published *Orphée* PWYS29, 1993.

Vega, Aurelio de la, 1925– . *Homenagem: In memoriam Heitor Villa Lobos* (1987). Piano. Unpublished. Source: *ConCom*. First performance 1987, São Paulo, by José Eduardo Martins. Recorded 1990 by Max Lifchitz on *Max Lifchitz plays American piano music* (Vienna Modern Masters VMM CD 2002, 1991).

VIÑES, RICARDO, Spanish pianist; b. Feb. 5, 1875; d. Apr. 29, 1943.

Rodrigo, Joaquin, 1901–1999. *A l'ombre de Torre Bermeja: A la memoria de Ricardo Viñes* (1945). Piano. Published *Schott-M* 7454, 1987.

VIOZZI, GIULIO, Italian composer; b. July 5, 1912; d. Nov. 29, 1984.

Zanettovich, Daniele, 1950– . *Suite per cinque: Alla memoria di Giulio Viozzi* (1985). Quintet for oboe, clarinet, violin, viola, double bass. Published *Pizzicato* N038.

VISÉE, ROBERT DE, French guitarist, composer; b. 1650?; d. 1725?

Jolivet, André, 1905–1974. *Le tombeau de Robert de Visée* (1972). Suite for guitar. Published *EMT* TRGC1576, 1980.

VITOLS, JAZEPS, Latvian composer, teacher; b. July 26, 1863; d. Apr. 24, 1948.

Ivanovs, Janis, 1906–1983. *Piano trio: To the memory of my professor Jasep Vitol* (1976). Published Moscow: Sov. Kompozitor 667, 1979.

VIVIER, CLAUDE, Canadian composer; b. Apr. 14, 1948; d. Mar. 7, 1983.

Brégent, Michel-Georges, 1948–1993. *Swiateo: Un pas vers la lumière: In memoriam Claude Vivier* (1985). Mixed chorus with orchestra. Unpublished. Source: *Canadian*. Text by Vivier and Plato.

VOLK, ARNO, German music publisher; b. Jan. 14, 1914; d. July 6, 1987.

Penderecki, Krzyzstof, 1933– . *Der unterbrochene Gedanke: Arno Volk in memoriam* (1988). String quartet. Published *Schott-M* 7640, 1991.

VÖTTERLE, KARL, German music publisher; b. Apr. 12, 1903; d. Oct. 29, 1975.

Bialas, Günter, 1907–1995. *Introitus-exodus: In memoriam Karl Vötterle* (1976). Organ and orchestra. Published *Bärenreiter* BA6716, 1976.

VYNER, MICHAEL, British violinist, arts administrator; b. Jan. 3, 1943; d. Oct. 19, 1989.

Benjamin, George, 1960– . *Upon silence: A setting of Yeats' "Long-legged fly": In memory of Michael Vyner 1943–1989* (1990). Mezzo-soprano and viols (5). Published *Faber* 0571512518, 1991. Second version (1992; published 1995) for mezzo-soprano and violas (2), violoncellos (3), double bass.

Berio, Luciano, 1925– . *Leaf: To Michael Vyner in memoriam* (1990). Piano. Published *UE* 19590, 1990.

Birtwistle, Harrison, 1934– . *Ritual fragment* (1990). Ensemble of flute, oboe, clarinet, bassoon, horn, trumpets (2), bass drum, piano, string quartet, double bass. Published *UE-L* 19413, 1990. Written for the Michael Vyner Memorial Concert, London, Royal Opera House Covent Garden, May 6, 1990.

Davies, Peter Maxwell, 1934– . *Threnody on a plainsong: For Michael Vyner* (1989). Orchestra. Published *Chester* 60356, 1992.

Gorecki, Henryk Mikolaj, 1933– . *Good night = Dobranoc,* op. 63: *In memoriam Michael Vyner* (1990). Soprano with alto flute, tam-tams (3), piano. Published *Boosey* VAB315, 1995. Vyner's name is encoded in the piano part. "Good night . . . flights of angels sing thee to thy rest"— quote from Shakespeare's *Hamlet* in score.

Henze, Hans Werner, 1926– . *Requiem: Neun geistliche Konzerte: In memoriam Michael Vyner* (1990–92). Piano solo, trumpet concertante, large chamber orchestra. Published *Schott-M* 8198, 1993. "The movements of the Requiem can be played separately or in any desired combinations"—note in score.

Knussen, Oliver, 1952– . *Secret song* (1990). Violin solo. Unpublished. Source: *Opera* 41, no. 291 (Mar. 1990): concert announcement.

Osborne, Nigel, 1948– . *Eulogy for orchestra.* Published *UE-L,* 1990. "This piece was written for the Michael Vyner memorial concert on 6th May 1990" at the Royal Opera House, Covent Garden (broadcast by BBC2)—note in score.

Takemitsu, Toru, 1930–1996. *Litany: In memory of Michael Vyner* (1990). Piano. Published *Schott-J* SJ1057, 1990. "This is a re-composition of *Lento in due movimenti* (1950) from the memory of the composer, since the original score has been lost"—note in score.

————. *My way of life: In memory of Michael Vyner* (1990). Baritone solo, chorus, orchestra. Published *Schott-J.*

WAGNER, RICHARD, German composer; b. May 22, 1813; d. Feb. 13, 1883.

Bruckner, Anton, 1824–1896. *Symphony no. 7 in E major* (1883). Published Vienna: A. Gutmann AJG576, 1885. The news of Wagner's death reached Bruckner while he was composing the Adagio of this symphony, and it is generally regarded as a lament over his death.

Glazunov, Aleksandr Konstantinovich, 1865–1936. *La mer: Fantaisie,* op. 28: *À la mémoire de Richard Wagner* [Morye]. Orchestra. Published *Belaieff* 302, 1890. Reprint: *Kalmus* 5349, 1980.

Holbrooke, Joseph Charles, 1878–1958. "Hommage à Wagner," in his *Hommages: Grand suite no. 3* (1905). Orchestra. Published *Novello,* 1910. CONTENTS: Festival: Hommage à Wagner—Serenata: Hommage à Grieg—Elegia e poem: Hommage à Dvorak—Introduction and Russian dance: Hommage à Tchaikovsky.

Kistler, Cyrill, 1848–1907. *Trauer-Musik,* op. 60: *Zum Andenken an Richard Wagner.* Piano. Also in a version for brass band. Published Munich: C. Werner; Bad Kissingen: Verlag des Tagesfragen VT11, 1885.

Koetsier, Jan, 1911– . *Skurrile Elegie auf Richard W.,* op. 86, no. 2 (1981). Tenor tuba (i.e., "Wagner" tuba, or bass clarinet) with string quartet (or string orchestra). Published *Donemus,* 1982.

Lessana, Antonio. *Un profondo sospiro in morte del celebre M. Riccardo Wagner: Marcia funebre,* op. 7. Piano. Published Milan: Domenico Vismara 8135.

Liszt, Franz, 1811–1886. "Am Grabe Richard Wagners" (May 22, 1883), in his *Early and late piano works,* Liszt Society publications, vol. 2. Piano or organ. Published *Schott-L* 5645, 1952. Another version is for string quartet with harp.

———. "Richard Wagner: Venezia" (Mar. 1883), in his *Verschiedene Werke für Pianoforte,* Musikalische Werke, ed. Franz Liszt-Stiftung, Ser. II, vol. 9. Published *Breitkopf* FL65, 1927. Later edition in Liszt, *Late piano works,* Liszt Society publications, vol. 1 (*Schott-L,* 1952). Composed to commemorate Wagner's funeral procession in Venice.

———. "Trauergondel = Lugubre gondola" (version 1, Dec. 1882), in his *Pianofortewerke,* Musikalische Werke, ed. Franz-Liszt Stiftung, Ser. II, vol. 9. Piano. Published *Breitkopf,* 1927. New edition in Liszt, *Einzelne Charakterstücke,* Neue Ausgabe sämtliche Werke, Ser. I, vol. 12 (*EMB* Z6217, 1978). Composed by some premonition in Venice six weeks before Wagner's death.

————. *Trauergondel = Lugubre gondola* (version 2, 1885?). Piano (or violin and piano). Published Leipzig: E. W. Fritzsch 430, 1886. New edition in Liszt, *Einzelne Charakterstücke,* Neue Ausgabe sämtliche Werke, Ser. I, vol. 12 (*EMB* Z6217, 1978).

Mascagni, Pietro, 1863–1945. *Elegia: In morte di Riccardo Wagner* (1883). Orchestra. Unpublished. Source: *NGrove.*

Ostendorf, Jens-Peter, 1944– . *Mein Wagner: Zum 100. Todestag von Richard Wagner* (1983). Orchestra. Published *Sikorski* 1933, 1983, in series Exempla nova, no. 233. Written for and first performed on the 100th anniversary of the death of Wagner, February 13, 1983, Hamburg, Musikhalle, Norddeutscher Rundfunk Sinfonie-Orchester, cond. by Hiroshi Wakasugi.

Popp, Wilhelm, 1828–1903. *Erinnerung an Richard Wagner,* op. 409, no. 6. Flute and piano. Published Berlin: Carl Simon.

WAGNER-RÉGENY, RUDOLF, Rumanian-German composer, keyboardist; b. Aug. 28, 1903; d. Sep. 18, 1969.

Schubert, Manfred, 1937– . *Hommage à Rudolf Wagner-Régeny: Konzertante Meditationen über Themen des Meisters* (1972). Harp solo, string orchestra, percussion, celesta. Published *DVfM* 1437, 1980.

WALLACE, CHRIS, American rap musician; b. 1972; d. Mar. 9, 1997. See: **NOTORIOUS B. I. G.**

WALTON, SIR WILLIAM, English composer; b. Mar. 29, 1902; d. Mar. 8, 1983.

Bennett, Richard Rodney, 1936– . *Reflections on a theme of William Walton: Dedicated to the memory of Sir William Walton* (1985). Solo strings (11). Published *Novello.*

Mathias, William, 1934–1992. *Missa Aedes Christi,* op. 92*: In memoriam William Walton* (1984). Chorus (SATB) and organ. Published *OUP* S616, 1985.

WARLOCK, PETER (PHILIP HESELTINE), English composer, author; b. Oct. 30, 1894; d. Dec. 17, 1930. Philip Heseltine used the pen name "Peter Warlock" on all his musical works.

Delius, Frederic, 1862–1934. *Cynara: Dedicated to the memory of Philip Heseltine* (1907). Baritone voice with orchestra. Published London: Winthrop Rogers H&S6961, 1931. Composed and first performed prior to Warlock's death; dedication added for publication.

Lambert, Constant, 1905–1951. *Concerto for solo pianoforte and nine players: To the memory of Philip Heseltine* (1931). Piano solo with flute/piccolo, clarinets (3), trumpet, trombone, violoncello, double bass, percussionist. Published *OUP* 0193652730, 1933.

WEBBE, SAMUEL, English composer; b. 1740; d. May 25, 1816.

Requiem to the memory of the late Samuel Webbe, the words by Mr. [William] Linley, and set to music severally by Lord Burghersch [i.e. John Fane], Messrs. Linley, Knyvett, Hawes, Elliott, Beale & Evans. Mixed voices. Published London: Welsh & Hawes, 1818? CONTENTS: Requiem I / by John Fane—Requiem II / by William Linley, 1771–1835—Requiem III / by Charles Smart Evans, 1778–1849—Requiem IV / by William Knyvett, 1773–1859—Requiem V / by James Elliott, 1783–1856—Requiem VI / by William Beale, 1784–1854—Requiem VII / by William Hawes, 1785–1846. Text incipit: "Chant we the requiem."

Horsley, William, 1774–1848. *Elegiac ode.* Voices (4). Published London: Clementi, 1817. Text by the Rev. Thomas Beaumont. "Inscribed to the memory of the late Samuel Webbe" —note in score.

WEBER, CARL MARIA VON, German composer; b. Nov. 18, 1786; d. June 5, 1826.

Schultheiss, Ulrich, 1956– . *String quartet no. 1: In memoriam Carl Maria von Weber* (1983). Published *Peters.*

Wagner, Richard, 1813–1883. *An Webers Grabe* (1844). Men's chorus (TTBB). Published Leipzig: E. W. Fritzsch, 1872. New edition in Wagner's *Chorwerke,* ed. Reinhard Kapp, Sämtliche Werke, Ser. A, vol. 16 (*Schott-M*, 1993). Composed in November 1844 for the ceremony on December 15, 1844, to rebury Weber's remains in Dresden. Text is by Wagner.

————. "Trauermusik nach Motiven aus Carl Maria von Webers Euryanthe" (1844), in his *Orchester Werke,* Richard Wagners Musikalische Werke, vol. 20, ed. Michael Balling. Winds and percussion. Published *Breitkopf,* 1926. Also separately published: *Breitkopf* PB3045. A version for piano was published as *Trauersinfonie zur feierlichen Beisetzung der Asche Carl Maria von Webers* (Dresden: C. F. Meser, 1860). Composed in November 1844 and first performed on December 14, 1844, during the processional on the day prior to the reburial of Weber's remains in Dresden. Based on themes from Weber's opera *Euryanthe*

WEBERN, ANTON, Austrian composer; b. Dec. 3, 1883; d. Sep. 15, 1945.

Bresgen, Cesar, 1913–1988. *Requiem für Anton Webern* (1945; rev. 1972). Solo voices (ST), chorus (SATB), string orchestra. Published *Gerig* HG1231, 1976. First performed 1945 in Mittersill, Austria, Bresgen's home and the site of Webern's death.

Brooks, William, 1943– . *In memoriam reducere studemus: To mark the 50ᵗʰ anniversary of Anton Webern's death* (1996). Soloists (SATB), Chorus (SATB), piano. Unpublished. Source: *IUL*. Text based in part on the poem "Anton Webern's birthday" by Pierre Joris. Thematic material derived in part from a tetrachord based on the initials of Anton Webern and of Heinrich Isaac, whose *Choralis Constantinus*, book 2, Webern edited, and from music by Notker Balbulus and Isaac.

Dallapiccola, Luigi, 1904–1975. *Sex carmina Alcaei: Una voce canenda, nonnullis comitantibus musicis* [Liriche greche. Carmina Alcaei] (1943). Soprano and chamber orchestra. Published *Zerboni* 4181, 1946. "Quest'opera, dedicata ad Anton Webern nel giorno del suo sessantesimo compleanno (3 dicembre 1943), offro oggo, con umiltà e devozione, alla di Lui memoria, 15 settembre 1945"— dedication in score. Dedicated in 1943 to Webern on his 60ᵗʰ birthday, and rededicated in 1945 to his memory.

Garant, Serge, 1929–1986. *Nucléogame: In memoriam Anton Webern* (1955). Sextet for flute, oboe, clarinet, trumpet, trombone, piano with electronic tape. Unpublished. Source: *Canadian*.

Gismonti, Egberto, 1947– . *Variations for guitar: À la mémoire d'Anton Webern* (1970). Published *Eschig* ME8424, 1982.

Homs, Joaquin, 1906– . *In memoriam Anton Webern: Three inventions* (1959). Orchestra. Unpublished. Source: *Homs*. Based on a tone series by Webern.

Krajev, Faradz, 1943– . *Concerto grosso for chamber orchestra: In memoriam Anton Webern* (1967). Published *Sikorski*.

Krenek, Ernst, 1900–1992. *Symphonic Elegy, op. 105: In memoriam Anton Webern* (1946). Published *E-V*, 1947.

Pousseur, Henri, 1929– . *Quintette: À la mémoire d'Anton Webern* (1955). Quintet for clarinet, bass clarinet, piano, violin, violoncello. Published *Zerboni* 5428, 1958.

Scelsi, Giacinto, 1905–1988. *Variazioni e fuga: Alla memoria di Anton Webern* (1940). Piano. Published Rome: De Santis EDS706, 1947. Later edition: *Salabert* EAS18375, 1986. Dedication is a post-composition addition.

Searle, Humphrey, 1915–1982. *Symphony no. 5, op. 43: In memory* *of Anton Webern* (1964). Published *Schott-L* 6662, 1966.

Whittenberg, Charles, 1927–1984. "Sostenuto (in memory of Anton Webern)," in his *Triptych for brass quintet* (1962). Suite for quintet of trumpets (2), horn, trombones (2). Published Hastings-on-Hudson, NY: Joshua Music, 1970. CONTENTS: Rotational games: Scherzo—Sostenuto (in memory of Anton Webern)—Canonic fanfares.

WEBSTER, BEN, American jazz saxophonist; b. Feb. 27, 1909; d. Sep. 20, 1973.

Reilly, Jack, 1932– . "In memoriam Ben Webster" (1974), recorded on *Tributes* (Carousel Records CLP1002, 1976). Jazz piano.

WEISS, SILVIUS LEOPOLD, German lutenist, composer; b. Oct. 12, 1686; d. Oct. 16, 1750.

Sexton, Brian, 1953– . *Le tombeau sur le mort de Sylvius Leipold Weiss* (1973). Guitar and harpsichord. Unpublished. Source: *Canadian.* Inspired by Weiss's "Tombeau sur la mort de M. Comte de Losy."

WEISSE, HANS, Austrian composer, theorist; b. Mar. 31, 1892; d. Feb. 10, 1940.

Rochberg, George, 1918– . *Two preludes and fughettas (from Book of contrapuntal pieces): To the memory of Hans Weisse* (1946). Keyboard instrument. Published *Presser* 110-40627, 1980.

WENZEL, ERNST FERDINAND, German pianist; b. Jan. 25, 1808; d. Aug. 16, 1880.

Kirchner, Theodor, 1823–1903. "Commodo," in his *Gedenkblätter: Zwölf Musikstücke zur Erinnerung an die Einweihung des neuen Königl. Conservatoriums für Musik zu Leipzig,* op. 82 (1843–87). Piano. Published Leipzig: J. Rieter-Biedermann 1508, 1887. No. 10 of 12 short piano pieces memorializing Conrad Schleinitz, Felix Mendelssohn, Robert Schumann, Moritz Hauptmann, Ferdinand David, Ignaz Moscheles, Ernst Friedrich Richter, Carl Ferdinand Becker, Ernst Ferdinand Wenzel, and Louis Plaidy.

WESLEY, CHARLES, English organist; b. Dec. 11, 1757; d. May 23, 1834.

Wesley, Samuel, 1766–1837. *Funeral anthem on the death of Charles Wesley* (1834). Soloists, chorus, organ. Published *Novello,* 1834. Modern edition in Holmes Ambrose, *The Anglican anthems and Roman Catholic motets of Samuel Wesley,* Boston University (Ph.D. thesis), 1969, available in reprint from University Microfilms. "All go unto one place"—anthem text incipit.

WEYSE, CHRISTOPH ERNST FRIEDRICH, German composer; b. Mar. 5, 1774; d. Oct. 8, 1842.

> Hartmann, Johan Peter Emilius, 1805–1900. *Weyses minde: Cantate, opfört: Musikforeningen d. 24de Janvar 1843,* op. 36 (1843). Vocal soloists, chorus, orchestra. Published Copenhagen: Udgivet af Musikforeningen, 1843. Text by Henrik Hertz.

WHITE, CLARENCE CAMERON, American violinist, composer; b. Aug. 10, 1880; d. June 30, 1960.

> Smith, Hale, 1925– . *Contours: In memory of my two friends Dr. Clarence Cameron White and Dr. Wallingford Riegger* (1961). Orchestra. Published *Peters* 6503, 1962.

WHITING, GRAHAM, English trumpeter; d. 1983.

> Barratt, Carol, 1945– . *Fanfare for a friend* (1983). Trumpets (3). Published *Chester* 55620, 1983. Whiting died of a brain tumor; proceeds from the sale of this work are donated to brain tumor research at the Royal Marsden Hospital.

WHITTENBERG, CHARLES, American composer; b. July 6, 1927; d. Aug. 22, 1984.

> Trombly, Preston, 1945– . *Duo for flute and percussion: In memory of Whittenberg* (1984). Published *ACA*, 1984.

WIECHOWICZ, STANISLAW, Polish composer; b. Nov. 27, 1893; d. May 12, 1963.

> Meyer, Krzysztof, 1943– . *Symphony no. 2: Epitaphium Stanislaw Wiechowicz in memoriam* (1967). Chorus (SATB) and orchestra. Published *PWM* 7134, 1971.

WILDER, ALEC, American composer; b. Feb. 16, 1907; d. Dec. 22, 1980.

> Benson, Warren, 1924– . *Beyond winter: Sweet aftershowers — In memoriam Alec Wilder* (1981). String orchestra. Published *Presser*, 1984.
>
> Levy, Robert. "Elegy: In memory of Alec Wilder," in his *Gestures: For trumpet alone* (1990). Published *Nichols* 31, 1992. CONTENTS: Assertively—Graciously—Elegy: In memory of Alec Wilder—Energetically.
>
> Schuller, Gunther, 1925– . *In praise of winds: Symphony for large wind orchestra* (1981). Published *AMP*. Second movement is inscribed "To the memory of Alec Wilder."

WILK, MAURICE, American violinist; b., 1923; d. 1963.

> Luening, Otto, 1900–1996. *Elegy for violin solo: In memory of Maurice Wilk* (1963). Published *Peters* 6893, 1965.

WILLAERT, ADRIAN, Flemish composer; b. 1490?; d. Dec. 17, 1562.
Benvenuti, Lorenzo, fl. 1560–1570. "Giunto Adrian fra l'anima beate," in his *Secondo libro delle fiamme.* Voices (5). Published Venice: Scotto, 1567. *RISM-B1*: 1567/13. Modern edition in *Fünf Madrigale venezianischer Komponisten um Adrian Willaert: zu 4–7 Stimmen,* ed. Helga Meier (*Möseler,* 1969).
Conforti, Giovanni Battista, fl. 1558–1567. "S'hoggi con senz'honor," in his *Madrigali a cinque voci: Libro primo.* Voices (5). Published Venice: s.n., 1567. *RISM-A1*: C-3497. New edition in Conforti, *Ricercare (1558) und Madrigale (1567),* ed. Dietrich Kämper, Concentus musicus, vol. 4 (Cologne: Arno Volk, 1978).
Gabrieli, Andrea, 1510–1586. "Sassi, Palae, Sabbion, del Adrian lio: Sopra la morte d'Adriano," in his *Di Manoli Blessi: Il primo libro delle Gregesche con la musicha disopra.* Voices (5). Published Venice: A. Gardano, 1564. *RISM-B1*: 1564/16. Modern edition in *Grechesche libro I (1564): 39 composizioni di diversi autori su testi poetici di Manoli Blesi detto il Burchiella: Edizione in trascrizione moderna a 4–5 voci,* ed. Sira Cisillino (*Zanibon,* 1974).
Rore, Cipriano de, 1516–1565. "Concordes adhibete animos, In mortem Adriani Willaert," in *Di Cipriano de Rore, Il quinto libro di madrigali a cinque voce.* Voices (5). Published Venice: A. Gardano, 1566. *RISM-B1*: 1566/17. Modern edition in Rore, *Madrigali 3–8 vocem,* Opera omnia, vol. 5, ed. Bernhard Meier (*AIM,* 1971).
Willaert, Alvise, fl. 1547–1564. "Pianza'l Grego Pueta: Sopra la morte d'Adriano," in *Di Manoli Blessi: Il primo libro delle Gregesche con la musicha disopra.* Voices (5). Published Venice: A. Gardano, 1564. *RISM-B1*: 1564/16. Text by Manoli Blessi (i.e. Antonio Molino). Modern edition in *Grechesche libro I (1564): 39 composizioni di diversi autori su testi poetici di Manoli Blesi detto il Burchiella: Edizione in trascrizione moderna a 4–5 voci,* ed. Sira Cisillino (*Zanibon,* 1974). Also published in Adrian Willaert, *Madrigali e conzoni villanesche,* ed. Helga Meier, Opera omnia, vol. 14, Corpus mensurabilis musicae, vol. 3, no. 14 (*AIM,* 1977). Alvise was a nephew of Adrian.

WILLIAMS, GRACE, Welsh composer; b. Feb. 19, 1906; d. Feb. 10, 1977.
Mathias, William, 1934–1992. *Helios,* op. 76: *In memoriam Grace Williams* (1977). Orchestra. Published *OUP J5673,* 1987.

WILSON, JACKIE, American rock vocalist; b. June 9, 1934; d. Jan. 21, 1984.

Commodores (Musical group). "Nightshift," song recorded on *Nightshift* (Motown Records 6124ML, 1984). Also released on single 45rpm recording (Motown 1773MF). Also dedicated to the memory of vocalist Marvin Gaye. Words and music by W. Orange, D. Lambert, F. Golde.

WINHAM, GODFREY, English-American composer, computer specialist; b. Dec. 11, 1943; d. Apr. 26, 1975.

Babbitt, Milton, 1916– . *Solo requiem: In memory of Godfrey Winham* (1977). Soprano and pianos (2). Published *Peters* 66877, 1981. Texts from Shakespeare (Sonnet 71), Dryden, and others.

WINNER, SEPTIMUS, American song composer; b. May 11, 1827; d. Nov. 22, 1902.

Sims, Ezra, 1928– . *In memoriam Alice Hawthorne* (1967). Vocal soloists (TBar) and narrator with septet of clarinets (4), horn, marimba 4-hands (or 2 marimbas). Published *ACA*, 1967. Alice Hawthorne was a pen name of Winner.

WOLPE, STEFAN, German composer; b. Aug. 25, 1902; d. Apr. 4, 1972.

Cage, John, 1912–1992. *Five⁴ [i.e. Five to the 4ᵗʰ power]: In memory of Stefan Wolpe* (1991). Quintet for saxophones (SA), percussion (3). Published *Henmar* 67430, 1991.

Carter, Elliott, 1908– . "Inner song: In memory of Stefan Wolpe," in his *Trilogy* (1992). Published *Hendon* WOB60, 1993. CONTENTS: Bariolage [oboe and harp]—Inner song: In memory of Stefan Wolpe [oboe solo]—Immer neu [oboe and harp].

Feldman, Morton, 1926–1987. *For Stefan Wolpe* (1986). Chorus (SATB) and vibraphones (2). Published *UE* 18493, 1986?

Pleskow, Raoul, 1931– . *Epitaphium: Stefan Wolpe in memoriam* (1985). Orchestra. Published *ACA*, 1985.

Rovics, Howard, 1936– . *Haunted objects: In memoriam Stefan Wolpe* (1974). Soprano, male narrator, oboe, English horn/oboe, hecklephone/English horn, bassoon, electronic tape. Published *ACA*, 1974. Text by Johanna Pragh and Stefan Wolpe.

WOOD, SIR HENRY JOSEPH, English conductor; b. Mar. 3, 1869; d. Aug. 19, 1944.

Lucas, Clarence, 1866–1947. "Elegy: In memoriam Henry J. Wood (ob. 1944)," in his *Seven short pieces for organ,* op. 75. Published London: Ascherberg, Hopwood & Crew 42428c, 1945. CONTENTS: Preludio eroico—Spring song—Elegy—Aubade—By the rivers of Babylon—Super hanc Petram—Benediction.

Walton, Sir William, 1902–1983. *Memorial fanfare for Henry Wood* (1945). Orchestra. Unpublished. Source: *Walton.*
————. *Where does unuttered music go?* (1946). Mixed chorus un-acc. Published *OUP*, 1947. Text by John Masefield was specially written and set to music by Walton for the unveiling on April 26, 1946, of the Memorial Window in St. Sepulchre's Church, Holborn, London.

WRÓBEL, FELIKS, Polish composer; b. May 15, 1894; d. Apr. 15, 1954.

Bloch, Augustyn, 1929– . *Dialoghi: Feliks Wrobel in memoriam* (1964). Violin and orchestra. Published *PWM* 6305, 1967.

WURLITZER, REMBERT, American string instrument historian; b. Mar. 27, 1904; d. Oct. 21, 1963.

Piston, Walter, 1894–1976. *Piano trio no. 2: Commissioned in memory of Rembert Wurlitzer by his family* (1966). Published *AMP* 7402, 1974.

WYSCHNEGRADSKY, IVAN, Russian composer; b. May 16, 1893; d. Sep. 29, 1979.

Leroux, Philippe, 1959– . *Hommage à Ivan Wyschnegradsky.* Guitars (2). Published *Billaudot* 4710, 1989.

YOUNG, LESTER, American jazz saxophonist; b. Aug. 27, 1909; d. Mar. 15, 1959.

Mingus, Charles, 1922–1979. "Goodbye pork pie hat" (1959), re-corded on *Mingus ah um* (Columbia Records CL1370, 1959). Jazz ensemble, featuring Mingus (double bass), John Handy (tenor sax), Booker Ervin (saxophone), Horace Parlan (piano), Dannie Rich-mond (drums), Shafi Hadi (saxophone), Willie Dennis (trombone), Jimmy Knepper (trombone). CONTENTS: Better git it in your soul—Goodbye pork pie hat—Boogie stop shuffle—Self-portrait in three colors—Open letter to Duke—Bird calls—Fables of Faubus—Pussy cat dues—Jelly roll.

YUN, ISANG, Korean-born German composer; b. Sep. 17, 1917; d. Nov. 3, 1995.

Brandmüller, Theo, 1948– . *Monodie für I.: In memoriam Isang Yun* (1995). Organ. Published *Bote* M202518557, 1996.

Hosokawa, Toshio, 1955– . *Memory: In memory of Isang Yun* (1996). Piano trio. Published *Schott-J* SJ1101, 1997.

ZAMACOIS, JOAQUIN, Spanish composer, teacher; b. Dec. 14, 1894; d. Sep. 8, 1976.

> **Palomo, Lorenzo.** *Scherzando: A la memoria de mi querido maestro, Joaquin Zamacois.* Piano. Unpublished. Source: *IUL.* CONTENTS: En jouant la danse—Danse de l'écureuil à ma fenêtre.

ZAPPA, FRANK, American rock musician; b. Dec. 21, 1940; d. Dec. 4, 1993.

> **Dyens, Roland, 1955– .** *Hommage à Frank Zappa* (1994). Guitar. Published *Lemoine* 26186, 1994.
>
> **Eötvös, Peter, 1944– .** *Psalm 151: In memoriam Frank Zappa* (1993). Percussion solo (or 4 percussionists). Published *Ricordi* SY3211, 1994.
>
> **Heider, Werner, 1930– .** "Zappa: In memoriam Frank Zappa," in his *Z Z Z: Zeus–Zappa–Zorro: Trilogie* (1998). Baritone saxophone solo. Published *Gravis* EG630, 1999. The subtitle is comprised of the titles of the three movements.

ZIEGLER, DOROTHY, American pianist, trombonist, opera coach; b. 1923; d. Mar. 1, 1972.

> **White, Donald H., 1921– .** "In memory of Dottie," in his *Tetra ergon: Four pieces* (1972). Bass trombone and piano. Published Nashville, TN: Brass Music Press, 1975. CONTENTS: For Van [Haney]—In memory of "The Boss" [i.e. William Bell]—In memory of "The Chief" [i.e. Emory Remington]—In memory of "Dottie".

ZILCZ, GYÖRGY, Hungarian trombonist; d. before 1976.

> **Kurtág, György, 1926– .** "In memoriam György Zilcz" (1975), in *Einführung in die Praxis des gemeinsamen Musizierens für Blechbläser = An introduction to ensemble playing for brass instruments*, by György Zilcz et al., vol. 2. Quintet for trumpets (2), trombones (2), tuba. Published EMB, 1977–1984.

ZIMMERMANN, BERND ALOIS, German composer; b. Mar. 20, 1918; d. Aug. 10, 1970.

> **Baur, Jürg, 1918– .** *Giorno per giorno: In memoriam B. A. Zimmermann* (1971). Orchestra. Published *Breitkopf* PB4850, 1971. CONTENTS: Giorno per giorno—Allegria di naufragi—La terra promessa—Soldati. "After Ungharetti" [sic]—caption in score, referring to Italian poet Giuseppe Ungaretti.
>
> **Denhoff, Michael, 1955– .** *Umbrae: In memoriam Berndt Alois Zimmermann* (1976). Violin and violoncello soloists with orchestra. Published *Breitkopf* 1252.

Fénelon, Philippe. *Helios (Mythologie III) pour clavecin: À la mémoire de Bernd Alois Zimmermann.* Harpsichord. Published *Amphion* A529, 1990. CONTENTS: Hélios traverse le ciel—L'île de Rhodes—Actis enseigne l'astrologie aux Egyptiens—Phaéton conduit le char du soleil.

Lonquich, Heinz Martin, 1937– . *Emanation: In memoriam Bernd Alois Zimmermann* (1971). Guitar, piano, electronics. Published *Gerig.*

Medek, Tilo, 1940– . *Stele für Bernd Alois Zimmermann* (1976). Violoncello solo. Published *Hansen* EHF1040, 1980.

Reinhardt, Bruno, 1929– . *Music for violin and guitar: In memoriam Bernd Alois Zimmermann* (1967). Published *Israeli* IMI253, 1972. Memorial dedication added for publication.

Terzakis, Dimitri, 1938– . *Katawassia: In memoriam Bernd Alois Zimmermann* (1972). Solo voices (SSATTB). Published *Bärenreiter* BA5425, 1974. Published twith Terzakis's *Ikos* (SSAATTBB).

ZIMMERMANN, FREDERICK, American double bassist; b. 1906; d. Aug. 3, 1967.

Green, Barry. *Fundamentals of double bass playing.* Published Cincinnati: Piper, 1971. "To my mother, my father, and my brother—and in memory of Fred Zimmermann"—composer's note in publication.

ZINGARELLI, NICOLA ANTONIO, Italian composer; b. Apr. 4, 1752; d. May 5, 1837.

Donizetti, Gaetano, 1797–1848. *Messa de requiem* (May 1837). Unpublished. Source: *Donizetti.* The work is lost.

ZIPOLI, DOMENICO, Italian composer, organist; b. Oct. 17, 1688; d. Jan. 2, 1726.

Siccardi, Honorio, 1897–1963. *Suite a la memoria de Domenico Zipoli* (1921). Piano. Unpublished. Source: *CompAmer*, vol. 2.

ZUCKERKANDL, VICTOR, Austrian musicologist; b. July 2, 1896; d. Apr. 24, 1965.

Allanbrook, Douglas, 1921– . *40 changes: In memoriam Victor Zuckerkandl.* Piano. Published *Boosey* PIB241, 1971.

ZULAWSKI, WAWRZYNIEC, Polish composer; b. Feb. 14, 1916; d. Aug. 18, 1957.

Rudzinski, Witold, 1913– . *Dach swiata = Dach der Welt: In memoriam W. Zulawski* (1960). Monologue with orchestra. Published *PWM* 4543, 1961. Title means "The roof of the world." Text by Bogdan Ostromecki.

Select Bibliography

Listed here are writings that discuss musical memorials in general, and also writings that discuss some specific types of musical memorials. It is not a comprehensive bibliography of writings on these topics, but is provided as a convenience for those who wish to read further.

Abbate, Carolyn. "Outside Ravel's tomb." *Journal of the American Musicological Society* 52/3 (1999): 465–530.

Bergmann, Walter. "Three pieces of music on Henry Purcell's death." *The consort* 17 (1960): 13–19.

Borren, Charles van den. "Esquisse d'une histoire des 'tombeaux' musicaux." *Studien zur Musikwissenschaft* 25 (1962): 56–67.

Brenet, Michel. "Les 'tombeaux' en musique." *La revue musicale* 3 (1909): 568–75, 631–38.

Burke, Richard N. "The March funèbre from Beethoven to Mahler." City University of New York, Ph.D. thesis, 1991.

Daverat, Xavier. "La déploration comme esthétique de la mort dans le jazz." In *Jazz*. La revue d'esthetique, v. 19, pp. 147–151. Paris: Editions Jean-Michel, 1991.

Duckles, Vincent. "The English musical elegy of the late Renaissance." In *Aspects of Medieval and Renaissance music*, pp. 568–75, 631–38. Ed. by Jan LaRue. New York: Norton, 1966.

Geary, Robert Aiken. "An Introduction to the Renaissance déploration." California State University, Fullerton, M.A. thesis, 1980.

Goldberg, Clemens. *Stilisierung als kunstvermittelnder Prozess: Die französischen Tombeau-Stücke im 17. Jahrhundert*. Neue Heidelberger Studien zur Musikwissenschaft, v. 14. Laaber: Laaber-Verlag, 1987.

Hilfiger, John Jay. "Funeral marches, dirges, and wind bands in the nineteenth century." *Journal of band research* 28/1 (fall 1992): 1–20.

Hudson, Barton. "Obrecht's tribute to Ockeghem." *Tijdschrift van de Vereniging voor Nederlandse Muziekgeschiedenis* 37 (1987): 3–13.

Johnston, Gregory Scott. *Protestant funeral music and rhetoric in seventeenth-century Germany: A musical-rhetorical examination of the printed sources*. University of British Columbia, Ph.D. thesis, 1987.

————. "Rhetorical personification of the dead in 17th-century German funeral music: Heinrich Schütz's *Musikalische Exequien* (1636) and three works by Michael Wiedemann (1693)." *The journal of musicology* 9/2 (spring 1991): 186–213.

————. "Musical-rhetorical prosopopoeia and the animation of the dead in 17th-century German funeral music." *Canadian university music review = Revue de musique des universites canadiennes* 10/1 (1990): 12–39.

Kappner, Gerhard. "Deutsche Begrabnismusik von Schütz, Bach, und Handel: Theologische Grundlagen, liturgische Funktionen und musikalische Formen." In *Alte Musik als asthetische Gegenwart: Berich über den internationalen musikwissenschaftlichen Kongress Stuttgart 1985,* v. 2, pp. 112–18. Ed. Dietrich Berke and Dorothee Hanemann. Kassel: Bärenreiter, 1987.

Mies, Paul. "Trauermusik von Heinrich Schütz bis Benjamin Britten: Probleme und Gestaltungen." *Musica sacra* 99/4 (1973): 206–14.

Die Musik in Geschichte und Gegenwart, s.v. "Elegie," by Willi Kahl.

Mussat, Marie-Claire. "Le tombeau dans la musique du XXème siècle." In *Tombeaux & monuments,* pp. 134–44. Ed. by Jacques Dugast and Michèle Touret. Rennes: Presses de l'Université Rennes 2, 1992.

Piccardi, Carlo. "Marche funèbre et conception laïque de la mort." *Dissonanz/Dissonance* 23 (Feb. 1990): 4–11.

Reich, Wolfgang. *Die gedruckten Leichenpredigten des 17. Jahrhunderts als musikalische Quelle.* Leipzig University, thesis, 1962.

————. *Threnodiae sacrae: Katalog der gedruckent Kompositionen des 16.–17. Jh. in Leichenpredigtsammlungen innerhalb der DDR.* Veröffentlichungen der Sächsischen Landesbibliothek, v. 7. Dresden: Sächsische Landesbibliothek, 1966.

————, ed. *Threnodiae sacrae: Beerdigungskompositionen aus gedruckten Leichenpredigten des 16. und 17. Jahrhunderts.* Das Erbe deutscher Musik, v. 79; Abteilung Motette und Messe, v. 9. Wiesbaden: Breitkopf & Härtel, 1975

Rice, Eric. "Tradition and imitation in Pierre Certon's *déploration* for Claudin de Sermisy." *Revue de musicologie* 85/1 (1999): 29–62.

Riedel, Friedrich. "A propos de l'Heroide funèbre: Quelques caracteristiques stylistiques des musiques funèbres de Liszt, de ses predecesseurs et de ses contemporains." In *Actes du Colloque international Franz Liszt, 1811–1886: Tenu dans le cadre de l'Université de Paris IV–Sorbonne sous la présidence de Serge Gut, 17–30 octobre 1986,* pp. 29–35. La revue musicale, v. 405–407. Paris: Richard Masse: La Revue musicale, 1987.

Robertson, Alec. "Memorial music and laments." In *Requiem: Music of mourning and consolation,* pp. 213–35. New York: Praeger, 1968.

Rollin, Monique. "Le 'tombeau' chez luthistes Denys Gautier, Jacques Gallot, Charles Mouton." *XVIIe siècle: Bulletin de la Société d'Étude du XVIIe Siècle* 21–22 (1954): 463–79.

————. "Les tombeaux de Robert de Visée." *XVIIe siècle: Bulletin de la Société d'Étude du XVIIe Siècle* 34 (1957): 73–78.

Rownd, Gary R. "Musical tombeaux and hommages for piano solo." University of Kentucky, D.M.A. thesis, 1990.

Rubin, Frances Anne. "Car atropos: A study of the Renaissance *déploration.*" University of North Carolina at Chapel Hill, M.A. thesis, 1978.

Schneider, Hans Wolfgang. *Instrumental Trauermusik im 19. und frühen 20. Jahrhundert: Dargestellt an 18 Klavierkompositionen zwischen 1797 und 1936.* Kölner Beiträge zur Musikforschung, v. 148. Regensburg: Bosse, 1987

Schrade, Leo. "The tragic pathos in music." In *Tragedy in the art of music*, pp. 83–105. Cambridge, MA: Harvard University Press, 1965.

Schuhmacher, Gerhard. "Begrabniskompositionen für einzelne Personen zwischen 1635 und 1670 aus Konigsberg, Leipzig, und Nurnberg in sozialgeschichtlicher Sicht." In *Bericht über den Internationalen musikwissenschaftlichen Kongres Bayreuth 1981*, pp. 314–20. Ed. Christoph-Hellmut Mahling and Sigrid Wiesmann. Kassel: Bärenreiter, 1984.

————. "Musikbeilagen in Leichenpredigten und selbständig veröffentlichte Sterbekompositionen." In *Leichenpredigten als Quelle historischer Wissenschaften*, pp. 408–25. Ed. By Rudolf Lenz. Vienna: Böhlau Verlag, 1975.

Simon, Damien. "La musique funèbre en France aux XVIIe- et XVIIIe siècles." Univ. of Strasbourg II, thesis (Maitrise, sciences humaines), 1993.

Traub, Andreas. "Kunst–Handwerk: Trauer-Musiken in Leichenpredigten." *Würtembergisch Franken: Jahrbuch des Historischen Vereins für Württembergisch Franken* (1994): 229–78.

Vendrix, Philippe. "Le tombeau en musique en France à l'époque baroque." *Recherches sur la musique française classique* 25 (1987):105–38.

————. "Il 'tombeau' in musica nel periodo barocco." *Nuova rivista musicale italiana* 23 (1989): 326–41.

————. "La transfiguration du poetique: Le tombeau en musique." *Le Licorne* 29 (1994): 217–27.

Weinhold, Liesbeth. "Die Gelegenheitskompositionen des 17. Jahrhunderts in Deutschland." In *Quellen Studien zur Musik: Wolfgang Schmieder zum 70. Geburtstag*, pp. 171–96. Frankfurt ; New York: C. F. Peters, 1972.

Abbreviations of Publishers and Sources

ACA	American Composers Alliance, 170 W. 74th St., New York, NY 10023, USA. URL: //www.composers.com. E-mail: info@composers.com.
ACC	Associació Catalana de Compositores, Passeig de Colom 6, Espai IV, 08002 Barcelona, Spain. URL: //www.accompositores.com.
ACE	American Composers Edition. Distributed in USA by *ACA*. E-mail: 75534.2232@compuserve.com.
Achron	Philip Moddel. *Joseph Achron: With a complete catalogue of Achron's works.* Tel Aviv: Israeli Music Publications, 1966.
ACoeur	Éditions A Coeur Joie, Les Passerelles, BP 9151, 24 ave. Joannès Masset, 69009 Lyon, France. URL: //edacj.musicanet.org.
AIM	American Institute of Musicology, 3773 W. 95th St., Leawood, KS 66206, USA. URL: //www.tempomusic.com/aim. E-mail: aim@tempomusic.com.
Alwyn	Stewart Craggs and Alan Poulton. *William Alwyn: A catalogue of his music.* Hindhead: Bravura Pubs., 1985.
Alpuerto	Editorial Alpuerto, S.A, calle Caños del Peral, 7, 28013 Madrid, Spain.
AMC	American Music Center, 30 W. 26th St., Suite 1001, New York 10010-2011, USA URL: //www.amc.net. E-mail: center@amc.net.
AMP	Associated Music Publishers. Distributed in USA by *Leonard*. URL: //www.schirmer.com. E-mail: amp@msc-gs.com.
Amphion	Amphion Éditions Musicales, 215 rue du Faubourg St.-Honoré, 75008 Paris, France.
APNM	APNM Music, 236 West 26th St., Suite 11S, New York, NY 10001.

Arcana	Arcana Editions, Indian River, Ontario KOL 2B0, Canada. URL: //www.patria.org/arcana.
Arnold	Alan Poulton. *The music of Malcolm Arnold: A catalogue.* London: Faber Music, 1986.
ASCAP	American Society of Composers, Authors, and Publishers. *ASCAP symphonic catalog.* 3rd ed. New York: Bowker, 1977.
Aureus	Aureus Publishing, 24 Mafeking Rd, Cardiff CF23 5DQ, Wales, UK. URL: //www.aureus.co.uk. E-Mail: meuryn.hughes@aureus.co.uk.
Australia	Australia Music Centre Ltd., Grosvenor St., Box N9, Sydney NSW 2000, Australia. URL: //www.amcoz.com.au. E-Mail: info@amcoz.com.au.
B&S	Boccaccini & Spada Editori, Via F. Duodo 10, 00136 Rome, Italy. Distributed in the USA by *Presser.* URL: //www.boccacciniespada.com. E-mail: webmaster@boccacciniespada.com.
Banks	Banks Music Publications, The Old Forge, Sand Hutton, Yorkshire YO4 1LB, UK. E-mail: banksramsey@mcmail.com.
Bardic	Bardic Edition, 6 Vairfax Crescent, Aylesbury, Buckinghamshire HP20 2ES, UK. URL: //www.bardic-music.com. E-mail: info@bardic-music.com.
Bärenreiter	Bärenreiter-Verlag, Heinrich-Schütz Allee 35, 34131 Kassel, Germany. URL: //www.baerenreiter.com. E-mail: info@baerenreiter.com.
Baron	M. Baron Co. Inc., Box 149, Oyster Bay, NY 11771, USA.
Bax	Graham Parlett. *A catalogue of the works of Sir Arnold Bax.* Oxford, UK: Clarendon Press, 1999.
BCP	*Boston composers project: A bibliography of contemporary music.* Compiled by Boston Area Music Libraries, Linda I. Solow, editor. Cambridge, Mass.: MIT Press, 1983.
Beckmann	Klaus Beckmann. *Repertorium Orgelmusik: Komponisten – Werke – Editionen 1150–1998: 41 Länder: Eine Auswahl = A bio-bibliographical index of organ music: Composers – works – editions 1150–1998: 41 countries: A selection.* 2nd ed. Mainz: Schott, 1999.

Bedford	Frances Bedford. *Harpsichord and clavichord music of the twentieth century.* Fallen Leaf reference books in music, v. 22. Berkeley: Fallen Leaf Press, 1993.
Belaieff	M. P. Belaieff, Postfach 700851, 60558 Frankfurt am Main, Germany. Distributed in USA by *Peters.* URL: //www.edition-peters.de.belaieff.
Belati	Casa Editrice Tito Belati, via della Scuola 59/ E, 06087 Ponte San Giovanni PG, Italy.
Bella	Bella Musica Edition, Eisenbahnstrasse 30, 77815 Bühl, Germany.
Belwin	Belwin-Mills Music. 15800 N.W. 48th Ave., Miami, FL 33014, USA.
Bennett	George Joseph Ferencz. *Robert Russell Bennett: A bio-bibliography.* New York: Greenwood Press, 1990.
Berandol	Berandol Music Ltd., 110A Sackville St., Toronto, Ontario M5S 3ET, Canada. URL: //www.mayfiarmusic.com. E-Mail: sales@mayfairmusic.com.
Berben	Berben, via Redipublia 65, 60122 Ancona, Italy. Distributed in USA by *Presser.* URL: //www.berben.it. E-mail: info@berben.it.
Bergamo	Arrigo Gazzaniga. *Il fondo musical Mayr della Biblioteca civica de Bergamo.* Bergamo: Biblioteca civica, 1963.
Berger	Dieter Siebenkäs. *Berger: Sein Leben und sein Werke unter besonderer Berücksichtigung seiner Liedschaffens.* Berlin: Merseburger, 1963.
Billaudot	Éditions Musicales Gérard Billaudot, 14, rue de l'Échiquier, 75010 Paris, France. URL: //www.billaudot.com.
BMI-71	Broadcast Music Inc. *BMI symphonic catalogue.* New York: BMI, 1971.
BMI-78	Broadcast Music Inc. *BMI symphonic catalog: Supplement number one.* New York: BMI, 1978.
BMIC	British Music Information Centre. *Keyboard solos and duos by living British composers.* London: BMIC, 1974.
BMms	Augustus Hughes-Hughes. *Catalogue of manuscript music in the British Museum,* v.2: *Secular vocal music.* London: British Museum, 1908.
Böhm	Anton Böhm & Sohn, Lange Gasse 25, Postfach 110369, 86152 Augsburg, Germany.

Boileau	Editorial de Música Boileau, calle Provenza 287, 08037 Barcelona, Spain. URL: //www.cambrabcn.es/boileau. E-mail: boileau@cambrabcn.es.
Bolamar	Bolamar Ediciones Musicales, S.A, c/o Aurea Ruiz, Azor, 5, Molino de la Hoz, 28230 Las Rozas Madrid, Spain. URL: //personal.redestb.es/bolamar. E-mail: bolamar@redestb.es.
Boosey	Boosey & Hawkes Inc., 35 East 21st St., New York, NY 10010, USA. URL: //www.ny.boosey.com. E-mail: bhsales@ny.boosey.com.
Bornemann	Bornemann Editions, Alphonse Leduc, 175, rue Saint-Honoré, 75001 Paris, France. Distributed in USA (non-exclusive) by *Presser*.
Bosse	Gustav Bosse Verlag, Box 101420, Heinrich-Schütz-Allee 35, 34014 Kassel, Germany. URL: //www.bosse-verlag.de. E-mail: info@bosse-verlag.de.
Bote	Bote & Bock Musikverlage, Lützowufer 26, 10787 Berlin, Germany. Distributed in USA by *Boosey*.
BPL	Boston Public Library. *Dictionary catalog of the music collection*. 20 vols. Boston: G. K. Hall, 1972– .
Brazilian	Brazilian Music Enterprises, Box 442, Moriches, NY 11955, USA. URL: //www.brazmus.com.
Breitkopf	Breitkopf & Härtel, Postfach 1707, 65007 Wiesbaden, Germany. URL: //www.breitkopf.com. E-mail: info@breitkopf.com.
Brenet	Michel Brenet. "Les tombeaux en musique: Les origines de la musique funèbre." *La Revue musicale* 3 (1902): 568-75, 631-38.
Broekmans	Broekmans & Van Poppel, Van Baerlestraat 92-94, 1071 BB Amsterdam, Netherlands. URL: //www.broekmans.com. E-mail: music@broekmans.com.
Broude	Broude Brothers Limited, 141 White Oaks Road, Williamstown, MA 01267, USA. E-Mail: broude@sover.net.
Burke	Richard N. Burke. "The marche funèbre from Beethoven to Mahler." City University of New York, Ph.D. thesis, 1991.
Camerica	Camerica Inc., Penthouse, 535 Fifth Ave, New York, NY 10017, USA.

Canadian	Canadian Music Centre / Centre de Musique Canadienne, Chalmers House, 20 St. Joseph, Toronto, Ontario M4Y 1J9, Canada. URL: //www.musiccentre.ca. E-mail: cmc@interlog.com.
Castle	Castle Enterprises, 3478B Pleasantbrook Village Lane, Atlanta, GA 30340, USA.
Catalan	*68 Compositors Catalans.* Barcelona: Generalitat de Catalunya, Departament de Cultura, 1989.
CeBeDeM	Centre belge de documentation musicale, rue d'Arlon 75-77, 1040 Brussels, Belgium. Distributed in USA by *Elkan.* URL: //www.cebedem.be. E-mail: music-centre@cebedem.be.
Cesky	Cesky hudebni fond, Besedni 3, 118 01 Prague, Czechoslovakia.
CFE	Composers Facsimile Edition. Distributed in USA by *ACA.*
CFischer	Carl Fischer Inc., 65 Bleecker St., New York, NY 10012, USA. URL: //www.carlfischer.com. E-mail: cf-info@carlfischer.com.
Chanterelle	Chanterelle Verlag, Postfach 103909, 69029 Heidelberg, Germany. URL: //www.chanterelle.com. E-mail: chanterelle@chanterelle.com.
ChantM	Chant du Monde, 31/33 rue Vandrezanne, 75013 Paris, France.
Chantraine	Editions Chantraine, 7 ave. Henri-Paris, 7500 Tournai, Belgium. URL: //www.angelfire.com/oh/chantraine.
Chappell	Chappell Music. Distributed in USA by *Leonard.*
Chester	J. & W. Chester Ltd., 8-9 Firth St., London W1V 5TZ, UK. Distributed in USA by *MusSales.*
Chile	Roberto Escobar and Renato Yrarrazaval. *Musica compueste in Chile, 1900–1968.* Santiago, Chile: Eds. de la Biblioteca nacional, 1969.
Choudens	Choudens, 38, rue Jean-Mermoz, 75008 Paris, France. Distributed (non-exclusive) in USA by *Peters* and *Presser.*
CMC	Contemporary Music Centre, 19 Fishamble St., Temple Bar, Dublin 8, Ireland. URL: //www.cmc.ie. E-mail: info@cmc.ie.
Combre	Editions Combre, 24 blvd. Poissonnière, 75009 Paris, France. Distributed in USA by *RKing.*
CompAmer	Pan American Union, Music Section. *Compositores de América: Datos biográficos y catálogos de sus obras =*

	Composers of the Americas: Biographical data and catalogs of their works. 20 v. Washington, D.C.: Organization of American States, 1955–1977.
ConBrio	ConBrio Verlagsgesellschaft, Postfach 100245, 93002 Regensburg, Germany.
ConCom	*Contemporary composers.* Ed. Brian Morton and Pamela Collins. Chicago; London: St. James Press, 1992.
Costallat	Costallat, 50 rue des Tournelles, 75003 Paris, France. Distributed in USA by *Presser.*
CPM	*Catalogue of printed music in the British Library to 1980.* Ed. Laureen Baillie. 62 v. London; New York: Saur, 1981–1987.
Curci	Edizioni Curci, Galleria del Corso 4, 20122 Milan, Italy. URL: //www.edizionicurci.it. E-mail: info@edizionicurci.it.
Dantalian	Dantalian Inc., 11 Pembroke St., Newton, MA 02158, USA. URL: //www.dantalian.com. E-mail: dantinfo@dantalian.com.
Davidge	Davidge Publishing, 990 Glenhill Rd, Shoreview, MN 55126, USA. URL: //www.davidgepublishing.com.
Diethelm	*Caspar Diethelm: Werkverzeichnis.* Zürich: Schweizerisches Musik-Archiv, 1989.
Doberman	Les editions Doberman-Yppan, BP 2021, Saint-Nicolas QC G7A 4X5, Canada. URL: //pages.infinit.net/doyp. E-mail: doberman.yppan@videotron.ca.
Doblinger	Musikhaus & Verlag Ludwig Doblinger, Postfach 882, Dorotheergasse 10, 1010 Vienna, Austria. URL: //www.doblinger.co.at.
Donemus	Donemus Stichting, Paulus Potterstraat 14-16, 1071 CZ Amsterdam, Netherlands. URL: //www.donemus.nl. E-mail: info@donemus.nl.
Donizetti	Herbert Weinstock. *Donizetti and the world of opera in Italy, Paris and Vienna in the first half of the nineteenth century.* New York: Pantheon, 1963.
DTÖ	*Denkmäler der Tonkunst in Österreich.* Vienna: Österreichischer Bundesverlag, 1894–1959; Graz: Akademische Druck- und Verlagsanstalt, 1960– .
Duma	Duma Music Inc., 580 Alden St., Woodbridge, NJ 07095, USA. URL: //www.dumamusic.com. E-mail: dumamuse@aol.com.

Durand	Durand Éditions musicales, 215 rue du Faubourg St.-Honoré, 75008 Paris, France. E-mail: durand-eschig@wanadoo.fr.
DVfM	Deutsche Verlag für Musik, Postfach 147, 04001 Leipzig, Germany.
Eben	Katerina Vondrovicova. *Petr Eben: Leben und Werk.* German trans. from the Czech by Silke Klein and Jan Kühmeier. Mainz: B. Schott, 2000.
EBMarks	Edward B. Marks Music Co., c/o Carlin America Inc., 126 E. 38th St., New York, NY 10016, USA. URL: //www.carlinamerica.com. E-mail: bgolden@carlinamerica.com.
ECS	E. C. Schirmer Music Co. Inc., 138 Ipswich St., Boston, MA 02215, USA. URL: //www.ecspublishing.com. E-mail: office@ecspublishing.com.
EdiPan	Edi-Pan s. r. l, viale Mazzini 6, 00195 Rome, Italy.
EditMuz	Editura Muzicala, Str. Doiana Narciselor 6. Bucurest Sector I. Romania.
EitnerQL	Robert Eitner. *Biographisch-bibliographcher Quellen-Lexikon der Musiker und Musikgelehrten.* 10 v. Leipzig: Beitkopf & Härtel, 1898–1904.
Elkan	Henri Elkan Music Publishing Co. Inc., Box 965, New York, NY 10024, USA.
ELWE	ELWE-Musikverlag, Zelgrankstrasse 1, Postfach 68, 8965 Rudolfstetten, Switzerland.
EMB	Editio Musica Budapest, Box 322, 1370 Budapest, Hungary. E-mail: musicpubl@emb.hu.
EMC	European Music Centre, Ambachsweg 42, 1271 AM Huizen, Netherlands.
EMEC	Editorial de Música Española Contemporánea, calle Alcalá 70, 28009 Madrid, Spain.
Emerson	Emerson Edition Ltd., Windmill Farm, High St., Ampleforth, Yorkshire YO6 4HF, UK.
EMT	Éditions musicales transatlantiques, 151-153 ave. Jean-Jaurès, 75019 Paris, France.
Eschig	Éditions Max Eschig, 215 rue du Faubourg St.-Honoré, 75008 Paris, France.
Eshpai	Laurel E. Fay. *Andrei Eshpai: A complete catalog.* New York: G. Schirmer, 1988.

Euphonia	Euphonia-Musikverlag, Bellevuestrasse 2, Postfach 14, 6280 Hochdorf, Switzerland.
EurAmer	European American Music Distributors Corp., 15800 N. W. 48th Ave., Miami, FL 33014. URL: //www.eamcd.com. E-mail: eamdc@eamdc.com.
E-V	Elkan-Vogel Inc. Distributed in USA by *Presser*.
EWP	Edition Wandelweiser GmbH, Lorenzstrasse 57, 12209 Berlin, Germany. URL: //www.timescraper.de/wandelweiser.html.
Everett	Thomas G. Everett. *Annotated guide to bass trombone literature*. 2nd ed. Nashville: Brass Press, 1978.
Faber	Faber Music Ltd., 3 Queen Square, London WC1N 3AU, UK . URL: //www.fabermucic.co.uk. E-mail: information@fabermusic.com.
Falcón	Belén Pérez Castillo and Julio Arce Bueno. *Juan José Falcón Sanabria*. Madrid: SGAE, 1997.
Fazer	Fazer Music, c/o Warner/Chappell Music Finland oy, POB 169, 02101 Espoo, Finland. Distributed in USA by *Boosey*. E-mail: fazer@warnerchappell.com.
Fétis	François Joseph Fétis. *Biographie universelle des musiciens*. 2nd ed. 8 v. Paris: Firmin-Didot, 1860–1865.
FIMIC	Finnish Music Information Centre = Suomalaiser musiikin tiedotuskeskus, Lauttasaarentie 1, 00200 Helsinki, Finland. E-mail: info@mic.teosto.fi.
Finnissy	Tom Morgan. "A catalogue of the works of Michael Finnissy," *Contemporary music review* 13 (1995): 159-243.
Forberg	Musikverlag Robert Forberg, Mirbachstrasse 9, 53173 Bonn, Germany.
FrogPeak	Frog Peak Music, Box 1052, Lebanon, NH 03766, USA. URL: //www.frogpeak.org. E-mail: fp@frogpeak.org.
Furore	Furore-Verlag, Naumburger Strasse 40, 34127 Kassel, Germany. URL: //www.furore-verlag.de. E-mail: FuroreVerlag.Kassel@t-online.de.
Fuzeau	Editions J. M. Fuzeau, BP 6, 79440 Courlay, France. URL: //www.fuzeau.com. E-mail: jmfuzeau@wanadoo.fr.
Gallot	*Oeuvres des Gallot*. Ed. Monique Rollin. Paris: Editions du Centre National de la Recherche Scientifique, 1987.
Geary	Robert Aiken Geary. "An introduction to the Renaissance déploration." California State University at Fullerton, M.A. thesis, 1980.

Gee	Harry R. Gee. *Saxophone soloists and their music, 1844– 1985: An annotated bibliography.* Bloomington, IN: Indiana University Press, 1986.
Gendai	Gendai Guitar Co. Ltd., 1-16-14 Chihaya, Toshima-ku, Tokyo 171, Japan. URL: //www.gendaiguitar.com/eng.
General	General Music Publishing. Distributed by *BostonMus.*
Gerig	Hans Gerig Musikverlage, Postfach 100435, 51404 Bergische Gladbach, Germany.
Gravis	Edition Gravis, Adolfstrasse 71, 65307 Bad Schwalbach, Germany.
Gray	H. W. Gray Publications. Distributed in USA by *Belwin.*
GunMar	GunMar Music Inc. Distributed in USA by *Margun.*
Hampton	Hampton Music Publishers, Hampton House, 84 Clare St., Northampton NN1 3JD, UK .
Hansen	Wilhelm Hansen Musik-Forlag, Gothersgade 9-11, 1123 Copenhagen, Denmark.
Heinrich	William Treat Upton. *Anthony Philip Heinrich: A nineteenth-century composer in America.* New York: Columbia University Press, 1932.
Helicon	Helicon Music Corp. Distributed in USA by *EurAmer.*
Hendon	Hendon Music Inc. Distributed in USA by *Boosey.*
Henmar	Henmar Press Inc. Distributed in USA by *Peters.*
Henze	*Hans Werner Henze: Ein Werkverzeichnis 1946–1996 = A catalogue of works 1946–1996.* Mainz; New York: Schott, 1996.
Heugel	Heugel et Cie, Editions Heugel, 175 rue Saint Honoré, 75001 Paris, France. Distributed in USA (non-exclusive) by *Presser.*
Highgate	Highgate Press. Distributed in USA by *ECS.*
Hildegard	Hildegard Publishing Co., Box 332, Bryn Mawr, PA 19010. URL: //www.hildegard.com. E-mail: sglickman@hildegard.com
Hinshaw	Hinshaw Music Inc., Box 470, Chapel Hill, NC 27514-0470, USA. URL: //www.hinshawmusic.com. E-mail: hinshaw@interpath.com.
Holbrooke	Kenneth L. Thompson. "Holbrooke: Some catalogue data." *Music & letters* 46 (1965): 297-305.
Homs	Piedad Homs Fornesa. *Catalogo de obras de Joaquin Homs.* Madrid: Fundacion Juan March, 1988.

Homuth	Donald Homuth. *Cello music since 1960: A bibliography of solo, chamber & orchestral works for the solo cellist.* Berkeley, CA: Fallen Leaf Press, 1994.
Hopkinson	Oscar Sonneck. *Francis Hopkinson, the first American poet-composer (1737–1791) and James Lyon, patriot, preacher, psalmodist, (1735–1794).* New introd. by Richard A. Crawford. New York: Da Capo Press, 1967. Reprint of the first edition of 1905.
Houdoy	Jules Houdoy. *Histoire artistique de la cathedrale de Cambrai, ancienne eglise metropolitaine Notre-Dame.* Paris, 1880; reprint: Geneva: Minkoff, 1972.
Hudobny	Hudobny fond, Medená 29, 81102 Bratislava, Slovakia. URL: //www.his.sk. E-mail: his@his.sk.
Hudson	Barton Hudson. "Obrecht's tribute to Ockeghem." *Tijdschrift van de Vereniging voor nederlandse Muziekgeschiedenis* 37 (1987): 3-13.
Hulme	Derek Hulme. *Dmitri Shostakovich: A catalogue, bibliography, and discography.* Oxford: Clarendon Press; New York: Oxford University Press, 1991.
Hungar	*Contemporary Hungarian composers.* 3rd ed. Budapest: Edition Musica, 1974.
IMIC	Islensk tónverkamiostöd = Iceland Music Information Centre, Sidumúli 34, 108 Reykjavik, Iceland. URL: //www.vortex.is/ITM. E-mail: icemi@vortex.is.
Impero	Impero Verlag, Postfach 620, 26354 Wilhelmshaven, Germany.
Ione	Ione Press Inc. Distributed in USA by *ECS.*
Irish-82	*A catalogue of contemporary Irish music.* Ed. Bernard Harrison. Dublin: Irish Composers' Centre, 1982.
Irish-96	*Irish composers: 1996–1997.* 4th ed. Dublin: Contemporary Music Centre, 1996.
Israeli	Israel Music Institute, Box 3004, 61030 Tel Aviv, Israel. Distributed in USA by *Presser.* URL: //www.aquanet.co.il/vip/imi. E-Mail: 035245275@doar.net.
ITG	International Trumpet Guild, 241 E. Main St., Westfield, MA 01086, USA. URL: //www.trumpetguild.org. E-mail: website@trumpetguild.org.
IUL	William and Gayle Cook Music Library, School of Music, Indiana University, Bloomington, IN 47405, USA.

	URL: //www.music.indiana.edu/muslib.html.
	E-Mail: libmus@indiana.edu.
Jalni	Jalni Publications Inc. Distributed by *Boosey*.
Jerona	Jerona Music Corp. Box 671, Englewood, NJ 07631, USA.
	URL: //host.mpa.org/agency/203p.html.
	E-mail: maasturm@sprynet.com.
Jobert	Editions Jobert et Cie. Distributed in USA by *Presser*.
Johnston	Heidi Van Gunden. *The music of Ben Johnston*. Metuchen, NJ: Scarecrow, 1986.
Kallisti	Kallisti Music Press, 810 S. Saint Bernard St., Philadelphia, PA 19143, USA.
	URL: //www.netcom.com/~kallisti/voice.html.
	E-mail: kallisti@ix.netcom.com.
Kalmus	Edwin F. Kalmus & Co., Box 5011, Boca Raton, FL 33431, USA. URL: //www.kalmus-music.com.
	E-mail: info@kalmus-music.com.
Kaltenecker	*Gertraud Kaltenecker*. Komponisten in Bayern, v. 37. Tutzing: H. Schneider, 1999.
Katzbichler	Bernd Katzbichler, Wilhelming 7, 83112 Frasdorf, Germany. URL: //www.ourworld.compuserve.com/homepages/katzbichler_musikverlag.
	E-mail: 101700.2410@compuserve.com.
KdG	*Komponisten der Gegenwart*. Ed. Hanns-Werner Heister and Walter-Wolfgang Sparrer. Munich: Edition Text & Kritik, 1992– . Continuing loose-leaf.
Kendor	Kendor Music Inc., Main and Grove Sts., Box 278, Delevan, NY 14042, USA. URL: //www.kendormusic.com. E-mail: kendor@wycol.com.
Kistner	Musikverlag Kistner & Siegel & Co, Aggerweg 6, 51149 Cologne, Germany.
Koshgarian	Richard Koshgarian. *American orchestral music: A performance catalog*. Metuchen, NJ: Scarecrow Press, 1992.
Kraus	Bertil H. van Boer. *Die Werke von Joseph Martin Kraus: systematisch-thematisches Werkverzeichnis*. Stockholm: Kgl. Schwedischen Musikakademie, 1988.
Leduc	Alphonse Leduc et Cie, 175 rue St.-Honoré, 75040 Paris, France. URL: //www.alphonseleduc.com/english.
	E-mail: AlphonseLeduc@wannado.fr.
	Distributed in the USA (non-exclusive) by *Presser*.

Lemoine	Editions Henry Lemoine, 41 rue Bayen, 75017 Paris, France. URL: //www.editions-lemoine.fr.
Leonard	Hal Leonard Corp., 7777 W. Bluemound Road, Box 13819, Milwaukee, WI 53213, USA. URL: //www.halleonard.com. E-mail: halinfo@halleonard.com.
Lesueur	Jean Mongrédien. *Catalogue thématique de l'oeuvre complète du compositeur Jean François Le Sueur: 1760–1837.* New York: Pendragon, 1980.
Lingua	Lingua Press. Distributed by *FrogPeak.* URL: //www.gamelan.org/fpartists/fplingua.html.
Litolff	Henry Litolffs Verlag, Postfach 700851, 60588 Frankfurt am Main, Germany. Distributed in the USA by *Peters.*
Londeix	Jean Marie Londeix. *Music for saxophone*, v. 2. Cherry Hill, NJ: Roncorp, 1985.
Loos	*Armin Loos, 1904–1971: A catalog of his music.* Ship Bottom, NJ: Association for the Publication of New Music, n.d.
Lopes	Filipe de Sousa. "O In memoriam Bela Bartok de Fernando Lopes-Graça." In *Uma homenagem a Fernando Lopes Graça,* pp. 17-21. Portugal: Camara Municipal de Matosinhos: Edicoes Afrontamento, 1995.
Ludwig	Ludwig Music Publ. Co. Inc., 557 East 140th St., Cleveland, OH 44110, USA. URL: //www.ludwigmusic.com. E-mail: Ludwig@cybergate.net.
Lundquist	Abraham Lundquist Musikförlag AB, Box 93, 18211 Danderyd, Sweden. URL: //www.smff.se/abr.lundquist-musikforlag-AB-2.htm. E-mail: info@abrahamlundquist.se.
Lunssens	Raymond Moulaert. "Notice sur Martin Lunssens." *Annuaire de l'Académie royale de Belgique* 127 (1961): 3–13.
Lyche	Harald Lyche & Co. A/S musikkforlaget, Box 2171 Stromso, 3001 Drammen, Norway. URL: // www.lyche.no.
Lyra	Lyra Music Co., 133 W. 69th St., New York, NY 10023, USA. URL: //www.lyramusic.com.
Malipiero	John C. G. Waterhouse. *Gian Francesco Malipiero (1882–1973): The life, times and music of a wayward genius.* Amsterdam: Harwood Academic Publishers, 1999.
Margaux	Margaux Edition, An den Kolonaden 15, 10117 Berlin, Germany. URL: //www.verlag-neue-musik.de.

Margun	Margun/Gunmar Music Inc., 167 Dudley Rd., Newton Centre, MA 02159, USA. URL: //members.aol.com/margunmus. E-mail: MargunMus@aol.com.
Martin	Editions Robert Martin, 106 grande rue de la coupée, 71850 Charnay-lès-Maçon, France. URL: //www.edmartin.com.
Masters	Masters Music Publications Inc., Box 810157, Boca Raton, FL 33481, USA. URL: //www.masters-music.com. E-mail: webmaster@masters-music.com.
Mayr	John Allitt. *J. S. Mayr: Father of 19th century Italian music.* Longmead, England: Element Books, 1989.
MCA	MCA Music Publishing, 8th Floor, 1755 Broadway, New York, NY 10019, USA.
McGinnis	McGinnis & Marx Music Publishers, 236 W. 26th St., New York, NY 10001, USA.
Media	Media Press Inc., Box 3937, Champaign, IL 61826, USA.
Méfano	*Paul Méfano.* Paris: Salabert, 1974.
MelBay	Mel Bay Publications Inc., 4 Industrial Dr., Box 66, Pacific, MO 63069, USA. URL: //www.melbay.com. E-mail: email@melbay.com.
Menotti	Donald L. Hixon. *Gian Carlo Menotti: A bio-bibliography.* Bio-bibliographies in music, v. 77. Westport, CT: Greenwood Press, 2000.
Mercury	Mercury Music Corp. Distributed in USA by *Presser.*
Merion	Merion Music Inc. Distributed in USA by *Presser.*
Merseburger	Verlag Merseburger Berlin, GmbH, Postfach 103880, 34038 Kassel, Germany. URL: //www.merseburger.de. E-mail: mail@merseburger.de.
Mesangeau	René Mesangeau. *Oeuvres.* Ed. André Souris. Paris: CNRS, 1971.
Mettraux	Laurent Mettraux SME/EMS, BP 7851, 6000 Lucerne 7, Switzerland. URL: //www.musicedition/ch/composers/98f.htm.
Mexicanas	Ediciones Mexicanas de Musica, avda. Juarez 18, despacho 206, Mexico City, Mexico.
MGG	*Die Musik in Geschichte und Gegenwart: Allgemeine Enzyklopadie der Musik.* 17 v. Ed. Friedrich Blume. Kassel: Bärenreiter, 1949–1986.

Migot	Marc Honegger. *Catalogue des oeuvres musicales de Georges Migot*. Strasbourg: Amis de l'oeuvre et de la pensée de Georges Migot, Institut de musicologie, 1977.
Milgra	Milgra-Edition, Box 137, 8820 Zurich Wädenswil, Switzerland.
Milhaud	Paul Collaer. *Darius Milhaud*. Trans. and ed. by Jane Hohfeld Galante. San Francisco, CA: San Francisco Press, 1988.
Minkoff	Editions Minkoff, 8 rue Eynard, 1211 Geneva, Switzerland. URL: //www.minkoff-editions.com.
MMB	MMB Music Inc., Contemporary Arts Building, 3526 Washington Ave., St. Louis, MO 63103, USA. URL: //www.mmbmusic.com. E-mail: mmbmusic@mmbmusic.com.
Mobart	Boelke-Bomart/Mobart Music Publishers, c/o Music Associates of America, 224 King St., Englewood, NJ 07631, USA.
Modern	Edition Modern – Tre Media Musikverlag, Amalienstrasse 40, 76133 Karlsruhe, Germany. URL: //members.aol.com/tremedia. E-mail: tremedia@aol.com.
Moeck	Moeck Verlag, Postfach 3131, 29231 Celle, Germany. Contemporary concert works distributed in USA by *EurAmer*. URL: //www.moeck-music.de. E-mail: info@moeck-music.de.
Möseler	Karl Heinrich Möseler Verlag, Postfach 1661, 38286 Wolfenbüttel, Germany.
Molenaar	Molenaar Edition B.V, Box 19, 1520 AA Wormerveer, Netherlands. URL: //www.molenaar.com.
Mollberg	Mollberg Music Media, Box 529, 451 21 Uddevalla, Sweden. URL: //www.mollberg.o.se.
Monge	Monge y Boceta Asociados Musicales, c/o Inmaculada Monge, calle Goya, 103-2 dcha, 28009 Madrid, Spain.
Montsalvatge	Francesc Taverna-Bech, Carles Guinovart and Francesc Bonastre. *Xavier Montsalvatge*. Barcelona: Generalitat de Catalunya ; Casa editorial de Musica Boileau, 1994.
Müller	Musikverlag Müller & Schade AG, Kramgasse 50, 3011 Bern, Switzerland.

MusicaRara	Musica Rara, Le Traversier, cemin de la Buire, 84170 Monteux, France; 2 Great Marlborough St., London W1, UK.
Musicus	Edition Musicus Inc., Box 1341, Stamford, CT 06904, USA.
MusSales	Music Sales Corporation, 20th floor, 257 Park Ave. South, New York, NY 10010, USA. URL: //www.musicsales.com.
Mussat	Marie-Claire Mussat. "Le tombeau dans la musique du XXème siècle." In *Tombeaux & monuments*. Ed. Jacques Dugast and Michele Touret. Rennes: Presses de l'Université, Rennes II, 1992.
Muzica	*Muzica: Revista Uniunii Compozitorilor din R. P. R. si a Comitetului de Stat pentru Cultura si Arta*. Bucurest: Uniunea si Comitetul, 1951– . Journal.
Muzyka	Muzyka, ul. Neglinnaja 14, 103031 Moscow, Russian Federation.
Neukomm	Sigismund Neukomm. *Werkverzeichniss, Autobiographie, Beziehung zu seinen Zeitgenossen*. Ed. Rudolph Angermüller. München: Katzbichler, 1977.
NewWest	New Music West, 1437 Crest Dr., Altadena, CA 91001, USA.
NGrove	*New Grove dictionary of music and musicians*. Ed. Stanley Sadie. 20 v. London: Macmillan; Washington, D.C.: Grove's Dictionaries, 1980.
Nichols	Nichols Music Co., 49 Tomlin St., Waltham, MA 02154, USA. E-mail: jwelts@aol.com. URL: //www.concentric.net:80/~Drwelts/Nichols/abtNMC.html.
Nielsen	Dan Fog and Torben Schousboe. *Carl Nielsen Kompositioner: En Bibliografi*. Copenhagen: Nordisk Forlag, 1965.
NMIC	Norsk Musikkinformasjon = Norwegian Music Information Centre, Tollbug 28, 0157 Oslo, Norway. URL: //www.mic.no. E-mail: info@mic.no.
No/Gro	*Norton/Grove dictionary of women composers*. Ed. Julie Anne Sadie and Rhian Samuel. New York: W. W. Norton, 1995.
NorO	*Contemporary Norwegian orchestral and chamber music*, supplement 1. Oslo: Society of Norwegian Composers, 1972.

NorP	Bjarne Kortsen. *Contemporary Norwegian piano music: A catalogue.* 3rd ed. Bergen: Forf., Ortustranden 45, 1976.
Norsk	Norsk musikforlag A/ S, Box 1499 Vika, 0116 Oslo, Norway.
Novello	Novello & Co. Ltd., 8-9 Frith St., London W1V 5TZ, UK. E-mail: music@musicsales.co.uk. URL: //www.firthview.freeserve.co.uk/HAVELOCK/novello.htm
NZ	Philip Norman. *Bibliography of New Zealand compositions.* Christchurch, NZ: Nota Bene Music, 1980; 2nd ed. 1982; 3rd ed. 1991.
NZfM	*Neue Zeitschrift für Musik.* 140. Jahrg. (continuing the earlier publication with the same title). Mainz: Schott's Söhne, 1979– . Journal.
OCLC	Online Computer Library Center Inc. (online database of over 42 million cataloging records created by more than 36,000 libraries around the world). URL: //www.oclc.org. E-mail: oclc@oclc.org.
Oecumuse	Oecumuse, 52A Broad St., Ely, Cambridgeshire CB7 4AH, UK .
Oiseau-L	Editions de l'Oiseau-Lyre, BP 515, 98015, Monaco. E-mail: 100525.3123@compuserve.com.
Ollone	Max d'Ollone. *Catalogue des oeuvres de Max d'Ollone.* Bibliothèque nationale (France), Manuscript Rés. 2690.
Olms	Georg Olms Musikverlag, Hagentorwall 7, 31134 Hildesheim, Germany. URL: //www.olms.de. E-mail: info@olms.de.
Opus	Opus – Ceskoslovenské hudobné vydavatelstvo, Mlynské nivy 73, 82799 Bratislava, Slovakia.
Orlando	Orlando Musikverlag, Kaprunerstrasse 11, D08000 Munich, Germany.
Orphée	Editions Orphée, Suite 400, 407 N. Grant Ave., Columbus, OH 43215, USA. URL: //www.orphee.com. E-mail: m.ophee@orphee.com.
OUP	Oxford University Press, Music Dept., Great Clarendon St., Oxford OX2 6DP, UK. URL: //www4.oup.co.uk/music. E-mail: enquiry@oup.co.uk; 198 Madison Ave., New York, NY 10016, USA. URL: //www.oup-usa.org/music. E-mail: webmaster&oup-usa.org.

Oz	Les Productions d'Oz, 1367 rue du Cran, Saint Romuald, Québec, Canada. URL: //pages.infinit.net/doz. E-mail: productionsdoz@videotron.ca.
OZOK	Österreichischer Komponistenbund. *Orchesterkatalog zeitgenossischer österreichischer Komponisten.* Vienna: E. Lafite, 1978?
Pan	Pan Educational Music, 40 Portland Rd., London W11 4LG, UK.
Panton	Panton, Radlicka 99, 150 00 Prague, Czechoslovakia. URL: //www.supraphon.cz. E-mail: supraphon@bonton.cz.
Papaioannou	Kostos Moschos and Haris Xanthoudakis. *Yannis A. Papaioannou: Complete catalogue of works.* 2nd ed. by Anargyros Deniosos. Athens: Philippos Nakas The Music House, 1990.
Parow'sche	Parow'sche Musikalien, Buchklinger Weg 12, 69517 Gorxheimertal, Germany.
Parry	Jeremy Dibble. *C. Hubert H. Parry: His life and music.* Oxford, Eng.: Clarendon Press, 1992.
Pazdirek	*Universal-Handbuch der Musikliteratur aller Zeiten und Völker: als Nachschlagewerke und Studienquelle der Welt-Musikleteratur.* 14 v. Vienna: Pazdirek & Co., 1904–10.
Peer-I	Peer International Corp. A division of *Peermusic.* Distributed in USA by *Presser.*
Peer-S	Peer-Southern Concert Music, 810 Seventh Ave., New York, NY 10019, USA. Distributed in USA by *Presser.*
Peermusic	Peermusic Classical, 810 Seventh Ave., New York, NY 10019, USA. Distributed in USA by *Presser.* URL: //www.peermusic.com. E-mail: peerEARS@peermusic.com.
Pembroke	Pembroke Music Inc. Distributed in USA by *CFischer.*
Penderecki	Ray Robinson. *Krzysztof Penderecki: A guide to his works.* Princeton, NJ: Prestige Publications, 1983.
Perkins	Francis Perkins. "Music in Portugal today." *Musical quarterly* 51 (1965): 38-43.
Perspectives	*Perspectives of new music.* Annandale-on-Hudson, NY: Perspectives, 1962– . Journal.
Peters	C. F. Peters Corp, 373 Park Ave., New York, NY 10016, USA. URL: //www.edition-peters.com. E-mail: sales@cfpeters-ny.com.;

	C. F. Peters Musikverlag, Box 700851, Frankfurt am Main, Germany. E-mail: info@edition-peters.de.
Picker	Martin Picker. "Josquiniana in some manuscripts at Piacenza." In *Josquin des Prez: Proceedings of the International Josquin Festival-Conference held at the Juilliard School at Lincoln Center in New York City, 21-25 1971*, pp. 247-260. Ed. Edward E. Lowinsky and Bonnie J. Blackburn. New York: Oxford University Press, 1976.
Pierre	Constant Pierre. *Histoire du Concert spirituel, 1725–1790.* Paris: Société Française de Musicologie, 1975.
Piles	Editorial de Musica Piles, S.A, calle Archena 33, 46014 Valencia, Spain. URL: //www.pilesmusic.com. E-mail: info@pilesmusic.com.
Pizzicato	Pizzicato, via Monte Ortigara 10, 33100 Udine, Italy. URL: //space.tin.it/musica/anfasan. E-mail: pizzikat@tin.it.
Plymouth	Plymouth Music Co. Inc., 170 NE 33rd St., Fort Lauderdale, FL 33334, USA.
Pocci	Vincenzo Pocci. *Guida al repertorio della chitarra nel novecento = The guitarist's 20th century repertoire guide.* Rome: VP Music Media, 2000.
Ponchielli	Licia Sirch. *Catalogo tematico delle musiche de Amilcare Ponchielli.* Cremona: Fondazione Claudio Monteverdi, 1989.
Presser	Theodore Presser Co., 1 Presser Place, Bryn Mawr, PA 19010-3490, USA. URL: //www.presser.com. E-mail: webmaster@presser.com.
ProOrgano	Musikverlag Pro Organo, Brühlstrasse 42, 88299 Leutkirch, Germany.
Purcell	Walter Bergmann. "Three pieces of music on Henry Purcell's death." *The consort* 17 (1960): 13–19.
PWM	Polskie Wydawnictwo Muzyczne, Al.Krasinskiego 11a, Krakow, Poland. URL: //www.pwm.com.pl. E-mail: cbn@pwm.com.pl.
Ramsey	Basil Ramsey Publisher of Music Ltd., 604 Rayleigh Rd., Eastwood, Leigh-on-Sea, Essex SS9 5HU, UK. URL: //www.mvdaily.com/basil_ramsey. E-mail: basil@mvdaily.com.
Rangel	Victor Rangel-Ribeiro and Robert Markel. *Chamber music: An international guide to works and their instrumentation.* New York: Facts on File, 1993.

Redcliffe	Redcliffe Edition, 68 Barrowgate Rd., London W4 4QU, UK.
Rehrig	William H. Rehrig. *Heritage encyclopedia of band music.* Ed. by Paul E. Bierley. 2 v. Westerville, OH: Integrity Press, 1991.
Reicha	Olga Sotolova. *Antonin Reicha: A biography and thematic catalogue.* Trans. Deryck Viney. Prague: Supraphon, 1990.
RevueMus	*La revue musicale.* Paris: Editions Richard-Masse; Editions de la Nouvelle revue française, 1920–1940, 1946–1949, 1952–1990. Journal.
Rhétorique	Denis Gaultier. *La rhétorique des dieux et autres pièces de luth.* Ed. David J. Buch. Recent researches in the music of the Baroque Era, v. 62 (transcription) and v. 62 supp. (facsimile). Madison, WI: A-R Editions, 1989. Facsimile and transcription of the manuscript lute source Staatliche Museen Preussischer Kulturbesitz, Kupferstichkabinett, MS 78 C 12, made for Anne de Chambré, probably in 1652. Also known as the "Hamilton Codex." Originally published in modern notation in: Oskar Fleischer, "Denis Gaultier," *Vierteljahresschrift für Musikwissenschaft* 2 (1886): 1-180. References herein are to the Buch edition.
Ricordi	Ricordi – BGM Ricordi, via Berchet 2, 20121 Milan, Italy. Rental and contemporary music distributed in USA by *Boosey*; general distribution in USA by *Leonard*.
Ricordi-BA	Ricordi Americana, Tte. Gral, Peróo 1558 Piso 2, 1037 Buenos Aires, Argentina.
Ricordi-P	Ricordi Paris, 22 rue Chauchat, 75009 Paris, France. Rental and contemporary music distributed in USA by *Boosey*; general distribution in USA by *Leonard*.
Ries	Ries & Erler, Charlottenbrunner Strasse 42, 14193 Berlin, Germany. URL: //www.rieserler.de. E-mail: verlag@rieserler.de.
RISM-A1	*Einzeldrucke vor 1800.* Ed. Karlheinz Schlager. Répertoire international des sources musicales, Pt. A1. 11 v. Kassel: Bärenreiter, 1971–.
RISM-B1	*Recueils imprimés XVIe–XVIIe siècles.* Ed. François Lesure. Répertoire international des sources musicales, Pt. B1. Munich: G. Henle, 1960.
RKing	Robert King Music Sales Inc., 29 Main St., North Easton, MA 02356, USA. URL: //www.rkingmusic.com.

	E-mail: commerce@rkingmusic.com.
RLIN	Research Libraries Information Network (online database of the Research Libraries Group Inc., containing more than 22 million cataloging records created by member libraries).
Roberton	Roberton Publications, The Windmill, Wendover, Ayles- bury, Buckinghamshire HP22 6JJ, UK. URL: //www.impulse-music.co.uk/roberton.htm.
Rossini	Herbert Weinstock. *Rossini: A biography.* New York: Knopf, 1968.
Rownd	Gary R Rownd. "Musical tombeaux and hommages for pi- ano solo." University of Kentucky, D.M.A. thesis, 1990.
Ruh	Emil Ruh Musikverlag, Zürichstrasse 33, 8134 Adliswil, Switzerland.
Salabert	Éditions Salabert, 22 rue Chauchat, 75009 Paris, France. E-mail: salabert@hol.fr.
Satorius	Richard Henry Satorius. *Bibliography of concertos for or- gan and orchestra.* Evanston, IL: The Instrumentalist, 1961.
Sauguet	David L. Austin. *Henri Sauguet: A bio-bibliography.* New York: Greenwood Press, 1991.
SBN	Servizio bibliotecario nazionale = National library service of Italy (online database of the Istituto Centrale per il Cata- logo Unico delle Biblioteche Italiane e per le Informazioni Bibliografiche: ICCU). URL: //www.iccu.sbn.it.
Schirmer	G. Schirmer Inc., 257 Park Ave. South, New York, NY 10010, USA. Distributed in the USA by *Leonard.* URL: //www.schirmer.com. E-mail: 102336.1611@compuserve.com.
Schoenberg	H. H. Stuckenschmidt. *Schoenberg: His life, world and work.* Trans. from the German by Humphrey Searle. Lon- don: John Calder, 1977.
Schott-J	Schott Japan Company Ltd., Kasuga Bldg. 2-9-3 Iidabashi, Chiyoda-ku, 102 Tokyo, Japan. Distributed in the USA by *EurAmer.* URL: //www.schott-music.com.
Schott-L	Schott & Co. Ltd., 48 Great Marlborough St., London W1V 2BN, UK. Distributed in the USA by *EurAmer.* URL: //www.schott-music.com.
Schott-M	Schott Musik International GmbH, Postfach 3640, 55026 Mainz, Germany. Distributed in the USA by *EurAmer.* URL: //www.schott-music.com.

	E-mail: schott.smd@t-online.de.
Schuberth	J. Schuberth & Co., Marienstrasse 13, 99817 Eisenach, Germany.
SCI	Society of Composers Inc., Box 296 Old Chelsea Station, New York, NY 10113. URL: //www.societyofcomposers.org.
Scotus	Scotus Music Publications Ltd., 28 Dalrymple Crescent, Edinburgh EH9 2NX, Scotland, UK. E-mail: secretary@societyofcomposers.com.
Seesaw	Seesaw Music Corp., 2067 Broadway, New York, NY 10023, USA.
SFC	Society of Finnish Composers, Runeberginkatu 15 A 11, 00100 Helsinki, Finland.
Shawnee	Shawnee Press Inc., 49 Waring Drive, Delaware Water Gap, PA 18327. USA. URL: //www.shawneepress.com. E-mail: shawneepress@noln.com.
Sikesdi	Sikesdi Press, 1102 Bellevue Ave. S.E., Calgary, Alberta T2G 4L1, Canada. URL://www.cadvision.com/Home_Pages/accounts/liszt/SikesdiPressWebpage.html.
Sikorski	Internationale Musikverlage Hans Sikorski, Johnsallee 23, Postfach 132001. 20148 Hamburg, Germany. Distributed in USA by *Leonard*. URL: //www.sikorski.de. E-mail: webmaster@sikorski.de.
Simrock	N. Simrock Musikverlag, Werderstrasse 44, 20144 Hamburg, Germany. London imprints distributed in USA by *Presser*.
Sinfonica	Edizioni Musicali Sinfonica, Box 70, 20047 Brugherio (MI), Italy. URL: //www.sinfonica.com. E-mail: sinfonica@sinfonica.com.
Siwe	Thomas Siwe. *Percussion ensemble and solo literature.* Champaign, IL: Media Press, 1993.
SKZ	*Schweizer Komponisten unserer Zeit: Biographien, Werkverzeichnisse mit Diskographie und Bibliographie = Swiss contemporary composers: biographies, list of works with discographies and bibliographies.* Winterthur, Switzerland: Amadeus, 1993.
Slovensk	Drustvo slovenskih skladateljev, Trg Francoske revolucile 6, 1000 Ljubljana, Slovenia.

SmithPubs	Smith Publications, 2617 Gwynndale Ave., Baltimore, MD 21207, USA.
SMT	Suomalaisen Musiikin Tiedotuskeskus, Lauttasaarentie 1, 00200 Helsinki, Finland.
SNB	*Das schweizer Buch: Schweizerische Nationalbibliographie = Le livre suisse: Bibliographie nationale suisse.* Zurich: Schweizerischer Buchhändler- und Verleger-Verband, 1943–.
Soler	Alvaro Garcia Estefania and Angel Medina. *Josep Soler.* Madrid: SGAE, 1995.
Southern	Southern Music Co., Box 329, San Antonio, TX 78292, USA. URL: //www.southernmusic.com. E-mail: info@southernmusic.com.
Squirrel	Black Squirrel Music Inc., Box 346, Kent, OH 44240, USA. E-mail: blksqmus@aol.com.
Stainer	Stainer & Bell Ltd., Box 110, 23 Gruneisen Road, London N3 1DZ, UK. URL: //ww.stainer.co.uk. E-mail: post@stainer.co.uk.
Still	William Grant Still Music, 4 South San Francisco St., Suite 422, Flagstaff, AZ 86001, USA.
STIM	Swedish Music Information Centre, Sandhamnsgatan 79, Box 27327, 10254 Stockholm, Sweden. URL: //www.mic.stim.se. E-mail: swedmic@stim.sw.
Stoneham	Marshall Stoneham, Jon A. Gillaspie and David Lindsey Clark. *Wind ensemble sourcebook and biographical guide.* Westport, CT: Greenwood, 1997.
Stravinsky	Clifford Caesar. *Igor Stravinsky: A complete catalogue.* San Francisco, CA: San Francisco Press, 1982.
StudiVerdi	Istituto Nazionale Studi Verdiani, Strada della Reppubblica 56, 43100 Parma, Italy. URL: Distributed in USA by Leonard. E-mail: studiver@iol.it.
SUDM	Samfundet til Udgivelse af Dansk Musik = The Society for the Publication of Danish Music, Grabrodrestraede 18, 1154 Copenhagen, Denmark.
Suisse	Société Suisse pour les Droits des Auteurs d'Oeuvres Musicales, Bellariastrasse 82, Postfach 782, 8038 Zurich, Switzerland.
Tag	Heinz Joachim Vieweg. *Christian Gotthilf Tag (1735–1811) als Meister der nachbachischen Kantate.* Leipzig: Druck von Thomas & Hubert, 1933.

Tailleferre	Robert Shapiro. *Germaine Tailleferre: A bio-bibliography.* Bio-bibliographies in music, v. 48. Westport, CT: Greenwood Press, 1994.
TCL	Transcontinental Music Publications, 838 Fifth Ave, New York, NY 10021, USA. URL: //www.etranscon.com.
Tempo	*Tempo: A quarterly review of modern music.* London: Boosey & Hawkes, 1939– . Journal.
Tenuto	Tenuto Publications. Distributed in USA by *Presser.*
Thiasos	Thiasos Musikverlag, Birkenweg 15G, 64295 Darmstadt, Germany. URL: //home.t-online.de/home/thiasos/main.htm.
Thompson	Gordon V. Thompson Music, 29 Birch Ave, Toronto, Ontario M4V 1C8, Canada.
Tonger	P. J. Tonger Musikverlag, Postfach 501818, 50978 Cologne, Germany. URL: //music-tonger.de. E-mail: tonger@musik-tonger.de.
Tonos	Tonos Musikverlags GmbH, Holzhofallee 15, 64295 Darmstadt, Germany. URL: //www.tonos-online.de. E-mail: mail@tonos-online.de.
Tre Media	Tre Media Musikverlage, Amalienstrasse 40, 76133 Karlsruhe, Germany.
Tripharia	Arte Tripharia, Apartado de Correos 14622, 28080 Madrid, Spain.
Tuba	Tuba-Euphonium Press, 3811 Ridge Road, Annandale, VA 22003, USA. URL: //www.tubaeuphoniumpress.com.
UE	Universal Edition AG, Postfach 3, 1010 Vienna, Austria. Distributed in the USA by *EurAmer.* URL: //www.uemusic.at. E-mail: uemusic@uemusic.co.at.
UE-L	Universal Edition Ltd., 48 Great Marlborough St., London W1V 2BN, UK. Distributed in the USA by *EurAmer.*
Ukraina	Muzycna Ukraina, Ul. Puskinskaia 32, 252004 Kiev, Ukraine.
UME	Unión Musical Ediciones, calle Blanca de Navarra 3, 28010 Madrid, Spain.
UMEsp	Union Musical Española, Avenida de la Fereria, Calle del Gas, 08001 Montcada i Rexiac, Barcelona, Spain.
UMP	United Music Publishers, 42 Rivington St., London EC2A 3BN, UK. URL: //www.ump.co.uk.
UNAM	Universidad Nacional Autónoma de México, Ciudad Universitaria, Del. Coyoacán, 04510 México, DF.

VNM	Vereniging Nederlandse Muziekgeschiedenis, Box 1514, 3500 BM Utrecht, Netherlands.
Walton	Stewart Craggs. *William Walton: A thematic catalog of his works.* London: Oxford University Press, 1977.
Warner	Warner Brothers Publications Inc., 15800 N.W. 48th Ave., Miami, FL 33014, USA.
Weinberger	Josef Weinberger Ltd., 12–14 Mortimer St., London W1N 7RD, UK. Distributed in the USA by *Boosey.*
Welsh	Guild for the Promotion of Welsh Music, 94 Walter Rd., Swansea SA1 5QA, UK.
WholeSum	Whole Sum Productions. Distributed in the USA by C. Alan Publications, Box 29323, Greensboro, NC 27429, USA. URL: //www.c-alanpublications.com. E-mail: calanp@earthlink.net.
Wimbledon	Wimbledon Music Inc., 1888 Century Park East, Suite 1900, Century City, CA 80067, USA. URL: //www.wimbtri.com. E-mail: webmaster@wimbtri.com.
WSF	Téodor de Wyzewa and Georges Poullain de Saint-Foix. *W.-A. Mozart: Sa vie musicale et son oeuvre de l'enfance a la pleine maturite.* 5 v. Paris: Desclée de Brouwer et Cie, 1937–1946.
Yayincilik	Pan Yayincilik, Barbaros Bulvan, 74/4 Besiktal/Istanbul, Turkey. URL: //www.pankitap.com.
Zanibon	Casa Musicale G. Zanibon, Piazza Signori 24, 35100 Padua, Italy.
Zerboni	Edizioni Suvini Zerboni, Via Quintiliano 40, 20138 Milan, Italy. URL: //www.sugarmusic.com/esz/esz_home.html. E-mail: suvini.zerboni@sugarmusic.com.
Zimmermann	Zimmermann Musikverlag, Postfach 940183, 60459 Frankfurt am Main, Germany. E-mail: 101572@compuserve.com.
Zurfluh	Zurfluh, 13 ave. du Lycée Lakanal, 92340 Bourg Reine, France.

Chronological Index

Arranged by year (first column) and by month/day (second column) of births (b) and deaths (d) of dedicatees.

	07/07	: Caamaño, Roberto (b)
	09/15	: Heiller, Anton (b)
	10/25	: Banks, Don (b)
	10/31	: Maynard, Paul (b)
1924 :	01/29	: Nono, Luigi (b)
	02/17	: Merikanto, Oscar (d)
	03/27	: Vaughan, Sarah (b)
	03/29	: Stanford, Sir Charles Villiers (d)
	04/15	: Caudella, Edoardo (d)
	05/14	: Santos, Joly Braga (b)
	05/31	: Presti, Ida (b)
	07/27	: Busoni, Ferruccio Benvenuto (d)
	11/04	: Fauré, Gabriel (d)
	11/14	: Kogan, Leonid (b)
	11/25	: Desmond, Paul (b)
	11/29	: Puccini, Giacomo (d)
	11/30	: Shand, Ernest (d)
1925 :		: Howell, Almonte (b)
	03/22	: Hoffnung, Gerard (b)
	06/11	: Fleury, Louis (d)
	06/23	: Chatzidakes, Manos (b)
	07/01	: Satie, Erik (d)
	07/04	: Berberian, Cathy (b)
	07/28	: Pruden, Larry (b)
	12/02	: Garreta, Julio (d)
	12/16	: Fisk, Charles Brenton (b)
1926 :		: Falabella, Roberto (b)
	01/08	: Chrestou, Giannes (b)
	01/12	: Feldman, Morton (b)
	02/11	: Gibson, Sir Alexander (b)
	02/28	: Shifrin, Seymour J. (b)
	03/26	: Kneisel, Franz (d)
	05/25	: Davis, Miles (b)
	07/15	: Lambert, John (b)
1927 :		: IUrlov, Aleksandr Aleksandrovich (b)
	01/12	: Martirano, Salvatore, (b)

	02/19	: Fuchs, Robert (d)
	03/08	: Berg, Josef (b)
	03/10	: Benz, Albert (b)
	05/20	: Barlow, David (b)
	07/06	: Whittenberg, Charles (b)
	07/07	: Casadesus, Jean (b)
	07/15	: Pack, Rowland (b)
	09/23	: Coltrane, John (b)
	10/01	: Kaufmann, Harald (b)
1928 :	01/17	: Barraqué, Jean (b)
	02/13	: Romann, Jack (b)
	03/12	: Bausznern, Dietrich von (b)
	06/20	: Dolphy, Eric (b)
	07/26	: Baird, Tadeusz (b)
	08/12	: Janacek, Leos (d)
	11/25	: Andersen, Alf (b)
1929 :		: Brennand, Charles (b)
	04/06	: Denisov, Edisson Vasilevich (b)
	05/17	: Craxton, Janet (b)
	06/09	: Ace, Johnny (b)
		: Ordzhonikidze, Givi (b)
	07/15	: Hofmannsthal, Hugo von (d)
	08/16	: Evans, Bill (b)
	08/19	: Diaghilev, Serge (d)
	09/22	: Garant, Serge (b)
	10/02	: Leighton, Kenneth (b)
	12/04	: Berger, Wilhelm Georg (b)
1930 :	03/09	: Schippers, Thomas (b)
	06/22	: Jacobs, Paul (b)
	10/08	: Takemitsu, Toru (b)
	10/30	: Brown, Clifford ("Brownie") (b)
	10/31	: Ervin, Booker (b)
	11/23	: Farnam, W. Lynnwood (d)
	12/05	: Miller, Robert (b)
	12/17	: Warlock, Peter (d)

Calendar-Year Index

Arranged by month/day of birth and death dates of dedicatees.

01/00   : Févin, Antoine de (d. 1512)
            : Gaultier, Denis (d. 1672)
            : Ramovs, Primoz (d. 1999)

01/01   : Bach, Johann Christian
             (d. 1782)
            : Goldman, Edwin Franko
             (b. 1878)
            : Racquet, Charles (d. 1664)

01/02   : Balakirev, Mily (b. 1837)
            : Stevens, Bernard (d. 1983)
            : Tippett, Michael (b. 1905)
            : Zipoli, Domenico (d. 1726)

01/03   : Hauptmann, Moritz (d. 1868)
            : Jaubert, Maurice (b. 1900;
             d. 1940)
            : Liatoshynskyi, Borys
             Mykolaiovych (b. 1895)
            : Pack, Rowland (d. 1964)
            : Pugno, Raoul (d. 1914)
            : Vyner, Michael (b. 1943)

01/04   : Anderson, Bruce C. (d. 1991)
            : Newton, Frankie (b. 1906)
            : Pergolesi, Giovanni Battista
             (b. 1710)
            : Tabuteau, Marcel (d. 1966)

01/05   : Gerhard, Roberto (d. 1970)

01/06   : Abravanel, Maurice (b. 1903)
            : Bruch, Max (b. 1838)
            : Esplá, Oscar (d. 1975)

            : Gillespie, John Birks
             ("Dizzy") (d. 1993)
            : Scriabin, Alexander (b. 1872)

01/07   : Poulenc, Francis (b. 1899)

01/08   : Albrecht, Johann Lorenz
             (b. 1732)
            : Bülow, Hans von (b. 1830)
            : Chrestou, Giannes (b. 1926,
             d. 1970)
            : Corelli, Arcangelo (d. 1713)
            : Fornerod, Aloys (d. 1965)
            : Kindler, Hans (b. 1892)
            : Presley, Elvis (b. 1935)
            : Schlesinger, Daniel (d. 1838)
            : Silberman, Aaron (b. 1916)
            : Thalberg, Sigismond (b. 812)
            : Tippett, Michael (d. 1998)
            : Vaet, Jacobus (d. 1567)

01/09   : Gianneo, Luis (b. 1897)
            : Greenberg, Noah (d. 1966)
            : Marbé, Myriam (b. 1931)
            : Serocki, Kazimierz (d. 1981)

01/10   : Belaiev, Mitrofan Petrovich
             (d. 1904)
            : Deans, Kenneth N. (Buddy)
             (d. 1984)
            : Donostia, José Antonio de
             (b. 1886)
            : Meyer, Wolfgang Sebastian
             (d. 1966)

03/18 : Jaeger, August Johannes
(b. 1860)
: Pijper, Willem (d. 1947)
: Rimsky-Korsakov, Nikolai
(b. 1844)

03/19 : Reger, Max (b. 1873)

03/20 : Buzzolla, Antonio (d. 1871)
: Dussek, Johann Ladislaus
(d. 1812)
: Hollingsworth, John
(b. 1916)
: Neruda, Franz Xaver
(d. 1915)
: Nordraak, Rikard (d. 1866)
: Ramovs, Primoz (b. 1921)
: Zimmermann, Bernd Alois
(b. 1918)

03/21 : Bach, Johann Sebastian
(b. 1685)
: Consolo, Ernesto (d. 1931)
: Maderna, Bruno (b. 1920)
: Mussorgsky, Modest
(b. 1839)
: Skalkottas, Nikos (b. 1904)

03/22 : Hoffnung, Gerard (b. 1925)
: Lully, Jean Baptiste
(d. 1687)

03/23 : Muench, Gerhart (b. 1907)
: Petri, Egon (b. 1881)
: Reubke, Julius (b. 1834)
: Rubinstein, Nikolai (d. 1881)

03/24 : Freitas Branco, Pedro de
(d. 1963)
: Granados, Enrique (d. 1916)
: Malibran, Maria Felicita
(b. 1808)
: Nanny, Édouard (b. 1872)
: Scheidt, Samuel (d. 1654)
: Shkolnik, Sheldon (d. 1990)

: Stewart, Sir Robert Prescott
(d. 1894)

03/25 : Bartók, Béla (b. 1881)
: Debussy, Claude (d. 1918)
: Ghedini, Giorgio Federico
(d. 1965)
: Heiller, Anton (d. 1979)
: Toscanini, Arturo (b. 1867)

03/26 : Beethoven, Ludwig van
(d. 1827)
: Kaprál, Václav (b. 1889)
: Kneisel, Franz (d. 1926)
: Sokolov, Nicolai (b. 1859)

03/27 : Bliss, Sir Arthur (d. 1975)
: Kincaid, William (d. 1967)
: Sokolov, Nicolai (d. 1922)
: Vaughan, Sarah (b. 1924)
: Wurlitzer, Rembert (b. 1904)

03/28 : Adaskin, John (b. 1908)
: Capuzzi, Giuseppe Antonio
(d. 1818)
: Dinicu, Grigoras (d. 1949)
: Mussorgsky, Modest
(d. 1881)
: Rachmaninoff, Sergei
(d. 1943)

03/29 : Guilmant, Alexandre (d.
1911)
: Stanford, Sir Charles Villiers
(d. 1924)
: Szymanowski, Karol
(d. 1937)
: Walton, Sir William
(b. 1902)

03/30 : Pollikoff, Max (b. 1904)

03/31 : Diaghilev, Serge (b. 1872)
: Haydn, Joseph (b. 1732)
: Weisse, Hans (b. 1892)

04/00 : Chambonnières, Jacques
Champion de (d. 1672)

04/01 : Busoni, Ferruccio Benvenuto
        (b. 1866)
      : Gaye, Marvin (d. 1984)
      : Joplin, Scott (d. 1917)
      : Pasta, Giuditta (d. 1865)
      : Rachmaninoff, Sergei
        (b. 1873)
04/02 : Gaye, Marvin (b. 1939)
      : Little, Booker (b. 1938)
      : Riegger, Wallingford
        (d. 1961)
04/03 : Brahms, Johannes (d. 1897)
      : Dinicu, Grigoras (b. 1889)
      : Foss, Aage (d. 1894)
      : Gilson, Paul (d. 1942)
      : Vaughan, Sarah (d. 1990)
04/04 : Monteux, Pierre (b. 1875)
      : Wolpe, Stefan (d. 1972)
      : Zingarelli, Nicola Antonio
        (b. 1752)
04/05 : Lieberson, Goddard (b. 1911)
      : Mammot, Isaac (d. 1964)
      : Mazzeo, Rosario (b. 1911)
04/06 : Denisov, Edisson Vasilevich
        (b. 1929)
      : Kaprál, Václav (d. 1947)
      : Nabokov, Nicolas (d. 1978)
      : Salzedo, Carlos (b. 1885)
      : Stravinsky, Igor (d. 1971)
04/07 : Holiday, Billie (b. 1915)
04/08 : Dilherr, Johann Michael
        (d. 1669)
      : Donizetti, Gaetano (d. 1848)
      : Koldofsky, Adolph (d. 1951)
04/09 : Greenberg, Noah (b. 1920)
      : Richter, Ernst Friedrich
        (d. 1879)
04/10 : Rota, Nino (d. 1979)
04/11 : Ginastera, Alberto (b. 1916)

      : Raff, Joseph Joachim
        (b. 1822)
      : Richard I, Coeur de Leon
        (d. 1199)
04/12 : Amati, Nicola (d. 1684)
      : Vötterle, Karl (b. 1903)
04/13 : Danzi, Franz (d. 1826)
04/14 : Handel, George Frideric
        (d. 1759)
      : Vivier, Claude (b. 1948)
04/15 : Caudella, Edoardo (d. 1924)
      : Liatoshynskyi, Borys
        Mykolaiovych (d. 1968)
      : Matamoros, Miguel (d. 1971)
      : Wróbel, Feliks (d. 1954)
04/16 : Mompou, Federico (b. 1893)
04/17 : Burkhard, Willy (b. 1900)
      : Lauro, Antonio (d. 1986)
      : Merritt, Thomas (d. 1908)
      : Nabokov, Nicolas (b. 1903)
      : Naumann, Johann Gottlieb
        (b. 1741)
      : Piatigorsky, Gregor (b. 1903)
04/19 : Melanchton, Philippe
        (d. 1560)
04/21 : Dupont, Jacques (d. 1978)
04/22 : Barié, Augustin (d. 1915)
      : Ferrier, Kathleen (b. 1912)
      : Gluck, Marianne Nanette
        (d. 1776)
      : Hartmann, Georges (d. 1900)
      : Motta, José Vianna da
        (b. 1868)
04/23 : Prokofiev, Sergey (b. 1891)
04/24 : Dieren, Bernard van
        (d. 1936)
      : Hilsberg, Alexander
        (b. 1897)
      : Martini, Giovanni Battista
        (b. 1706)

: Ponce, Manuel Maria
  (d. 1948)
: Presti, Ida (d. 1967)
: Vitols, Jazeps (d. 1948)
: Zuckerkandl, Victor
  (d. 1965)

04/25 : Glenn, Carroll (d. 1983)

04/26 : Kincaid, William (b. 1895)
: Winham, Godfrey (d. 1975)

04/27 : Messiaen, Olivier (d. 1992)
: Scriabin, Alexander (d. 1915)
: Simmons, Calvin (b. 1950)
: Thalberg, Sigismond
  (d. 1871)

04/28 : Sacher, Paul (b. 1906)

04/29 : Clark, Edward (d. 1962)
: Ellington, Edward K.
  ("Duke") (b. 1899)
: Riegger, Wallingford
  (b. 1885)
: Viñes, Ricardo (d. 1943)

04/30 : Elkus, Albert (b. 1844)

05/00 : Battishill, Jonathan
  (b. 1738)

05/01 : Dvořák, Antonín (d. 1904)
: Lawes, William, (b. 1602)
: Leifs, Jón (b. 1899)

05/02 : Haney, Lewis Van (d. 1991)
: Krumpholz, Wenzel
  (d. 1817)
: Meyerbeer, Giacomo
  (d. 1864)
: Rawsthorne, Alan (b. 1905)

05/03 : Adam, Adolphe (d. 1856)
: Dupré, Marcel (b. 1886)
: Fox, Virgil (b. 1912)
: Marcus, Adele (d. 1995)
: Seiber, Mátyás (b. 1905)

05/04 : Enesco, Georges (d. 1955)
: Noble, T. Tertius (d. 1953)

: Seiber, Mátyás (b. 1905)

05/05 : Barrios Mangoré, Agustin
  (b. 1885)
: Freudenthal, Josef (d. 1964)
: Noble, T. Tertius (b. 1867)
: Romann, Jack (d. 1987)
: Zingarelli, Nicola Antonio
  (d. 1837)

05/06 : Salzedo, Carlos (b. 1885)
: Smythe, Patrick (d. 1983)

05/07 : Brahms, Johannes (b. 1833)
: Burgmüller, Norbert
  (d. 1836)
: Cardew, Cornelius (b. 1936)
: Froberger, Johann Jakob
  (d. 1667)
: Tchaikovsky, Piotr Ilyich
  (b. 1840)

05/08 : Beeler, Walter (b. 1908)
: Gottschalk, Louis Moreau
  (b. 1829)
: Israel, Brian (d. 1986)
: Jarocinski, Stefan (d. 1980)
: Langlais, Jean (d. 1991)
: Matamoros, Miguel (b. 1894)
: Nono, Luigi (d. 1990)
: Premru, Raymond Eugene
  (d. 1998)
: Surdin, Morris (b. 1914)

05/09 : Bucchi, Valentino (d. 1976)
: Buxtehude, Dietrich
  (d. 1707)
: Cliquet-Pleyel, Henri
  (d. 1963)
: Henselt, Adolf von (b. 1814)
: Maciunas, George (d. 1978)
: Paisiello, Giovanni (b. 1740)

05/10 : Clark, Edward (b. 1888)
: Feltkamp, Johannes
  Hendricus (d. 1962)

05/11
: Jones, David Roger (d. 1965)
: Leclair, Jean Marie (b. 1697)
: Gaviniés, Pierre (b. 1726)
: Reger, Max (d. 1916)
: Winner, Septimus (b. 1827)

05/12
: Berkeley, Sir Lennox (b. 1903)
: Bordes, Charles (b. 1863)
: Busoni, Ferdinando (d. 1909)
: Fauré, Gabriel (b. 1845)
: Smetana, Bedrich (d. 1884)
: Stoessel, Albert (d. 1943)
: Wiechowicz, Stanislaw (d. 1963)

05/13
: Beaucamp, Albert Maurice (b. 1921)
: Pollikoff, Max (d. 1984)
: Riadis, Emilios (b. 1855)
: Schleinitz, Heinrich Conrad (d. 1881)
: Sullivan, Sir Arthur Seymour (b. 1842)

05/14
: Hartmann, Johan Peter Emilius (b. 1805)
: Hensel, Fanny Mendelssohn (d. 1847)
: Klemperer, Otto (b. 1885)
: Santos, Joly Braga (b. 1924)

05/15
: Monteverdi, Claudio (b. 1567)
: Munrow, David (d. 1976)
: Wróbel, Feliks (b. 1894)

05/16
: Liberace (Wladziu Valentino Liberace) (b. 1919)
: Reinhardt, Django (d. 1953)
: Wyschnegradsky, Ivan (b. 1893)

05/17
: Brain, Dennis (b. 1921)
: Craxton, Janet (b. 1929)

: DeLamarter, Eric (d. 1953)
: Dukas, Paul (d. 1935)
: Gagnon, Henri (d. 1961)
: Köhler, Ernesto (d. 1907)
: Satie, Erik (b. 1866)

05/18
: Albéniz, Isaac (d. 1909)
: Bergenson, Aron Victor (d. 1914)
: Jaeger, August Johannes (d. 1909)
: Mahler, Gustav (d. 1911)
: Sauguet, Henri (b. 1901)

05/19
: Bukowski, Ryszard (d. 1988)
: Froberger, Johann Jakob (b. 1616)
: Hawkins, Coleman (d. 1969)
: Ives, Charles (d. 1954)
: Rosenberg, Hilding (d. 1985)
: Sikorski, Tomasz (b. 1939)

05/20
: Barlow, David (b. 1927)
: Bellasio, Paolo (b. 1554)

05/21
: Gilles, Joseph (b. 1903)
: Gonzales, Victor (b. 1877)

05/22
: De Groote, Steven (d. 1989)
: Fleuret, Maurice (d. 1990)
: Preusensin (Preiss), Gerhard (d. 1672)
: Scionti, Silvio (d. 1973)
: Tulder, Louis van (b. 1892)
: Wagner, Richard (b. 1813)

05/23
: Moscheles, Ignaz (b. 1794)
: Samuel, Harold (b. 1879)
: Wesley, Charles (d. 1834)

05/24
: Ellington, Edward K. ("Duke") (d. 1974)
: Fleury, Louis (b. 1878)
: Leduc, Emile Alphonse III (d. 1951)

05/25
: Davis, Miles (b. 1926)

06/11 : Fleury, Louis (d. 1925)
: Lokshin, Aleksandre
(d. 1987)
: Lukashevskii, Ilia Avseevich
(d. 1967)
: Strauss, Richard (b. 1864)
06/12 : Nordraak, Rikard (b. 1842)
: Scherchen, Hermann
(d. 1966)
: Tansman, Alexandre
(b. 1897)
06/13 : Chávez, Carlos (b. 1899)
: Goossens, Sir Eugene
(d. 1962)
: Mariani, Angelo (d. 1873)
: Michael, Tobias (b. 1592)
06/14 : Bourdin, Roger (b. 1900)
: Haney, Lewis Van (b. 1920)
: Lasso, Roland de (d. 1594)
: Maynard, Paul (d. 1998)
Rubinstein, Nikolai (b. 1835)
: Sacchini, Antonio (b. 1730)
06/15 : Chatzidakes (Hadzikakis)
Manos (d. 1994)
: Danzi, Franz (b. 1763)
: Gilson, Paul (b. 1865)
: Grieg, Edvard (b. 1843)
: Luening, Otto (b. 1900;
d. 1996)
: Montgomery, Wes (d. 1968)
06/16 : Duruflé, Maurice (d. 1986)
: Eller, Heino (d. 1970)
: Huntley, David (b. 1947)
: Kaprólová, Vitezslava
(d. 1940)
: Schiske, Karl (d. 1969)
: Sjögren, Johann Gustav Emil
(b. 1853)
06/17 : Rath, Felix von (b. 1866)
: Stravinsky, Igor (b. 1882)

06/18 : Burkhard, Willy (d. 1955)
: Pearson, William (d. 1995)
: Pleyel, Ignaz (b. 1757)
06/19 : David, Ferdinand (b. 1810)
: Surdin, Morris (d. 1979)
06/20 : Abel, Carl Friedrich (d. 1787)
: Alain, Jehan Ariste (d. 1940)
: Dolphy, Eric (b. 1928)
: Fink, Reginald H. (b. 1931)
: Groves, Sir Charles (d. 1992)
06/21 : Hába, Alois (b. 1893)
: Rimsky-Korsakov, Nikolai
(d. 1908)
: Rosenberg, Hilding (b. 1892)
: Scherchen, Hermann
(b. 1891)
06/22 : Bruna, Pablo (b. 1611)
: Fleuret, Maurice (b. 1932)
: Garland, Judy (d. 1969)
: Jacobs, Paul (b. 1930)
: Méhul, Étienne-Nicolas
(b. 1763)
: Milhaud, Darius (d. 1974)
: Sauguet, Henri (d. 1989)
: Talvela, Martti (d. 1989)
06/23 : Chatzidakes (Hadzikakis),
Manos (b. 1925)
: Gallon, Jean (d. 1959)
: Pugno, Raoul (b. 1852)
06/24 : Andersen, Alf (d. 1962)
: Busoni, Ferdinando (b. 1834)
: Raff, Joseph Joachim
(d. 1882)
06/25 : Gallon, Jean (b. 1878)
: Ginastera, Alberto (d. 1983)
: Partch, Harry (b. 1901)
: Senn, Kurt Wolfgang
(d. 1965)
: Szervánszky, Endre (d. 1977)

: Lamas, José Angel (b. 1775)
: Mercuri, Agostino (b. 1839)
: Smolensky, Stepan
  Vassilievich (d. 1909)

08/03 : Howe, Marvin Clarence
  (d. 1994)
: Lane, Lewis (b. 1901)
: Lauro, Antonio (b. 1909)
: Martini, Giovanni Battista
  (d. 1784)
: Zimmermann, Frederick
  (d. 1967)

08/04 : Anderson, Marian (d. 1993)

08/05 : Butterworth, George Sainton
  Kaye (d. 1916)
: Esplá, Oscar (b. 1886)
: Litaize, Gaston (d. 1991)
: Merikanto, Oscar (b. 1868)
: Paz, Juan Carlos (b. 1901)

08/06 : Chance, John Barnes
  (d. 1972)
: Piatigorsky, Gregor (d. 1976)
: Rhaw, Georg (d. 1548)
: Ronnefeld, Peter (d. 1965)

08/07 : Barrios Mangoré, Agustin
  (d. 1944)
: Bell, William (d. 1971)
: Berg (Montanus), Johann van
  (d. 1563)
: Dahl, Ingolf (d. 1970)

08/08 : Heusser, Hans (b. 1892)
: Jolivet, André (b. 1905)
: Miaskovsky, Nicolai
  (d. 1950)

08/09 : Shostakovich, Dmitri
  (d. 1975)

08/10 : Arnold, Samuel (b. 1740)
: Edwards, John S. (d. 1984)
: Haydn, Michael (d. 1806)

: Hilsberg, Alexander
  (d. 1961)
: White, Clarence Cameron
  (b. 1880)
: Zimmermann, Bernd Alois
  (d. 1970)

08/11 : Litaize, Gaston (b. 1909)
: Peaker, Charles (d. 1978)
: Sumsion, Herbert (d. 1995)

08/12 : Cage, John (d. 1992)
: Janacek, Leos (d. 1928)
: Munrow, David (b. 1942)

08/13 : Nikolayev, Leonid (b. 1878)

08/14 : Böhm, Karl (d. 1981)
: Cristini, Cesare Mario
  (d. 1970)
: Fabricius, Jakob (d. 1652)
: Persichetti, Vincent (d. 1987)
: Schaeffer, Pierre (b. 1910)
: Spilling, Willy (Karl
  Wilhelm) (d. 1965)
: Venuti, Joe (d. 1978)

08/15 : Bakfark, Bálint. (d. 1576)
: Gianneo, Luis (d. 1968)
: Hughes, Edwin (b. 1884)
: Ibert, Jacques (b. 1890)
: Joachim, Joseph (d. 1907)
: Marais, Marin (d. 1728)

08/16 : Boskovich, Alexander Uriah
  (b. 1907)
: Evans, Bill (b. 1929)
: Jarocinski, Stefan (b. 1912)
: Poradowski, Stefan Boleslaw
  (b. 1902)
: Presley, Elvis (d. 1977)
: Shirinsky, Vasili Peotrovich
  (d. 1965)
: Wenzel, Ernst Ferdinand
  (d. 1880)

08/17   : Barraqué, Jean (d. 1973)
         : Bull, Ole (d. 1880)
         : Mossman, Sheila (d. 1971)
         : Salzedo, Carlos (d. 1961)

08/18   : Zulawski, Wawrzyniec
           (d. 1957)

08/19   : Diaghilev, Serge (d. 1929)
         : Enesco, Georges (b. 1881)
         : Parlow, Kathleen (d. 1963)
         : Pedrell, Felipe (d. 1922)
         : Schaeffer, Pierre (d. 1995)
         : Wood, Sir Henry Joseph
           (d. 1944)

08/20   : Dadi, Marcel (b. 1951)
         : Harder, Paul O. (d. 1986)
         : Lukashevskii, Ilia Avseevich
           (b. 1892)
         : Miaskovsky, Nicolai
           (b. 1881)

08/21   : Boulanger, Lili (b. 1893)
         : Guarneri, Giuseppe Antonio
           (b. 1698)
         : Hildesheimer, Wolfgang
           (b. 1916; d. 1991)
         : Simmons, Calvin (d. 1982)
         : Thomson, César (d. 1931)

08/22   : Debussy, Claude (b. 1862)
         : Steinfirst, Donald (d. 1972)
         : Whittenberg, Charles.
           (d. 1984)

08/23   : Kalnins, Alfreds (b. 1879)

08/24   : Leighton, Kenneth (d. 1988)
         : Marliave, Joseph de (d. 1914)
         : Schoemaker, Maurice
           (d. 1964)

08/25   : Bernstein, Leonard (b. 1918)
         : Jommelli, Nicolò (d. 1774)
         : Mangeot, André (b. 1883)
         : Paz, Juan Carlos (d. 1972)
         : Rath, Felix von (d. 1905)

         : Valen, Fartein (b. 1887)
         : Wolpe, Stefan (b. 1902)

08/26   : Vaughan Williams, Ralph
           (d. 1958)

08/27   : Josquin des Prez (d. 1521)
         : Young, Lester (b. 1909)

08/28   : Böhm, Karl (b. 1894)
         : Corigliano, John (elder)
           (b. 1901)
         : Dietrich, Albert Hermann
           (b. 1829)
         : Gail, Edmée-Sophie
           (b. 1775)
         : Khachaturian, Aram
           (d. 1978)
         : Leibowitz, René (d. 1972)
         : Martinu, Bohuslav (d. 1956)
         : Wagner-Régeny, Rudolf
           (b. 1903)

08/29   : Guézec, Jean Pierre (b. 1934)
         : Parker, Charlie (b. 1920)
         : Teagarden, Jack (b. 1905)
         : Touche, Jean-Claude
           (d. 1944)

08/30   : Donostia, José Antonio de
           (d. 1957)
         : Kindler, Hans (d. 1949)
         : Silberman, Aaron (d. 1993)

08/31   : Ervin, Booker (d. 1970)
         : Ponchielli, Amilcare
           (b. 1834)
         : Rist, Johann (d. 1667)

09/00   : Bremner, James (d. 1780)
         : Richard I, Coeur de Leon
           (b. 1157)
         : Tunnell, John (d. 1988)

09/01   : Brain, Dennis (d. 1957)
         : Corigliano, John (elder)
           (d. 1975)
         : Venuti, Joe (b. 1903)

: Wagner-Régeny, Rudolf
(d. 1969)

09/19 : Lokshin, Aleksandre
(b. 1920)

: Skalkottas, Nikos (d. 1949)

09/20 : Binchois, Gilles (d. 1460)

: Kapell, William (b. 1922)

: Mul, Jan (b. 1911)

: Parlow, Kathleen (b. 1890)

: Sarasate, Pablo de (d. 1908)

: Sibelius, Jean (d. 1957)

: Webster, Ben (d. 1973)

09/21 : Brain, Aubrey (d. 1955)

: Holst, Gustav (b. 1874)

: Pastorius, Jaco (John Francis)
(d. 1987)

: Thurston, Frederick (b. 1901)

09/22 : Abravanel, Maurice (d. 1993)

: Beaucamp, Albert Maurice
(d. 1967)

: Garant, Serge (b. 1929)

: Potter, A. J. (Archibald
James) (b. 1918)

: Sicotte, Lucien (b. 1902)

: Sullivan, Thomas (d. 1866)

09/23 : Bellini, Vincenzo, (d. 1835)

: Coltrane, John (b. 1927)

: Hinrichsen, Walter (b. 1907)

: Malibran, Maria Felicita
(d. 1836)

: Sicotte, Lucien (d. 1943)

09/24 : Grétry, André Ernest
Modeste (d. 1813)

: Panufnik, Andrzej (b. 1914)

: Seiber, Mátyás (d. 1960)

09/25 : Bonham, John Henry
(Bonzo) (d. 1980)

: Gerhard, Roberto (b. 1896)

: Gould, Glenn (b. 1932)

: Jacobs, Paul (d. 1983)

: Lejeune, Claude (d. 1600)

: Rameau, Jean-Philippe
(b. 1683)

: Shostakovich, Dmitri
(b. 1906)

09/26 : Bartók, Béla (d. 1945)

: Gershwin, George (b. 1898)

: Marlowe, Sylvia (b. 1908)

: Munch, Charles (b. 1891)

: Shifrin, Seymour J. (d. 1979)

09/27 : Finzi, Gerald (d. 1956)

: Tomkins, John, (d. 1638)

09/28 : Davis, Miles (d. 1991)

: Fromm, Paul (b. 1906)

: Hoffnung, Gerard (d. 1959)

: Jara, Victor (b. 1932)

09/29 : Merikanto, Aarre (d. 1958)

: Tcherepnin, Alexander
(d. 1977)

: Wyschnegradsky, Ivan
(d. 1979)

09/30 : Stanford, Sir Charles Villiers
(b. 1852)

10/00 : Fennelly, Priscilla Proxmire
(d. 1978)

: Morley, Thomas (d. 1602)

: San Miguel, Mariano
(d. 1935)

: Tulder, Louis van (d. 1969)

10/01 : Dukas, Paul (b. 1865)

: Kaufmann, Harald (b. 1927)

: Krzanowski, Andrzej
(d. 1991)

: Partos, Oedoen (b. 1907)

: Pruden, Larry (d. 1982)

: Stasov, Vladimir (d. 1906)

10/02 : Bergenson, Aron Victor
(b. 1848)

: Bruch, Max (d. 1920)

: Grunwald, Hugo (d. 1956)

Composer Index

Under each composer name entry are listed the names of musicians to whom that composer dedicated memorial compositions. "In" references are to titles of collections of memorials to the dedicatee.

Abbott, Alain, 1938–
    Bach, Johann Sebastian
Abeliovich, Lev, 1912–1985
    Shostakovich, Dmitri
Absil, Jean, 1893–1974
    Berg, Alban
Achron, Joseph, 1886–1943
    Scriabin, Alexander
Adams, John, 1947–
    Feldman, Morton
    Koussevitzky, Serge
Adler, Samuel, 1928–
    DeGaetani, Jan
    Glenn, Carroll
    Koussevitzky, Serge
    List, Eugene
    Saminsky, Lazare
Ahle, Johann Georg, 1651–1706
    Ahle, Johann Rudolph
Alain, Olivier, 1918–
    Gonzales, Victor (in *Le Tombeau de Gonzalez*)
Alary, Giulio, 1814–1891
    Bellini, Vincenzo
Albright, William, 1944–1998
    Albrecht, Johann Lorenz
    Koussevitzky, Serge

Alcock, Walter Galpin, Sir, 1861–1947
    Parry, Sir Charles Hubert Hastings (in *Little organ book*)
Alexander, Peter, 1959–
    Koussevitzky, Serge
Alfvén, Hugo, 1872–1960
    Sjögren, Johann Gustav Emil
Ali-Sade, Frangis, 1947–
    Berg, Alban
    Mahler, Gustav
Allanbrook, Douglas, 1921–
    Zuckerkandl, Victor
Alwyn, William, 1905–1985
    Holst, Gustav
Amadei, Roberto, 1840–1913
    Brizzi, Gaetano
Ambrosioni, Pietro
    Donizetti, Gaetano
Amengual Astaburuaga, René, 1911–1954
    Ravel, Maurice
Amlin, Martin, 1953–
    Boulanger, Nadia
Amram, David, 1930–
    Monk, Thelonious
    Pozo, Chano
    Tabuteau, Marcel

Garcia Laborda, José Maria, 1946–
  Granados, Enrique
Garcia Roman, José, 1945–
  Albéniz, Isaac
  Campo, Conrado del
  Falla, Manuel de
  Granados, Enrique
  Turina, Joaquin
Gárdonyi, Zoltán, 1906–1986
  Bach, Johann Sebastian
  Kodály, Zoltán
Gárdonyi, Zsolt, 1946–
  Dupré, Marcel
Gariboldi, Giuseppe, 1833–1905
  Bellini, Vincenzo (in *Alla memoria di Vincenzo Bellini*)
Garrido Vargas, Pablo, 1905–1982
  Liszt, Franz
Gaspari, Gaetano, 1808–1881
  Rossini, Gioachino (in *Messa per Rossini*)
Gaubert, Denis
  Grétry, André Ernest Modeste
Gaubert, Philippe, 1879–1941
  Taffanel, Paul
Gaucelm Faidit, fl.1156–1209
  Richard I, Coeur de Leon
Gaultier, Denis, d.1672
  Blancrocher
  Enclos, Henri de l'
  Gaultier, Denis
  Racquet, Charles
Gaultier, Enemond, ca.1575–1651
  Mesangeau, René
Gaviniés, Pierre, 1726–1800
  Gaviniés, Pierre
Genge, Anthony, 1952–
  Feldman, Morton

Genzmer, Harald, 1909–
  Lasso, Roland de
Geraci, Bernardo, 1825–1889
  Bellini, Vincenzo (in *Alla memoria di Vincenzo Bellini*)
Gerber, René, 1908–
  Grigny, Nicolas de
Gianella, Louis, ca.1778–1817
  Cimarosa, Domenico
Giazotto, Remo, 1910–
  Ravel, Maurice
Ginastera, Alberto, 1916–1983
  Casals, Pablo
Giner, Salvador, 1832–1911
  Rossini, Gioachino
Giosa, Nicola de, 1820–1885
  Donizetti, Gaetano
Girod-Parrot, Marie-Louise, 1915–
  Gonzales, Victor (in *Le Tombeau de Gonzalez*)
Gismonti, Egberto, 1947–
  Webern, Anton
Gladd, Neil Laurence, 1955–
  Scarlatti, Domenico
Glazunov, Aleksandr Konstantinovich, 1865–1936
  Belaiev, Mitrofan Petrovich
  Borodin, Alexander
  Chopin, Frédéric
  Liszt, Franz
  Rimsky-Korsakov, Nikolai
  Stasov, Vladimir
  Wagner, Richard
Glick, Srul Irving, 1934–
  Adaskin, John
  Bernstein, Leonard
  Mammot, Isaac
  Pack, Rowland

Grunenwald, Jean-Jacques, 1911–1982
   Gonzales, Victor
Guarnieri, Camargo, 1907–1993
   Villa Lobos, Heitor
Gustavson, Mark
   Koussevitzky, Serge
Gut, Serge
   Liszt, Franz

Haas, Joseph, 1879–1960
   Schittler, Ludwig
Hahn, Reynaldo, 1874–1947
   Haydn, Joseph (in *Hommage à Haydn*)
Haieff, Alexei, 1914–1994
   Poulenc, Francis
Hailstork, Adolphus C., 1941–
   Johnson, Thor
Hainlein, Paul, 1626–1686
   Dilherr, Johann Michael (in *Tauben-Rast*)
Hakim, Naji, 1955–
   Langlais, Jean
   Messiaen, Olivier
Halffter, Cristobal, 1930–
   Mompou, Federico
Halffter, Ernesto, 1905–1989
   Cassado, Gaspar
   Ravel, Maurice
Halffter, Rodolfo, 1900–1987
   Chávez, Carlos
Hall, Henry, 1655–1707
   Purcell, Henry
Hambraeus, Bengt, 1928–
   Messiaen, Olivier
   Reger, Max
Hamburg, Jef, 1956–
   Ast, René van

Hamilton, David B., 1955–
   Ives, Charles
Hamilton, Iain, 1922–2000
   Bach, Johann Sebastian
   Leno, Dan
   Mahler, Gustav
Hammond, Richard, 1896–
   Paderewski, Ignacy Jan (in *Homage to Paderewski*)
Hanard, Martin, fl.1465–1500
   Ockeghem, Johannes
Hanson, Howard, 1896–1981
   Chopin, Frédéric
   Hughes, Edwin
   Koussevitzky, Serge
Harbin, Juanita
   Presley, Elvis
Harbison, John, 1938–
   Schubert, Franz
   Sessions, Roger
Harper, Edward, 1941–
   Dallapiccola, Luigi
   Leighton, Kenneth
Harries, David, 1933–
   Jones, David Roger (in *Violin music for young players*)
Harrison, Lou, 1917–
   Chávez, Carlos
   Cowell, Henry
   Ives, Charles
   Milhaud, Darius
   Simmons, Calvin
Hartke, Stephen Paul, 1952–
   Koussevitzky, Serge
Hartley, Walter S., 1927–
   Deans, Kenneth N. (Buddy)
   Fink, Reginald H.
   Hanson, Howard
   Israel, Brian

About the Author

R. Michael Fling is the music bibliographer and head of acquisitions at the William and Gayle Cook Music Library of Indiana University. He received his M.A. in musicology and M.L.S. degrees from the University of Iowa. As a member of the Music Library Association he has served as editor of the *MLA Index and Bibliography Series*, the *MLA Technical Reports Series*, and the second edition of the association's *A Basic Music Library: Essential Scores and Books*.